ASSESSING WAR

ASSESSING WAR

THE CHALLENGE OF MEASURING SUCCESS AND FAILURE

Leo J. Blanken, Hy Rothstein,
Jason J. Lepore, EDITORS

Foreword by Gen. George W. Casey Jr. (USA, Ret.)

Georgetown University Press / Washington, DC

Library of Congress Cataloging-in-Publication Data
Assessing war : the challenge of measuring success and failure / Leo J. Blanken,
Hy Rothstein, Jason J. Lepore, editors.
    pages cm
  Summary: Are we winning? Combatants often find themselves asking this question, especially during today›s protracted asymmetrical conflicts where victory and defeat are not clear or easy to measure. Also, too often politics or wishful thinking take the place of objective assessment. Assessing War explores how the trajectory of war has been analyzed in conflicts throughout American history. The book brings together military historians, political scientists, and military officers to examine wartime assessment in theory, in practice through historical and contemporary cases, and through alternative dimensions of assessment such as justice and proportionality, the war of ideas, and economics. The cases start with the Seven Years' War and cover all major US conflicts through the war in Afghanistan. There are also unique examinations of how Al Qaeda has assessed its war on the United States and how assessment might be conducted in cyber war. Wartime assessment is critical because forming an accurate picture is essential to developing the right strategy. This book concludes with advice for practitioners about best approaches, though it also offers sobering conclusions about the difficulty of assessing war objectively and without politicization or self-delusion.
  Includes bibliographical references and index.
  ISBN 978-1-62616-245-7 (hc : alk. paper) — ISBN 978-1-62616-246-4 (pb : alk. paper) — ISBN 978-1-62616-247-1 (eb)
  1. Military planning—United States. 2. War—Decision making. 3. Strategy. 4. United States—Military policy. 5. United States—History, Military. I. Blanken, Leo J. (Leo James), editor. II. Rothstein, Hy S., editor. III. Lepore, Jason J., editor.
  U153.A87 2015
  355'.033073—dc23
                        2015007438

16 15   9 8 7 6 5 4 3 2 First printing

Printed in the United States of America

Cover design by Faceout Studio, Charles Brock. Cover images courtesy of sergeyskleznev/Thinkstock (aged vintage calipers) and Albert Smirnov/Thinkstock (weapon).

CONTENTS

FOREWORD

LIKE STRATEGIC LEADERS IN PAST ERAS, today we live, compete, and lead in a volatile, uncertain, complex, and ambiguous world in which we constantly struggle to stay abreast of our rapidly changing environment. This will be even more true in wars in the twenty-first century—a fact that I can attest to from my time in Iraq. It will continue to be even harder for leaders to antici- pate opportunities and challenges in conducting military operations.

The extraordinary value of *Assessing War: The Challenge of Measuring Success and Failure* is its focus on the challenge of assessing military operations during their execution. The editors—Leo J. Blanken, Hy Rothstein, and Jason J. Lep- ore—have assembled contributions from scholars and practitioners, many of whom are leading experts in their fields and some of whom are veterans of our most recent wars in Iraq and Afghanistan. They provide a wide-ranging anal- ysis of assessment processes across almost three centuries of armed conflicts, from colonial North America to Afghanistan today.

The historical cases of successes and failures in wartime assessment have direct and immediate application in twenty-first-century conflict. British flexibility in using colonial militias in the Seven Years' War (French-Indian War) holds lessons for proxy forces today. There is a strong cautionary mes- sage in the examination of the optimistic assumptions and dogmatism that undermined German strategy in World War II. The United Nations faced a formidable task of calibrating the effect of combat operations on truce negoti- ations during the Korean War. The assessment task became only harder in the subsequent series of limited wars and counterinsurgencies as regular military forces were forced to assess political, economic, and informational impacts on their military efforts. This volume's accounts and analyses comprehensively reveal both the difficulties of assessment amid the chaos of war and the value of this essential endeavor.

From my own experience in Iraq, I used assessment processes to help me "see" myself and my enemies, to evaluate and communicate the progress of the campaign, and to identify the need for and to drive change. I cannot overstate the importance of commanders establishing formal and informal assessment processes concurrently with the development of their campaign plans. In war the only constant is change, and without effective assessment processes, commanders are unable to effectively measure and report progress, identify opportunities, anticipate challenges, and adjust their effort. I felt that this process was the commander's business, and I worked painstakingly with my assessment staff to identify and measure the key elements of success. It took a year, and continuous adjustments after that, to build an assessment process with which I was satisfied.

While military assessment processes should focus on the military campaign's progress toward achieving national strategic objectives, military leaders will be called on to provide candid assessments to their civilian superiors and to the American public on the progress of the campaign. The book also looks at the civil-military dynamics of assessments, an area that serious military and civilian leaders cannot ignore.

This exceptional volume provides insights for military and civilian security professionals and leaders. Its breadth, detail, clarity, and relevance commend it to required reading lists at service staff and war colleges. I believe *Assessing War: The Challenge of Measuring Success and Failure* will also serve policymakers charged with the oversight of military operations. It is a very useful handbook for leaders who hope to be successful at sustained efforts in our volatile, uncertain, complex, and ambiguous world.

Gen. George W. Casey Jr. (USA, Ret.)

INTRODUCTION

THE CHALLENGE OF WARTIME ASSESSMENT

Leo J. Blanken and Jason J. Lepore

ASSESSMENT DURING WAR IS CRITICAL, and in the wake of the frustrating—and often bewildering—conflicts in Iraq and Afghanistan there should come a serious reappraisal of this aspect of modern conflict. What constituted progress? Which units performed well? What lines of operation were effective? What aspects of victory, if any, were achieved? How do these issues impact our policy, force structure, strategy, doctrine, and technology choices? The seemingly inscrutable nature of these particular conflicts raises the deeper issue of how wartime progress has been measured in the past and, more important, how it should be measured in the future. Some conflicts, such as the Second World War, seemed to have been "simple" in retrospect while others, such as Vietnam, consistently befuddled observers at the time. Why was this the case? What explains this variation? And how can we move forward from the assessment challenges of current conflicts to craft better policy and strategy in the future?

The challenge has grown far beyond the simple metrics of combat. As current conflicts expand to "military operations other than war"—peacekeeping, cyber warfare, and information campaigns—the tasks of operational and strategic assessment may change and expand in kind. As a result, evaluating the ethical, social, and human development dimensions of such campaigns further complicates the assessment challenge. This work seeks to address the issue in several ways. The first goal is to generate recommendations to assist in establishing future policy, strategy, and doctrine. Another goal is to compile a rich set of in-depth historical accounts of a crucial, yet neglected, aspect of military history. The final goal is to refresh our current understanding of the assessment problem in an academic sense by refining our general models in light of the evolving wartime environments we observe today and are likely to see in the future.

THE PUZZLE

This project was motivated by a series of pronouncements regarding the conflict in Afghanistan that were all published within months of the ten-year anniversary of the beginning of the war. The following quotes are all from observers or participants who analyzed the war from positions of considerable access.

- Counterinsurgency expert John Nagl argued, "We are on the verge of breaking the insurgency. It's exactly the wrong time to change horses."[1]
- Secretary of Defense Leon Panetta later asserted that "[one should] make no mistake: We are succeeding. . . . We are closer than ever to achieving our strategic objectives."[2]
- Gen. Stanley McChrystal, former commander of the Coalition forces, argued that they were "only 'a little better than' 50% of the way to reaching their war goals."[3]
- Col. Don Bolduc, then commander of Combined Joint Special Operations Task Force–Afghanistan (CJSOTF-A), wrote in a memo to his troops: "Pick your sport: 'fourth and long,' 'bottom of the ninth,' 'overtime' . . . [all appropriately convey where the effort is at]. The context we are operating under is one of urgency."[4]

The significance of this series of pronouncements on the progress of the conflict is their wild divergence; ten years into the conflict, highly placed experts could not begin to agree on the status of the war effort. Nagl's quote conveys optimistic certitude. Secretary Panetta's quote contains hopeful sentiment, echoing the "we have turned the corner/light at the end of the tunnel" tone of Gen. William Westmoreland in Vietnam. The quotes from McChrystal and the CJSOTF-A commander, however, descend into something more akin to desperation.

Ironically these four drew very different conclusions even though this conflict has benefited from an unprecedented amount of dedicated assessment resources in the form of drones, satellite surveillance, signals intelligence, population surveys, and social science "human terrain teams"—all of which produced a staggering amount of data. For example, in 2009 one of the editors of this book was offered access to a computer hard drive being flown back from Afghanistan that contained forty-seven terabytes of metrics data characterizing the war (for some perspective on this figure, ten terabytes would constitute the entire printed collection held by the US Library of Congress). Upon inquiring whether a briefer summary or outline of that data was available, the response was that no one had even attempted to do it. Since no human has the capacity to absorb such a vast amount of information, the utility of the impressive collection of data is called into serious question. This anecdote illustrates a central problem for the United States in modern conflicts: Amassing vast amounts of assessment data is easy, but making sense of it poses serious difficulties.

WHAT IS ASSESSMENT?

We take *wartime assessment* to mean the act of gathering information to update one's beliefs about a war. At the most basic level, wartime assessment answers whether we are winning.[5] Beyond that question, it may involve several lines of effort including measures of effectiveness (what impact specific lines of operational effort are having) and measures of performance (how specific units are succeeding or failing in their allotted tasks). In expanding the concept we can add military intelligence, which uncovers aspects of the enemy to understand how the war is affecting him. Intelligence also assists in updating our strategy (what is now referred to as "red" intelligence) and in assessing both the human terrain in which the conflict takes place ("white" information) and the status of allies and partners ("green" intelligence).[6] These efforts may then be applied at the political, strategic, operational, or tactical level and may take into account numbers, reports, radio messages, images, or other forms of data.[7] Once again these various foci and diverse efforts can be roughly boiled down to that single crucial question: Are we winning?

ASSESSING WHAT?

Once a war is undertaken, the question arises as to which aspects of it should be assessed. In his classic treatment of the problem of conflict termination, Fred Charles Iklé warns us that war is an exceedingly complex environment. It provides an infinite number of data streams that could be gathered, counted, sifted, and analyzed; then decision makers must decide "which data to ignore as trivial, and which to interpret as important signals. They must reconcile conflicting evidence. They must amalgamate into a single answer the most diverse indicators: reports from the battlefield, statistics on potential military resources, and impressionistic predictions."[8] The consensus answer to this challenge is "strategy." In other words, *strategy* serves as "the bridge between military tool and political purpose. . . . [T]he forecasted cause-effect relationships that are used to link military effort and political goal ex-ante is the theory of victory. It has to encompass the overall effort and describe how the tactics used will lead to operational success, and how operational success will force the enemy to do one's will."[9] Strategy, therefore, provides benchmarks of military action that are set with the underlying belief that once achieved, they will create sufficient conditions for the war's political goals to be realized. This establishment of operational tasks constitutes a crucial aspect of strategy as it dedicates material resources—and soldiers' lives—to the theoretical argument that links their sacrifice to the needs of the state. It is the core of Carl von Clausewitz's insight that "war is a continuation of politics by other means" and serves as the foundation for a broad approach to wartime assessment.

ASSESSING HOW?

Once these military tasks have been determined, it becomes necessary to operationalize the assessment effort. This effort systematically gathers data to inform the leadership as to how units and commanders are performing and what impact their efforts are having toward the achievement of the strategic goals. Both types of information are important as they allow the leader to mark progress and to ascertain whose efforts led to such progress.

These data-gathering efforts may take several forms. The first method is direct observation. On July 3, 1863, Robert E. Lee ordered roughly three divisions of infantry to take the high ground of Cemetery Ridge on the third day of the Battle of Gettysburg. Conducted uphill, across an open field, and into prepared defensive positions, the attack resulted in tactical failure for the Southern units, which suffered 50 percent casualties in the attempt. This action, known as Pickett's Charge, provided immediate and directly observable information for the participants that allowed them to update their beliefs regarding the prospects of Southern victory in the campaign as well as the war. One participant, Union soldier Levi Baker of the Ninth Massachusetts Light Artillery, recognized the gravity of the failed assault: "I recognized then and there that this battle was to be, in all probability, regarded as a great turning point in history. I did not believe the Confederates would ever surpass their efforts on that gory field. . . . [This was] the high water mark of the Rebellion."[10] Observers could immediately verify the effects of military efforts—in this case, the relative effectiveness of the Southern and Northern armies' abilities to take or hold territory and inflict casualties on one another's forces.

Sometimes direct observation of the wartime environment is not feasible. Consider, for example, a strategic bombing campaign. According to

Robert Ehlers, "Unlike ground and naval campaigns, in which the parties involved generally know whether the battle was a victory, draw, or defeat, air campaigns are prone to uncertainty. . . . [P]hotos, signals intercepts, and ground sources never [tell] the whole story."[11] In such cases, evidence gathering becomes removed from direct verification of effects and must rely more and more on theoretical constructs to link indirect evidence to conclusions about the impact of military activities. In the Second World War, for example, the reporting method that the Royal Air Force's Research and Experiments Department 8 (RE 8) used to estimate bomb damage of German factories relied on photographic evidence coupled with elaborate mirror-imaging models based on previous German bombing of British factories. It used "comparisons of those bombs to British bombs of similar size; susceptibility of various industries to blast, fragmentation, and fire damage; comparison of British and German building construction to optimize bomb choice; and assessments of railroad damage and delays." The results also benefitted from the input of economists and industry experts to determine how such damage would impact various aspects of the German economy (petroleum refining, chemical production, railroad functioning, et cetera). This method was vindicated at the end of the war, when survey teams in 1945 determined that RE 8 reports "were always within a few percentage points of figures quoted in captured German damage records."[12] Thus indirect evidence buttressed by theorizing was used to overcome the lack of direct observation.

Sometimes actors rely on even less direct methods to surmise information of the battle space. As assessment efforts become more removed from the evidence, they must rely more on assumptions.[13] Take, for example, the German attack on the French forts of Verdun in 1916. German chief of staff Erich von Falkenhayn planned the attack to "bleed the French army white" in an effort to bring France to the negotiating table. To do so, rather than actually conquer the forts, he sought to turn Verdun into a meat grinder for French forces. He wrote later that "our object . . . was to inflict upon the enemy the utmost possible injury with the least expenditure of lives on our part."[14] The difficulty for the Germans, however, was that their efforts relied largely on artillery to inflict casualties and that they could not take the territory necessary to verify the lethality of their efforts. Falkenhayn, therefore, relied on a simple assumption to deduce French casualties, or the ratio of 2:5: "Even though the German units were suffering horribly, the General Staff Chief maintained that the French were suffering more; 'for two Germans put out of action five Frenchmen had to shed their blood.'"[15] According to this assumptive model, the Germans should have been able to simply count their own casualties and calculate the enemy's losses. Unfortunately the assumed ratio was wildly inaccurate; the Germans suffered 281,000 casualties in the battle compared to 315,000 French.[16]

These examples demonstrate the variety of approaches actors can take in creating assessment mechanisms. It further illustrates that as we move from direct observation of effects to less direct methods, the challenge of assessment grows and presents more interesting difficulties for participants. Finally it shows how abstract theorizing inherently asserts its place—either beneficially or pathologically—in the assessment process.

WHAT PREVENTS EFFECTIVE ASSESSMENT?

Beyond the inherent difficulties of measurement in wartime environments, other systematic difficulties might arise in the assessment process. They can be driven by bureaucratic processes, by political friction, and from actors' cognitive and motivational biases. While obviously not an exhaustive list of the hindrances to assessment, it introduces some common themes that have been identified.

Scott Sigmund Gartner examines the impact of factors from the bureaucratic/organizational level of analysis on the assessment problem. An important conclusion that he draws in his study is that modern militaries comprise multiple, heterogeneous bureaucratic organizations that, in turn, view the war through their respective organizational lens: "Because the organization sees the health of the larger unit, such as the nation, in terms of success of its own policies, organizations are capable of drawing significantly different conclusions about the general likelihood of success."[17] The implication of Gartner's analysis is that bureaucratic interests and organizational processes may play a hand in driving assessment efforts.[18] It may result in disagreement about the progress of the war and the performance of units despite well-meaning assessment efforts. Further, disagreements among the various bureaucratic entities in the military that are driven by rivalry, most famously at the interservice level, may stem from competition over resources, recognition, or control over various aspects of the conflict.[19] This contention may result in a willful clouding or manipulation of assessment efforts to favor one bureaucratic entity over others.

A second critical institutional juncture that may pose a challenge to assessment is in civil-military relations. The relationship between the military bureaucracy and its political master has generated many important studies.[20] This institutional link has two important implications for the study at hand. The first implication involves the establishment of strategic goals; in particular, the political leadership needs to determine how military activity might serve the nation's interest, while military experts need to vet the feasibility of the military's attainment of such goals and to provide specific military strategies to do so. As Allan Millett, Williamson Murray, and Kenneth Watman note, "Strategic objectives chosen in a political vacuum possess no meaning. Political goals chosen without reference to what is strategically possible are futile at best and disastrous at worst."[21] The second implication is that militaries are intrinsically invested in the process of providing the political leadership with the information and analysis that constitute assessments of how wars are proceeding. Problems may arise in this relationship, however, if the military has preferences that diverge from that of the political leadership. One obvious reason for preference divergence is that the military often relies on the political leadership for "the resources required to maintain, expand, and reconstitute itself"; as such, this asymmetric relationship (one side has the purse strings while the other controls information) may present challenges for unbiased assessment.[22] Murray and Mark Grimsley summarize this tension succinctly: "The structure of government and military institutions plays a crucial role in the formulation of strategy and its adaptability to actual conditions. The form of government effects [sic] the ability of decision-makers to analyze and interpret the external environment . . . [while] officials in any system are highly skilled at telling leaders what they want to hear."[23] Risa Brooks focuses on this problem as well, arguing that "[c]lashes over security and other corporate issues and the balance of power between military and political leaders affect the routines through which they share and analyze information, consult with one another, and . . . engage in strategic assessment."[24] She identifies the balance of power, as well as the degree of preference divergence, between the political and military leaders as the relevant variable that determines the quality of strategic assessment. This discussion highlights the Janus-faced nature of strategic assessment, as it must satisfy both the external observation of the wartime environment as well as the internal navigation of the politicized realm of civil-military relations.

A third challenge to assessment may arise from cognitive and cultural biases that may be inherent to militaries in general and to the US military in particular.[25] Modern professional militaries are culturally attuned to desire offensive operations, decisive battles, and therefore short wars.[26] A complicated assessment apparatus would not be necessary if war consisted of one or two massive battles of annihilation, for "the boys would be home by Christmas." The German Army that fought in the First World War, for example, had built its professional identity around rapid, offensive operations that were designed to decisively disarm the enemy military and occupy its territory.[27]

This vision failed to come to fruition after the collapse of the Schlieffen Plan: "The failure of Germany's initial plans to win the war in a few rapid, decisive battles represented the failure of the 'traditional' German approach to warfare and left Germany in a precarious strategic position. Germany now found itself surrounded by enemies who possessed far greater resources. . . . [T]hese challenges called for a new way of thinking about warfare."[28] The German military leaders, however, were unable to build such an alternative strategic vision—to include an appropriate assessment apparatus—to rationally prosecute the long-term conflict in which they found themselves.

Such proclivity for decisive operations and the attendant lack of a long-term assessment apparatus may still exist. Early operational success in Iraq, for example, seemed to follow this pattern. As Richard Sinnreich notes, "In mid-2003, an unexpected and expanding insurgency followed the initial tactical success. Weeks went by before anyone in uniform was willing to acknowledge that what Defense Secretary Donald Rumsfeld had cheerfully dismissed as 'post-war untidiness' was neither post-war nor merely untidy."[29] As Ben Connable points out, the tendency has also been reflected in the paucity of resources dedicated to assessment efforts: "Despite the critical role that assessments play, organizations frequently treat assessments as an afterthought. Assessment capabilities are often recognized as lacking well after deployment and are subsequently generated out of the institutional force as a temporary loan."[30] Such cognitive biases toward short, violent, decisive wars, therefore, may prevent actors from confronting the realities of complex, enduring conflicts—and hence from developing the necessary assessment apparatus to measure the environment appropriately.

These challenges to effective wartime assessment create important areas of study for academics, strategists, and policymakers. Academics can assess these challenges across the historical record with a descriptive framework in mind, policymakers can focus on prescriptions derived from such analyses to improve the effects of US military actions, and strategists can develop options that most effectively achieve political aims.

REASSESSING WARTIME ASSESSMENT

Given this discussion, we have assembled several scholars to analyze the task of assessment in cases drawn from history and recent and ongoing wars, and to focus on emerging aspects of conflict that may figure prominently in the future landscape of war. The authors were guided by the following initial questions in preparing their work:

- What were the context and the origin of the conflict?
- What were the aims or goals of the actors? Did they change over the course of the conflict?
- What types of assessments were made? Why were they chosen? How were they conducted? What challenges or frictions arose?
- How did those assessments affect the actors' conduct in the war?

The first section of the book features work that expands the theoretical understanding of the assessment process. In the leading chapter, Leo J. Blanken and Jason J. Lepore discuss the *metrics triangle* as a base model to understand problems with assessment mechanisms. Consisting of *operational benchmarks, incentives,* and *information,* this construct illuminates the fact that the information obtained from a measure and the incentives the measurement effort gives to soldiers are fundamentally connected and jointly determine the utility of an assessment mechanism of military operations. Above this triangle there can be a critically important separation between operational benchmarks and the state's political goals, and this is denoted as the *Clausewitzian gap.* In the next chapter Hy Rothstein focuses on explaining this Clausewitzian gap, which is exacerbated by the failure to make clear strategic goals, and he provides suggestions to narrow this fissure. A well thought-out strategy should function as the bridge between political goals and operational benchmarks, but in democratic societies, bureaucratic and institutional factors serve as roadblocks to good strategy. The divergence between the backgrounds and experiences of political leaders and military leaders, for example, feeds this gap. Thus Rothstein argues that increasing the quality (not quantity) of officer education about geopolitical issues should enable military leaders to help close the gap. In the final chapter of the section, Gartner brings to the front the three primary problems with making assessment productive: information overload, decision making without sufficient information, and large amounts of uncertainty. He suggests using the *dominant indicator* approach to help mitigate these problems. The idea is to rely on quantitative measures that can provide easily processed insights into the success or failure of a campaign. Gartner uses examples from the Second World War, the Korean War, and the Vietnam War to illustrate the utility of this approach to assessment.

The nine historical chapters in the second section cover major American conflicts through the Vietnam War and offer a vivid picture of how assessment was done in a variety of contexts. Three primary themes come out of these cases. First, the accuracy of the conflict model dictates the value of an assessment system. On the one hand, incorrect models of the conflict are shown to drive assessment problems that limit campaign success in the chapters by John Grenier (Seven Years' War), Brooks D. Simpson (Civil War), Brian McAllister Linn (Philippines), D. Scott Stephenson (First World War), and Conrad C. Crane (Korea). In most of these conflicts, the bad assumptions were eventually revised, the conflict model updated, and the assessment system reconstructed. On the other hand, Col. Michael Richardson argues in chapter 7 (western Indian wars) that a deep understanding of the conflict environment allowed for a parsimonious assessment mechanism that simplified operational goals and provided a clear path to campaign success. The second theme of these cases is that political and bureaucratic interests can skew the assessment process. In the chapter on Vietnam, Gregory A. Daddis provides a mass of evidence that not only was the assessment process highly politicized but also the internal assessments were far different than those presented to the American public. Stephenson (First World War) shows assessment schemes being used to fight internal bureaucratic, political, and alliance games while Crane (Korea) highlights the Cold War's bigger backdrop as a player in assessment decisions. In Edward G. Lengel's chapter on the Revolutionary War, the system of assessment had to be completely developed during the conflict, resulting in a highly political and bureaucratic process. The third theme is that of large changes in policy stemming from assessment. Most of the chapters highlight situations where critical changes in policy are made based on assessment information. In Gerhard L. Weinberg's chapter (Second World War), information from assessments induced both Adolf Hitler and Winston Churchill to make critical policy changes.

In the third section of the book, the recent conflicts that motivated this work in the first instance are critically analyzed. First, Maj. Gen. William C. Hix and Kalev I. Sepp offer a detailed narrative of the establishment of the assessment process in Iraq. In particular, they relay their personal experiences in establishing the assessment effort under Gen. George W. Casey Jr. in 2004 and share important insights about the realities of the assessment challenge in a complex conflict environment. Next, Alejandro S. Hernandez, Julian Ouellet, and Christopher J. Nannini look at the conflict in Afghanistan. They argue that social science tools were borrowed to structure assessments of the counterinsurgency campaign there, but these tools were often used without the necessary epistemological and contextual understanding to use them correctly. They then attempt to fit the Afghanistan case within a larger prescriptive scheme for assessing counterinsurgency campaigns. Mark Stout, in turn, tackles a novel subject by asking how al-Qaeda assesses its progress in its jihad. In exploring this question, he analyzes the degree to which al-Qaeda's organizational structure allows for coherent goals and assessment mechanisms, as well as the underlying goals of such an organization and how they fit into our notions of wartime assessment.

The nature of war is not static. It changes with developments in technology, ethical considerations, and the political context. The authors in this book's final section address these evolving aspects of war and how they impact the tasks of assessment. Bradley J. Strawser and Russell Muirhead open this section by showing the intersection of strategic assessment and just war theory. They explore the impact of assessing the physical manifestation of the "goodness" (moral benefits) and "badness" (moral costs) that wars may generate and how weighing these assessments impacts the central just war concept of proportionality. Dorothy E. Denning examines the challenge of assessment in an emerging war-fighting environment—namely, the cyber dimension. Her analysis provides a framework for measuring two critical aspects of this domain—assessing battle damage and weighing the relative strengths of opponents in a potential cyber conflict. Robert Reilly's chapter on assessing the "battle of the narrative" in wartime again picks up on the just war thread. He argues that assessment is crucial for understanding the relative justness of one's own wartime cause vis-à-vis that of the enemy. He further explores how one would assess the operational effectiveness of the strategic communication that would disseminate this narrative—both to bolster one's own side and to undermine the enemy's narrative. Aric P. Shafran's chapter examines a growing yet surprisingly immature aspect of the current operational environment—that is, assessing the impact of economic development efforts in occupied territory. He shows that existing efforts at assessing such work are insufficient, and he offers ways forward for more thoughtful assessment in this area. Finally, Anthony H. Cordesman and Hy Rothstein conclude the book with lessons culled from all of the chapters and provide recommendations for future decision makers who must face the challenge of assessment.

NOTES

1. Quoted in Michael Hirsh and Jamie Tarabay, "Washington Losing Patience with Counterinsurgency in Afghanistan," *National Journal*, June 23, 2011, http://www.nationaljournal.com/magazine/washington-losing-patience -with-counterinsurgency-in-afghanistan-20110623?page=1.
2. Testimony before the House Armed Services Committee as delivered by Secretary of Defense Leon E. Panetta, October 13, 2011 (Washington DC).
3. Quoted in Associated Press, "Stanley McChrystal: After 10 Years, Afghan War Only Half Done," *The Guardian*, October 7, 2011, http://www.guard ian.co.uk/world/2011/oct/07/stanley-mcchrystal-afghanistan-us.

4. Quoted in Sean D. Naylor, "Program Has Afghans as First Line of Defense," *Army Times,* July 20, 2010, http://www.armytimes.com/article/20100720/NEWS/7200336/Program-has-Afghans-first-line-defense.

5. See Emily Mushern and Jonathan Schroden, *Are We Winning? A Brief History of Military Operations Assessment* (Arlington VA: Center for Naval Analyses, 2014).

6. See John Wilcox, "The Information Barber Pole: Integrating White Information and Red Intelligence in Emerging Conflicts" (thesis, Naval Postgraduate School, 2013).

7. On the definition of these levels of analysis and their relationship to assessing effectiveness, see Allan R. Millett, Williamson Murray, and Kenneth H. Watman, "The Effectiveness of Military Organizations," in *Military Effectiveness,* vol. 1, *The First World War,* ed. A. R. Millett and W. Murray (Boston: Unwin Hyman, 1988).

8. Quoted in Scott Sigmund Gartner, *Strategic Assessment in War* (New Haven CT: Yale University Press, 1997), 9.

9. Stephan Frühling, "Uncertainty, Forecasting, and the Difficulty of Strategy," *Comparative Strategy* 25 (2006): 19–31, 21.

10. Quoted in Richard Rollins, introduction, in *Pickett's Charge: Eyewitness Accounts at the Battle of Gettysburg,* ed. R. Rollins (Mechanicsburg PA: Stackpole Books, 2005), 1.

11. Robert S. Ehlers Jr., *Targeting the Third Reich: Air Intelligence and the Allied Bombing Campaigns* (Lawrence: University of Kansas Press, 2009), 9–10.

12. Ibid., 126.

13. Leo J. Blanken and Justin Overbaugh, "Are We Assuming the Worst about Assumptions? Induction, Deduction, and Military Intelligence in Counterinsurgency," *Inteligencia Y Seguridad* 13 (January–June 2013).

14. Robert T. Foley, *German Strategy and the Path to Verdun: Erich von Falkenhayn and the Development of Attrition, 1870–1916* (New York: Cambridge University Press, 2005), 211.

15. Ibid., 231.

16. This figure comes from Hermann Wendt, *Verdun, 1916: Die Angriffe Falkenhayns im Maasgebiet mit Richtung auf Verdun als strategisches Problem* (Berlin: E. S. Mittler, 1931), 243–44.

17. Gartner, *Strategic Assessment,* 46.

18. For a classic treatment, see James G. March and Herbert A. Simon, with Harold Guetzkow, *Organizations* (New York: John Wiley and Sons, 1958).

19. On these dynamics, see Graham T. Allison and Morton H. Halperin, "Bureaucratic Politics: A Paradigm and Some Policy Implications," *World Politics* 74 (1972): 40–79.

20. The foundational work remains Samuel P. Huntington's *Soldier and the State: The Theory and Politics of Civil-Military Relations* (Cambridge MA: Belknap Press, 1981); and an important recent work is Peter D. Feaver's *Armed Servants: Agency, Oversight, and Civil-Military Relations* (Cambridge MA: Harvard University Press, 2005).

21. Millett, Murray, and Watman, "The Effectiveness of Military Organizations," in Millett and Murray, *Military Effectiveness*, 1:8.

22. Ibid., 1:4.

23. Williamson Murray and Mark Grimsley, "On Strategy," in *The Making of Strategy: Rulers, States, and War*, ed. W. Murray, M. Knox, and A Bernstein (New York: Cambridge University Press, 1994), 19.

24. Risa Brooks, *Shaping Strategy: The Civil-Military Politics of Strategic Assessment* (Princeton NJ: Princeton University Press, 2008), 3.

25. For an essay on how cognitive biases are formed in militaries, see Peter Paret, *The Cognitive Challenge of War: Prussia, 1806* (Princeton NJ: Princeton University Press, 2009); and on the impact of culture on military organizations, see Morton Halperin, *Bureaucratic Politics and Foreign Policy*, 2nd ed. (Washington DC: Brookings, 2006), 27–36.

26. See Jack Snyder, *The Ideology of the Offensive: Military Decision Making and the Disasters of 1914* (Ithaca: Cornell University Press, 1989); and Beatrice Heuser, *The Evolution of Strategy: Thinking War from Antiquity to the Present* (New York: Cambridge University Press, 2010), 137–51.

27. See L. L. Farrar Jr., *The Short War Illusion: German Policy, Strategy and Domestic Affairs, August–December 1914* (Santa Monica: ABC Clio, 1973); and Jehuda L. Wallach, *The Dogma of the Battle of Annihilation: The Theories of Clausewitz and Schlieffen and Their Impact on the German Conduct of the Two World Wars* (Westport CT: Greenwood Press, 1986).

28. Foley, *German Strategy*, 124.

29. Richard Hart Sinnreich, "That Accursed Spanish War: The Peninsula War, 1807–1814," in *Hybrid Warfare: Fighting Complex Opponents from the Ancient World to the Present*, ed. W. Murray and P. R. Mansoor (New York: Cambridge University Press, 2012), 105.

30. Quoted in Ben Connable, *Embracing the Fog of War: Assessments and Metrics in Counterinsurgency* (Santa Monica: RAND, 2012), 6.

PART I: THEORY

1

PRINCIPALS, AGENTS, AND ASSESSMENT

Leo J. Blanken and Jason J. Lepore

WARTIME ASSESSMENT INVOLVES the gathering and analyzing of information to update a decision maker's understanding of an ongoing conflict. Throughout the chain of command, data is gathered, vetted, synthesized, packaged, and interpreted. The resulting products are then delivered to the political leadership that oversees management of the conflict, often thousands of miles removed from the fighting. Finally the political leadership must, to some degree, report on the status of the conflict to the ultimate judge of their efforts, their domestic constituency.

Conceiving of the assessment challenge as a series of nested relationships allows for the utilization of theoretic tools and insights from the field of economics. These tools, bundled under the general moniker *principal-agent* (P-A) *modeling*, were developed to analyze such hierarchical structures. More specifically these models analyze relationships characterized by an informational asymmetry between actors along with the incentives engendered by some divergence of interests. In other words, the subordinate may know information that the boss does not know, and the subordinate may have interests that do not fully accord with the boss's vision of "getting the job done." These two aspects—information and incentives—taken together provide a powerful foundation for thinking about wartime assessment.

This chapter proceeds as follows. First, we introduce the P-A model and highlight some relevant results from this research agenda, expounding on the relationship between information and incentives in the task of assessment. Second, we focus on the central P-A relationship that exists between the military and the political leadership. This relationship is presented conceptually as a triangle. This *metrics triangle* sits distinctly beneath the leadership's

3

political goals, which are translated into *operational benchmarks* (the apex of the triangle) for the agent to pursue on the battlefield. The measurement of progress toward such benchmarks is then characterized by the search for *information* and by the *incentives* this effort generates for the subordinate military agent; these factors form the two subordinate points of the triangle. Finally, we consider the political constraints under which the leadership operates in the face of its domestic constituency in constructing and monitoring the military agent.

THE PRINCIPAL-AGENT MODEL

At the core of the principal-agent approach are the problems that may arise from delegation.[1] A principal may contract an agent to execute a task because the principal lacks the time or expertise or because of the increasing returns associated with the division of labor. If there is a divergence of interests between the two parties, as well as informational asymmetry, an opportunity will arise for exploitation. In economic analyses, this is commonly conceived of as an "information rent"; that is, the agent is able to extract additional surplus from the principal (wages, for instance) by concealing aspects of its activities: effort level, progress, resource use, et cetera. The principal, in turn, may use monitoring mechanisms or the strategic construction of contracts to reduce the impact of the agent's informational advantage. Such microeconomic models seek to show the basic dynamics of contracting that exists among bosses, managers, and employees throughout a firm.

Increasingly such economic principal-agent models have been adapted for application to the public sector. Initially these P-A models focused on the relationship between Congress and the body of federal bureaucracies to execute national policy.[2] Such efforts centered on the essential question of whether the behavior of the bureaucratic agent faithfully reflects the intent of the legislative principal and the degree to which the agent can use informational asymmetries to exploit its political master.[3] It is worth noting explicitly that a central aspect of the original P-A model (actors maximizing wealth through wages or profits) had to be modified for the public sector. If Weberian bureaucrats cannot directly enrich themselves, then the divergence of their preferences from those of the principal need to be predicated on other features of the contract: benefits for their organization (increased resources or autonomy), professional interests (promotions or awards), or a preference ordering over the actual range of political outcomes that may induce manipulation of policy to their liking.[4]

Only rarely have principal-agent models been modified to deal with the specifics of war.[5] This is unfortunate as the attributes of the P-A tool kit could greatly illuminate many features of the subject matter: from command decisions to tactical innovations to force structure planning. The problem of wartime assessment is particularly suited to P-A analysis, for the model's emphasis on information asymmetry and monitoring rises to the forefront.[6] Soldiers in the trenches answer to noncommissioned officers and junior officers who work beneath the local commander responsible for that portion of the battlefield. The local commanders are monitored by multiple levels of authority throughout the battle space, in oft-labyrinthine structures. The uniformed military leadership in the theater of operations, in turn, answers to civilian superiors in the seat of political power. Finally the elected officials answer to the domestic constituency, or the spouses, parents, and siblings of those soldiers sent to fight.[7] Each layer executes tasks under the watchful eye of its superior, which seeks to know how the subordinate agent is performing and what progress is being made. We now turn to a discussion of assessment that utilizes the insights of P-A analysis, conceived of here as a triangle of considerations.

THE PRINCIPAL MONITORS THE AGENT

We argue that the P-A assessment challenge in wartime revolves around three primary considerations: *operational benchmarks, information*, and *incentives*. These elements form a triangle that, first and foremost, must be situated beneath the *political goals* of the war (see figure 1.1).

At the top of the figure is the desired political end state determined by the principal, which is in this case the state leadership. This hierarchically superior position accords with Clausewitz's dictum that war is a continuation of politics by other means. This insight—that war does not serve its own purpose but rather exogenous political goals—generates profound implications for the metrics issue. These implications are represented in figure 1.1 by the space, which we refer to as the Clausewitzian gap, between the top of the metrics triangle and the political goals beneath which it sits.

Once the leadership decides on a *political goal* and crafts a plan of specific operational benchmarks to create sufficient conditions for success, it must then choose metrics to assess the progress toward completion of those tasks. This act of choosing a set of metrics must satisfy the dual requirements of revealing information about the nature of the wartime environment and recognizing the incentives that any assessment instrument will create for the military agent. We now turn to a fuller discussion of each of these points.

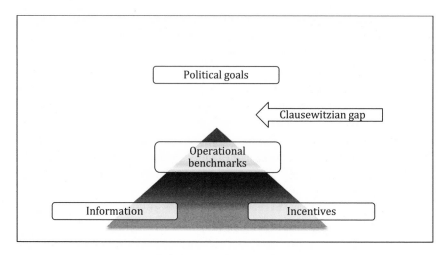

Figure 1.1. The metrics triangle

POINT ONE: OPERATIONAL BENCHMARKS

The top point of the triangle consists of the operational benchmarks of the conflict, or the set of military tasks that are designed by the leadership—or more often the result of a dialogue between political and senior military personnel—to establish a set of battlefield outcomes that would constitute sufficient conditions for political success.[8] In other words, if the political goal of a war is to "secure natural resources," "stabilize a region," or "end human rights violations," then these political outcomes must be linked to particular tasks that the military can execute such as "establish air superiority" or "destroy enemy armored units."[9] Clausewitz was sensitive to this disjoint, arguing that "[t]he political object . . . will thus determine both the military objective to be reached and the amount of effort it requires. . . . Sometimes the political and military objective is the same—for example, the conquest of a province. In other cases, the political object will not provide a suitable military objective."[10]

We refine Clausewitz's insight by highlighting the conceptual seam that separates political objectives from all military activities; we label these concrete military tasks as *operational benchmarks*. Even Clausewitz's straightforward example of "the conquest of a province" could involve a variety of specific military operations involving disparate activities designed to render the province conquered, from a population-centric counterinsurgency campaign to outright genocide. This raises two points for discussion. First, the sufficiency argument that links operational benchmarks to political goals may not hold true. If this is the case, then a military can succeed operationally without winning a war. The second, and more fundamental, point concerns the principal-agent interaction that determines which operational benchmarks are selected and how military strategy might link them to underlying political goals.[11] If one considers that the military agent has professional expertise regarding the use of force and that the agent may have divergent preferences from the principal—perhaps for increased budget, autonomy, or prestige—then room for agent "drift" may occur during this dialogue. This would accord with the central insight of the P-A model: The agent's private information and the incentive to misrepresent itself are fundamental problems of delegation.

In sum, operational benchmarks need to be in place for effective monitoring to occur; however, where divergence between principal and agent preferences and information may skew the process, establishing such benchmarks may be a challenge in and of itself. After these benchmarks are set, one must turn to the task of gathering information to monitor the agent's efforts and progress in the war.

POINT TWO: INFORMATION

The informational point of the triangle—that is, the search for data that will allow the principal to gain insight into the wartime environment and to evaluate the performance of the agent—is central to the principal's effort at monitoring the agent. The US military provides two umbrella terms to define the informational tasks of agent monitoring—measure of performance (MOP) and measure of effectiveness (MOE). Current doctrine defines a *measure of performance* as "a criterion used to assess friendly actions that is tied to measuring task accomplishment" and a *measure of effectiveness* as a "criterion used to assess changes in system behavior, capability, or operational environment that is tied to measuring the attainment of an end state, an objective, or the creation of an effect. It measures the relevance of actions being performed."[12] In other words, the MOP determines whether we "are doing things right," and the MOE answers whether we "are doing the right things." The former is internally focused (are agents performing tasks to standards?) while the latter is externally focused (how are agent activities impacting the battle space?).[13]

Ease of monitoring can vary across wartime environments. In conventional wars, it may be easy to establish both MOPs and MOEs. One can measure agent performance (number of enemy submarines sunk) and link it to a measurable desired effect (stop the enemy from interdicting allied shipping), because in high-intensity, force-on-force combat, the environment is relatively free of extraneous variables. Soldiers and weapons platforms compete in a relatively straightforward contest of attrition to kill, capture, or otherwise render ineffective enemy soldiers and platforms. This type of warfare characterized the majority of combat in the Second World War, as well as the projected Fulda Gap battles that were envisioned if the Soviet Union invaded Western Europe.

In irregular conflicts such as counterinsurgency, however, establishing MOPs and MOEs may be much more difficult due to the cacophony of confounding variables introduced by the social context in which the operations take place. Isolating the effect of agent activity in such a complex environment is very difficult. In fact, this measurement effort constitutes the most difficult aspect of social science, and the fields of political science, sociology, and economics have struggled with it for decades.[14] These efforts include creating appropriate concepts (social capital, network cohesion, reconciliation), selecting valid and reliable indicators, arduously searching for data, and designing elaborate research to control for a myriad of confounding factors. In such difficult cases MOPs may devolve into simply measuring input activity (number of leaflets dropped, number of patrols conducted) that is entirely disengaged from progress toward operational benchmarks. Conversely MOEs may devolve into simply gauging the environment, with little understanding as to how changes in that environment are the result of military activities. Given the direction of current doctrine, irregular missions in the "human domain" will likely be increasing in the future, and the challenge of measuring such efforts will increase proportionally.[15]

Another distinct dimension to this problem is determining how the principal's monitoring efforts impact the nature of the agent's battlefield activity (as opposed to simply its reporting effort). Even if a wartime environment could be accurately measured without agent distortion, the measurement apparatus itself will impact the nature of the agent's behavior. We now turn to the implications of this influence—that is, how the assessment effort directs the activities of the agent on the battlefield—in the incentives point of the metrics triangle.

POINT THREE: INCENTIVES

The third, and most commonly neglected, aspect of the metrics triangle is made up of incentives, or, more specifically, how the principal's assessment mechanism can affect agent behavior on the battlefield. This effect is driven by the degree to which rewards and punishments are linked to the assessment of actor performance. Depending on whether the principal understands the causal relationship between agent activity and battlefield effect, this incentive system can either be a powerful tool for wartime success or a source of serious pathological behavior.

To examine the role of incentives, we must focus again on the causal impact of agent activity on the wartime environment. We can conceive of MOEs as measures of an outcome, or dependent variable, and MOPs as measures of causes, or independent variables; and "[w]ell-devised measures can help the commanders and staffs understand the causal relationship between specific tasks and desired effects."[16] As outlined previously, in a conventional war scenario this measurement task may be simple. An activity such as shooting down enemy aircraft has a positive causal effect on an operational benchmark, such as establishing air superiority. This, in turn, is assumed to form part of the sufficient conditions for the ultimate political goal of the principal—that is, the capitulation of the enemy state. In this case, the agent can be rewarded for achieving higher and higher levels of the MOP (shooting down enemy aircraft), and the principal is confident that such incentives will foster success in the war effort.

In irregular warfare environments, however, such causal relationships between agent activity and its effect may be more difficult to discern.[17] Current doctrinal sources emphasize measuring behavioral inputs—such as routes cleared, leaflets disseminated, key leader engagements, or schoolhouses funded—as appropriate MOPs in irregular warfare, but it may be problematic if there is a disconnection between the activity and its desired effects.[18] Jack Kem notes this issue: "A unit may be tasked to conduct at least ten patrols a day in a neighborhood in order to gain the confidence of the local populace. Even though the unit might conduct the requisite number of patrols to standard, it still may not result in confidence. From an MOP standpoint, the unit is successful; from an MOE standpoint, it may not be."[19] So if the relationship between increased activity and effect is not positive, what is it? For one, the relationship may be orthogonal; that is, agent activity could have no systematic impact on progress toward operational benchmarks. If that is the case, then increased effort along that line of operation is simply wasteful. Worse, it may even have a negative effect; that is, increased activity may inhibit or reverse progress toward operational benchmarks and ultimately hinder the war effort.

Understanding the relationship between agent activity and outcomes is crucial when agent incentives are taken into consideration. If agents are rewarded with medals, promotions, and attractive assignments for higher levels of a particular activity, then they will respond accordingly by directing their effort to maximize that metric. If the relationship between the rewarded activity and desired effect is positive, it can be a potent device in helping the principal achieve success in the war. If the relationship is orthogonal, then inefficiencies are introduced into the war effort, and as resources are finite, this increased effort is detrimental. If the relationship is negative, then the agent is working directly against the principal's desired end state. It is worth pointing out that in this line of reasoning, negative incentives (punishments) can have just as serious an impact as rewards do. If outcomes associated with an activity (such as losing men or causing civilian casualties) can end an officer's career, the officer may become so risk averse as to not engage in any fruitful activity whatsoever.

In sum, as long as an agent is rewarded or punished according to the metric, the nature of the measurement apparatus will shape the level and direction of the agent's efforts on the battlefield. Can the measurement effort similarly impact the principal? We now turn to this point by considering the web of political and diplomatic constraints in which the principal resides.

CONSTRAINTS ON THE PRINCIPAL

Until now we have assumed that the principal is motivated exclusively by the desire to achieve the stated political goals in the war. By assuming away all other political context, the argument has focused solely on the bilateral relationship between the political principal and the military agent, but in doing so, it loses much of the richness of wider wartime political dynamics. When taken into account, the wider aperture through which assessment can be viewed allows for a fuller treatment of the subject. In a famous 1988 article, Robert Putnam introduced the term "two-level game" while drawing attention to the fact that political leaders make foreign policy decisions that have important impacts both in the domestic political arena and on the international stage.[20] This point has serious implications for the challenge of wartime assessment.

The political principal not only has to monitor the progress of an ongoing war but also has to contend with domestic and foreign audiences. Managing the perception of wartime progress by domestic constituents involves a trade-off between sustaining morale and managing ambition. If a principal emphasizes that the war is going well, morale may be buoyed, but domestic pressures may seek a ratcheting up of war aims. If a principal announces that a war is going poorly, morale may deflate—even to the point of demanding the war's termination on unfavorable strategic terms and damaging the nation's reputation for resolve. Perception of the war's progress is also of concern on the international stage. A nation's foreign allies, its foreign rivals, and its current enemy will all be interested in how the war is progressing, what costs have been incurred, and how it will be terminated—in victory, defeat, or negotiated settlement.[21] This perception, in turn, may deter or invite aggression elsewhere, induce additional states to enter the conflict, or cause coalitions of allies to fall apart.[22]

Does manipulation of the assessment mechanism become part of the principal's strategy in the war effort? If so, then the problem of the principal is to design an assessment system that maximizes success in terms of the war's aims while keeping the support of the constituency sufficiently high. If the public approval constraint is binding, then by definition the principal must implement an assessment mechanism that is suboptimal in achieving war aims. That is, the principal may be forced to produce an assessment mechanism that makes the progress look good enough for the public while simultaneously providing as much true information as feasible. It becomes a challenging balancing act: If the principal chooses to misrepresent the war, it risks losing credibility as the truth becomes more difficult to hide; however, the principal may lose office as a war's costs and failures become more apparent.

CONCLUSIONS

The crux of the principal-agent approach to assessment is that the agent has an informational advantage over the principal. If the agent also has any divergent interests, then room for manipulation is created. The argument proposed here is that viewing wartime assessment through the lens of principal-agent modeling provides new insights into structuring the problem. We now summarize these insights and propose policy recommendations.

The formulation of operational benchmarks is intimately enmeshed in the initial choice to use force. Here the civil-military relationship is crucial for the optimal establishment of such benchmarks. Ideally the political leadership exerts its authority to ensure political control over the military bureaucrats, whereas the military bureaucrat offers an honest assessment of what is militarily possible. The agent's military expertise, however, constitutes private information about the impending war. Given this informational asymmetry, therefore, it is in the political principal's interest to ensure that there is little divergence of interests. In other words, senior military leaders should be incentivized to give honest pronouncements as to (a) which benchmarks are possible given the military's capabilities and (b) the degree to which the accomplishment of said benchmarks will create the necessary conditions for achieving the political goals.[23]

The search for information is also informed by the divergence of interests between the principal and the agent as the war unfolds. As long as a competition for rewards or avoidance of punishments exists, a reasonable agent can manipulate the information-gathering and reporting process. When one considers that many thousands (perhaps millions) of agents in a cascade of principal-agent relationships constitute the war effort, even a small incentive to inflate numbers across the battle space can create a large-scale torrent of systematically distorted information. It may occur not only through qualitative self-reporting but also through the choice of self-serving quantitative metrics by subordinate agents. This problem can be mitigated through several minor policy changes that adjust the type of contract that the principal (or senior agents) has with subordinates. For example, simply adjusting the rotation of military units into and out of the theater of operations can radically change the incentives for junior agents to misrepresent themselves. Rather than creating a "renter's mentality" of making a portion of the battle space look good for six months or a year, differing rotation mechanisms could match the agent's time horizon to that of the principal and reduce the incentive to plump numbers in the short term.[24]

Beyond the impact it has on the reporting process, the assessment mechanism may also drive the agent's substantive behavior on the battlefield. One must recognize that when agents drive up their performance metrics to be rewarded by their boss, they may not only fudge the numbers to do so but also actually produce a higher volume of that activity. This incentive for increased output can help guide the war effort in positive directions or create wide-scale pathology. The starkest example was the emphasis on body counts in Vietnam in which rewards for producing Vietnamese casualties helped foster a massive amount of killing, which ultimately worked against the strategy of winning the people's hearts and minds. Even seemingly benign behaviors, however, can similarly be overproduced through performance incentives.[25] For example, humanitarian assistance projects in Afghanistan ultimately have served to retard the healthy growth of the local economy. The gravest policy recommendation here is for the principal to understand, and revise its understanding if necessary, how the agent's behavior impacts the battle space. If this link between effort and effect is poorly understood, one can be left with a massive military effort that churns uselessly—or counterproductively—on some foreign battlefield.[26]

Finally the entire war takes place within a broader political arena. The principal may choose to manipulate revelations concerning the war's costs and progress to both foreign and domestic audiences. This insight connects the wartime assessment problem to fundamental issues of political office holding and international diplomacy. The best one can hope for from the political leaders on this point is that they will choose wars carefully, weighing the stakes and costs before entering into a costly conflict. Doing so may help alleviate the incentives for misrepresentation and reduce unnecessary bloodshed.

NOTES

1. For a comprehensive presentation of this approach, see Jean-Jacques Laffont and David Martimort, *The Theory of Incentives: The Principal-Agent Model* (Princeton NJ: Princeton University Press, 2002).

2. See, for example, Arthur Lupia and Mathew D. McCubbins, "Designing Bureaucratic Accountability," *Law and Contemporary Problems* 57, no. 4 (1994): 91–126; and Terry M. Moe, "The Politics of Structural Choice: Toward a Theory of Public Bureaucracy," in *Organization Theory: From Chester Barnard to the Present and Beyond*, ed. O. E. Williamson (New York: Oxford University Press, 1990).

3. For a nontechnical overview of this literature, see Kenneth A Shepsle, *Analyzing Politics: Rationality, Behavior, and Institutions*, 2nd ed. (New York: W. W. Norton, 2010).

4. The seminal work on this topic remains William A. Niskanen, *Bureaucracy and Representative Government* (1971; repr., Chicago: Aldine, 2007). For nonmaterial incentives, see Morton H. Halperin, Priscilla A. Clapp, and Arnold Kanter, *Bureaucratic Politics and Foreign Policy*, 2nd ed. (Washington DC: Brookings, 2006).

5. One notable exception is Peter D. Feaver, *Armed Servants: Agency, Oversight, and Civil-Military Relations* (Cambridge MA: Harvard University Press, 2005).

6. For a deeper discussion of the modifications necessary for a P-A analysis of wartime assessment, see Leo J. Blanken and Jason J. Lepore, "Performance Measurement in Military Operations: Information versus Incentives," *Defence and Peace Economics*, 2014 (on Taylor & Francis website); forthcoming in print, http://www.tandfonline.com/doi/abs/10.1080/10242694.2014.949548#preview.

7. In a democracy, this "looping" of the principal-agent ladder from the common soldier to the citizen serves to shape and temper the instigation and prosecution of wars. On the instigation of wars, see Kenneth A. Schultz, *Democracy and Coercive Diplomacy* (New York: Cambridge University Press, 2001); on the prosecution, see Dan Reiter and Allan C. Stam, *Democracies at War* (Princeton NJ: Princeton University Press, 2002); and on war termination, see H. E. Goemans,

War and Punishment: The Causes of War Termination and the First World War (Princeton NJ: Princeton University Press, 2000).

8. On this point, see chapter 2 by Hy Rothstein in this volume.

9. Our concepts of political goals and operational benchmarks parallel the "operational" and "nonoperational" goals in the seminal work of James G. March and Herbert A. Simon, with Harold Guetzkow, *Organizations* (New York: John Wiley and Sons, 1958).

10. Carl von Clausewitz, *On War*, trans. Michael Howard and Peter Paret (Princeton NJ: Princeton University Press, 1976), 81. See also Peter Paret, *The Cognitive Challenge of War: Prussia, 1806* (Princeton NJ: Princeton University Press, 2009), 122.

11. For classic treatments of the issues surrounding civil-military relations, see Samuel Huntington, *The Soldier and the State: The Theory and Politics of Civil-Military Relations* (1957; repr., Cambridge MA: Harvard University Press, 1985); and Richard K. Betts, *Soldiers, Statesmen, and Cold War Crises* (Cambridge MA: Harvard University Press, 1977).

12. US Joint Chiefs of Staff, JP-05, *Joint Operation Planning* (Washington DC: Department of Defense, August 11, 2011), III-45.

13. Jack D. Kem, "Assessment: Measures of Performance and Measures of Effectiveness," *Military Intelligence Professional Bulletin* 35, no. 2 (2009): 48–50.

14. See, for example, Richard A. Zeller and Edward G. Carmines, *Measurement in the Social Sciences: The Link between Theory and Data* (New York: Cambridge University Press, 1980).

15. This is a core concept in the new strategic landpower initiative currently being proposed by the US Army, US Marine Corps, and Special Operations Command. See Raymond T. Odierno, James F. Amos, and William H. McRaven, *Strategic Landpower: Winning the Clash of Wills* (Washington DC: Department of Defense, 2013), available at http://www.tradoc.army.mil/FrontPageContent/ Docs/Strategic%20Landpower%20White%20Paper.pdf.

16. US Joint Chiefs of Staff, JP-05, *Joint Operation Planning*, III-45.

17. On this point, see Jonathan Schroden, Rebecca Thomasson, Randy Foster, Mark Lukens, and Richard Bell, 2014, "A New Paradigm for Assessment in Counterinsurgency," *Military Operations Research* 18, no. 3 (2014): 5–20.

18. US Joint Chiefs of Staff, JP-05, *Joint Operation Planning*, appendix D.

19. Kem, "Assessment," 49.

20. Robert D. Putnam, "Diplomacy and Domestic Politics: The Logic of Two-Level Games," *International Organization* 42, no. 3 (1988): 427–60.

21. See Allan C. Stam, *Win, Lose, or Draw: Domestic Politics and the Crucible of War* (Ann Arbor: University of Michigan Press, 1999).

22. See Randolph M. Siverson and Harvey Starr, *The Diffusion of War: A Study of Opportunity and Willingness* (Ann Arbor: University of Michigan Press, 1991).

23. The strategic choice and utilization of senior advisers present additional dynamics. See Marissa Myers, "When Biased Advising Is a Good Thing: Information and Foreign Policy Decision Making," *International Interactions* 24, no. 4 (1998): 379–403; and Andrew Farkas, *State Learning and International Change* (Ann Arbor: University of Michigan Press, 1998).

24. Steven Kerr was the first to note the impact of time horizons on wartime behavior. He compared the soldiers of World War II, who were in "for the duration," to the soldiers of Vietnam, who served one-year tours, in the seminal article "On the Folly of Rewarding A, While Hoping for B," *Academy of Management Journal* 18 (1975): 769–83.

25. On this point, see Aric Shafran's work in chapter 19 of this volume.

26. See Leo J. Blanken and Justin Overbaugh, "Looking for Intel? . . . Or Looking for Answers? Reforming Military Intelligence for a Counter-Insurgency Environment," *Intelligence and National Security* 27, no. 4 (2012): 559–75; and John Bleigh, Justin Hufnagel, and Curt Snyder, "Institutional Challenges to Developing Metrics of Success in Irregular Warfare" (thesis, Naval Postgraduate School, 2011), accessible at http://www.soc.mil/SWCS/SWEG/AY_2011/Bleigh,%20J%202011.pdf.

2

CIVIL–MILITARY RELATIONS AND ASSESSMENTS

Hy Rothstein

WHEN A PRESIDENT SENDS AMERICAN TROOPS to war, a hidden timer starts to run. He has a finite period of time to win the war before the people grow weary of it.

Richard Nixon

Political and public support for an ongoing war is tied to proof of progress. In the past winning and losing were relatively easy to measure, especially in wars for national survival. However, the wars in Afghanistan and Iraq have proven very difficult to assess, and victory remains beyond reach. Perhaps the nature of these wars made campaign assessments more difficult than in the past. Maybe the war planning was flawed or the doctrine was inadequate. Possibly political goals were unclear, changing, or unrealistic, or execution on the ground was less than razor sharp. It could be, as former secretary of defense Donald Rumsfeld's famous memo to senior defense civilians and military leaders stated, the fact that we "lack metrics to know if we are winning or losing the global war on terror" accounts for the shortfalls in data necessary to guide the decisions of political and military leaders.[1] The problem goes beyond the issue of metrics, however, and is rooted in impaired strategic planning and bureaucratic governmental politics, contemporary civil-military relations, and the American way of war. These matters obscured rather than clarified what was to be accomplished. In other words, it was unclear what the United States was trying to do.

Risa Brooks has recently addressed the issue of assessment and civil-military politics. Brooks challenges the widely held belief that democracies

16

make better strategic decisions as a result of free and open debate. She argues that a better gauge to predict the quality of strategic assessment lies in a country's civil-military relations; specifically, she asserts conflicting civilian and military preferences coupled with ambiguous coordination, consultation, and decision-making processes undermine strategic assessment. For Brooks clear lines of authority are an anecdote to these damaging influences.[2]

While Brooks's focus is on the political-military calculation leading to the decision to go to war, Scott Sigmund Gartner examines the assessment issue while the war is being fought. Gartner posits that judgments about how well the military campaign is progressing can be made using a few quantitative measurements, referred to as dominant indicators, plus any significant rapid change of these indicators.[3] Of course, selecting the correct dominant indicators and making necessary adjustments over time are nontrivial matters with grave consequences should the wrong indicators persist.

Leo Blanken and Jason Lepore, in chapter 1 of this volume, offer a different model for conducting wartime assessments. Like Gartner, Blanken and Lepore focus mostly on military units operating in combat theaters. Their assessment model, however, clearly recognizes that war does not serve its own purpose, and political goals both propel military operations and ultimately must be satisfied. Accordingly their model relies on three considerations for effective assessment: *operational benchmarks*, *information*, and *incentives*. These considerations form the *metric triangle* that falls under, and is subordinate to, political goals. While the metric triangle is the centerpiece of Blanken and Lepore's work, they clearly acknowledge the underappreciated implications of unfilled space between the triangle and the political goals of the state. They aptly label this space as the *Clausewitzian gap*. The nature of this gap has weighty repercussions for any assessment process designed to guide the military to effectively secure the state's expressed political goals. The reasons for this gap and the way to minimize it are the subject of this chapter.

THE CLAUSEWITZIAN GAP

What exactly is the Clausewitzian gap? Clausewitz held that wars were fought for objectives that arose from the political sphere; therefore, political objectives shaped the course of military operations. Strategic failure was inevitable whenever political ends and military means were disconnected. He also recognized that war was one of several alternatives available to political leaders. More important, the key characteristic of war rested not in its destructiveness but in the violent, irrational emotions that the use of force could stimulate. Such emotions on the part of political and military leaders could change and even overpower the strategic logic that originally connected the ends and means for all involved. The resulting escalatory dynamic could make war alien to its original intended purpose.[4] This partially accounts for the subsequent strategic and assessment challenges associated with the Clausewitzian gap. But there is more.

IMPAIRED STRATEGIC PLANNING AND BUREAUCRATIC GOVERNMENTAL POLITICS

Strategic success and failure seem obvious in hindsight.[5] Good strategy starts with an understanding of what is to be accomplished. In other words, what are we trying to do? Failure to clearly answer this question at the outset may be the most egregious strategic error of all. For the military strategist, identifying the obstacles separating political objectives from the achievement of those objectives is the most urgent issue. Strategy functions as the purpose-built bridge connecting policy goals with policy ends, using mostly military tools. It is expressed in the form of a plan—that is, a clear articulation of how successful military operations would conclude the war and, most important, satisfy policy objectives. It is, in essence, a theory of victory. Clausewitz offers the simplest yet most complete definition of strategy: "the art of the employment of battles as a means to gain the object of war."[6] Yet the strategist is always operating against severe odds, especially in contemporary, democratic societies. Besides the enemy, political, bureaucratic, and institutional factors can quickly turn a good strategy into a bad one.[7]

But even if we understand the essence of strategy, we still need a way to make it, a means to execute the plan, and a method to measure progress. The image of political and military leaders coming together for a deliberative process with frank and open consultation leading to clear decisions may be the good intentions of all actors involved. The actual process is not so simple or clear-cut.[8]

Clean models for developing strategy exist only in theory. Egos, institutional agendas, current crises, personal relationships, budget constraints, domestic and reelection politics, and media leaks—all frustrate formal processes. Small politics can trump overarching national interests.[9] As a result, actual strategy making is suboptimal, and politics are always in flux. Good military leaders and strategists attempt to overcome this reality and create order through a comprehensive, deliberate planning process involving research and analysis and detailed planning. Although plans rarely survive initial contact with the enemy, they still are the basis for developing flexible options.[10]

By contrast, political leaders usually approach strategic problems differently as a result of their own backgrounds and experiences. Mostly they are successful lawyers or businessmen. They may distrust strong-minded military officers and do not hesitate to exert civilian control over the military. They might focus on the big picture and lack patience for military detail. They have little doubt that the past experiences and processes that brought them success can be directly applied to military problems and deliver equally successful results. Tangible cultural differences and perceived roles between civilian and military leaders can result in an unequal dialogue that undermines effective teamwork. Asserting complete civilian control of everything that is military is as dangerous as the military ignoring its civilian masters. The inevitable result of either will be bad strategy and possibly policy overreach.[11]

CIVIL-MILITARY RELATIONS

The central issue in civil-military relations involves a simple paradox: Because people fear others, they create an institution of violence for protection; but then this very institution becomes a source of fear.[12] The concern about civil-military relations dates back at least to Plato's *Republic* in which he debates the difficulties of creating a guardian class that would be both "gentle to their own and cruel to enemies."[13] For the United States, the fundamental issue of civil-military relations—preventing a military takeover of the state— has not been the concern. Not having to fear a coup has left serious thinking about the subject wanting for too long. Samuel P. Huntington's *The Soldier and the State*, originally published in 1957, set the terms of debate about civil-military relations in this country. Huntington recognized that the military mind-set was realistic and conservative. More important, the military ethos is a source of strength for both the military and society. His recipe for ensuring civilian dominance over the armed forces involved a clearly delineated partition between civilian and military roles. For Huntington objective civilian control of the military required increased professionalism of the officer corps that would result in a separate sphere of action independent of politics. Objective control recognized autonomous military professionalism and acknowledged that politicians should leave purely military matters to officers.[14] So for Americans, this national security dilemma seems to be resolved.

While there are boundaries that differentiate appropriate civilian and military areas of responsibility and expertise, significant areas also overlap. Civilian leaders are responsible for setting the policy goals, providing resources, establishing strategic priorities, and even levying operational constraints.

Military leaders must insist on clarity regarding the purpose of the military operation and must object when, in their best military judgment, the use of force, the constraints applied, or the resources provided are unlikely to deliver the expressed policy goals. This duty to object is not insubordination. It is part of the necessary dialogue and overlap of responsibilities between civilian and military leaders. Absent this dialogue, the level of political ambition or changing politics can become disconnected from the resources provided and the strategy designed to use military power to achieve political ends. The result will be a costly, protracted, and open-ended venture with an unsatisfying outcome.[15] This disconnect also wreaks havoc on any assessment process.

THE PERMANENT GAP AND THE AMERICAN BIFURCATION OF STRATEGY

A Clausewitzian gap is inevitable with the days of the statesman and military commander being the same person long gone. The military can easily perfect "doing things right." The more important question, and the one at the center of wartime assessments, is whether the military is "doing the right thing" for accomplishing policy objectives. Any provisional strategy or theory of victory requires periodic updating, not only because the enemy has a vote, but also because of the ever-changing nature of politics. The greatest challenge for the strategist is not designing a campaign plan to achieve set goals but to anticipate what the goals ought to be based on inevitable political change and newfound insights about the logic of the ongoing struggle. Therefore, in recognizing the dynamic nature of war and minimizing the Clausewitzian gap, the role of the strategist may be above that of all others.[16]

Still the American strategic culture makes developing strategy difficult. In a political system where power is shared, authority fragmented, and consensus rarely achieved, crafting clear national policies is challenging. And if strategy exists to support the attainment of policy, then any good Clausewitzian must accept that politics does more than intrude in strategy and war. However, while most military officers can quote Clausewitz regarding the indispensable connection between politics and war, they do not seem to accept the full implications of his logic.[17] As Sir Lawrence Freedman notes, one finds among American military thinking that "politics is often treated [by] . . . military theory as an awkward exogenous factor, at best a necessary inconvenience and at worst a source of weakness and constraint."[18]

The US military displayed its aversion to policy and politics during World War II when Gen. George Marshall bristled at presidential guidance intended to shape operations in North Africa. Marshall felt that the direction reflected a sensitivity more to electoral cycles than to the exigencies of the war. During Operation Just Cause in 1989, military planners showed little appreciation for the political conditions necessary to establish a legitimate government after Manuel Noriega was ousted. Likewise not only did planners in 2003 barely consider the basic requirements to maintain order after Saddam Hussein and the Iraqi army fell, but it is also now clear that the war itself never fully attained its political objectives. After more than thirteen years in Afghanistan, either our strategy was inadequate or our political goals were poorly conceived. This aversion to big politics breaks Colin S. Gray's proverbial "strategy bridge." The rational and perhaps linear way that military leaders develop strategy contrasts with the policy creation process that is inevitably the product of negotiation and compromise. Strategy making can never be a politics-free enterprise.[19]

To be sure, on the civilian side of Gray's bridge, the policy community, today more than ever before, seems to distance itself from the realities and limitations of the use of force. Even worse it may leave the war fighting to the generals and never ask the hard questions about how a given strategy will deliver policy objectives. Contemporary American military strategists, however, tend to shy away from the complicated process of turning military successes into policy victories. The focus for the military professional is on winning battles and campaigns while policymakers concentrate on the political struggles preceding and during the war. This bifurcation is both a matter of preference and a by-product of American civil-military relations. As a result, two separate spheres of responsibility exist—one for politics and one for military operations.[20]

THE AMERICAN WAY OF WAR

Two centuries after its founding, scholars were able to look back and study America's approach to war. Russell Weigley's *The American Way of War* is a comprehensive examination of the approach Americans took for exercising military power from the American Revolution through the Vietnam War.[21] He concluded that with the exception of the Revolution, American-style warfare sought to crush opponents through strategies of attrition or annihilation. Generally the destruction of the enemy's capacity to wage war and the occupation of his capital marked the end of the war and the beginning of postwar political and diplomatic dialogues.[22] This conception evaded the true logic of war by rarely thinking beyond winning battles and campaigns and on to the ultimate political objective of the struggle, or the only measure that matters. Antulio Echevarria, rephrasing Weigley, calls the American approach to war "a way of battle" more than a way of war.[23]

The current American approach to war that emphasizes the employment of Special Forces, precision firepower, psychological operations, and joint and combined task forces is not a significant departure from slightly older concepts that highlighted the qualities of speed, jointness, knowledge, and precision. Underlying both concepts is the belief that delivering a series of coordinated strikes (kinetic and non-kinetic) against an adversary's center of gravity will paralyze his ability to wage war. Both concepts assume that America's asymmetric technical advantage will deliver the same outcomes that Weigley described as America's style of war but now at much less cost.[24] The commonality between the contemporary and traditional views of the American approach to war unfortunately displays a similar weakness—that is, a lack of emphasis on the endgame. It confuses winning battles and campaigns with winning wars. This confusion inevitably leads to assessment models that are destined to measure the wrong things.

BETTER WARTIME ASSESSMENT REQUIRES BETTER POLICY-STRATEGY FORMULATION

We're lost, but we're making good time!

Yogi Berra

Famed baseball player Yogi Berra is credited with many comical remarks. Yogi was driving to the Baseball Hall of Fame in Cooperstown, New York, with some other players. After passing the same landmark three times, Joe Garagiola said, "Yogi, you're lost." Berra replied, "Yeah, I know it. But we're making good time, ain't we?"[25] Yogi's assessment was accurate but irrelevant to the undertaking. Policy is also meaningless without a mechanism to sanction it.

Any meaningful wartime assessment concept must follow a policy formulation process that includes a more balanced dialogue between civilian and military leaders. Military leaders should have a role in shaping foreign policy, in setting the conditions under which the military is expected to act, in creating the forces and equipment appropriate for its missions, and in mobilizing civil support for its activities.[26] After all, policy is nothing by itself. These issues are contentious, but the military strategist has a duty to encroach on political decision making to convey what is within reach through military operations. The necessary dialogue does not change who has the last word in civil-military relations. Good strategy requires this dialogue, and meaningful wartime assessment demands better strategy.

Moving forward will require a significant effort to reduce the bifurcation of policy-strategy formulation. The custom of senior military leaders fixating on the actual conduct of war hinders the translation of military victory into policy success. In Clausewitzian terms, it subordinates the logic of war to its grammar. Many will view moves to reduce this bifurcation as attempts to weaken civilian control of the military; however, the historic and proper dominant civilian role in decision making will not change because it has become a part of the American military officers' DNA. So while tension will exist between preserving civilian control and giving military officers a greater voice in policy decisions, closing the gap between policy and power demands adjustment.[27] The following thoughts are offered.

Professional military education must be modified. Senior military officers will need to know more to have a greater voice in policy formulation. To a large degree, the wars in Afghanistan and Iraq were fought to bring about a political and economic order favorable to the United States. Whether these goals were ever possible to achieve at an acceptable cost is open to debate, but senior military officers should have had more to say. What is less debatable is the preparedness of military leaders to go beyond military success. Some suggest that planning for post-conflict operations was inadequate because of the rapid collapse of organized resistance resulting from modern, quick-paced US military maneuvers. In other words, unlike during World War II, planners simply did not have time to plan for post-conflict requirements. A more plausible explanation is the policy-strategy bifurcation already discussed. After all in an era of fast-paced military operations, there is no reason why post-conflict planning cannot start simultaneously with the planning of combat operations.[28]

A better-educated senior military officer is necessary but not enough to sufficiently reduce the gap created by the separate spheres through bifurcation. Political-military aptitude is not present in every well-educated and operationally effective officer. For the most part, officer evaluation reports do not screen for aptitude in policy formulation and international politics. In fact, too much aptitude in these areas may flatten an officer's career progression curve. A process is needed to identify and reward talented officers who possess both soldier and statesman qualities and to develop these people through carefully selected assignments and education. This will not be easy because it will create friction in both the civilian and military ranks. It is also not clear that the military is prepared to properly identify these officers.

Not all education is equal. Historically highly regarded education programs that have kept officers away from the trenches for a few years may have done more to damage an officer's career than to help it. More education rather than better education seems to be the norm. To illustrate, in early 2014 the chief of staff of the US Air Force said that he wanted officers to have master's degrees as a requirement for promotion to colonel, but he did not comment on the quality and relevance of that education. He went on to say that officers selected for professional military education (PME) schools would be able to get degrees while attending these schools.[29] Most high-quality master's programs require two years of study while senior officer PME may last for ten months. So in ten months, an officer will study a military-specific curriculum and study the brainy topics found in quality two-year master's programs. The message is clear for US Air Force officers: Get a degree and check the box. The quality of the education associated with the degree doesn't matter. This standard must change.

More than ever before, an officer's effectiveness not only will depend on his knowledge, skills, and character but also will require an understanding of the changing geopolitical environment and its impact on conflict. But officers, past and present, faithfully keep their noses to the bureaucratic grindstone, focusing on day-to-day operations and housekeeping tasks, and seldom look up. They deal with increasingly more sophisticated equipment, logistics, and budget issues. Both senior and junior officers generally focus on the same categories of knowledge—leadership, weapons, tactics, techniques and procedures, and administration—but at what point in someone's career do these activities become a distraction from more important duties?[30]

When day-to-day activities and grindstone work schedules dominate, creativity is often suppressed. The Defense Department must go beyond the routine of PME and assist the most talented officers to break away from simply solving daily problems. Selected officers must occupy themselves with the higher problems of war, so when war comes, they know what to do rather than default to doing the housekeeping that they know how to do. The strategists in uniform must provide advice to political leaders in the development of national policy—what is to be achieved—because they are in the best position to convey to political leaders what can be achieved using the military instrument.[31]

The scope of this chapter does not permit offering a detailed agenda for identifying and developing military strategists, but one thing is clear: Trying to create "instant strategists" in time of war is too costly. We must break out of established patterns that focus attention on mundane activities that suffocate the ability to think. Time must be put aside to study with the right scholars, to seek council from successful leaders, to read, to train, and to learn from maneuvers, war, and trial and error in the school of hard knocks. Taking a strategy elective at a ten-month PME school coupled with a "shake and bake" master's program as a means of developing senior military thinkers is farcical. Reducing the bifurcation requires strengthening both military and civilian education and ensuring officers are taught by first-rate faculty. Though difficult, the military has the means to effect meaningful change within its ranks. No similar means exist to change the way political leaders behave.

The second and perhaps more difficult problem is the flip side of the first and is directly related to the question of civilian control of the military. Even though the threat of a military coup in the United States is almost nonexistent, what is possible is an overly influential military either draining society of limited resources as a hedge against real and perceived enemies of the state or, perhaps, pressing the state to go to war or to continue the fight contrary to society's interest.

In democracies the prerogatives of the protected always trump those of the protector. It is the case even when the military expert understands the issue best. It is the politician who must determine the value the people attach to a particular matter and the level of risk acceptable to society. Military leaders may quantify risk, but politicians judge it and decide how much security to buy and how much risk to accept.[32]

Therefore, the need for society to be protected *by* its military is in constant tension with society's need to be protected *from* its military. Vulnerability to outside threats increases at one end of the by–from continuum while susceptibility to military seizure of political power exists at the other. While a balance is clearly possible (and is the norm in the United States), fear of an imbalance tilting toward the military has resulted in political leaders getting what they ask for even if the end result is not what they had envisioned. Political leaders have the right to be wrong, and they even have the right to use the military to advance any number of societal goals.[33] But if the military becomes so pliant at the behest of the politician that the balance tilts too far, then all will be lost. Sometimes the military needs protection from the politicians. Thus, because educating political leaders about a healthy balance between protection *by* the military and protection *from* the military is impractical, the burden remains with senior officers to be well educated and articulate enough to shape policy for the national defense.

Educating political officials may be impractical, but acknowledging their shortcomings cannot be ignored. Civilian leaders are almost always less prepared for service to the nation than senior military officers are. Huntington recognized that the military is a profession. Accordingly, it is founded upon specialized education and training along with relevant professional qualifications necessary for advancement. No such standards exist for elected public officials or for political appointees. The qualifications for president and for members of Congress are minimal and specified in the Constitution. Perhaps this is partly because the founding fathers never considered political office as a career choice or a profession. Today, however, it is a career choice. Career politicians and professional staffs are the norm in Washington. But the characteristics of a true profession never materialized.

One can only hope that elected officials might be mindful of Plato's law that they must know war if they want peace. If this awareness is too much to expect, then there is truth to the old adage that the people deserve the politicians they elect (along with the people the Senate consents to hold appointed positions).

So even if the military does its job well, politicians who fail to cash in on the blood spilled and treasure spent in a successful military campaign can still lose the peace. Military leaders must live with this reality, but politicians and their professional staffs need to recognize their responsibilities and deficiencies and to be better prepared for their positions.

IS EFFECTIVE OPERATIONAL ASSESSMENT IN WAR POSSIBLE?

Effective wartime assessment can only be a by-product of effective policy-strategy formulation. Yet the obstacles standing in the way of policy-strategy formulation remain formidable. The tension between the demands of military security and the values and traditions that frame American civil-military relations will only be relieved by the weakening of the security threat or the weakening of America's liberal traditions; neither of which is likely to occur. When the United States moves closer to war, military officers exert significant influence and authority. It is also at this point that military officers focus their efforts more on the military task of defeating the threat and less on winning the war. At other times when the threat seems minimal, military leaders lose their influence, and political leaders look for "peace dividends" and ways to advance domestic agendas, sometimes using the military as a weather gauge. The irony is that an influential military officer corps historically has been a force for caution, sanity, and realism. The stronger the military voice, the less the likelihood of conflict. There is little doubt that strong American officership does more good than harm.[34]

The need to reduce the bifurcation between policy formulation and strategy development seems evident. Undoubtedly something should be done. The larger questions of whether the bifurcation can be significantly reduced and if it is desirable to do so are at the core of American democracy and civil-military relations.

Samuel Huntington, in the closing pages of his classic book on civil-military relations, gives us perhaps the best insight into the possibility of attaining a more synchronized civil-military dialogue. He describes the town of Highland Falls, New York, the village just south of the main gate to the US Military Academy at West Point. The town is a mosaic of small banks, real estate and insurance offices, barbershops, Victorian homes with faded porticoes, and old wooden churches. Overhead telephone and electrical wires connect the structures in an attempt to make something whole of the motley disconnected nature of this small town, but the incredible variety of structures and small-town commercialism reveal a lack of common purpose or unity. A short distance away, on the other side of West Point's South Gate, exists a different world. There is order, even serenity. The academy's individual parts do not exist on their own but are subordinate to the whole. Both beauty and utility are merged into the gray stone walls and neatly landscaped surroundings. Rhythm, harmony, and collective will displace individual impulse. The West Point community has a purpose, and the behavior of its citizens is governed by a code. The spirit of Highland Falls is embodied in Main Street. The spirit of West Point is found in a military life that subordinates the soldier to duty for society's purposes, reflecting the military ideal at its best. While this discipline, order, and selfless devotion have much to offer Main Street, we must remember that the virtues of West Point have been democracy's vices, and the vices of the military, democracy's virtues.[35]

NOTES

For the epigraph, Richard Nixon, *No More Vietnams* (New York: Arbor House, 1985), 88.

1. Donald Rumsfeld, "Rumsfeld's War-on-Terror Memo," *USA Today*, October 16, 2003, http://usatoday30.usatoday.com/news/washington/executive/rumsfeld -memo.htm.

2. Risa A. Brooks, *Shaping Strategy: The Civil-Military Politics of Strategic Assessment* (Princeton NJ: Princeton University Press, 2008), 4–9, 15–18.

3. Scott Sigmund Gartner, *Strategic Assessment in War* (New Haven CT: Yale University Press, 1997), 4–5.

4. Daniel Moran, "The Instrument: Clausewitz on Aims and Objectives in War," in *Clausewitz in the Twenty-first Century,* ed. Hew Strachan and Andreas Herberg-Rothe (Oxford: Oxford University Press, 2007), 91–92.

5. This section's subtitle reflects the ideas in *Essence of Decision: Explaining the Cuban Missile Crisis* by Graham T. Allison, 2nd ed. (New York: Longman, 1999). This book is an analysis of decision making during the Cuban missile crisis. The book's title is based on a speech by John F. Kennedy, who said, "The essence of ultimate decision remains impenetrable to the observer—often,

indeed, to the decider himself." The book says that decisions are the cumulative result of rational thinking, organizational processes, and governmental or "palace" politics. Allison's model is useful in helping to decipher past decisions. It also illuminates the difficulties in predicting policy.

6. Carl von Clausewitz, *On War*, trans. Michael Howard and Peter Paret (Princeton NJ: Princeton University Press, 1976), 177.

7. Colin S. Gray, "The Strategist as Hero," *Joint Forces Quarterly* 62 (July 2011): 38–40.

8. Richard D. Hooker, "The Strange Voyage: A Short Précis on Strategy," *Parameters* 42, no. 4/43, no. 1 (Spring 2013): 59–60.

9. I differentiate between "big politics," which is about international power and order, and "small politics," which would include political posturing by a politician or by the armed services to get a bigger share of the defense budget.

10. Hooker, "Strange Voyage," 61.

11. See ibid.; and Eliot Cohen, *Supreme Command* (New York: Free Press, 2002), 208–11.

12. Peter D. Feaver, "The Civil-Military Problematique: Huntington, Janowitz, and the Question of Civilian Control," *Armed Forces & Society* 23, no. 2 (Winter 1996): 152–54.

13. Quoted from Cohen, *Supreme Command*, 225.

14. See Samuel P. Huntington, *The Soldier and the State: The Theory and Politics of Civil-Military Relations* (Cambridge MA: Harvard University Press, 1981), 83; and Cohen, *Supreme Command*, 226–27.

15. Hooker, "Strange Voyage," 62.

16. Brig. Gen. Huba Wass de Czege (USA, Ret.), "Systemic Operational Design: Learning and Adapting in Complex Missions," *Military Review* 89, no. 1 (January–February 2009): 5.

17. Frank Hoffman, "Politics and the American Way of War (and Strategy)," *War on the Rocks* (blog), October 15, 2013, http://warontherocks.com/2013/10/politics-and-the-american-way-of-war-and-strategy/.

18. Sir Lawrence Freedman is quoted in ibid.

19. Ibid.

20. Antulio J. Echevarria II, *Toward an American Way of War* (Carlisle PA: Strategic Studies Institute, March 2004), 7.

21. Russell F. Weigley, *The American Way of War: A History of United States Military Strategy and Policy* (Bloomington IN: Indiana University Press, 1973).

22. See ibid., 475; and Echevarria, *Toward an American Way*, 1.

23. Echevarria, *Toward an American Way*, 1.

24. See ibid., 8; and Max Boot, "The New American Way of War," *Foreign Affairs* 82, no. 4 (July/August 2003): 41–58.

25. Yogi Berra, as identified in *Quote Investigator*, http://quoteinvestigator.com/
    2012/07/11/making-good-time/.
26. Cohen, *Supreme Command*, 226.
27. Echevarria, *Toward an American Way*, 16–17.
28. Ibid., 13–14.
29. Gen. Mark A. Welsh III (USAF), quoted by Rich Lamance in "CSAF: Taking
    Care of Airmen, Future Roadmap Key to AF Success," *Air Force News Service*,
    February 21, 2014, http://www.af.mil/News/ArticleDisplay/tabid/223/Article/
    473391/csaf-taking-care-of-airmen-future-roadmap-key-to-af-success.aspx.
30. John R. Galvin, "Uncomfortable Wars: Toward a New Paradigm," *Parameters*
    16, no. 4 (1986): 2–3.
31. John R. Galvin, "What's the Matter with Being a Strategist?," *Parameters* 20,
    no. 4 (Winter 2010–11): 82–84.
32. Feaver, "Civil-Military Problematique," 152–54.
33. Ibid., 154.
34. Huntington, *Soldier and the State*, 456, 463.
35. Ibid., 464–66.

3

WARTIME STRATEGIC ASSESSMENT
CONCEPTS AND CHALLENGES

Scott Sigmund Gartner

THE MAXIM "WIN THE BATTLE, BUT LOSE THE WAR" captures the challenge of evaluating wartime performance. As US Air Force colonel (and former dean of the School of Advanced Airpower Studies) Philip Meilinger wrote, "One of the most vital yet difficult tasks a wartime commander must perform is strategic assessment."[1] Strategic assessment affects decisions about changing and retaining strategies, war duration, war outcomes, and the costs and patterns of war. Despite its importance, strategic assessment in war and the conduct of war have generally received minimal analytical study, with most systematic research focusing "almost exclusively . . . with the subject of initial war outbreak."[2] The result is that critical, elemental questions remain unanswered or understudied. One of the most important of these questions addresses the topic of strategic assessment: How does war information affect leaders' assessments of strategy performance? This question is fundamental to understanding the dynamics that shape the conduct and outcomes of war.

One reason that assessment receives little study is that strategic assessment is also hard to do. On the one hand, the task seems simple and clear. As Leo Blanken and Jason Lepore write, "Wartime assessment involves the gathering and analyzing of information to update a decision maker's understanding of an ongoing conflict."[3] In practice, however, the task is daunting. Three factors make strategic assessment especially difficult: wartime information accrues faster than wartime analytical capacity, leaders need to make decisions before they have a clear picture of what is going on, and the information environment contains tremendous uncertainty and noise.

INFORMATION OVERLOAD

Wartime performance information accumulates too quickly for decision makers to analyze it all.[4] War answers dozens of questions and raises many others: Did allies on either side fight? What strategy did the adversary use? Are new weapons on both sides as effective as claimed? Will troops fight hard for a new country? Have the changes implemented since the last war improved or deteriorated fighting capacity? At the same time these questions are being answered, fighting raises new information about tactical, operational, and strategic effectiveness. It is likely that a war between these militaries with these weapons in this situation has never occurred before. Every maneuver, battle, and logistic effort exposes new problems and questions. All of this information washes down upon the leaders who are looking to figure out what is going on and, critically, whether they are winning or losing.

THE NEED FOR SPEED

Leaders collect wartime intelligence so quickly that it almost always exceeds a military organization's capacity for thorough and comprehensive analysis. The rapid rate of conflict data generation places a premium on the ability to identify and interpret relevant information. A quick decision can lead to victory (e.g., Israel's attack on the Egyptian Air Force in the 1967 Six-Day War), but it also can be disastrous (e.g., Egypt's decision to go beyond the Sinai passes in the 1973 Arab-Israeli War). The dilemma is that waiting until the situation becomes clear is often too late. As Gen. Colin Powell states, "We do not have the luxury of collecting information indefinitely. At some point, before we can have every possible fact in hand, we have to decide. The key is not to make quick decisions, but to make timely decisions."[5] In August 1990 when an adviser suggested that Saudi Arabian king Fahd wait to learn more about the Iraqis' intent before inviting American forces into his country, he replied, "The Kuwaitis did not rush into a decision, and today they are guests in our hotels!"[6] Strategic assessment always reflects a trade-off between accuracy and speed, a choice made even more difficult by the uncertainty of wartime information.

CERTAIN ABOUT UNCERTAINTY

In a linear battle, the front line moving forward means you are winning, and backward movement means you are losing. Measuring performance is less clear, however, in other types of conflict, such as an insurgency.[7] Daniel Byman notes, "Counterinsurgency is difficult for even the best militaries."[8] For example, conditions in the Vietnam War did not lend themselves to traditional military measurement of ground warfare. "In a conventional war, possession of real estate has generally been the measure of success, but progress in the Vietnam War was not to be assessed in the straightforward manner."[9] The problem was that "looking at maps of the war in Vietnam never told anybody what was really happening until the very end."[10] The mission thus required other types of performance measures, notably the enemy body count. The war in Afghanistan was equally challenging to assess, but here the enemy body count plays a much smaller role.[11] These examples demonstrate the potential for measurement variation between seemingly similar conflicts. Much of this variation has to do with the rudimentary uncertainty and difficulty of strategic assessment.

War has no scoreboard; rather, it has multiple measures of performance. After the war the best measures may be clear, but confusion reigns during the conflict. Carl von Clausewitz stated that "a great part of the information obtained in War is contradictory, a still greater part is false, and by far the greatest part is of a doubtful character."[12] The strategic assessment challenge is thus highly formidable; leaders must "decide which data to ignore as trivial and which to interpret as important signals. They must reconcile conflicting evidence. They must amalgamate into a single answer the most diverse indicators: reports from the battlefield, statistics on potential military resources, and impressionistic predictions of how friend and foe will bear the costs and suffering of further fighting."[13]

The assessment process is also hindered by the nature of the data; in war people die, putting tremendous pressure on leaders to "get it right fast." Unlike peacetime, merely the presence of death and destruction tells a leader little about a policy's performance. Given the costs of defeat, leaders try to implement the best strategies available. As a result strategic assessment is also a stressful, uncertain, political, and deadly serious business.

Strategy is the plan that connects means to ends. I define *strategy* as the way an organization operates a class of military forces to achieve specific aims against an adversary.[14] Organizations implement and assess strategy. For example, it would be difficult to discuss US strategy in the Gulf War. Instead, one could say that the US Air Force's strategy was to gain and maintain air superiority and to attack the Iraqi command and control apparatus, and the US Army and Marine Corps's strategy was to bluff a coastal, frontal assault and instead assail Iraqi forces indirectly. Put simply, organizations—not nations—implement, assess, and fight. Strategy plays a key role in affecting a war's outcome.[15] Both military and civilian actors, as well as analysts, frequently view the choice of strategy as one of the most critical decisions made in war.

MY APPROACH

How do decision makers then select and use wartime information to evaluate a strategy's performance, and how can we as analysts systematically represent that process? I show that we can capture organizations' strategic assessment beliefs with the *dominant indicator* approach.[16] The dominant indicator approach focuses on wartime performance metrics and their movement. Indicators—quantitative, time-based measures of performance such as the number of enemy dead—reflect an organization's mission. If an indicator moves in the desired direction (e.g., the monthly number of enemy dead increases), it suggests the strategy is performing well. Conversely, when the indicator moves in an undesired direction (e.g., monthly enemy dead decreases), leaders view their policy as failing.

ORGANIZATIONS, INTERESTS, AND MISSIONS

Organizations impose their identity on individuals through recruitment, training, and incentives: "Governments perceive problems through organizational sensors."[17] Leaders thus represent and reflect their organization. Individuals naturally have their own idiosyncratic interests and traits, but because organizational interests are systematic and general, a group's and a leader's preferences tend to be highly correlated. For example, when he was at the Office of Management and Budget (OMB), Caspar Weinberger was called Cap the Knife because he was so adamant about cutting budgets, reflecting the OMB's organizational objective during the Nixon administration. In the next decade when Weinberger was secretary of defense, David Stockman referred to him as Cap the Shovel because he oversaw the largest US peacetime military buildup and was so unwilling to cut the Department of Defense's budget.[18] At both jobs Weinberger displayed certain individual characteristics, such as intelligence, stubbornness, and bureaucratic effectiveness, but in each position he clearly reflected the preferences and objectives of the organizations that he led.

Organizations' behavior derives from their pursuit of intrinsic interests, which include such factors as autonomy, budget, prestige, and essence (the image that an organization has of itself).[19] In addition, each organization has an assigned objective. The objectives lay out the basic goals that an organization's supervisory agency (sometimes called the principal) expects the organization to accomplish.[20] Organizations are unable to do whatever they want; instead, they try to make choices that pursue their interests within the objectives imposed upon them. Organizations combine their basic interests with their assigned objective to form a "mission," which in turn provides them with operable goals upon which they can direct their efforts. Herbert Simon wrote, "Most organizations are oriented around some goal or objective which provides the purpose toward which the organization decisions and activities are directed."[21] Missions represent what the organization sees as its purpose. The organization then chooses the strategy it thinks is most likely to achieve the mission. Because the mission contains the organization's interests and objective, the organization's leaders believe that a policy that is good for the mission is good for their organization and for their country. For example, "military officers tend to see the health of their institution as a determining condition of the health of national security."[22]

Abstract notions such as "do a good job" and "win the war" are too broad to be well suited for assessment. Organizations require goals to be observable, clear, and measurable. As Simon notes, "High-level goals provide little guide [sic] for action because it is difficult to measure their attainment and difficult to measure the effects of concrete actions upon them."[23] Victory and defeat also occur too late; decision makers want to know how well they are doing before they win or lose. "Victory is an outcome of a battle; it is not what a military organization does in battle."[24] Even when leaders win a war, they might evaluate their performance as poor. For example, in 1941 German airborne forces defeated the British forces on Crete and took possession of the island in a "highly ambiguous victory" that led to Adolf Hitler's displeasure despite the outcome. After Israel's "victory" in the 1973 war, the Israeli government created a commission to study why it had been surprised and why casualties were so high.

Given that their missions are organization specific, leaders from the same country might rely on different types of information to assess their individual performance.[25] Because they rely on a different organizational lens, two leaders who hold common high-level goals might reach conflicting evaluations of their "nation's" performance. Each of them might be unable to recognize that the other is using different criteria to assess the situation. In these circumstances, different organizational lenses might result in leaders talking completely past each other.

THE DOMINANT INDICATOR APPROACH

To assess their performance, organizations need to analyze information generated by their behavior. Organizations may rely on a variety of different types of information for formulating beliefs about the likely outcomes of their implemented policies. Among the types of information they employ are quantitative indicators, or time-specific measures of complex information, to assess policy performance. "Even a cursory examination of other historical examples suggests that a tendency toward the use of indicators is widespread across time and in different countries."[26] In making all types of choices, decision makers frequently rely on indicators. "People typically make predictions about the behavior of the economy and the behavior of individuals based upon a limited number of easily observable characteristics. We say that such a prediction is based upon an *indicator*."[27] Indicators represent cognitive shortcuts that actors use in the face of an overwhelmingly complex reality.

Modern warfare generates many different types of indicators. For example, naval leaders concerned with the effectiveness of a blockade might look at how many ships they were able to sink. Naturally they do not assume that each ship is equivalent, as some ships carry supplies that are clearly more important than others. But as a general measure of the success or failure of a blockade strategy, the number of ships sunk represents a reasonable, and useful, gauge of blockade effectiveness. This is especially true given that they cannot observe effectively the number of ships that make it through their blockade and reach enemy ports. But all other things being equal, as the number of enemy ships sunk increases the adversary obtains fewer supplies. This example closely resembles the way that the US Navy operated in World War II. It measured the success of its blockade on Japan through the number of Japanese ships sunk. "Submarine skippers were simply told to sink ships, any kind of ships, or they would be relieved of command."[28] Ships sunk provided a measure of policy success, yet an exact estimate of what supplies were destroyed was impossible to determine. The number of ships sunk thus represented a quantitative measure of success, or an indicator.

Indicators that leaders rely on for evaluating their strategies are called dominant indicators.[29] They are dominant in the sense that they represent the most important quantitative data used by the group, and they capture the primary forces that structure an organization's strategic assessment: "*The indicators made discussion possible while simultaneously distorting and ultimately dominating it.*"[30] Dominant indicators represent an organization's central measure of performance.[31] In the naval example, "sinking enemy ships, seizing key ports, and establishing patrolled areas that friendly unarmed ships can safely use are linked to winning control of sea lines of communication. These relationships define measures that determine whether the military organization is performing the way it is supposed to perform."[32] Dominant indicators reflect the decision makers' dynamic information environment.

The dominant indicator approach, as shown in figure 3.1, is similar to other strategic assessments (e.g., see Blanken and Lepore's figure 1.1 in chapter 1), but it has several distinguishing features. First, *organizational interests* (such as maximizing budget, autonomy, and prestige) combine with the *assigned objective* to form the organization's *mission*. Organizations then select *strategies* that they think are most likely to meet their mission's requirements. Based on their mission, organizations choose the *dominant indicators* that they think will most likely reflect success (note this model is changed from an earlier version presented in Gartner's *Strategic Assessment in War* [1997]). Observing the movements of their dominant indicators, organizations form *strategic assessments* regarding the performance of their strategies.

Indicators not only provide insight into leaders' strategic incentives, they help to explain the dynamics of military organizations. Because they link actions to success and failure, performance measures create incentives and disincentives for particular types of behavior, translating abstract goals into operational objectives. Conversely, "imperfect measures of success may have deleterious externalities by creating unintended incentive structures for agents within the organization."[33] Clear objectives and measures of success

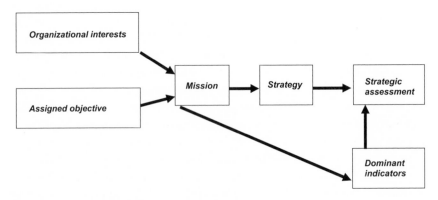

Figure 3.1. Dominant indicators and strategic assessment

are critical for military operations.[34] Military leaders use these indicators to form assessments and make necessary changes.[35] Gen. William Westmoreland, head of US forces in Vietnam during the fiercest fighting of the war, noted that "statistics were, admittedly, an imperfect gauge of progress, yet in the absence of conventional frontlines, how else [were we] to measure it?"[36] He was not alone; leaders routinely employ and trust quantitative performance data to form their strategic assessments.[37]

Organizations evaluate their performance to maximize their likelihood of accomplishing missions. Whether we identify this behavior as learning, Bayesian updating, cybernetics, or feedback, organizations assess and often alter their policies and resource distributions on the basis of their experiences and assessments. Put simply, organizations "keep tabs on their own performance."[38] Dominant indicators link battlefield information and organizational performance assessments. Organizations form their assessments of whether strategies are succeeding or failing based on the direction of these indicators. Movement of the indicators in the desired direction suggests positive performance; the opposite direction results in the opposite assessment.

ALTERNATIVES

It is important to distinguish between *quantitative goals*, which are static, numerical descriptions of objectives, and *indicators*, which are variable measures of strategic performance. For example, the Germans believed in World War I that if they sank about 600,000 tons of British shipping per month, they would win the war.[39] Similarly Secretary of Defense Robert McNamara identified the minimum amount of damage US nuclear weapons had to be able to inflict on the Soviet Union for "assured destruction" as destruction of 30 percent of its population and 60 percent of its industrial capacity.[40] In both examples, the leaders defined their goals quantitatively. These benchmarks may play a role in measuring success, but they are not measures of policy performance as they neither vary nor reflect the organization's behavior.

Some scholars disagree with this dominant indicator perspective and argue that organizations fail to assess their policies and behavior. "Evaluation and organization, it turns out, are to some extent contradictory terms."[41] Historically, however, organizations frequently evaluate their performance, and military and civilian organizations in war conduct and act on their strategic assessments. While this volume contains several critical in-depth studies of wartime performance evaluation, I will now briefly relate three vignettes that demonstrate some of the variable strategic assessment behavior observed in war.

THE BATTLE OF BRITAIN TO THE BLITZ

On July 16, 1940, Adolf Hitler issued Führer Directive No. 16, which ordered the German Air Force, or the Luftwaffe, to destroy virtually all British military capabilities on land, sea, and air before the planned German invasion of Great Britain (Operation Sea Lion).[42] Hermann Göring, head of the Luftwaffe, translated these objectives into a strategy that used bombers to destroy all elements of the British Royal Air Force (RAF). Göring stated, "As long as the enemy air force is not destroyed, it is the basic principle of the conduct of air war to attack the enemy air units at every possible favorable opportunity—by day and night, in the air, and on the ground—without regard for other missions."[43] In July the Luftwaffe began the Battle of Britain, an intense bombing effort designed to destroy all RAF facilities, planes, and personnel. To bomb the RAF targets accurately, most of the Luftwaffe raids occurred during daylight hours, which facilitated bombing accuracy but also allowed British antiaircraft efforts to be most effective. The German attack was enormous, employing a substantial portion of the Luftwaffe's planes. The effort was also extremely costly to both sides: In August the Luftwaffe lost 774 planes, or 18.5 percent of its total strength, while the RAF lost more than 25 percent of its fighter pilots.[44] Between August 24 and September 6, the Luftwaffe lost 380 aircraft and the RAF 290.[45] Losses were running too high for the Luftwaffe to sustain this effort, and at the same time the RAF's capabilities did not seem to weaken fundamentally.

As a result, "the Germans changed their air strategy."[46] On September 7, the Luftwaffe instituted a strategic shift. "Attacks on Britain's air defense system through September 6 had given no indication that Fighter Command was weakening. Göring—at [Albert] Kesselring's urging and with Hitler's support—turned to a massive assault on the British capital."[47] The Luftwaffe thus turned the Battle of Britain into the London Blitz, as it altered its strategy from one of counterforce to countervalue and switched from attacking the RAF to bombing London. The Luftwaffe increasingly bombed London at night, leading to a much more sustainable loss rate than their daylight raids against air defense targets had. Despite the improved loss rate, however, the Blitz was not successful in destroying enough of London either for the British to sue for peace or for the RAF to be annihilated in its defense of London. As a result, the Germans called off the Blitz and the invasion of the United Kingdom, and they never again threatened to invade Britain during the war.[48]

Two aspects of the Battle of Britain and the Blitz deserve special attention. First, the Blitz represented a strategic change for the Luftwaffe because it switched its target category from air defense to attacking London's civilian and industrial targets. Second, during the campaigns, the Luftwaffe performed two strategic assessments. When the leadership determined that the Battle of Britain was not successful, it changed its strategy to the London Blitz. Next, when the Blitz was not successful, the leadership terminated it.

During the Luftwaffe's switch from attacking British air defense forces to bombing the capital, London, the basic German political objectives remained the same. Changes in strategy were driven largely by battlefield assessments and not by the introduction of new goals. But sometimes changes in strategy result from the selection of new political goals. Such was the case for the Americans in the Korean War.

MacARTHUR VERSUS RIDGWAY

During its first six months, the Korean War was a highly mobile, rapidly shifting conflict.[49] On June 25, 1950, North Korean forces crossed the thirty-eighth parallel and attacked South Korea. US troops arrived in Korea on July 1, but they began to retreat rapidly with Republic of Korea (ROK) forces to the Pusan perimeter on the southern tip of the peninsula. On September 15, US and ROK forces landed at Inchon, severed the North Korean lines of supply and communication, and crossed the thirty-eighth parallel northward. This effort was consistent with US political objectives, which called for occupying North Korea and "rolling back" the Communists. The Chinese, however, became fearful as US and ROK troops approached their border, and on October 25, China attacked. By December Chinese and North Korean forces had pushed the UN troops back to the thirty-eighth parallel. At this point President Harry Truman, with the support of the Joint Chiefs of Staff, altered US political objectives from retaking North Korea to ending the war and returning to the prewar political status quo.

At the beginning of the war, the US Army employed a strategy of annihilation and maneuver. Led by Gen. Douglas MacArthur, US forces attempted to locate and destroy Communist forces. "Under MacArthur's direction, the army pursued a strategy of 'annihilation,' which was an attempt to destroy the adversary's military capacity to wage war. This strategy required that military forces seek out and annihilate the sources of enemy military capability."[50] This highly mobile strategy exploited the Americans' superiority in trucks, planes, and helicopters.

This strategy, however, did not work well with the new political objectives. Instead of penetrating into North Korea, the president wanted to end the war with a return to the thirty-eighth parallel. MacArthur, however, was not willing to change strategies. He believed "that Red Chinese aggression could not be stopped by killing Chinese, no matter how many, in Korea, so long as her power to make war remained inviolate."[51] In the ensuing political fight, Gen. Matthew Ridgway, Truman, and the Joint Chiefs won. In April 1951 Truman replaced MacArthur with Ridgway, and the United States began to follow a new strategy of attrition. In this strategy US forces dug in and used their superiority in firepower, and not their maneuverability, to kill Communist soldiers. Ridgway instituted a "meat grinder, to chew up Chinese manpower at a rate even the Chinese could not afford."[52] The idea was to create a killing machine that would eliminate vast numbers of Communist forces. This death toll would raise the costs of fighting so that the Communists would negotiate and return to the prewar political status quo. The war thus became entrenched and positional, although it became even more deadly, particularly for the Communists.

Two aspects of the American switch from a strategy of annihilation and maneuver to attrition and position are worth noting. First, this change represents a switch in strategy because it consisted of a fundamentally different way of using a class of forces—in this case, infantry and armor divisions. Rather than having the units attempt to find, circle, and destroy critical North Korean and Chinese war-fighting matériel (supply depots, bases, factories, military units), US troops largely confined themselves to a geographic region and attempted to kill as many Communists who entered that region as possible. Thus the strategic change resulted primarily in an alteration in operations.

Second, the American strategy change was a direct result of a revision of US political goals and not of a critical strategic assessment. Unlike the Germans' strategic change from the Battle of Britain to the Blitz, which resulted from a negative assessment, the shift from annihilation to attrition was exogenous, or a function of a new set of goals.

The Luftwaffe shifted its aims while the Americans altered the way they operated. In some cases, however, a new strategy incorporates changes in both how forces operate and how specific aims are pursued. The North Vietnamese 1972 Easter Offensive represents such a situation.

THE EASTER OFFENSIVE

Between March 30 and April 8, 1972, the North Vietnamese Army (NVA) launched the Easter Offensive, a conventional, large unit, armored attack across the demilitarized zone into South Vietnam.[53] The North Vietnamese decision to use major troop concentrations represented a fundamental strategy shift from their previous, small unit, guerrilla-oriented strategy.[54] In this case the NVA changed both the way that it operated (from guerrilla to large-scale conventional maneuvers) and its aim. Unlike the previous guerrilla strategy, which aimed to whittle away the South Vietnamese government's control of the state, the new strategy was a "massive conventional invasion that aimed to win a series of limited victories and lead ultimately to decisive victory."[55]

The NVA changed its strategy because it believed that its insurgent strategy was leading toward defeat. It attacked "to reverse the deteriorating battlefield prospects of Communist forces. Despite the withdrawal of nearly all American combat forces, the North's influence over territory had waned, principally because the combination of Vietnamization and pacification had by 1972 become effective."[56] The NVA also hoped its action would "neutralize the diplomatic blow dealt by Nixon's impending visits to China and the Soviet Union."[57] The Easter Offensive was the result of a negative North Vietnamese strategic assessment.

The US response, a massive aerial bombing campaign named Operation Linebacker, had greater impact than a similar, earlier effort (Operation Rolling Thunder) because of the interaction of the two strategies—US bombing and Communist conventional attack. Both Rolling Thunder and Linebacker demolished military-related targets in North Vietnam, yet one failed while the other succeeded. The key difference lay in the connection between the air offensive and Hanoi's battlefield strategy. Thus the success and failure of coercive bombing depended not only on the assailant's choice of strategy but also on the strategy employed by the opponent.[58] The ways that both countries fought influenced each other's effectiveness, demonstrating the critical, interactive dynamic of strategies and strategic assessments.[59]

CONCLUSION

These examples each represent a different type of strategy change. When the Luftwaffe shifted from the Battle of Britain to the Blitz, it altered its target category and specific aims; when the US Army moved from maneuver to attrition, it changed the way it operated its forces; and the NVA changed both its specific aims and the operation of its forces when it used conventional forces to attack South Vietnam. In addition, these cases show that strategic change may occur as a result of a negative strategic assessment or new political objectives. These cases demonstrate the challenge of strategic assessment and its critical importance.

Dominant indicators provide a powerful tool for understanding wartime strategic assessment. Identifying the current and possible future roles of strategic assessment is vital for understanding the dynamics of counterinsurgency conflicts such as the war in Afghanistan.[60] Strategic assessment represents a fundamental factor in war termination, war outcomes, the diffusion of military ideas, and other critical war dynamics.[61] It is vital that we examine not just a military organization's behavior but also its incentives and measures of success, for only then will we be able to make predictions about its wartime behavior and develop more comprehensive understanding of the factors that drive its choices and behaviors.

NOTES

1. Col. Philip S. Meilinger (USAF, Ret.), review of *Strategic Assessment in War*, by Scott Sigmund Gartner, *Naval War College Review* 51, no. 4, sequence 364 (Autumn 1998): 129–30.

2. Scott Sigmund Gartner, "Opening up the Black Box of War," *The Journal of Conflict Resolution* 42, no. 3 (1998): 252–58; and Randolph M. Siverson and Harvey Starr, *The Diffusion of War: A Study of Opportunity and Willingness* (Ann Arbor: University of Michigan Press, 1991), 3.

3. See Leo Blanken and Jason Lepore's work in chapter 1 of this volume.

4. W. S. Murray, "A Will to Measure," *Parameters* 31, no. 3 (2001): 134–47.

5. Colin Powell, *My American Journey*, with Joseph E. Persico (New York: Ballantine Books, 1995), 380.

6. H. Norman Schwarzkopf, *It Doesn't Take a Hero*, with Peter Petre (New York: Bantam Books, 1992), 306.

7. J. J. Schroden, "Measures for Security in a Counterinsurgency," *The Journal of Strategic Studies* 32, no. 5 (2009): 715–44.

8. Daniel L. Byman, "Friends like These: Counterinsurgency and the War on Terrorism," *International Security* 32, no. 2 (2006): 79–115, 90.

9. L. E. Cable, *Unholy Grail: The US and the Wars in Vietnam, 1965–68* (New York: Routledge, 1991).

10. Thomas C. Thayer, *War without Fronts* (Boulder: Westview, 1985), 4.

11. Scott Sigmund Gartner, "Counter Insurgency Warfare and Suicide in the Military," presentation given at University of Southern California, Los Angeles, 2014.

12. Carl von Clausewitz, *On War* (New York: Penguin, 1985), 162.

13. Fred Charles Iklé, *Every War Must End* (New York: Columbia University Press, 1971), 35.

14. Scott Sigmund Gartner, *Strategic Assessment in War* (New Haven CT: Yale University Press, 1997).

15. P. Sullivan, *Who Wins? Predicting Strategic Success and Failure in Armed Conflict* (New York: Oxford University Press, 2012); and D. Reiter and A. C. Stam III, "Democracy, War Initiation, and Victory," *American Political Science Review 2*, no. 2 (June 1998): 377–89.

16. Gartner, *Strategic Assessment in War.*

17. Graham T. Allison, *Essence of Decision: Explaining the Cuban Missile Crisis* (Boston: Little, Brown, 1971), 67.

18. David Stockman, *Triumph of Politics* (New York: Harper & Row, 1986), 296–98.

19. Gartner, *Strategic Assessment in War.*

20. See Blanken and Lepore's work in chapter 1 of this volume.

21. H. A. Simon, *Administrative Behavior* (New York: Free Press, 1976), 3:112.

22. K. M. Zisk, *Engaging the Enemy: Organization Theory and Soviet Military Innovation, 1955–1991* (Princeton NJ: Princeton University Press, 1993), 13.

23. Simon, *Administrative Behavior*, 3:xxxiv.

24. Allan R. Millet, Williamson Murray, and Kenneth H. Watman, "The Effectiveness of Military Organizations," in *Military Effectiveness*, vol. 1, *The First World War*, ed. Allan R. Millet and Williamson Murray (Boston: Unwin Hyman, 1988), 3.

25. Gartner, *Strategic Assessment in War.*

26. A. L. Friedberg, *The Weary Titan: Britain and the Experience of Relative Decline, 1895–1905* (Princeton NJ: Princeton University Press, 1988), 285.

27. George Akerlof, "The Economics of Caste and of the Rat Race and Other Woeful Tales," *Quarterly Journal of Economics* 90, no. 4 (November 1976): 599. Italics in the original.

28. S. P. Rosen, *Winning the Next War: Innovation and the Modern Military* (New York: Cornell University Press, 1994), 146.

29. Gartner, *Strategic Assessment in War.*

30. Friedberg, *Weary Titan*, 284. Italics added.

31. Gartner, *Strategic Assessment in War.*

32. Rosen, *Winning the Next War*, 34.

33. Leo J. Blanken and Jason J. Lepore, "Performance Measurement in Military Operations: Information versus Incentives," *Defence and Peace Economics*, 2014, 24 (on Taylor & Francis website); forthcoming in print, http://www.tandfonline.com/doi/abs/10.1080/10242694.2014.949548#preview.

34. Leo J. Blanken and Justin Overbaugh, "Looking for Intel? . . . Or Looking for Answers? Reforming Military Intelligence for a Counter-Insurgency Environment," *Intelligence and National Security* 27, no. 4 (July 2012): 559–75.

35. Gregory A. Daddis, *No Sure Victory: Measuring US Army Effectiveness and Progress in the Vietnam War* (New York: Oxford University Press, 2011).

36. Gen. William C. Westmoreland, *A Soldier Reports* (Garden City NY: Doubleday, 1976), 332. See also Lt. Gen. Julian Ewell and Maj. Gen. Ira Hunt Jr.,

Sharpening the Combat Edge: The Use of Analysis to Reinforce Military Judgment (Washington DC: Department of the Army, 1974).

37. Director of Central Intelligence Richard Helms told President Lyndon Johnson that he "believed the enemy casualty counts to be reliable, conservative and verified" (Cable, *Unholy Grail*, 181).
38. Zisk, *Engaging the Enemy*, 15.
39. James L. Stokesbury, *A Short History of World War I* (New York: William Morrow, 1981), 203.
40. Lawrence Freedman, *The Evolution of Nuclear Strategy* (New York: St. Martin's Press, 1983), 246.
41. Aaron Wildavsky, "The Self-Evaluating Organization," *Public Administration Review* 32 (September/October 1972): 509.
42. John Keegan, *The Second World War* (New York: Viking, 1989), 91.
43. Quoted in Williamson Murray, *Luftwaffe* (Baltimore: Nautical & Aviation Publishing, 1985), 47.
44. Ibid., 53.
45. Keegan, *Second World War*, 96.
46. Gerhard L. Weinberg, *A World at Arms: A Global History of World War II* (Cambridge: Cambridge University Press, 1994), 149.
47. Murray, *Luftwaffe*, 54.
48. Ibid., 59.
49. Scott Sigmund Gartner and Marissa Edson Myers, "Body Counts and 'Success' in the Vietnam and Korean Wars," *Journal of Interdisciplinary History* 25, no. 3 (Winter 1995): 377–95.
50. Ibid., 382.
51. David Halberstam, *The Fifties* (New York: Villard Books, 1993), 83.
52. Russell Weigley, *The History of the United States Army* (Bloomington: University of Indiana Press, 1984), 521–22.
53. George Donelson Moss, *Vietnam: An American Ordeal* (Englewood Cliffs NJ: Prentice Hall, 1990), 395.
54. Gen. Bruce Palmer Jr., *The 15-Year War: America's Military Role in Vietnam* (Lexington: University of Kentucky Press, 1984).
55. Robert A. Pape Jr., "Coercive Air Power in the Vietnam War," *International Security* 15, no. 2 (Fall 1990): 144.
56. Scott Sigmund Gartner, "Differing Evaluations of Vietnamization," *Journal of Interdisciplinary History* 29, no. 2 (1998): 243–62.
57. Lien-Hang T. Nguyen, *Hanoi's War: An International History of the War for Peace in Vietnam* (Chapel Hill: University of North Carolina Press, 2012), 233.
58. Pape, "Coercive Air Power," 146.

59. Allan C. Stam, *Win, Lose, or Draw: Domestic Politics and the Crucible of War* (Ann Arbor: University of Michigan Press, 1999).

60. Scott Sigmund Gartner and Leo Blanken, "Beyond Victory and Defeat: Rethinking Outcome, Assessment, and Strategy in Afghanistan," in *Afghanistan Endgames: Strategy and Policy Choices for America's Longest War*, ed. Hy Rothstein and John Arquilla (Washington DC: Georgetown University Press, 2012), 127–50.

61. D. Reiter, *How Wars End* (Princeton NJ: Princeton University Press, 2009); B. L. Slantchev, "How Initiators End Their Wars: The Duration of Warfare and the Terms of Peace," *American Journal of Political Science*, 48, no. 4 (2004): 813–29; P. Sullivan, *Who Wins? Predicting Strategic Success and Failure in Armed Conflict* (New York: Oxford University Press, 2012); Reiter and Stam, "Democracy, War Initiation," 377–89; and M. C. Horowitz, *The Diffusion of Military Power: Causes and Consequences for International Politics* (Princeton NJ: Princeton University Press, 2010).

PART II: HISTORICAL CASES

4

ASSESSING PROXY FORCES

A CASE STUDY OF THE EARLY YEARS OF THE SEVEN YEARS' WAR (1754–63) IN NORTH AMERICA

John Grenier

ASSESSING THE EFFECTIVENESS AND EFFICIENCY of proxy forces marks one of the most difficult tasks commanders and their staffs face. Differences in languages, cultural norms, and war aims often complicate the ability of soldiers from one culture to work well with those from another. Long before the mid-twentieth century's codification of a doctrine of unconventional warfare—training and using indigenous and native troops to function alongside and independent of regular and conventionally focused forces—professional soldiers struggled to make the best use of proxy forces.

The early years (1755–57) of the Seven Years' War serve as a useful case study in which to examine how professional soldiers assessed their proxies. French and British commanders in North America made concerted efforts to assess the operational and strategic-level contributions of their proxies. Modern soldiers can learn three basic lessons from their efforts. First, proxy troops fight for different reasons than regulars do; thus, assessments must account for incentives among proxy troops that are very different than among regulars. Different motivations, as suggested in the incentive-versus-information part of the metrics triangle explained in this volume's chapter 1, create the need for consistent post-battle assessments, as well as interpretations of those assessments. Second, proxies are by default "outsiders" from the regular establishment, thus allowing commanders, as a function of being the voice that speaks for them, to manipulate reports and assessments of the proxies' worth.

Far too often commanders blame their failures on poorly trained, ill-motivated, or undisciplined proxies. Last, proxies can profoundly shape, either positively or negatively, a campaign's or a war's progression and outcome. Proxies on the periphery often refuse to embrace fully the conventional force's policies, strategies, and objectives, and their resistance, in turn, can widen the Clausewitzian gap between the political leadership and commanders in the field. It remains exceedingly difficult to keep proxies focused on and motivated toward accomplishing tasks that they do not judge as necessarily producing results in their best interests.

French and British assessments of their proxies' worth as partners changed dramatically between 1755 and 1757. The Canadian-born leadership of New France began the war convinced that Native Americans and colonial navy troops (les Troupes de la Marine) led by Canadian officers would prove adequate for victory. In early 1756, however, officers from metropolitan France decided that Native Americans were no longer worth the trouble to organize and equip, and perhaps most damagingly, they suggested that the Canadians "had gone native" and were little better than *les sauvages* (Indians). After Native Americans perpetrated a string of gruesome massacres, French officers became so disgusted with them that they chose to forgo their help. Ironically, at the start of the war, British soldiers openly disdained their American proxies. But victory in North America proved frustratingly elusive for the redcoats, and near the same time that the French abandoned irregular and unconventional warfare, British commanders embraced Anglo-American rangers. This chapter examines the train of events between 1755 and 1757 to show how the French found that they could not work with their proxies and how the British found that they could not do without them.

France began the war in North America with three distinct types of proxy forces. Since the early 1680s, the French Navy had maintained in the colonies several thousand long-service professional soldiers officered by Canadians. Les Troupes de la Marine served throughout France's sprawling North American empire, where they gained valuable experience fighting against and alongside Native Americans. While it took until the mid-1740s for Europe's leading theoreticians of war, most notably Hermann Maurice, comte de Saxe, to codify that kind of war as *petite guerre* (small war, from which the word "guerrilla"—the Spanish diminutive for *guerra* [war]—derived), the marines, who may not have known what to call it, knew it when they saw it. Aggressive, well trained, and experienced, the marines stood as the most fearsome and effective European soldiers on the North American continent. In 1756, for instance, the British commander in chief, John Campbell, the fourth earl of Loudoun, noted with barely hidden contempt how the thought of fighting the marines "frightened [Americans] out of their Senses."[1] French command-ers in Canada could also turn to *la milice* (the militia). The milice had devel-oped a proud tradition of defending its homes and communities, and it stood as an ideal defensive or partisan force. New France's third proxy asset—Native Americans—functioned as a wild card. Indians remained fiercely indepen-dent, even the thousands of *sauvages domiciliés* (domiciled Indians) who lived near and among the Canadians. But the Canadians worked tirelessly to build strong bonds with them. In time, generous annual outlays of presents and gifts from the governor of New France, whom the Indians called Onontio, helped inspire the sauvages domiciliés to promise fidelity to their "French Father."

The British forces in North America stood as no match for the Canadi-ans and Indians. The army maintained only the Fortieth Regiment at half strength (500 instead of 1,000 men) in Nova Scotia, four independent compa-nies (approximately 200 men combined) in New York, and three independent companies of around 150 troops total in South Carolina. The militia, as a result, functioned as the backbone of the colonial military establishment, but its effectiveness as a fighting force left much to be desired. Most professional army officers viewed the Yankees' victory at Louisbourg in 1745, for example, as merely a lucky roll of the dice by a pack of bumbling amateurs. The Yankees, in turn, spoke of arrogant and condescending British regulars who remained unappreciative of Americans' social mores as well as their sacrifices and services to the empire. "Familiarity breeds contempt" certainly rang true in the realm of Anglo-American civil-military relations in the mid-eighteenth century.

American rangers occupied a middle ground between the militia and Brit-ish professionals. Since the late seventeenth century, Americans had turned to men who self-selected and specialized in fighting Indians. The typical ranger was a volunteer who served for high wages and the hope of collecting lav-ish bounties—upwards of several years' pay for a typical laborer—on Indian scalps. Ranger companies became the first line of defense in tight-knit back-country communities. The popular heroes of American military history before the War for Independence were mostly ranger officers to whom their enlisted men—often their friends and extended family members—remained fiercely loyal. British officers deemed the rangers, regardless of rank, as undisciplined, insubordinate, and unruly. The rangers often were all those things, but they also understood war much differently than a British officer who demanded unquestioned obedience and obsequiousness from his social inferiors. In the summer of 1755 the disorder of tin ear that afflicted British regular officers became readily apparent in the opening campaigns of the Seven Years' War.

Planners on both sides designed the operations for 1755 as sideshows to buy time for their armies and navies to prepare for war on the Continent.

They hoped that their proxy forces could fight the North American campaigns, ones frankly focused on third- and fourth-level strategic objectives, "on the cheap." Pierre François de Rigaud de Vaudreuil de Cavagnial, marquis de Vaudreuil, New France's native-born governor-general, expected only minimal support from Europe, but he assumed that his marines and many Indian "children" offered a sufficient force to defend the periphery of Canada from British and American attacks. He focused on using his proxies in the strategic and operational defensive to bloody and blunt any Anglo-American forces that crossed into French-claimed territory. In the end Great Britain's plan played directly to French strengths. Maj. Gen. Edward Braddock was to transport two understrength regiments from Ireland to North America, raise them to full strength with levies from the militia, and march into the heart of Indian country and take Fort Duquesne at today's Pittsburgh. Governor William Shirley of Massachusetts, the administrator-politician who organized the Yankee victory at Louisbourg in 1745 but who never had led troops in the field, received a major general's commission. He was instructed to reactivate two previously disbanded regular infantry regiments, fill their rolls with militia, and advance from Albany to Oswego on Lake Ontario, cross the lake, and capture Niagara. William Johnson, a trader who lived near the Mohawks, garnered a major general's commission and command of more than five thousand militia placed in "provincial" regiments that would muster in Albany, like Shirley's army, and then take Fort Saint-Frédéric on Lake Champlain. The British also formed a five-hundred-man battalion of regulars from the Fortieth Regiment and the independent companies to join the two thousand provincials who moved against the Acadian homelands in Nova Scotia.

The war started terribly for the British. Braddock expected to encounter Indians and possibly Frenchmen on his march against Fort Duquesne, yet he dismissed suggestions to augment his forces with more than a handful of American rangers. Benjamin Franklin later wrote how Braddock "Smiled at my Ignorance, & replied 'These Savages may indeed be a formidable Enemy to your raw American Militia; but upon the King's regular & disciplined Troops, Sir, it is impossible they should make any Impression.'"[2] The Indians, marines, and milice nevertheless left a lasting mark on the British Army when they met near the Monongahela River on July 9. Braddock's advanced party under Lt. Col. Thomas Gage fired on the Indians and French at long range, killed their commander, and as their training dictated, deployed in a line fit for a European battlefield. Gage initially assumed the Indians and marines had scattered, but he was shocked to see them sweep down and begin to encircle the entire British column. Gage "fell back upon the van, which very much disconcerted the Men," and the British column bunched up, whereupon Braddock ordered his artillery pieces into action. But the Indians and marines, "whether ordered or not," recalled a British officer, "kept an incessant fire on the Guns & killed the Men very fast. These Indians from their irregular method of fighting by running from one place to another obliged us to wheel from right to left, to desert the Guns and then hastily return & cover them." The redcoats held their ground in the charnel house for four hours before they broke. The Indians, the British officer continued, then "pursued us[,] butchering as they came."[3] George Washington, who had volunteered to serve without pay or rank as one of Braddock's aides-de-camp, recalled that the British soldiers became "struck with a deadly *Panic*" while the handful of Virginians who had joined Braddock "behaved like men, and died like Soldiers."[4] At the end of the day, the French and Indians killed or wounded 977 regulars, including Braddock and 59 of his 85 officers. Col. Thomas Dunbar led the survivors on a headlong retreat to Philadelphia.

The army placed Gage and Dunbar in charge of conducting the post-battle assessment. They categorically refused to say or write anything that one could construe as a criticism of Braddock. If American proxies had served with them, no doubt Gage and Dunbar would have placed the blame on them. Instead, they mendaciously insisted the French and Indians outnumbered the British on the Monongahela and, worse, blamed the disaster on the "misconduct" of the British enlisted men and noncommissioned officers. Franklin perhaps made the best assessment of Braddock, and the reasons for the British defeat, when he described the general as "a brave Man, and [who] might probably have made a Figure as a good Officer in some European War. But he had too much self-confidence, too high an Opinion of the Validity of Regular Troops, and too mean a One of both Americans and Indians."[5] Several marine prisoners agreed with Franklin. "None of their Officers," they told William Shirley, "were in the least Surprised at it [their victory], as it was a Maxim with them never to Expose Regulars in the Woods without a sufficient Number of Indians and irregulars for any Attack that might be Expected."[6]

Anglo-American forces in Nova Scotia also encountered difficulties in dealing with French proxies. During the removal of the Acadians, marine ensign Charles Deschamps de Boishébert and disparate groups of refugees and métis (offspring of European and Indian unions) joined forces. Boishébert's guerrillas doggedly fought the Anglo-Americans until 1760, and only after Anglo-American rangers under Joseph Gorham enabled the British to penetrate the Acadian sanctuaries in present-day New Brunswick did the British suppress the insurgency. In 1755 no one expected it would take five years to crush the opposition of a bunch of poorly armed and starved peasants. The Clausewitzian gap had widened to a chasm in the Maritimes.

Shirley, meanwhile, stalled at Oswego. Upon hearing of Braddock's disaster and the arrival in Canada of two thousand European regulars under Jean-Armand Dieskau, baron de Dieskau—a respected protégé of Saxe—Shirley knew better than to press across Lake Ontario. He found only eighteen Indians and no rangers to serve with his army. He decided to build Fort Ontario at the eastern end of the lake and leave his two regular regiments, with only the barest stock of provisions and supplies, to winter over while he and the bulk of the provincials returned to the comforts of New England. It proved exceedingly easy for Shirley to blame his inaction on the militia's poor preparation to conduct expeditionary operations.

Vaudreuil initially planned to use Dieskau's troops to destroy Shirley's army on Lake Ontario, but the French victory on the Monongahela allowed him to reassess his courses of action and make better use of his resources. Among the flotsam and jetsam the Indians found on the battlefield a detailed summary of the British plan for 1755. It confirmed that William Johnson intended to lead a provincial army against Fort Saint-Frédéric. Vaudreuil and Jacques Legardeur de Saint-Pierre, one of New France's most experienced and well-respected marine officers and diplomats to the Indians, easily convinced Dieskau to take a page from the petite guerre handbook. Dieskau agreed to leave the majority of his regular forces in New France and use only his elite grenadier companies with marines, milice, and sauvages domiciliés on a raid against the British supply lines north of Albany. The Canadians understood that Dieskau need not meet Johnson's army in an open-field battle. Winter was coming, and if they cut his supply lines, Johnson's army would stall in the snow and cold.

While Dieskau's main objective remained the supply depot at Fort Lyman, he was not above attacking Johnson's army if the opportunity presented itself. Coincidently near the same time that Dieskau set out with fifteen hundred men for Fort Lyman, Johnson left its safety and marched his army of twenty-five hundred provincials, with one regular officer (Capt. William Eyre) as an adviser, for the head of Lake George. On September 7 the French and Indians arrived outside Fort Lyman, whereupon the Kanawakes (Mohawk sauvages domiciliés) categorically refused to attack an entrenched and fortified position. Legardeur and the other marine officers, however, knew how to properly incentivize their proxies. They suggested that Johnson's army near the lake stood ripe for picking, and they promised all the booty, plunder, and scalps the Indians could carry if they agreed to attack the Americans.

Hendrick Theyanoguin, a septuagenarian Mohawk sachem and longtime friend and business associate of Johnson's, had convinced his people to join the British. But both Johnson and Hendrick failed to grasp that all the Mohawks might not be as fully interested in helping them as Hendrick was.

Several younger Mohawks in fact had met their Kanawake cousins in the woods to discuss the difficult position in which their respective leaders had placed them. Johnson, in the meantime, barricaded his army with its back to Lake George and prepared to send out at first light on September 8 a reconnaissance in force to find Dieskau's army.

New Englanders came to call the battle into which the provincials and Mohawks marched the Bloody Morning Scout. Dieskau had deployed his forces in an ambush about four miles south of Johnson's Great Camp, and shortly after 10:00 A.M., just before all hell broke loose, someone from the French side called out to Hendrick to warn or perhaps taunt him of his doom. Someone then fired his musket, and a volley of fire erupted from the grenadiers. Hendrick and thirty Mohawks were killed on the spot, and another dozen were gravely wounded. Col. Ephraim Williams tried to lead the provincials to safety, but the marines and sauvages domiciliés cut him down along with nearly fifty of his men. The surviving Mohawks retreated and protected each other and the few provincials who joined them with covering fire. Most of the provincials simply ran for their lives.

The sauvages domiciliés and Canadians chased the Yankees, caught and killed dozens of them, and stopped only when they arrived within range of the cannon behind Johnson's barricade. The Kanawakes again refused to attack a fortified position, plus they had gained what they wanted from the fight—scalps and prisoners whom they could "caress" (torture) to ritualistically "cover their dead" at their villages. They also wanted to mourn Legardeur, who had fallen while leading from the front during the ambush. The Kanawakes announced that they were going home, and the other sauvages domiciliés followed suit. The milice then decided that their work was done, too. Dieskau had gotten all he was going to get from his native proxies.

Dieskau nonetheless hoped to convert his petite victory in the woods into a grand one at the Great Camp. He ordered the grenadiers to fix bayonets and breach the barricade, a task for which they specifically had trained. As the marines stepped aside, the grenadiers, in the white uniforms of France's regulars, marched into the 150-yard-wide clearing in front of the Yankee breastwork. At 75 yards, Eyre (Johnson had taken to his tent after having been shot through the thigh and buttocks) opened fire with grapeshot. It "made Lanes, Streets and Alleys thro' their army."[7] The grenadiers understandably buckled, and with the wounded Dieskau prostrated in the dirt, they frantically tried to catch up with the sauvages domiciliés and Canadians. The last thing they wanted was for the Mohawks or rangers to catch them alone in the woods.

The battles on the Monongahela and at Lake George, as well as Shirley's stalled expedition at Oswego, marked major strategic and operational victories for the French. New France's proxies had so bloodied British forces that they spent the second half of the 1755 campaigning season licking their wounds and building a fort—Fort William Henry—on the site of the Great Camp. The marines and Indians had shown that, although mere proxies, they stood as masters of the war in the wilds of eastern North America.

European soldiers' assessments of the campaigns of 1755 nonetheless focused on the wrong points. On the British side, the army placed the blame for its multiple defeats and inaction on the provincials instead of its convoluted campaign plans or its regulars, who could not execute them. One anonymous correspondent, for example, wrote from North America: "Nothing will ever be done here without veteran [regular] troops."[8] The king thus sent Loudoun to the colonies with reinforcements of regular regiments and instructions to place all forces in North America under regular officers. On the French side, King Louis XV picked a favorite of his court, Louis-Joseph de Montcalm, marquis de Montcalm, to replace Dieskau. Montcalm epitomized the military courtier of the ancien régime who owed his rank to his family connections and political patrons as much as to his talents as an officer. Although he had seen a great deal of service during campaigns in Western and Central Europe, his familiarity with petite guerre remained, as he preferred, limited. Montcalm had seen French troops regularly beat the best regular troops the other European nation-states could offer, and he determined he would direct the war in North America as if he were in the Low Counties or Germany. Both sides had planted seeds from which huge Clausewitzian gaps could grow.

The British Army's disregard for its American proxies' wants and needs doomed the Anglo-American war effort in 1756. At this early stage of the war, the British did not understand how to properly incentivize their proxies. Loudoun announced that all provincials must serve under regular officers. When Americans considered the implications of the "merger," the central issue understandably became the army's so-called Rule of 1754, which read that every British officer, regardless of rank, outranked every provincial officer. Under the rule, for example, a sixteen-year-old British ensign whose family had purchased a commission for him received the authority to issue orders to a provincial general. Not surprising, most American officers refused to abide by such an arrangement. More disconcerting for the provincial enlisted men, the merger made them subject to the British Rules and Articles of War rather than the campaign-specific contracts under which they had enlisted in their respective colonies' service. The Rules and Articles of War allowed the king's officers to inflict the most severe punishments, including death, for the most minor infractions. As a result nearly half of the provincial regiments threatened to throw down their arms and go home. Loudoun compromised and gave American field grade officers (majors and above) seniority and rank as the eldest captains while on joint service. His "compromise of 1756" temporarily mollified the Americans, but in an age in which deference to one's social superiors shaped interpersonal relations, the army refused to treat even proxy field graders as anything more than second-class subjects.

Fortuitously for the British in the spring of 1756, William Shirley created several of His Majesty's Independent Companies of Rangers. Capt. Robert Rogers spent most of the year bringing the companies of his brother Richard and other officers under first his direction and then his outright command. Rogers was not the first American ranger, but he was certainly a charismatic and capable leader. Throughout 1756 and 1757 Rogers's Rangers stood as the only Anglo-American troops who took the war to the French and Indians on the Lake George–Lake Champlain front. Without the rangers' strategic reconnaissance, Loudoun would have been blind and deaf to French movements and intentions. The rangers also engaged the marines and sauvages domiciliés in a petite guerre, and by the end of 1756 at least, they seemed to have gained the upper hand. In fact, the rangers' many raids far behind French lines flummoxed regular French officers. Montcalm's young aide-de-camp, Louis Antoine de Bougainville, assumed that the Highlanders (Scottish regulars with a well-earned reputation as troops who often doubled as irregulars) and Indians "had established a flying camp behind the mountains north of the lake [George] which supplies and shelters all these little parties."[9] He wanted to hunt down and destroy them. Vaudreuil knew better than to chase a phantom army across the Adirondack Mountain range; it stood abundantly clear to him that "the English have formed a corps of volunteers who are Independents and go forth like the Indians."[10] Loudoun, meanwhile, recognized that "there is no carrying on the Service here, without Rangers; for it is only by them, we can have Intelligence of what motion the Enemy are making and by them, that we can secure our Camps and Marches from Surprises; from where it appears to me that till we can regain the Indians, which can only be done by beating the Enemy, no Army can Subsist in this Country without Rangers."[11] His plan for 1757 therefore called for two operations—a massive regular expedition against Louisbourg and a petite guerre that New England rangers would lead against French positions south of Montreal.

While British regulars' attitudes toward their indigenous forces were beginning to change for the better, the same could not be said in the French camp. The mutual contempt that Vaudreuil and Montcalm shared for each other quickly became palpable, in large part because Montcalm refused to consider the possibility that the colonial troops or sauvages domiciliés offered anything of value to him. Vaudreuil pleaded with Montcalm to focus on petite guerre, which had to this point in the war paid huge dividends to the French, and to leave the bulk of the regulars on the strategic defensive on Lake Champlain. He eventually managed to convince Montcalm that the Oswego front offered the best opportunity for success, but when Montcalm developed his operational plan to take the British outpost, he gave the sauvages domiciliés and marines no role. Montcalm had no idea how to properly incentivize his proxies. Vaudreuil suggested that Montcalm leave the task to his younger brother, François-Pierre de Rigaud de Vaudreuil (known simply as Rigaud), who easily enlisted hundreds of Indians to serve as Montcalm's regulars. The French-born officers on Montcalm's staff scoffed at the necessity of such measures, and they openly disparaged Rigaud as "shallow brained" because he had little interest in fighting a regular-style war.[12] They did not understand that Rigaud was a skilled practitioner of petite guerre and that the milice and sauvages domiciliés respected him immensely, a fact that had become increasingly important after Legardeur's death. Montcalm, in the end, grudgingly agreed to send Rigaud, 250 sauvages domiciliés, and marines ahead as his advance guard.

The events outside Oswego showed the dangerous fissures in Montcalm's relationship with New France's proxies. Rigaud's Indians and marines skillfully isolated the British forces in Oswego, enabling Montcalm to lay siege to the fort as if it were child's play. After offering only the most halfhearted defense, the half-starved and thoroughly demoralized Anglo-Americans gravely insulted Montcalm when they surrendered. Montcalm refused to grant them the honors of war (parole and the right of the officers to keep their side arms and the enlisted men to keep their personal property, for example) that he would have offered a vanquished foe in Europe, and he announced that he intended to take the entire garrison to Canada as prisoners of war. More ominously he gave the sauvages domiciliés nothing that they could take to their villages as recognition for their service. It was a mind-bogglingly stupid decision, and it seemed as if he purposely was trying to disrespect them. The sauvages domiciliés had literally begged to serve under Rigaud so they could grab the *gloire* (glory) for themselves and their clans, but Montcalm simply did not care.

The sauvages domiciliés swarmed into the fort soon after the garrison opened the gates to surrender. In the subsequent mini massacre, Montcalm's proxies killed and scalped between thirty and a hundred unarmed men and women and took an unknown number as captives. Montcalm and his officers were appalled. During the height of the massacre, he ordered Rigaud and the marine officers to control "their" Indians, but the Canadians knew better than to get between the sauvages and the booty and prisoners. The marines stood by and let the massacre run its course, and they then joined the Indians, not Montcalm, on the march to Montreal. Montcalm fumed in anger and disgust, but upon his arrival in Montreal, he decided not to invite trouble and suggest his proxies had sullied his victory. He instead tried to spin the events at Oswego as the most brilliant campaign ever waged on the North American continent. Rigaud, les sauvages, and the Canadians, nevertheless, collectively had become Montcalm's bête noir.

Yet to Montcalm's great displeasure, he could not do without Rigaud, the marines, or the sauvages domiciliés and milice, however much he despised them. Rogers's Rangers continued to poke and probe at the French positions at Fort Saint-Frédéric and Fort Carillon (Ticonderoga), keeping the garrisons continuously on the defensive. The war was devolving into one that looked radically different than how the European officers and their political masters in Europe had envisioned. The sauvages domiciliés and marines who raided to the south also informed Montcalm that Loudoun had begun to stockpile matériel and bateaux at Fort William Henry. That news proved most disconcerting for Vaudreuil and Rigaud. They knew time marked their enemy's greatest advantage; the British colonies' population was ten times larger than that of New France, which after nearly 150 years of existence still depended on the *metropole* for weapons, reinforcements, the trade goods to keep Onontio's children loyal, and, most important, food. Montcalm recognized that he needed to move against Fort William Henry before Loudoun's juggernaut built up enough steam to roll over him, but he refused to risk his regulars in the depths of winter in an operation distant from their supply bases, especially with Rogers's Rangers lurking in the no-man's land between the French and British forts.

Rigaud volunteered to lead the milice and sauvages domiciliés over the frozen surface of Lake George and destroy the British stores and bateaux at Fort William Henry. As Rigaud assembled his forces south of Montreal, he received encouraging news from the Lake Champlain forts. On January 21, 1757, a party of marines and Odawa warriors from the Great Lakes region had ambushed a large party of Rogers's Rangers—the French had begun referring to them as *les troupes d'élite* (the elite troops) of the British force—along La Barbue Creek between Fort Saint-Frédéric and Fort Carillon. Rogers lost thirty-one of the seventy-two men engaged and, more damaging, several of his most experienced noncommissioned officers and officers. Rogers, wounded badly in the hand, managed to lead the survivors to safety at Fort William Henry, but when he reported to the hospital in Albany, the medicos quarantined him because he had contracted smallpox (*Variola major*). The disease had cut such a large swath through the ranger companies at the northern forts that when Rigaud and his party of fifteen hundred raiders set out over the ice of Lake George in mid-March, only several dozen rangers remained standing to oppose them outside Fort William Henry's walls.

Rigaud's raid was a masterpiece of petite guerre. Because no Anglo-American forces screened the approaches to Fort William Henry, he nearly took the garrison by surprise. Although denied the satisfaction of capturing the fort, the Canadians and sauvages domiciliés spent four days and nights, including one in a blizzard, outside it. Rigaud's Canadians burned hundreds of tons of supplies, 230 bateaux, the forty-ton sloop *Loudoun*, and the post's three hundred cords of firewood. At the cost of less than a dozen causalities, Rigaud delayed the British forces' advance down the lake (Lake George flows from the south to north) by at least several months.

The two sides' assessments of the significance of Rigaud's raid were markedly different. The British findings proved spot on. Loudoun, from his New York headquarters, recognized that with the matériel and vessels at Fort William Henry having gone up in flames, he could not send forces that summer against Fort Carillon or Fort Saint-Frédéric without a massive influx of rangers. He therefore suspended all offensive operations on the Lake George–Lake Champlain corridor for 1757, but then he surprisingly announced his plan to take all the rangers—except for Richard Rogers's company, which would remain at Fort William Henry—to Halifax for his campaign against Louisbourg. Montcalm, meanwhile, failed to acknowledge the significance of Rigaud's efforts. He refused to give the Canadians and sauvages domiciliés anything but lukewarm recognition for their accomplishment; he even criticized Rigaud for wasting provisions by marching his force to Fort William Henry yet failing to draw out the garrison from behind its walls and engaging it in battle. It must have galled Montcalm greatly, therefore, when in the late spring and early summer more than a thousand western Indians presented themselves to him. They had heard of Onontio's great victories at Oswego and Fort William Henry, as well as the defeat his Odawa children had inflicted on Rogers at La Barbue Creek. They rushed to Montreal to join the war before it ended. Unfortunately for the French, Montcalm still had not learned how to properly incentivize his proxies.

The sauvages domiciliés and western Indians who joined Montcalm in 1757 did so solely on their terms, and by that point in the war, they frankly cared little for what Montcalm thought. Montcalm had no choice but to welcome them into his army. He tried unsuccessfully to organize them into companies with marine officers at their head, but the reality was that a huge Clausewitzian gap still separated the French and their proxies. The Indians did not care about the niceties of eighteenth-century European norms of restrained warfare; they envisioned war making as a much more feral undertaking. In late July, for example, 550 Great Lakes Indians and Canadians, nominally under the command of a marine ensign named Corbière, caught 350 men of the New Jersey Provincial Regiment (known as the "Jersey Blues") in bateaux on Lake George. "The English," Bougainville recalled, "terrified by the shooting, the sight, the cries, and the agility of these monsters, surrendered almost without firing a shot." In the slaughter that followed, the Indians killed more than 100 Jersey Blues and seized another 160 prisoners. Only one Indian suffered a slight wound. As the Anglo-Americans survivors rowed frantically for Fort William Henry, the horrors for the prisoners began. According to Bougainville, the Indians "put in the pot and ate three prisoners, and perhaps others were so treated. All have become slaves unless they are ransomed. A horrible spectacle to European eyes."[13]

The Fort William Henry massacre—the best-known event of the war in North America because of James Fenimore Cooper's dramatization of it in his book *The Last of the Mohicans*—signaled the end of the Franco-Indian union. The Indians' victory over the Jersey Blues effectively isolated Lt. Col. George Munro and his Anglo-American troops inside Fort William Henry. Maj. Gen. Daniel Webb, frightened to inaction by the events on the lake, refused to send reinforcements and thereby doomed Munro. Munro and the garrison valiantly held out for several days before they agreed to surrender, after which Montcalm gladly offered them the full honors of war. Nevertheless, he again failed to offer his Indian allies recognition, booty, or prisoners. The resulting massacre on August 10, 1757, in which the Indians murdered upwards of 185 Anglo-American soldiers and camp followers and took between 300 and 500 prisoners, was by this point hardly unexpected.

Both the French and their proxies assessed the events at Fort William in their own ways. For his part, Montcalm initially blamed the British for the massacre. He suggested that Munro had allowed the Indians unfettered access to the fort's rum supplies, making it impossible for the French to control their proxies. Montcalm also tried to wash away the stain of having "allowed" another massacre when he told Loudoun that "[I] Exposed myself personally as well as my Officers, in defense of Yours."[14] Within French circles, he refused to have anything more to do with his Native American allies. He barred them from the army's camps and insisted that they were little more than uncontrollable demons. Bougainville proved more realistic, as well as prescient, in his assessment: "All Europe will oblige us to justify ourselves."[15] Ill will emanated from the Indians. They eventually blamed Montcalm for the smallpox epidemic that ravaged their communities over the winter of 1757–58. They unknowingly had exposed themselves to the disease at Fort William Henry when they murdered and scalped the patients in the fort's smallpox ward. In 1758 they insisted that Montcalm's disrespect for them had angered their manitous, which subsequently had punished them for agreeing to help the ungrateful French in the first place. Canadians such as Rigaud and Vaudreuil faced an insurmountable obstacle in convincing les sauvages to again raise the hatchet for Onontio.

Assessments of the massacre helped the British refocus their strategy, operations, and tactics to give their proxies a larger role. Loudoun slipped into near-apoplectic anger upon hearing of the massacre, and he announced that henceforth he would use his rangers to raid deep into Canada and "teach them [the enemy] to comply with the Laws of Nations and Humanity." He continued, "For altho' I abhor Barbarity, the Murders committed at Oswego, and now at Forte [sic] William Henry, will oblige me, contrary to human nature, to make those above Gentlemen [Vaudreuil and Montcalm] sick of such inhuman Villany whenever it is in my Power."[16] Proxies, albeit primarily on the French side, had changed a limited war into an Old Testament–style conflict of an eye for an eye, a tooth for a tooth.

Throughout the war's remaining campaigns in North America, the British and Americans uniformly shared the opinion that the French had abdicated any right to humane treatment and instead must suffer under the hard hand of war. The British placed the blame for the war's gross violence on the French and not solely on the French proxies. So outside Louisbourg in the summer of 1758, when Maj. Gen. Jeffrey Amherst's army stood within hours of taking the fortress and the fort's French commander asked him to cease bombarding the hospital because sick and wounded soldiers and civilians filled it, Amherst mustered no mercy. James Wolfe, one of Amherst's brigadiers and who would soon be a hero of the empire, reminded him, "When the French are in a scrape they are ready to cry out [on] behalf of the human species; when fortune favors them—none [are] more bloody, more inhuman; Moncalm [sic] has chang'd the very nature of war, and has forced us, in some measure, to a deterring, and dreadfull [sic] vengeance."[17] Wolfe hoped his patron in Europe, Lord George Sackville, knew that he was "neither inhumane nor rapacious," but he wanted the "Canadian Vermin sack'd & pillage'd & justly repaid" for their "Creulity."[18] When Wolfe led the Anglo-American army against Quebec in the summer and autumn of 1759, he capitalized on what he viewed as the "barbarity which seems so natural" in the American rangers to cudgel the Canadian populace into submission. He ordered Joseph Gorham's rangers to "burn and lay waste the country for the future, sparing only churches."[19] Wolfe knew how to incentivize his proxies: he gave them carte blanche to scalp Indians and any Canadians dressed like Indians. In the end, even the sacred ground of churches became unsafe. The regulars of the Forty-third Regiment killed and scalped a priest and thirty parishioners inside the church at Ste. Anne des Pays-Bas. In September 1759, Amherst ordered Rogers's Rangers to destroy the village and Catholic mission at Saint-François, 150 miles behind French lines. He told Rogers, "Remember the barbarities that have been committed by the enemy's Indian scoundrels on every occasion where they had an opportunity of showing their infamous credulities on the King's subjects, which they have done without mercy."[20] The rangers did not need reminding. They enthusiastically put Saint-François to the torch and even killed women and children without abandon.

As Vaudreuil feared, the British eventually overwhelmed New France. British success after 1757 in large part resided with their ability to effectively use their proxies, while at the same time the French purposefully abandoned theirs. Both sides' assessments of their proxies evolved significantly over the war's early years, and the British proved much more adept at learning lessons from those assessments. The British grasped that proxies fight for different reasons than regulars do and offered Americans proper incentives. The French, as opposed to the Canadians, never fully accepted their proxies' needs and wants or their legitimacy as soldiers. Rather than work with them to find a middle ground between two apparently contradictory conceptualizations of war making, Montcalm adopted adversarial attitudes toward his proxies. He regularly blamed them, none more so than the sauvages domiciliés, for his failures to properly lead, motivate, and incorporate them into French strategic and operational designs. Although Montcalm would have been loath to admit it, proxies on both sides, despite the cost of widening the Clausewitzian gap, profoundly shaped the war's outcome. In the final analysis, the overarching lesson to be learned from this case study is that professional soldiers must always respectfully and judiciously deal with their proxies. To do otherwise is to invite disaster.

NOTES

1. John Campbell, the fourth earl of Loudoun, to Prince William Augustus, Duke of Cumberland, August 29, 1756, in Loudoun Manuscripts, Henry E. Huntington Library, San Marino CA (hereafter LO), number 1626.

2. Benjamin Franklin, *The Autobiography of Benjamin Franklin*, ed. Louis P. Masur (Boston: St. Martin's Press, 1993), 135.

3. "The Journal of a British Officer," in *Braddock's Defeat: The Journal of Captain Robert Chomley's Batman: The Journal of a British Officer; Halkett's Orderly Book*, ed. Charles Hamilton (Norman: University of Oklahoma Press, 1959), 50.

4. George Washington to Robert Dinwiddie, July 18, 1755, in the Colonial Office Class 5 Papers, volume 46, The National Archives of the UK, Surrey (hereafter CO 5). Italics in original.
5. Franklin, *Autobiography*, 135.
6. William Shirley to Thomas Robinson, November 5, 1755, CO 5:46.
7. Anon., September 10, 1755, in Edmund Bailey O'Callaghan, ed., *Documents Relative to the Colonial History of the State of New York*, 15 vols. (Albany: Weed, Parsons, 1853–87), 6:1005 (hereafter *DRCHSNY*).
8. Letter from Boston, December 6, 1755, LO 690.
9. Bougainville's journal entry, September 11, 1756, in Louis Antoine de Bougainville, *Adventure in the Wilderness: The American Journal of Louis Antoine de Bougainville, 1756–1760*, ed. and trans. Edward P. Hamilton (Norman: University of Oklahoma Press, 1964), 35.
10. Vaudreuil to Francis de Gaston, chevalier de Lévis, August 14, 1756, in *Lettres de Marquis de Vaudreuil au Chevalier de Lévis* (Quebec: L. J. Demers & Frère, 1895), 25.
11. Loudoun to Henry Fox, November 22, 1756, LO 2263.
12. *Dictionary of Canadian Biography*, s.v. "Rigaud de Vaudreuil, François-Pierre de."
13. Bougainville's journal entry, July 24, 1757, in Bougainville, *Adventure in the Wilderness*, 142–43.
14. Montcalm to Loudoun, August 14, 1757, LO 4182.
15. Bougainville's journal entry, August 12–31, 1757, in Bougainville, *Adventure in the Wilderness*, 172.
16. Loudoun to Webb, August 20, 1757, LO 4271.
17. Wolfe quoted in Stephen Brumwell, *Paths of Glory: The Life and Death of General James Wolfe* (Montreal: McGill-Queen's University Press, 2006), 157.
18. Wolfe to Sackville, July 1758, Sackville-Germain Manuscripts, vol. 1, William L. Clements Library, Ann Arbor MI.
19. General Wolfe's Proclamations to the Canadians, July 29, 1759, *DRCHSNY*, 10:1047–48.
20. Amherst to Rogers, September 13, 1759, in Robert Rogers, *Journals of Major Robert Rogers* (London: J. Millan, 1765), 145.

5

ASSESSING WAR

THE REVOLUTIONARY WAR

Edward G. Lengel

AMONG THE REVOLUTIONARY WAR's many complexities is the problem of American war aims, which were not always stable and rarely well defined. In 1775–76 no consensus yet existed as to whether the rebellion should aspire toward autonomy or independence from Great Britain. Fighting the British was in this context more a matter of survival than a means to establishing a particular end. The Declaration of Independence, which many Americans opposed and others welcomed cautiously, was a game changer. It firmly set the goal as independence.

George Washington stands as a central focus of any study of American military assessment in the Revolutionary War. It is tempting to see him as a constant among the shifting tides of war aims and strategy, yet he too underwent change. At the war's outset, he wrote little about strategy and nothing about war aims. His role, as he understood it, was to fight the British while Congress determined overall political and military objectives. Only later on—especially during the Trenton-Princeton campaign of 1776–77—did Washington begin to conceive of himself as responsible for guiding if not dictating all aspects of the war effort.

This chapter nevertheless posits the centrality of Washington's headquarters for American military assessment during the Revolutionary War. Changes in overall war aims, and the processes by which military strategy was formulated, tended to bring Washington's headquarters increasingly to the forefront. Whereas early in the war Washington deferred to Congress and his generals on many important matters, and exercised little oversight and no control on far-flung campaigns, by war's end he had assumed some level of responsibility for every military undertaking in North America.

Processes of operational and strategic assessment also changed. In 1775–76 the tools and processes of assessment were informal and personalized. Washington labored intensely to create clear procedures for information gathering and reporting, but this took time and intense effort as the Continental Army took shape. So too did Washington have to establish methods for evaluation and decision making. Not until at least 1778 was any semblance of a system in place that could operate simultaneously at all levels, from assessment to evaluation to decision in the context of clearly defined war aims. Even then much work remained to be done. That this system operated so effectively during the Yorktown campaign of 1781 is a testament to Washington's vision and hard work.

THE BOSTON CAMPAIGN, 1775–76

In the war's initial phases, rebellious colonists resisted British coercive measures aimed at enforcing Parliament's right to impose taxation. Local assemblies, particularly in New England, called out, armed, and trained bodies of militia. Exhorted by the Massachusetts convention to "be ready to act at a moment's warning," the so-called minutemen prepared to resist any British military sortie from Boston.[1] Gen. Thomas Gage's advance on Lexington and Concord on the night of April 18–19, 1775, provoked the minutemen to respond. The running battle that followed between the redcoats and militia severely bloodied Gage's force. News of the engagement spread via correspondence and word of mouth. The object of such communications was not to assess but to exhort patriotic feeling and to celebrate the fighting abilities of the American militia. Thus Pennsylvania delegate John Dickinson wrote on April 29 that "the Provincials . . . fought bravely . . . the Regulars have been defeated with considerable Slaughter, tho they behav'd resolutely."[2]

Confidence that the militia would thwart British oppression seemed justified. A "Grand American Army" of sixteen thousand militiamen from Massachusetts, New Hampshire, Rhode Island, and Connecticut assembled around Boston. To many members of Congress, this number seemed enough. Beholden to fears that standing armies led inevitably to military rule, the delegates did not heed calls for the formation of a regular army. Fortunately more realistic heads prevailed after eyewitnesses wrote to Philadelphia describing the chaotic state of the "army" around Boston. This situation—and indications that provincial armies would likely work at cross-purposes—led Congress on June 14 to vote for the formation of an American Continental Army.[3]

Four days later, the Battle of Bunker Hill took place. The discovery of British plans to occupy Charlestown peninsula north of Boston led American Maj. Gen. Israel Putnam to urge the fortification of Charlestown Heights. Militiamen holding fixed fortifications, he believed, could bloody and possibly repel the British. British assault troops commanded by Gen. William Howe did take heavy casualties—more than a thousand killed and wounded—as they stormed the works on June 17. The militiamen had entrenched inadequately and could not withstand British bayonets, however, and at battle's end they fled.

Once again information about the battle traveled informally. Washington, who had been appointed commander in chief of the new Continental Army on June 16, learned about the battle on June 25 while he was in New York and on his way to take command in Massachusetts. Encountering a dispatch rider with a letter from the Massachusetts provincial congress to the Continental Congress, Washington opened it. He later confessed to John Hancock that he was "induced to take that Liberty . . . agreeable to the Orders of many Members of Congress who judgd it necessary that I should avail myself of the best Information." The report emphasized the disparity in casualties and admitted only that "if any error has been made on our side, it was in taking a post so much exposed."[4] Washington was clearly impressed.

Washington's commission stated that he commanded the army "for the defence of American Liberty and for repelling every hostile invasion thereof." For the moment it was his only instruction.[5] His stance at Cambridge, Massachusetts, where he arrived to take command on July 2, was therefore defensive. The troops dug in while Washington visually assessed their situation and labored to establish a military administration. As verbal and written accounts of Bunker Hill continued to filter in, however, the outlines of a plan began forming in his mind. Noting reports of provision shortages in Boston—shortages that he sought to intensify by cutting the city off from civilian resupply—and recounting the heavy casualties suffered by the British at Bunker Hill, Washington wrote his brother on July 20 that "a few more such [pyrrhic] Victories would put an end to their army and the present contest."[6]

No coherent plan of operation would be possible, however, until Washington developed a clear vision of his own and the enemy's forces. To do so he needed information and the tools to procure it. When he took command, methods for information gathering were haphazard. He strove to make them clear and efficient. In deciding what to assess, he cast his net wide. Washington's demand for thorough and incisive knowledge arose from his belief that the most effective commander understood his own force, and as much as possible his opponent's, from top to bottom.

In his first general orders to his army, Washington defined the officers' duties and worked to establish a chain of command. He did so to enforce obedience and ensure the smooth flow of information. Simultaneously he established a system of reportage based on copious and regular paperwork. His first general orders demanded that his officers call and record rolls, and make "exact" and frequent returns of food, ordnance, clothing, equipment, and other supplies. Careful records were also to be kept of the sick and wounded. These reports were to be submitted to him via his aides-de-camp and secretaries. The work was not easy—repeated reminders had to be issued—but within a few days, Washington became reasonably well informed of the size of the force available to him and its many deficiencies. By the same process, so did his officers.[7]

Establishing a system for assessing the enemy took second place to the task of assessing his own army. Washington nevertheless issued orders respecting the duties of sentries and scouts, and he established posts to observe the enemy in Boston and at sea, with express riders to provide him with information of enemy movements. Verbal reports would not suffice. Instead, Washington demanded "a report every day in writing, sealed up, to the Commander in Chief at Head Quarters, in Cambridge, of all the material Occurrences of the preceeding day" with respect to the enemy's naval and land forces.[8]

No time was available for perfecting these tools of assessment before Washington considered what military steps he should take. He did not believe himself authorized to make such decisions on his own. His first council of war with his generals on July 9 began by reviewing the number, type, and dispositions of British and American land and naval forces in and around Boston. From that information the council considered military objectives and the steps to achieve them. Unanimously agreeing that aggressive steps were currently inadvisable but that "the publick Service requires the Defence of the present Posts," the generals turned to the urgent problem of recruiting.[9] As recruits appeared and the flow of information increased, Washington issued fresh guidelines for military organization, training, and supply.

Washington's headquarters was simultaneously evaluating and improving the tools of assessment. It was a learning process that would pay dividends as the war progressed and as Washington developed a strong if imperfect understanding of strengths and weaknesses on both sides. Thus he became aware, for example, of the limitations of the militia system and of the strategic advantages that the British enjoyed by virtue of their command of the sea.

As the campaign progressed, Washington and his officers thought increasingly of forcing the British out of Boston. Washington, still with Bunker Hill in his mind, hoped either to launch a direct assault on the city or to entice the

British into assaulting his own positions. Either event, he thought, might end the conflict. From the beginning, Washington sought not to outlast the enemy but to end the war as quickly as possible. Washington observed firsthand the ongoing challenges of military, political, and economic organization and the indications of the limited staying power of the civilian population. He also made assumptions—based on the aftermath of Bunker Hill and the records of the parliamentary debates that he perused assiduously throughout the war—that a steady rate of high combat casualties would undermine the British will to win. His own aggressive instincts occasionally put him at loggerheads with Congress and his officers. In every instance of substantive disagreement, however, he deferred to their cautious counsel.

By the time the British evacuated Boston on March 17, 1776, rudimentary tools of assessment were in place. During the bombardment of Boston, anticipating a possible land battle in case the British chose not to evacuate, Washington visited outposts and studied written reports from major generals and brigadier generals who had procured information from subordinate officers, scouts, and civilians.[10] Yet the refusal of the British army, now led by General Howe, to assault his positions left Washington unhappy. He could "scarce forbear lamenting the disappointment" that the "great event" he had sought in the form of a major military victory had not come to pass.[11]

NEW YORK AND NEW JERSEY, 1776–77

As the 1776 campaign began, the tools of assessment available to Washington remained imperfect. Widespread inexperience in the American officer corps exacerbated problems created by the need to rebuild the army at the conclusion of each year as the men's terms of enlistment expired. As a result the kind of organic improvements that a military force might normally expect to witness over time were not forthcoming. Washington would continue to have to make his assessments in great measure based on personal observation or instinct.

Even before the evacuation of Boston, Washington believed that the next British strike would fall at New York City. He therefore sent Maj. Gen. Charles Lee to inspect the defenses in and around the city. Lee, a man of some military experience and judgment, ran into the sort of trouble that would plague American intelligence-gathering and assessment efforts throughout the war. After his arrival on February 4, Lee found his "hands were effectually tied up from taking any step necessary for the public service" by interference from Congress and New York State government committees.[12] Only after long conferences and debates with these civilian officials—who had agents of their own trolling about the city and gathering information—could Lee get anything done.

Defending New York City was almost impossible. The task baffled Lee until he finally devised a plan focused not on holding the city permanently but on luring the enemy into attacking newly built fortifications on Brooklyn Heights and lower Manhattan. Washington declared himself "much pleas'd."[13] Following his arrival in the city on April 13, he barely assessed the city's defenses, choosing instead to accept Lee's plan with minor modifications. The commander in chief found almost all of his time taken up with trying to recruit and supply his army and to perfect its administration. Politics was also a distraction. Washington therefore felt compelled to defer to suggestions from overeager but ill-informed delegates on how to defend the city.[14]

The arrival of the British fleet off New York in late June found Washington and his generals poorly informed and overconfident. Washington's efforts to assemble and form his army had borne some fruit, giving him hope that the troops could carry out the defensive plan he envisioned. The Americans would occupy fixed defenses on Long Island and in and around Manhattan, and the British would "have to wade through much blood & Slaughter before they can carry any part of our Works, If they carry 'em at all, and at best be in possession of a melancholy and mournfull victory."[15] Unfortunately preoccupied as he was with problems of army administration, Washington had left the work of scouting terrain, building defenses, and deploying troops almost entirely in the hands of subordinates who were sometimes not up to the task.

When British troops began landing on Long Island on August 22, Washington had no effective scouting apparatus in place to assess enemy strength. Scouts underestimated the size of the British force, which in fact numbered about twenty thousand men, and Washington deployed a badly inferior force of only about eight thousand men to oppose them. Largely ignorant of Long Island's geography, Washington delegated to Rufus Putnam and James Sullivan the job of scoping out defensive positions and then retired to Brooklyn Heights to await events. The resulting Battle of Long Island on August 27, 1776, constituted a catastrophic American defeat. Only General Howe's decision not to storm Brooklyn Heights saved Washington from total defeat and probable capture.

Two days after the battle, Washington knew from reports and personal observation that "the great Loss sustained . . . had occasioned great confusion and discouragement among the troops." Their failure, he thought, had been the result of an inadequately prepared and dispersed system of defensive fortifications. Thus "the Divided state of the Troops rendered our defence very precarious."[16] In other words, the execution, and not the policy, of fixed defense had been to blame.

After withdrawing from Brooklyn Heights to southern Manhattan, Washington surveyed his strategic predicament. While refusing to admit the deficiencies of his own conduct, Washington considered intelligence from multiple sources—including scouts and spies—to gain a clear idea of British intentions. Juxtaposed with a dawning, yet imperfect, awareness of his army's weakness, this information exposed the dangers of his military position. "It is now extremely obvious from all Intelligence," he wrote President of Congress John Hancock on September 8, "that having landed their whole Army on Long Island . . . they mean to inclose us on the Island of New York by taking post in our Rear, while the Shipping effectually secure the Front; and thus either by cutting off our Communication with the Country oblige us to fight them on their own Terms or Surrender at discretion, or by a Brilliant stroke endeavour to cut this Army in peices."[17]

The army had to pull out of Manhattan—and quickly. Putting the army in danger to mount a last-ditch stand to save the city and inflict casualties on the enemy would serve no purpose, but civilian leaders hesitated to allow him to withdraw. It was in this context that Washington wrote his notorious passage on the "War of Posts." In it he explained to Congress the policies he had so far pursued and hinted toward what he might do in the future:

> On every side there is a choice of difficulties, & every measure on our part . . . to be formed with some apprehension that all our Troops will not do their duty. In deliberating on this great Question, it was impossible to forget that History—our own experience—the advice of our ablest Friends in Europe— The fears of the Enemy, and even the Declarations of Congress demonstrate that on our side the War should be defensive. It has been even called a War of posts, that we should on all occasions avoid a general Action or put anything to the risque unless compelled by a necessity into which we ought never to be drawn. . . . With these views & being fully persuaded that It would be presumption to draw out our young Troops into open Ground against their superiors both in number and discipline, I have never spared the Spade & Pickax: [However] I confess I have not found that readiness to defend even strong posts at all hazards which is necessary to derive the greatest benefit from them. The honour of making a brave defence does not seem to be a sufficient stimulus when the success is very doubtfull and the falling into the Enemy's hands probable.[18]

Washington was arguing that while the system of defending fixed posts had merit, it could not function effectively when the troops needed to carry it out were deficient or when the circumstances invited destruction.

Congress listened, and the army withdrew just in time. After subsequent engagements in upper Manhattan, Washington began pulling his army back across New Jersey. All of these battles had been defensive in character, and most had been defeats. Personal observation and evidence of increasing disorganization among both the militia and the Continentals took a further toll on Washington's confidence in his troops. He remarked to Congress that "any dependence upon Militia, is, assuredly, resting upon a broken staff."[19] Sensing the necessity of an overhaul of the army, he badgered Congress with prescriptions—as yet ignored—for reform.

Washington nevertheless was not yet ready to give up on a strategy based on defending fixed posts. As he pulled out from Harlem Heights in mid-October, Washington established two fortifications along the Hudson River— Fort Lee on the west bank in New Jersey and Fort Washington on Manhattan Island. He did so partly because of political pressure to delay the British and partly because, as he later wrote, "when I considered that our policy led us to waste the campaign without coming to a general action on the one hand, or to suffer the enemy to overrun the Country on the other I conceived that every impediment that stood in their way was a mean to answer these purposes."[20] Maj. Gen. Nathanael Greene's insistence that Fort Washington could be held convinced Washington to leave three thousand of his best Continentals there. From across the river at Fort Lee on November 16, the commander in chief witnessed Hessian troops storm the fort and capture the entire garrison. In a single stroke, many of the assumptions that he had carried since Bunker Hill went down in flames. Henceforward, given that the war's goal was now total separation from Great Britain and given his increasing independence of thought from Congress and his officers, he would adopt a new approach.

Washington's change in strategy is evident in his actions. Through November and early December, the British hustled his decaying force across New Jersey toward the Delaware River. December 7, 1776, found him in Trenton, with his baggage already across the river and the remainder of his troops ready to cross. But when the British pursuers paused, Washington incredibly prepared to counterattack. "I conceive it my duty, and it corresponds with my Inclination," he told Hancock, "to make head against them so soon as there shall be the least probability of doing it with propriety. . . . I shall now . . . face about with such Troops as are here fit for service, and march back to Princeton and there govern myself by circumstances."[21] But the British also chose that moment to resume the advance, and Washington backed off just in time to escape back across the river.

It had been a near-run thing but representative of a turnabout in Washington's attitude. Although some of his generals, such as Greene, encouraged a more aggressive posture, Washington came to this decision on his own. He did so based on observations he had made during the preceding campaign and on information gleaned from a variety of military and civilian sources. They indicated that the national will to continue the war was on the verge of collapse, with increasing numbers of civilians abandoning the cause or joining the enemy. Personal habits facilitated the acquisition of this information. First, Washington was a diligent reader of newspapers. Second, he was an avid correspondent with military officers and administrators, civilian officials, and private citizens at all levels. They responded by providing him with information from varying perspectives. Finally, while Washington did much of his information gathering from the command nerve center at headquarters, he also gathered facts in person. In a letter to John Hancock on December 20— typical of many lengthy epistles in which the commander in chief surveyed the cause at all angles—he concluded that "the Enemy are daily gathering strength from the disaffected; This strength, like a Snowball by rolling, will increase, unless some means can be devised to check effectually, the progress of the Enemy's Arms."[22] From this conviction came the dramatic turnarounds at Trenton and Princeton, demonstrating a far more aggressive war strategy.

THE PHILADELPHIA CAMPAIGN, 1777–78

The campaign of 1777 revealed how much had been accomplished and how much had yet to be done. During the winter of 1776–77, Washington identified problems in military organization and command structure that hindered control and the flow of information. His letters to Congress included complaints about the irksome necessity for consultation with that body before he formulated military policy. The day after the Battle of Trenton, Congress responded by investing Washington for six months with broad authority to determine military—and to an extent civil—policy on his own. Although this authority expired in principle after six months, it remained in fact throughout the war. Washington continued to consult with Congress as a matter of prudence, but he no longer felt himself bound to seek permission for everything he did. Washington used this authority in 1776–77 to initiate urgently needed army reforms that Congress later expanded and confirmed. These reforms included the establishment of a quartermaster department and commissariat whose duties included self-assessment and reportage through the chain of command. The capstone to these reforms was changing the term of enlistment to three years or the duration of the war, obviating the need to reinvent the army at the beginning of every year.

Yet Washington's tools of assessment—and therefore his understanding of tactical and strategic realities—remained imperfect. His successes at Trenton and Princeton with a small, highly motivated force encouraged him to overestimate his troops' capacity to execute complicated maneuvers in the campaign that followed. This overconfidence became particularly dangerous in light of the Continental Army's continuing lack of effective eyes and ears. Although Washington did begin to use cavalry, light infantry, and mobile militia bands more extensively in conjunction with his more aggressive war strategy, these formations remained poor at information gathering.

In July and August 1777, as General Howe conducted the naval movement of an expeditionary force from New York to the Chesapeake Bay, Washington got an inkling of how blind he was. Conflicting reports of British intentions and movements left the commander in chief in "constant perplexity and the most anxious conjecture" as he marched his army up and down the coastal mid-Atlantic.[23] When the British landed at Head of Elk, Maryland, on August 25 and marched toward Philadelphia, Washington discovered that he was ignorant of local military resources and terrain. Feeling it incumbent upon himself to assess the situation personally, he led scouting parties around the enemy positions and on one occasion was nearly captured.[24] On August 30 he ordered Col. Theodorick Bland, his cavalry commander, to keep "a diligent and constant watch on the motions of the enemy," but at the Battle of Brandywine on September 11, Bland's poor intelligence gathering nearly cost Washington his army.[25]

Brandywine represented a strange reversion to pre-Trenton concepts of defending fixed positions. This was partly dictated by Congress, which insisted on defending Philadelphia. Although seeking to harass the British with light infantry and militia, Washington ultimately decided to hold what he thought—incorrectly, thanks to poor local intelligence—was a strong position along Brandywine Creek. During the course of the battle, Washington was briefly tantalized by an apparent opportunity to attack Howe's divided force during its flank march, but then he pulled back and mounted a purely passive defense. The day ended with his army driven from the field. Washington initially attributed his defeat to "uncertain & contradictory" intelligence of the enemy. Later he recognized that another deficiency had allowed the British to outmaneuver his troops on the battlefield—poor training in drill and discipline.[26]

After the British captured Philadelphia on September 26, Washington chose to risk another Trenton-style surprise attack on the enemy. His explanation to Hancock of how he came to this decision reveals that he still used his personalized tools of information gathering and assessment and continued to rely on his officers in council: "Having received intelligence through Two intercepted Letters, that Genl Howe had detached a part of his force . . . I communicated the Accounts to my Genl Officers, who were unanimously of Opinion, that a favourable Opportunity offered to make an Attack upon the Troops, which were at & near German Town."[27] Unfortunately Washington devised a concentric plan of attack that was too complex for his poorly trained troops to handle, and the attack of October 4 soon broke down in confusion. Washington judged the results "rather unfortunate, than injurious," but he would soon take steps to correct those errors.[28]

The following winter encampment witnessed important developments in processes of assessment. First, the failures at Brandywine and Germantown revealed the Continental Army's tactical deficiencies and need for thorough training. Washington designated the Prussian Friedrich von Steuben to carry out this training and secured his appointment as inspector general. Second, the supply challenges at Valley Forge revealed problems in army administration that persisted despite previous reforms. Washington took it upon himself to study the problem from all angles and enact reforms (his forty-one-page manuscript letter of January 29, 1778, to a congressional committee on this subject is one of the most remarkable of his entire military career).[29] Finally Washington began moving away from the system of councils of war—which he called only irregularly thereafter—in preference for writing to his generals at moments of strategic decision and asking them to provide written assessments and suggestions. On April 20, 1778, for example, Washington wrote a circular letter to his generals, asking their opinions on the strategy for the coming campaign: attack Philadelphia, attack New York, or remain "quiet in a secure, fortified Camp, disciplining and arranging the army, 'till the enemy begin their operations and then to govern ourselves accordingly." The recipients provided responses that assessed the strategic situation from top to bottom. Washington studied these written assessments carefully and adopted the third option despite his own feelings that "the destruction of the Enemy in Philadelphia" was "undoubtedly, the most desirable object" and that of capturing New York only slightly less so.[30]

THE FRUITS OF FRENCH INTERVENTION, 1778–81

French intervention in the spring of 1778 changed the strategic game. In the short term, the primary consequence of France's appearance was the British withdrawal from Philadelphia toward Sandy Hook for evacuation to New York. Washington followed the British army, now under Gen. Henry Clinton, and succeeded in forcing an engagement at Monmouth Courthouse on June 28. Technically a draw, the battle displayed a Continental Army that moved more effectively on the field—thanks to Steuben's ministrations—and consisted of troops who felt personally connected to their commander in chief.[31] In the battle's aftermath, Washington and his aides worked to jettison one of his few remaining vocal detractors—Maj. Gen. Charles Lee—and to "spin" the battle as a victory, cementing Washington's position as the unchallenged leader of the army.[32]

After Monmouth the American war effort grew into an increasingly far-flung endeavor. French assistance appeared in the form of ill-fated efforts against British-occupied Rhode Island and Savannah, Georgia, in 1778–79. Some military and civilian leaders tried to push for a joint Franco-American invasion of Canada. Washington, however, quashed the scheme with a private letter to the president of Congress in which he weighed the strategic calculations of such an endeavor and concluded that a French move in Canada would leave it "in her power to give law to these States."[33] Indian pressures on the frontier led Washington to direct an expedition against the Iroquois Confederacy in the summer of 1779; he supervised it by correspondence although it took place at a distance. British efforts, meanwhile, increasingly focused on the South. Washington could not discount the possibility of their move from New York up the Hudson and so remained ensconced near there, fortifying West Point; nevertheless, he demanded constant reports of affairs in Georgia and the Carolinas. He now also sought reports from overseas on naval activities and on European politics and diplomacy. More than ever, he was thinking strategically.

Washington's ability to keep the big picture would save him from the potentially dangerous consequences of his conviction that the war would be brought to an end in New York City. Continuing troubles in the American political and economic structure—understood by virtue of Washington's broad correspondence with individuals at all levels of society—were worrying, as were problems in army morale consequent upon poor living conditions, low compensation, and long-term service. Just as in 1775, he sought the means to end the war as quickly as possible. From 1779 to 1781, therefore, he pondered the possibility of bringing New York under an all-out attack. In the summer and autumn of 1779, the prospect of a French fleet under Admiral d'Estaing sealing off the city from the sea led Washington to mobilize his forces and prepare attack plans. The French fleet did not arrive, but Washington's continuing interest in New York led him to devote prolonged attention to the need for improving his tools of assessment.

In considering an assault on New York City, Washington had to maximize his means of gathering intelligence. This effort included gathering minute details of British troop and ship deployments and information about affairs at sea. Riding about the city, reading newspapers, or taking in reports from scouts or civilians would not suffice for a full strategic assessment on this scale. Washington therefore constructed a well-organized intelligence-gathering apparatus, including the famed Culper spy ring, that reported directly to him. Espionage hitherto had been diffused and personalized; now Washington developed it into an actual network with himself at its head.

YORKTOWN, 1781

By the spring and summer of 1781, American and French forces had come into closer conjunction than ever before. A French fleet had arrived at Newport, carrying several thousand French troops under General Rochambeau, and there was the prospect for the arrival of another French fleet that could blockade the coast and support a land assault on some major British post. For Washington the obvious target was New York. In a conference at Wethersfield, Connecticut, on May 22, he and Rochambeau considered strategic opportunities for joint operations. Washington arrived clutching a paper detailing the strength of his army and other available military resources—a product of the system of returns and reporting that he had begun in 1775. He had also acquired, through his spies and scouts, a thorough knowledge of British defenses and military strength in New York, as well as some understanding of the goings-on at Clinton's headquarters. His tools of assessment were well honed by eighteenth-century standards. In his conference with Rochambeau, Washington made a strong argument in favor of attacking New York—his spies told him that Clinton had made several detachments there—and against the French general's preference for moving south.[34]

Washington provided an impressive display of his system of assessment at Wethersfield. Rochambeau agreed to focus on New York and even scouted the city with his American colleague. On one occasion, the two generals paused during a scout and took a nap under a hedge. They awoke only to find themselves caught alone on what was now an island because of the inrushing tide. Fortunately some dragoons brought them off before the British, who were nearby, noticed their predicament.[35] Secretly, however, Rochambeau urged the French fleet in the West Indies under Admiral de Grasse not to make for New York, as Washington had preferred, but to head for the Chesapeake and begin operations against the British garrison at Yorktown under Gen. Charles Cornwallis. On August 14 Washington discovered that de Grasse had arrived off the coast of Virginia.

A commander in chief who was too focused on local events to take stock of the wider strategic situation—or who lacked well-developed tools of strategic assessment—would have been ill equipped to handle this situation. Quick thinking was paramount as the French fleet would remain off the coast of Virginia for only a limited time, and a prospective march southward would take weeks. Fortunately even as Washington worried about New York, he had closely studied the course of the southern campaign. That some of his closest military associates—including Greene and the Marquis de Lafayette—were now operating in that region and that Benedict Arnold, one of his bitterest enemies, was ravaging Virginia while in a British uniform helped to fix his attention. Ultimately, though, what made the difference was Washington's understanding of the decisive, though fleeting, strategic opportunity that now appeared. He had gained this knowledge by developing an efficient intelligence apparatus that gathered information from multiple points and thus allowed him to form an accurate assessment of the situation.

A letter to Lafayette written on August 15, the day after receiving word from de Grasse, gives a sense of the wide array of information Washington had accumulated. He began by noting almost casually that the British did not seem to be sending troops from Virginia to New York because "a fleet of 20 sail came in last Saturday with troops, but they are said to be Hessian Recruits from Europe." He had doubtless learned this intelligence from spies. He then announced the arrival of de Grasse and communicated the size and origin of his fleet. Washington went on to tell Lafayette where to position his forces to prevent Cornwallis from slipping away, ordered the delay of forces now along the James River that were on their way to reinforce Greene in the Carolinas, and provided instructions on the disposition of the local militia in preparation for the dispatch of "aid from this quarter."[36]

Such a missive—typical of many that emanated from Washington's headquarters—was indicative of how much had changed in just a few years. In the summer of 1777, with Howe's fleet somewhere offshore, Washington had desperately sought information on British intentions and dispositions before being forced to campaign in a region where he possessed almost no local intelligence. Now in 1781 he was able instantaneously to call up detailed knowledge of American, French, and British land and naval resources, dispositions, and strategic intentions not only in New York but also in Virginia and the Carolinas. From this he was able to make an immediate decision to seize the brief opportunity that had appeared and move south. He also was able to conduct that march with alacrity and efficiency thanks to the regular flow of information that reached his headquarters.

The Continental Army's tools of assessment had undergone a transformation. Much still depended on personal observation and word of mouth; however, now Washington could acquire knowledge from multiple channels through extensive reports that he could classify, compare, and digest at leisure. The massive flow of correspondence with the general's many military and civilian contacts that his extensive "military family" of aides and secretaries handled also provided additional information (of the 140,000 documents in the papers of George Washington that cover his entire life span, almost half pertain to the eight years of the Revolutionary War). The apparatus of decision making had changed as well. For the first few years of the war, Washington had felt behooved to consult with the Continental Congress and councils of war before he made any important strategic decision. Now although he drew upon the knowledge and expertise of his subordinates and allies, he was able to come to quick decisions on his own. It was his ability to assess fully and execute promptly that, in the summer and autumn of 1781, ultimately won the Revolutionary War at Yorktown.

NOTES

1. John Ferling, *Almost a Miracle: The American Victory in the War of Independence* (New York: Oxford University Press, 2007), 27.
2. Paul H. Smith et al., eds., *Letters of Delegates to Congress, 1774–1789*, 26 vols. (Washington DC: Library of Congress, 1976–2000), 1:332.
3. Worthington Chauncey Ford, eds., *Journals of the Continental Congress, 1774–1789*, 34 vols. (Washington DC: Government Printing Office, 1904–37), 2:90; and Ferling, *Almost a Miracle*, 34–39.
4. W. W. Abbot et al., eds., *The Papers of George Washington*, Revolutionary War Series, 22 vols. (Charlottesville: University of Virginia, 1987–), 1:32–36.
5. Ibid., 1:7.
6. Ibid., 1:135.
7. Ibid., 1:54, 63, 73–74.
8. Ibid., 1:73–75, 79.
9. Ibid., 1:79–80.
10. Ibid., 3:399–428.
11. Ibid., 3:545.
12. Ibid., 3:250.
13. Ibid., 3:468.
14. Ibid., 4:355–56, 432.
15. Ibid., 5:260.
16. Ibid., 6:153–54.

17. Ibid., 6:248–49.
18. Ibid., 6:249.
19. Ibid., 6:396.
20. Ibid., 22:225.
21. Ibid., 7:262.
22. Ibid., 7:382.
23. Ibid., 10:410–12.
24. Edward G. Lengel, *General George Washington: A Military Life* (New York: Random House, 2005), 223.
25. Ibid., 11:91.
26. Ibid., 11:200.
27. Ibid., 11:393.
28. Ibid., 11:394.
29. Ibid., 13:376–409.
30. Ibid., 14:567, 641–47.
31. Lengel, *General George Washington*, 284–306.
32. Mark Edward Lender, "The Politics of Battle: Washington, the Army, and the Monmouth Campaign," in *A Companion to George Washington*, ed. Edward G. Lengel (Hoboken NJ: Wiley-Blackwell, 2012), 226–44.
33. Abbot et al., *Papers of George Washington*, 18:150.
34. John C. Fitzpatrick, ed., *The Writings of George Washington*, 39 vols. (Washington DC: Government Printing Office, 1931–44), 22:102–3, 105–7.
35. Lengel, *General George Washington*, 333.
36. Fitzpatrick, *Writings of George Washington*, 22:501–2.

6

ASSESSING ENEMY CIVILIAN WILL

THE UNITED STATES GOES TO WAR, 1861

Brooks D. Simpson

THE STORY OF HOW THE UNITED STATES framed a policy of subduing a rebellion in 1861 is one shaped in large part by how policymakers, led by President Abraham Lincoln, assessed white Southerners' support of secession. Waging a war to seek reunification, Lincoln, his advisers, and several of his generals weighed how best to erode secessionist support. Key to this strategy was leaving alone the institution of slavery and inflicting minimal damage upon the South. A guiding assumption was that, over time, secessionist fervor would subside, and cooler heads would eventually reunite the nation. Left unexamined was the way in which policymakers reached their assessments of white Southern attitudes. Several of these assumptions proved to be wishful thinking, for policymakers overlooked the agenda of other actors, notably black slaves. By the summer of 1862 policymakers revisited their assumptions and devised new assessments, which led to the escalation of the conflict and a limited embrace of emancipation.

Essential to understanding how policymakers assessed the attitudes of white Southerners in the first two years of the conflict is how they defined Southerners. Most policymakers believed that very few white Southerners were truly determined secessionists who would not abandon their dream of independence without a fight. A minority of white Southerners remained loyal to the United States, but no one knew how many of them would take action to maintain the Union. Policymakers paid most attention to two groups in the middle—reluctant secessionists, many of whom defined themselves as conditional Unionists during the secession crisis, and mainstream supporters of secession. Policymakers believed that it might not take much to persuade many people in both groups, especially reluctant secessionists, to abandon the struggle. So long as the conflict remained contained and limited, the fervor that had inspired many white Southerners to support secession might give way to a more dispassionate attitude that would consider reunion so long as the conflict did not devastate property or erode the foundations of slavery. Restraint was essential to foster this process of reconsideration; reconciliation would be facilitated by a "soft" war whose destructiveness was limited.

Policymakers arrived at these assessments impressionistically, not systematically. There were no public opinion polls or ways to gather data that would inform these understandings; rather, these assessments were largely exercises in deductive reasoning based on policymakers' assumptions about Southern attitudes. They were largely intuitive, based on what policymakers believed white Southerners would (and should) think and reinforced by an interpretation of fragmentary data, such as newspaper editorials, correspondence, and results from various elections and referenda concerning secession. Moreover, the only actors that policymakers considered were white. They did not think about what enslaved and free African Americans might do, unless it was to launch a slave insurrection that would have to be quelled immediately.

Assessing sentiment for secession was at the heart of Lincoln's policy during the first six weeks of his presidency. Lincoln believed that secession was the result of a temporary surge of irrational passions. Only the threat of anything that smacked of attacking slavery could inflame emotions yet again. Having repeatedly reassured Americans that he had no intention to touch slavery where it existed, Lincoln hoped that a wait-and-see posture would lead to negotiated compromise and the restoration of the Union.

The news that the US garrison at Fort Sumter in South Carolina's Charleston harbor had only six weeks' worth of provisions placed a time limit on a policy of masterful inactivity. Lincoln weighed whether to evacuate Sumter's garrison to eliminate the fort as a potential flashpoint of hostilities. That would violate his promise to retain possession of federal installations, but if he could swing a deal with the states of the upper South, especially Virginia, where secession had stalled, perhaps he could halt the spread of the Confederacy while buying much-needed time. Such efforts proved unsuccessful.[1]

One of the more puzzling aspects of this period is that in making his assessment of the Southerners' mood, Lincoln relied on very little information from the South itself. He refused to meet with the commissioners whom Confederate president Jefferson Davis appointed to resolve the Sumter crisis when they visited Washington. Secretary of State William Henry Seward was left to deal with them. The president dispatched Stephen A. Hurlbut and Ward Hill Lamon, two trusted friends from Illinois, to assess the public mood in South Carolina. Both returned convinced that secessionist sentiment remained strong. Nor is it clear whether a policy of delay was having the effect upon the Confederates and other secessionists that Lincoln believed it would. Confederate secretary of state Robert Toombs welcomed it as affording the Confederacy more time to make military preparations.[2]

Lincoln did nothing to provoke support for secession or to prepare for war during the first six weeks of his presidency. At first he contemplated reinforcing Fort Pickens outside Pensacola, Florida, while evacuating Sumter on grounds of military necessity given its vulnerable position. That way he could rid himself of the Sumter dilemma while acting forcefully to resist Confederate claims. Only when he learned that an effort to reinforce Pickens had failed did he decide to stand fast at Sumter by reprovisioning the garrison. Although he did not hope for war and certainly did not seek it, he realized that resupplying Sumter might lead to war should the Confederates seek to force its evacuation by firing the first shot. They did so on April 12, 1861, and two days later the garrison surrendered. On April 15 Lincoln issued a proclamation calling state militia regiments into federal service for ninety days, adding that while they would be employed to repossess those installations that had been lost, "the utmost care will be observed . . . to avoid any devastation, any destruction of, or interference with, property, or any disturbance of peaceful citizens in any part of the country."[3]

Virginia, North Carolina, and Arkansas hastened to join the new Southern republic, with Tennessee not far behind. Many white Southerners in those states who had previously leaned toward unionism cited Lincoln's call for the militias as decisive in their change of heart in favor of secession. Matters hung in the balance in Missouri and Maryland, where a vigorous response by US authorities barely retained both states in the Union, although a considerable number of residents in both states supported the Confederacy. In Kentucky the two sides were so closely matched that for several months the state sought refuge in a declaration of neutrality that Lincoln refused to violate in hopes that over time his native state would come around.

The president remained reluctant to accept the possibility of a costly conflict. "I have desired as sincerely as any man—I sometimes think more than any other man—that our present difficulties might be settled without the shedding of blood," he told a group of Kansans. "I will not say that all hope is gone." When Baltimore secessionists sought to block the passage of militia regiments to Washington, Lincoln rebuked them, declaring: " I have no desire to invade the South, but I must have troops to defend this Capital."

The implication was that he still was not sure how to undertake offensive operations without escalating the conflict and widening the breach. To Maryland senator Reverdy Johnson, the president reiterated, "I have no purpose to *invade* Virginia," although he would strike back if Virginia threatened Washington.[4]

Administration officials pondered how best to wage war. Aside from blockading Southern ports and halting postal service, Attorney General Edward Bates proposed securing the Mississippi River and defending St. Louis, Washington, and Fort Monroe in Virginia, but no more: "I think it would be wise and humane, on our part so as to conduct the war as to give the least occasion for social and servile war, in the extreme Southern States, and to disturb as little as possible the accustomed occupations of the people." Bates did not notice the irony when a week later, remarking on events in Maryland and Virginia, he wailed: "We hurt nobody; we frighten nobody; and do our utmost to offend nobody."[5]

Although Lincoln decided to blockade Southern ports, little else happened during the first three months of the war. Military operations were small in scale and did not involve major movements into enemy territory, except in Virginia, where Union forces secured positions south of the Potomac River from Washington to the Shenandoah Valley and advanced from the Ohio River into the western portion of the state. One event, however, had long-term implications. In May several slaves escaped to Union lines at Fort Monroe. After determining that the Confederates had used them to construct fortifications, Gen. Benjamin F. Butler declared them contraband of war and US property. Thus the war that was not supposed to undermine slavery slowly began to erode it, although a hands-off policy persisted toward the institution itself.[6]

The US high command was slow to develop a plan to defeat the Confederacy. Winfield Scott, the army's aging general in chief, had hoped that war would not come. When it did, he was not prepared to wage it. It took a letter from a major general of Ohio volunteers, George B. McClellan, to stir discussion. McClellan proposed to cross the Ohio River, invade western Virginia, and strike toward the Confederate capital at Richmond, with a secondary thrust toward Louisville. Should Kentucky side with the Confederacy, he would strike south and head toward Nashville.[7]

Scott rejected McClellan's plan. Invading Virginia, he thought, "would insure the revolt of Western Virginia"; moreover, the logistical obstacles to supplying an army across mountainous terrain were perhaps insurmountable. After all, the "three months' men" would be discharged before McClellan could undertake his ambitious endeavor. Building a new army would take time. Instead, Scott proposed strengthening the blockade and gaining control of the Mississippi, thus effectively quarantining the bulk of the Confederacy. This strategy, he claimed, would bring the seceded states "to terms with less bloodshed than by any other plan." It would be months before the plan would be put into operation as Scott maintained that "the greatest obstacle in the way" was "the impatience of our patriotic and loyal Union friends" who would "urge instant vigorous action, regardless, I fear, of consequences." Thus was born what would become known as the Anaconda Plan, although Bates had offered a similar strategy in mid-April.[8]

McClellan held his command in check until most Virginia voters cast their ballots for secession on May 23. Three days later, claiming that he was simply interested in protecting the rights and property of loyal Virginians, he entered the Old Dominion. "Your homes, your families & your property are safe under our protection," he announced. "All your rights shall be religiously respected. Notwithstanding all that has been said by the traitors to induce you to believe that our advent among you will be signalized by interference with your slaves, understand one thing clearly—not only will we abstain from all such interference but we will on the contrary with an iron hand, crush any effort at insurrection on their part."[9]

Congress defined the objective of the war that summer. On July 19, 1861, Kentucky congressman John J. Crittenden introduced a series of resolutions that the House of Representatives passed three days later. The Senate approved them with slight modifications on July 25, with Senator Andrew Johnson of Tennessee leading the way. The House version proclaimed "that this war is not waged upon our part in any spirit of oppression, or for any purpose of conquest or subjugation, or purpose of overthrowing or interfering with the rights or established institutions of those States, but to defend and maintain the supremacy of the Constitution, and to preserve the Union, with all the dignity, equality, and rights of the several States unimpaired; and that as soon as these objects are accomplished the war ought to cease." Many scholars point to the Crittenden-Johnson Resolutions as taking slavery off the table, but less than two weeks later the same Congress passed the Confiscation Act of 1861, rendering Butler's contraband argument as national policy.[10]

By the time Congress had addressed the issues of war aims and confiscation, US military forces had suffered their first serious setback near Manassas Junction on July 21, 1861, putting an end to the notion that the war would be short and decisive. Observers concluded that Irvin McDowell's men lacked the training to prevail on the battlefield. In contrast, McClellan received credit for a series of small victories that secured much of western Virginia, providing the foundation for the establishment of an independent state carved out of the rebellious Old Dominion. Pleased, Lincoln summoned McClellan to Washington. The general arrived determined to take his time to forge a real army. The ensuing pause in military operations effectively delayed implementing the administration's policy of a limited war that did not erode slavery.

McClellan approved the administration's assessment of the problem before it. The current conflict was unlike an "ordinary war," where nation-states looked "to conquer a peace and make a treaty on advantageous terms." Rather, it called upon the United States "not only to defeat [the Confederacy's] armed and organized forces in the field but to display such an overwhelming strength, as will convince all our antagonists, especially those of the governing aristocratic class, of the utter impossibility of resistance." Still the road to victory was a simple one to follow: "By thoroughly defeating their armies, taking their strong places, and pursuing a rigidly protective policy as to private property and unarmed persons, and a lenient course as to common soldiers, we may well hope for the permanent restoration of peaceful Union."[11]

In retrospect, it is interesting that Lincoln and his advisers did not consult with a man who had spent the secession winter of 1861 in Louisiana—William T. Sherman. Serving as president of a military academy, Sherman circulated among people who discussed whether Louisiana should leave the Union. While Sherman termed secession "all madness, all folly," and attributed it to an emotional outburst, he declared that "when People believe a delusion they believe it harder than a real fact." He said nothing about Unionist sentiment and much about the determination of secessionists to prevail; he understood that a war would follow. Nor did he think it would be a short conflict. White Southerners were going to pose a persistent threat until they were soundly defeated, and Sherman believed "the intense hatred bred at the South" would be hard to overcome. Although Sherman visited Washington and met with Lincoln several times in 1861, no one appears to have asked him what he thought, and he was unimpressed by the new president's awareness of what was before him.[12]

Among those Union officers who embraced a reconciliationist approach was Ulysses S. Grant, whose regiment of Illinois volunteers entered Missouri in July. At first "there was a terrible state of fear existing among the people," he told his wife, a native Missourian. As his men marched forth to meet the enemy, the houses along the way "appeared to be deserted." Once people discovered that Grant's men behaved "respectfully and respected private property," the residents returned, "and all the people turned out to greet us." He asserted, "I am fully convinced that if orderly troops could be marched through this country . . . , it would create a very different state of feeling from what exists now."[13]

That impression soon changed after news arrived in Missouri of the Confederate victory at Manassas. The enemy "are so dogged that there is no telling when they may be subdued," Grant observed (although he doubted the war would last past the following spring). "Send Union troops among them and respect all their rights, pay for everything you get and they become desperate and reckless because their state sovereignty is invaded."[14] Despite the concern Grant displayed about the behavior of his soldiers in irritating secessionist sentiment, other variables, including military success, also shaped civilian attitudes. In the face of persistent Confederate resistance, he worried less about how tougher actions might aggravate matters.[15]

The policy of reconciliation received a rude jolt at the end of August 1861 when John C. Frémont took firm measures in Missouri. Declaring martial law, he called for the confiscation of secessionists' property, including slaves. Coming just as Kentucky was deciding which side it would join, this proclamation was ill timed. After failing to secure Frémont's agreement to withdraw or modify the proclamation on his own, Lincoln rescinded it. Fortunately for him, Confederate forces entered Kentucky in early September, just days ahead of a planned Union incursion into the state. That act proved the last straw in moving Kentucky into the Union column.

As soon as he learned that Confederate forces had entered Kentucky, Grant occupied Paducah, thus gaining control of the mouths of the Cumberland and Tennessee Rivers. Like Frémont, Grant issued a proclamation, but it was far different. He assured Kentuckians that his men were there "to defend and enforce the rights of all loyal citizens" and nothing more. He ordered subordinates to make sure "that no harm is done to inoffensive citizens"; any soldier who destroyed private property or insulted citizens was subject to immediate disciplinary action.[16] Especially in a border state, where slavery remained a vibrant institution, Grant's caution and restraint aimed to appease and even woo civilians as he sought to minimize the change and destruction wrought by war.

Grant's Paducah declaration was in line with the prevailing attitude of the Union high command during the second half of 1861. Assuming the position of general in chief in November 1861, McClellan counseled his generals to fight a limited war. "I know that I express the feelings and opinion of the President," he told Don Carlos Buell, one of his western subordinates, "when I say that we are fighting only to preserve the integrity of the Union and the Constitutional authority of the General Government." This assertion was especially true when it came to slavery, and McClellan, aware that in Kentucky Buell was protecting slaveholding Unionists, also declared that Kentuckians "may rely upon it that their domestic institutions will in no manner be interfered with, and that they will receive at our hands every Constitutional protection." McClellan directed Buell to "be careful so as to treat the unarmed inhabitants as to contract, not widen, the breach existing between us & the rebels. . . . It should be our constant aim to make it apparent to all that their property, their comfort, and their personal safety will be best preserved by adhering to the cause of the Union."[17]

Thus, through the end of 1861, the US high command's assessment of Confederate civilian will had changed very little since the opening of hostilities. Aside from seizing several points along the Atlantic coast and in northern and western Virginia, US forces had not made significant inroads into Confederate territory. The lack of military operations meant that the administration's assessment and the underlying assumptions on which it was based had not been put to the test. Where the policy of conciliating civilians had borne fruit was in helping to keep the border states of Missouri, Kentucky, and Maryland in the fold, although significant pro-Confederate minorities continued to exist in each state. However, there was little evidence that the policy of conciliating civilians and respecting slavery had weakened Confederate resolve. Nor did there seem to be any systematic way of gathering and assessing such intelligence. What information passed through Washington seemed impressionistic, and policymakers chose to interpret it as simply reinforcing their preexisting assumptions.

As Union forces prepared to invade Confederate territory in 1862, McClellan repeated his warnings about the limited nature of the conflict. He advised Ambrose E. Burnside, who was about to embark on an expedition to capture Roanoke Island, North Carolina, to "say as little as possible about politics or the negro" in whatever proclamations he might issue.[18] But the assumptions shaping soft war policy unraveled during the first six months of 1862. As Union military forces penetrated Confederate territory, it soon became apparent that white Southerners were not responding to a policy of conciliation. Some of this resistance was due to the nature of the war; some was due to the black Southerners' asserting their own interests. Moreover, the assessment of white Southerners that had justified a soft war policy was flat wrong. While the resolve of Confederate civilians stiffened as war approached their front door, Southern white Unionists proved unequal to the task of reasserting themselves even while under the protection of Union arms.

Try as one might to fight a war that did not affect the civilian population, the mere presence of Union forces disrupted the lives and disturbed the property of white Southerners. Soldiers were not always on their best behavior; thousands of men marching, camping, and fighting were sure to leave their mark on the surrounding environment. The indecisive nature of battle also meant that no victory was conclusive enough to create long-lasting despair. News of defeats might cause some foreboding, but most white Southerners on the home front stood firm (even as the Confederacy's decision to resort to conscription in April 1862 suggested that such resolve did not translate into more enlistments). Meanwhile, Union forces found themselves moving into territory where support for the Confederacy remained high. For example, had they been able to conquer East Tennessee, where Unionist sentiment was strong, they might have found a different reception than what happened when they captured Confederate strongholds in the middle and western parts of the state. In North Carolina, landings along the eastern shore encountered more resistance among the population than an advance into the western portion of the Tar Heel State might have experienced.

Union strategy also failed to take into account black agency. The number of blacks seeking refuge in Union lines increased as those lines moved southward toward the slaves and as the slaves moved northward to greet their sometimes quite reluctant liberators. Congress instructed Union military personnel to cease returning fugitives, although that directive did not always reach the front. Where Union forces appeared, slavery was disrupted even if it was not destroyed. Secessionist slaveholders were understandably embittered, while Unionists (and a few pretend Unionists) were not always pleased, either.

Confederate civilians remained committed to the war effort even if they did not always rush to participate in it. During 1862 there was no sign of a significant long-term loss of faith in the cause. Although the series of Confederate setbacks in Tennessee were discouraging, Robert E. Lee's successful defense of Richmond revived morale. Union commanders soon learned that Confederate civilians resisted occupation with determination. Such behavior wore away at the willingness of some Union soldiers to let slavery alone; punishing the enemy became an apt excuse for welcoming refugees, as did the experience of seeing the horrors of slavery firsthand.

Grant's experience in Tennessee documents how commanders came to question the assumptions that underlay assessments of white Southern attitudes. While he agreed that if "it is necessary that slavery should fall that the Republic may continue its existence, let slavery go," he directed his men to leave private property alone because activities such as foraging were "apt to make open enemies where they would not otherwise exist." In early 1862 as his men advanced into Tennessee, he learned that one of his colonels had commandeered two slaves for his own use, spurring support for the Confederacy. Grant believed that "the return of those two negroes would do more good, & go further to cultivate a union sentiment" in the area "than any other act."[19]

Helping to explain Grant's moderation in early 1862 was his belief that the conflict was coming to a close. "With one more great success," he told his wife after he had captured Fort Donelson, "I do not see how the rebellion is to be sustained." After Shiloh he anticipated "a speedy move, one more fight and then easy sailing to the close of the war." He believed that many Tennesseans would welcome returning to the Union, but they bristled when Union soldiers seized their slaves (in many cases with the welcoming assistance of the slaves themselves). It would not be until he settled down as commander of occupied West Tennessee that summer that he began to change his mind. He had undertaken the task believing that shrewd and efficient management would leave citizens "loyal, or at lease law-abiding." He was wrong. Restless Confederate citizens resisted Union rule, no matter how gentle it was. By day they grumbled; by night and in areas far away from Union lines, they fought back. "We curry favor of these secessionists, and real Union men do not fare as well as they," reported a doctor who was close to Grant. "We are obsequious to them, we feed them, we guard their property; we humble ourselves to gain their favor, and in return we receive insult and injury." Soldiers "very naturally ask is this the way to crush the rebellion." Perhaps tougher measures were required, concluded the physician: "The iron gauntlet must be used more than the silken glove to crush this serpent."[20]

Grant began implementing tougher policies. He shut down newspapers critical of the United States, levied fines against Confederate sympathizers to pay off damages inflicted on Union forces, threatened to execute guerrillas, and accepted that he no longer cared about what might happen if slaves sought refuge in his lines. He realized that one assumption upon which soft war rested—that a generous policy would resuscitate unionism—was simply not true. The presence of Union armies inspired resistance, while few Unionists took advantage of the presence of friendly forces to exert themselves. By the summer of 1862 Grant was willing to wage hard war.[21]

So was Abraham Lincoln, although that change came slowly. In early 1862 he continued to hold fast to his assumptions. Surely Confederate civilians would respond favorably to gentle treatment; surely the presence of Union troops would inspire Unionists to reassert themselves. To foster this meant going slow on attacking slavery. While the president was now willing to consider the possibility of emancipating at least some slaves in support of the war effort, he wanted to make sure that the choice remained his as much as possible. Thus in May 1862 he immediately rescinded Gen. David Hunter's proclamation liberating slaves in Florida, Georgia, and South Carolina. Lincoln was still interested in wooing Southern Unionists and alienated Confederates, especially in the wake of recent Union military successes.

It soon became evident that most Confederate civilians persisted in resisting conquest. Even worse was the response of white Southern Unionists. In contrast to their resilient Confederate counterparts, they proved weak willed, even timid, while they sought protection behind Union bayonets. They seemed more interested in preserving slavery as an institution and did little to assist in the process of restoring their states to the Union.

Lincoln grew exasperated with the weak-kneed nature of unionism in Louisiana in the summer of 1862. He wrote: "The paralysis—the dead palsy—of the government in this whole struggle is, that this class of men will do nothing for the government, nothing for themselves, except demanding that the government shall not strike its open enemies, lest they be struck by accident!" Instead, Louisiana Unionists expressed frustration over how the army's presence disrupted master-slave relations. The president did not mince words in characterizing the Unionists: "a class of men who, having no choice of sides in the contest, were anxious only to have quiet and comfort for themselves while it rages, and to fall in with the victorious side at the end of it, without loss to themselves."[22]

"Of course the rebellion will never be suppressed in Louisiana," Lincoln archly observed, "if the professed Union men there will neither help to do it, nor permit the government to do it without their help." If they did not act quickly to restore a loyal civil government, the very changes they dreaded might well come to pass, because there remained a war to be won. "What would you do in my position?" he wrote one Louisiana official. "Would you drop the war where it is? Or, would you prosecute it in future, with elder-stalk squirts, charged with rose water? Would you deal lighter blows rather than heavier ones? Would you give up the contest, leaving any available means unapplied[?]" Lincoln refused to consider that last option.[23]

By the summer of 1862 Lincoln had seen enough. Confederate civilians remained determined to put up a fight, with the news of Lee's triumph outside Richmond inspiring them still more. White Southern Unionists, with a few exceptions, were undependable and unequal to the task before them. On July 17, 1862, Lincoln signed the Second Confiscation Act, which declared free those slaves owned by secessionists. The president was also willing to entertain the notion of mobilizing African Americans to fight for the Union, even though he knew that idea would infuriate many white Southerners who had always dreaded what might happen if their slaves secured firearms. Meanwhile he continued to ponder how to undertake an even more far-reaching measure, that of declaring free those slaves in areas under Confederate control on the grounds of military necessity. Lincoln bluntly explained his policy to New York Democrat August Belmont: "This government cannot much longer play a game in which it stakes all, and its enemies stake nothing. Those enemies must understand that they cannot experiment for ten years trying to destroy the government, and if they fail still come back into the Union unhurt." The time was coming to a close where the Union as it was might be preserved with at most minimal change; indeed, the war to preserve the Union, if it continued, would change it fundamentally.[24]

As Lincoln decried the frail nature of Southern unionism, one of his chosen generals set forth what a harsher war might look like. In June 1862 the president ordered John Pope to take charge of the newly formed Army of Virginia. Upon assuming command, Pope boldly announced that he was adopting a new approach to waging war. His men would live off the land where possible, he would take harsh measures against Confederate civilians who disrupted Union military operations, he would eject those civilians who did not take an oath of allegiance to the United States from their homes and send them toward Confederate lines, and he rejected the notion of using soldiers to protect private property.[25]

Opposed to escalating the conflict, McClellan explained his reasoning to Lincoln. The war being waged "should not be a War looking to the subjugation of the people of any state. . . . Neither confiscation of property, political executions of persons, territorial organization of states or forcible abolition of slavery should be contemplated for a moment." McClellan felt military forces should respect private property, that there was no need for martial law or loyalty oaths, and that slavery as an institution should be protected, although he accepted the necessity for the Confiscation Act of 1861. Nor was he simply concerned about the impact of a policy of emancipation upon the Confederates: "A declaration of radical views, especially upon slavery, will rapidly disintegrate our present Armies."[26]

McClellan found Pope's orders particularly objectionable. He had already warned the new general in chief, Henry W. Halleck, "that our efforts should be directed towards crushing the armed masses of the rebels, not against the people." Moreover, McClellan believed that "the question of slavery should enter this war solely as a military one" and that Union forces "should protect inoffensive citizens in the possession of that, as well as other kinds of property."[27] In promulgating Lincoln's order outlining the implementation of the Second Confiscation Act, the general reminded his men "that we are engaged in supporting the Constitution and laws of the United States and in suppressing rebellion against their authority; that we are not engaged in a war of rapine, revenge, or subjugation; that this is not a contest against populations, but against armed forces and political organizations; that it is a struggle carried on within the United States, and should be conducted by us upon the highest principles known to Christian civilization."[28]

Ironically it would be McClellan's performance on the battlefield that advanced the agenda he openly dreaded. His failure to take Richmond in the spring of 1862 ended any hope of a short, decisive conflict. In August 1862 Lee's Army of Northern Virginia moved northward to engage Pope, defeating him at the Battle of Second Manassas. Lee decided to take the war into the North by invading Maryland. McClellan took charge of Union forces around Washington and pursued Lee. A series of battles in mid-September, climaxing with a bloody slugfest along Antietam Creek near Sharpsburg, Maryland, induced Lee to return to Virginia.

Lincoln had been looking for just such a military triumph to issue a proclamation emancipating slaves in areas under Confederate control. He could no longer wait for Southern Unionism to reassert itself, especially as it showed no signs that it was capable of doing so. His preliminary proclamation, issued on September 22, 1862, just five days after Antietam, offered white Southerners one last opportunity to avoid emancipation by rejoining the Union by year's end. Having tried once to lure white Southerners back into the fold by reassuring them that he had no intention of abolishing slavery, Lincoln now declared that unless they abandoned their quest for independence, they would imperil slavery. Finding no takers, on January 1, 1863, he issued the Emancipation Proclamation. At the same time he welcomed efforts to enlist African Americans in US military service. Both steps infuriated Confederates, raised the stakes for victory and defeat, and promised to complicate the reconstruction yet to come.

In acting as he did, Lincoln confessed that the assessment he and others had made of white Southern sentiment had been far off the mark. While in the end the will of white Southerners seeking independence gave way, it did so after years of hard fighting that struck at Southern society and slavery as well as Confederate armies. Nor, in the end, should this failure in assessment come as much of a surprise. Very little had been done to ascertain the state and nature of Southern support for the war. Lincoln and others framed a policy that reflected their own assumptions about what would happen without determining whether white Southerners shared those same assumptions.

One wonders what would have happened had Lincoln correctly assessed Southern support for independence. Would he have been willing to wage hard war from the start to overcome the Confederate will to resist and to pay the price to achieve decisive victory? Could he have sold that approach to a Northern public that proved just as fickle as he supposed white Southerners to be? Perhaps in the end the decision to fight a war to preserve the Union would never have been fought had people known what it would cost; then again, it would not have been worth fighting a war that would have left largely untouched the underlying reasons why it was fought in the first place.

NOTES

1. James G. Randall, *Lincoln, the President* (New York: Dodd, Mead, 1945–55), 1:324–28. The most systematic examination of US policy is Mark Grimsley's *The Hard Hand of War: Union Military Policy toward Southern Civilians, 1861–1865* (Cambridge: Cambridge University Press, 1995). While I offer a different understanding of why conciliation failed in 1861–62, one can find his conclusions in brief on pages 92–95.
2. Randall, *Lincoln, the President*, 1:322, 329–30.
3. Abraham Lincoln, Proclamation, April 15, 1861, in Abraham Lincoln, *The Collected Works of Abraham Lincoln*, ed. Roy Basler (New Brunswick NJ: Rutgers University Press, 1953), 4:331–32.
4. In ibid., see: Lincoln, Reply to the Frontier Guard, April 26, 1861, 4:345; Lincoln, Reply to Baltimore Committee, April 22, 1861, 4:341–42; and Lincoln to Reverdy Johnson, April 25, 1861, 4:342–43.
5. Edward Bates, *The Diary of Edward Bates, 1859–1866*, ed. Howard K. Beale (Washington DC: Government Printing Office, 1933), 182–84.
6. On Butler, see Silvana R. Siddali, *From Property to Person: Slavery and the Confiscation Acts, 1861–1862* (Baton Rouge: Louisiana State University Press, 2005), 52–54.
7. George B. McClellan to Winfield Scott, April 27, 1861, in George B. McClellan, *The Civil War Papers of George B. McClellan: Selected Correspondence, 1860–1865*, ed. Stephen W. Sears (New York: Ticknor and Fields, 1989), 12–13. On McClellan, see Stephen W. Sears, *George B. McClellan: The Young Napoleon* (New York: Ticknor and Fields, 1988); and Ethan Rafuse, *McClellan's War: The Failure of Moderation in the Struggle for the Union* (Bloomington: Indiana University Press, 2005).
8. Winfield Scott to George B. McClellan, May 3, 1861, or Series 1, 51/1: 369–70; and Scott to McClellan, May 21, 1861, in War Department, *The War of the Rebellion: A Compilation of the Original Records of the Union and Confederate Armies*, 127 vols. (Washington DC: Government Printing Office, 1881–1901), 386–87.
9. McClellan to the Union Men of Western Virginia, [May 26, 1861], in McClellan, *Civil War Papers*, 26.
10. Crittenden-Johnson Resolutions, July 22–25, 1861, in Brooks D. Simpson, Stephen W. Sears, and Aaron Sheehan-Dean, eds., *The Civil War: The First Year Told by Those Who Lived It* (New York: Library of America, 2011), 522–23; and Siddali, *From Property to Person*, 59–94.
11. George B. McClellan to Abraham Lincoln, [August 2, 1861], in McClellan, *Civil War Papers*, 71–72.

12. William T. Sherman to Maria Sherman, December 15, 1860; and Sherman to Thomas Ewing Sr., January 8 and May 27, 1861, in William T. Sherman, *Sherman's Civil War: Selected Correspondence of William T. Sherman, 1860–1865*, ed. Brooks D. Simpson and Jean V. Berlin (Chapel Hill: University of North Carolina Press, 1999), 18, 32, 95; and Lloyd Lewis, *Sherman: Fighting Prophet* (New York: Harcourt, Brace, 1932), 149–50.

13. Ulysses S. Grant to Julia D. Grant, July 19, 1861, in Ulysses S. Grant, *The Papers of Ulysses S. Grant*, ed. John Y. Simon (Carbondale: Southern Illinois University Press, 1967–), 2:72–73.

14. Ulysses S. Grant to Mary Grant, August 12, 1861, in ibid., 2:105.

15. See, for example, Grant to Capt. R. Chitwood, [August 25, 1861], in ibid., 2:136–37, where Grant provides for foraging, confiscating secessionists' horses, and taking secessionist civilians hostage.

16. In ibid., see: Ulysses S. Grant, Proclamation, September 6, 1861, 2:194–95; and Grant to Eleazer A. Paine, September 6, 1861, 2:195.

17. In McClellan, *Papers of McClellan*, see: George B. McClellan to Don Carlos Buell, November 7,1861, 125; McClellan to Buell, November 12, 1861, 132; and McClellan to Henry W. Halleck, November 11, 1861, 130.

18. George B. McClellan to Ambrose E. Burnside, January 7, 1862, in ibid., 149–50.

19. Brooks D. Simpson, *Let Us Have Peace: Ulysses S. Grant and the Politics of War and Reconstruction, 1861–1868* (Chapel Hill: University of North Carolina, 1991), 18, 20, 22.

20. Ibid., 23–25.

21. Ibid., 25–27.

22. Abraham Lincoln to Cuthbert Bullitt, July 28, 1862, in Lincoln, *Collected Works*, 5:344–46.

23. Ibid.

24. Abraham Lincoln to August Belmont, July 31, 1862, in ibid., 5:350–51.

25. See Daniel E. Sutherland, "Abraham Lincoln, John Pope, and the Origins of Total War," *Journal of Military History* 56 (October 1992): 567–86.

26. George B. McClellan to Abraham Lincoln, July 7, 1862, in McClellan, *Papers of McClellan*, 344–45.

27. George B. McClellan to Henry W. Halleck, August 1, 1862, in ibid., 380–82.

28. General Orders No. 154, Army of the Potomac, August 9, 1862, in War Department, *War of the Rebellion*, Ser. 1, 11/3: 362–63.

7

"KEEP 'EM MOVING"

THE ROLE OF ASSESSMENT IN US CAVALRY OPERATIONS AGAINST THE PLAINS INDIANS

Michael Richardson

THE US ARMY EXECUTED CAMPAIGNS on the Great Plains as one means for the US government to accomplish the national strategic goal of subjugating the Plains Indian peoples to the political authority of the federal government. It was part of a political effort to consolidate all territorial claims across the North American continent. In this chapter I argue that measures for assessing combat operations played a significant role in conducting the campaigns of the Plains Indian Wars, and I illustrate this argument by focusing on the Red River War of 1874.

This chapter focuses on the linkage of assessment at the operational and tactical levels to the larger political goals. The strategy used in the conflict was built on reducing hostile Indians' resources by keeping the tribes constantly moving. This *societal disruption* strategy was based on the fact that the American Indian tribes' very limited production capabilities kept them existing close to subsistence level; they could not sustain themselves without time to farm, hunt, and gather in synchronization with the seasons. This plan, therefore, hinged on inducing a rate of movement for the tribes such that survivable living conditions were unsustainable and consequently forcing the Indians to choose surrender instead of extinction. This strategy in the Red River War was predicated on the heavy use of Indian scouts who were highly skilled in field craft and knowledgeable of the targeted tribe's customs and the territory in which they lived. To dramatically enhance the effectiveness of the strategy, the

US forces employed Native scouts to keep the Indian tribes moving at a pace that disrupted the functioning of their society. As such, the role of Lt. Richard Henry Pratt and his use of scouts serve as the focal point of this analysis.

Army leaders at every level understood that the attrition of Indian resources through societal disruption campaigns was the most effective means to subjugate tribes that resisted federal control. Based on that knowledge, the means to assess the effectiveness of societal disruption campaigns was also well known. Strategic commanders and operational-level commanders tracked the progress of campaigns through the reports and correspondence of their field commanders. Those reports provided information not only about the movements of army troop formations, the battles or skirmishes, and the number of Indian warriors ("military-age males" in twenty-first-century terminology) killed or wounded in those engagements, but more important those field reports routinely included the quantity of horses, mules, and livestock captured, as well as the number of weapons, teepees, buffalo hides, and foodstuffs destroyed by the soldiers. The most significant category in providing leaders an assessment of the campaign's effectiveness was the total number of Indians that surrendered and accepted federal control as symbolized by giving up their weapons and moving onto a reservation. Thus, army leaders recognized that the quantitative reporting of resources destroyed and adversaries killed, captured, or surrendered was an integral component to assess the progress of any ongoing societal disruption campaign.

The chapter is structured as follows. In the next section I provide a background for the Red River War and details of the campaign. I show the larger context of the deteriorating relations between the Native tribes and the federal government, the mobilization of resources under Lt. Gen. Philip H. Sheridan, and the critical contribution of Lieutenant Pratt and his Indian scouts to the campaign designed to implement the societal disruption strategy. I then focus on the assessment process used in the campaign and discuss the connection between observable military actions and their causal relationship to the underlying political goals of the war.

BACKGROUND

Since the initiation of the Indian reservation system on the Southern Plains following the Medicine Lodge Treaty of 1867, relations between American Indian tribes and the federal government steadily deteriorated. These failures were a consequence of overly ambitious treaty terms, lack of congressional funding, incompetent agents of the Office of Indian Affairs, unscrupulous contractors, racism on both sides, and miscommunication caused by differing values between the white and Indian cultures. The breakdown of the treaty was manifested in Indian depredations against white hunters, survey parties, travelers, and settlements in Kansas, the Indian Territory (present-day Oklahoma), and Texas during the spring of 1874 that resulted in a military response by the federal government.[1] In July 1874 General Sheridan, commander of the Division of the Missouri, issued orders for the consolidation of men and supplies to conduct a punitive expedition against the hostile Southern Plains tribes.[2]

The Red River War was in many ways typical of other major campaigns to subdue resisting tribes during the Plains Indian Wars. The acknowledged goal of the Red River War (as with those of other campaigns against resisting Indians) was to force the tribes to keep moving throughout the seasons and deny them opportunities to replenish the resources necessary to survive during the coming winter season. With the fiscal backing of Congress, the US Army would exercise its advantage over any resisting Indian tribe through a sophisticated logistical system that could sustain soldiers in the field year-round. Just as he did in the Winter Campaign of 1868–69 and in campaigns subsequent to the Red River War, Sheridan directed his subordinate commanders to maneuver their forces beginning from the exterior of the area of operations and move along major waterways or terrain features toward a central point. This method of converging columns maximized the soldiers' opportunities to make direct contact with the resisting tribes. The Indian leaders' fear of soldiers finding and directly attacking their villages kept them pushing their people to move.

The Red River War began on June 27, 1874, when warriors of the Southern Plains Indian confederation attacked the Adobe Walls trading post on the Canadian River in the Texas Panhandle.[3] Despite the minor number of settler casualties, the attack on Adobe Walls provided justification for a major military operation against the Southern Plains Indian confederation.[4] Shortly after receiving word regarding the attack on Adobe Walls, General Sheridan requested authority to deploy his command in battle against the southern tribes. The authority was granted on July 20, 1874, and included the concurrence of both the secretary of war and the secretary of the interior, who oversaw the Bureau of Indian Affairs. Along with authority to fight the Indian tribes, Sheridan and his soldiers were allowed to enter reservations when pursuing hostile Indians, an authorization that had been withheld since the start of President Ulysses S. Grant's Peace Policy in 1869. The authority for Sheridan to campaign without constraint was an admission of the Peace Policy's failure and marked the low point in the president's relationship with the East

Coast humanitarian movement that had advocated for the policy early in his presidency.[5]

In addition to deploying his troops to fight the southern tribes, Sheridan requested authority from the War Department to use special military commissions to try those Indians accused of murdering settlers. Indicative of Sheridan's intent was his specific request for the authority to impose the death penalty for those found guilty of sedition and murder. Beyond executing the most recalcitrant Indians, Sheridan proposed incarcerating other Indian leaders, notable warriors, and potentially rebellious men in a prison located on the East Coast far from their homeland. The removal of these men was expected to cause the remaining Plains Indians to assume a more compliant attitude toward American migration across and settlement on the plains.[6]

In less than ten days President Grant, Secretary of War William Belknap, General in Chief William T. Sherman, Secretary of the Interior Columbus Delano, and the Commissioner of Indian Affairs Edward P. Smith quickly approved Sheridan's proposed solution for ending resistance among the Southern Plains Indians despite protests from the eastern humanitarian movement. This rapid approval of major military operations was unprecedented for the Indian Wars. Sheridan wasted little time in issuing orders for his subordinate commanders to initiate the campaign. By July 25, 1874, infantry, cavalry, and artillery units throughout the Division of the Missouri and Department of Texas were preparing for war against all hostile Indians on the Southern Plains.

Later during the campaign, George Williams, the attorney general, ruled that military commissions could not try members of the southern tribes because the US government was not and could not be "at war" with people who were in their charge. According to Williams, the Indians within the boundaries of the United States and its territories were wards of the state. Beyond battle, the imprisonment of Indian leaders in the East remained the principal tool that Sheridan anticipated using to ultimately break the collective will of the Southern Plains tribes that continued to resist federal authority.[7]

PREPARING FOR THE CAMPAIGN

Officially recorded as the Indian Territory Campaign by the US Army, the Red River War of 1874–75 completed the subjugation of the confederation of Southern Plains Indians including the Kiowa, Comanche, Southern Cheyenne, and Southern Arapaho tribes. General Sheridan claimed the Red River War was the most important and successful campaign against the Indians since Europeans began settling North America.[8] Whether Sheridan's claim is accurate or bravado, the fact remains that the Red River War proved decisive in ending the threat of Indian attacks on American immigrants and settlements in the Southern Plains including Kansas, Texas, the Indian Territory (Oklahoma), and southeastern Colorado.[9]

The army's objective in the war was to force tribes that refused to return to their reservations in the Indian Territory back into the government-controlled enclaves permanently.[10] To achieve that goal, General Sheridan sent five columns, each consisting of cavalry and infantry soldiers, to find and if necessary attack the tribes along the Red River Valley south of the Indian Territory and on the Staked Plains of the Texas Panhandle. From the north, Col. Nelson A. Miles moved from Camp Supply, Indian Territory. From the west Maj. William R. Price rode from Fort Bascom, New Mexico. From Texas in the south, Col. Ranald S. Mackenzie marched from Fort Concho, and Col. George P. Buell departed from Fort Griffin. Finally from the east came Lt. Col. John Davidson from Fort Sill, Indian Territory. Each column included Indian scouts who were recruited to increase the likelihood of finding the resisting tribes.[11]

THE ROLE OF PRATT AND HIS SCOUTS

The national political leadership's rapid decision to authorize the campaign caught the army underprepared. The units responsible for the operation were widely dispersed and lacked adequate supplies. With the exception of the Tonkawa scouts permanently assigned to Fort Griffin and a small number of full-time white scouts, none of the columns had their own scout detachments on hand.[12] Soldiers and supplies would be consolidated at posts in Texas, New Mexico, and the Indian Territory; meanwhile, white and Indian scouts had to be enlisted for the duration of the campaign.

In preparation for the upcoming campaign, Lieutenant Pratt at Fort Griffin was ordered to consolidate with the main body of his regiment, the Tenth Cavalry, at Fort Sill in the Indian Territory. The Tenth Cavalry would make up the backbone of Davidson's column. Pratt departed Fort Griffin but left the detachment of Tonkawa Indian scouts he commanded for the previous two years behind. The Tonkawa scouts he formerly commanded would now support Mackenzie's and Buell's columns.[13]

Pratt headed north, expecting to lead the men of his regiment in the upcoming campaign; however, Colonel Davidson needed a man thoroughly familiar with raising, training, and leading Indian scouts. At Fort Sill, Davidson had already directed an infantry captain to raise a detachment of Indian scouts to guide his column during the campaign, but after a week on the job, that officer failed to recruit a single Indian. Upon Pratt's arrival, Davidson ordered him to take over the recruiting effort. In three days Pratt, who was already familiar with the Indians near Fort Sill, recruited, enlisted, and equipped fifteen Indian scouts for Davidson's column.

Pratt wrote on August 30, 1874, that Davidson authorized him to invite "from twenty to fifty volunteers" to accompany the column in addition to the fifteen scouts he was authorized to enlist for the duration of the campaign. Of the volunteers who came forward, Pratt wrote there are "a number of my old Caddo Scouts as volunteers and in the number [I] have already men from the Wichitas, Kechies, Tawankawas, Wacoes, Pawnees, and Delawares. And they are as fine a lot as I could wish: quite a number of the leading men, or the sons of Chiefs. As the General [Davidson] would only agree to take a limited number they sent their best men." Pratt noted in his letter that these volunteers "expect to pay themselves from the plunder" of the campaign. The response Pratt received from his invitation for scouts and volunteers indicates that the tribes near Fort Sill gave him a status akin to that of a tribal war chief whose exploits entitled him to invite warriors to follow him in raiding and war.[14] The volunteers included men from a variety of tribes who were familiar with the topography and the resisting tribes of the Red River Basin and Staked Plains. Even more valuable, several of the scouts were related by blood or marriage to Indians from the resisting tribes. The intimate knowledge that these scouts and volunteers possessed of individual Indians and tribal patterns represented another major contribution that Indian scouts brought with them to the frontier army.[15]

The day after enlisting his scouts and volunteers, Pratt set out to drill his new detachment before their departure for Davidson's first expedition of the Red River War. He wrote of riding across Fort Sill's parade ground and leading those scouts whom he had "organized and equipped in a manner eminently satisfactory (to myself) and must say I am not without pride in it. Think of a command of forty only two of whom can understand their commander and in which five nationalities are represented." Pratt was clearly motivated to lead such a diverse group of men to war.[16]

From September 10 to October 19, 1874, Pratt's scouts were critical to the success of Davidson's column. In the nearly six-week march from Fort Sill to the Staked Plains and back, Pratt's scouts were the only men in the column to make contact with hostile Indians. In one incident while scouting an unmapped branch of the Washita River, Pratt's scouts captured a lone, disoriented Cheyenne warrior. The warrior revealed he had been with a war party raiding along the Kansas border and had attacked a family in which everyone was killed except for four young sisters, who were taken captive. This information somewhat diverted the focus of the campaign as all the columns set off to find the captive girls. Finally after exhausting most of their supplies, Davidson ordered the scouts to lead his column back to Fort Sill.[17]

Upon the column's return to Fort Sill, General Sheridan, who was impressed with Pratt's leadership of the scouts, authorized him to enlist an additional sixty Indians for the second expedition. The order surprised Pratt both in its breadth of fiscal authority (since scouts were paid the same as regular army soldiers) and in that Sheridan expected results in just one day.[18] Pratt wrote that in less than twenty-four hours he rode eighty miles among the tribes around Fort Sill, "drumming [his] scouts together," and then selecting, enlisting, and provisioning them. More than two hundred Indian men responded to the call. To avoid resentment by those not selected and to further distance them from the resisting tribes, Pratt issued rations to all the Indian men who came to Fort Sill.[19]

Now with the additional Indian scouts, Davidson's column made another great sweep from Fort Sill to the Staked Plains and back between October 21 and November 29, 1874. During that march the scouts found several Indian camps abandoned by the now rapidly fleeing hostile tribes. As part of the societal disruption strategy to force the Indians back to the reservations and to accept federal authority, the army destroyed everything in the camps including teepees, clothing, food, and cooking equipment to preclude their use should the Indians return. Pratt's scouts led various sub-elements from the column and on several of these forays accepted the surrender of bands of Indians numbering from a few dozen to as many as four hundred individuals. The more resources destroyed and the more Indians who surrendered measured progress toward the ultimate objective.

During the second expedition, the main column arrived at a recently abandoned village with fires still hot and a fresh trail leading west. The find illustrated the work of Pratt's scouts, who kept the column in position to threaten the Indians. Davidson ordered an immediate pursuit of the former occupants. Pratt's scouts rapidly took up the chase of the Indian tribe. Near the Staked Plains, in an effort to stay close to the bulk of the fleeing Indians, Davidson reduced the size of the pursuing force, sending Pratt and his fifty strongest scouts to guide a squadron of 350 men to continue the chase. For two days and over ninety miles, Pratt's scouts trailed the tribe, always keeping them in sight. After exhausting what little supplies they carried, the squadron commander ended the pursuit in the face of an approaching "Norther" winter storm. Displaying the skills the army so valued in the Indians, two of the scouts broke from their winding pursuit trail and, through the storm, in less than a day led the command across the nearly featureless landscape and on the most direct route back to Davidson's camp below the escarpment. The scouts then led Davidson's entire command back to Fort Sill for refitting while the tribe they chased remained on the Staked Plains in the gathering winter.

Although Davidson's column fought no major battle with the hostile tribes, in concert with the other columns they were effective in achieving General Sheridan's objective of exhausting the hostile tribes by keeping them constantly moving during the fall and winter of 1874. During the course of the campaign, Davidson's column captured hundreds of Indians, weapons, and ponies and destroyed thousands of pounds of food, lodges, clothing, and equipment. Davidson along with Mackenzie and Buell, who were led by the Tonkawas, owed much of their success to Pratt's scouts, who effectively guided them and their soldiers to the hostile villages and back to their logistical camps through the fall and winter of 1874 and later the spring and summer of 1875.[20]

The efforts of Lieutenant Pratt were crucial to the Red River War. They provided the capability for the societal disruption strategy to be effective and efficient. Only through the efforts of the Indian scouts, trained and led by Pratt, could the cavalry units pursue the Indian tribes closely enough to disrupt their ability to sustain themselves. We now turn to a closer discussion of this military strategy and its relationship to political goals.

THE SOCIETAL DISRUPTION STRATEGY: OPERATIONAL BENCHMARKS AND ASSESSMENT

The US military had an enormous advantage in firepower over its Indian adversary. In an idealized confrontation, a column of federal troops might surprise a hostile camp and allow the army's overwhelming collective advantage in firepower to destroy any Indians who would stand and fight. But that scenario was both unlikely and unnecessary. It was unlikely because the Indian tribes were extremely difficult to track and trap in the vastness of the Western Plains. It also proved to be unnecessary because the concept of societal disruption allowed the federal troops to degrade the ability of the Indians to resist without having decisive combat engagements.[21]

To sustain themselves, the Indians needed to stop to hunt for game, preserve gathered foodstuffs, make clothes, and build shelter. In contrast, the army columns remained mobile as long as supply trains could reach them. If the army could keep the tribes moving through the fall season, the Indians would be unable to stop long enough to prepare for the coming winter.[22] Sheridan was aware of this fact and instructed his subordinate commanders accordingly.[23] The tactics employed during the societal disruption campaign presented the Indians with a dire dilemma. When the tribes set up their camps, the army columns guided by their Indian scouts could find and attack them. If the tribes kept moving, they would quickly exhaust their supplies. Without food and shelter the Indians would be forced to fight or submit. Sheridan's plan for the campaign depended on integrating the Indian scouts' unique knowledge of the Southern Plains and their tracking skills to maximize the army's collective advantages against the tribes.

This societal disruption strategy generated metrics of the success. They included the following:

- *Contacts or engagements with "hostile" Indians.* Commanders generally reported an estimated number of combatants engaged and killed or wounded.
- *Indian warriors.* Gatherings of military-aged males (in current parlance) were the focus of US Army attention, but the elderly, women, and children were also included in counts of those captured and in some (rare) cases killed. The Marias River attack in Montana Territory was one such case, where women and children were specified in the count of Indians killed during a winter raid.
- *Logistical stockpiles.* Meat, grain, corn, skins (largely buffalo), gunpowder, lead shot—all were often reported by gross tons seized or destroyed.
- *Villages.* The number of tepees or shelters seized (and generally destroyed by fire) was reported to indicate the significance of the location.
- *Horses, mules, and livestock.* Reports included identifying captured livestock as Indian versus those clearly stolen from settlers and the US government. Capturing the horses of horse-culture tribes was a means to damage the adversaries' mobility capabilities and to disrupt the tribe's economy and social order.
- *Tribes returned to or consolidated onto reservations.* Tribal leaders were forced to submit to military or Indian Bureau authorities.

This knowledge of Indian society, coupled with the scouts' capacity to pursue the tribes, allowed for an effective linkage of operational benchmarks and the underlying goals of the campaign. Sheridan's forces could forgo decisive battle for a campaign plan that degraded the tribes' ability to sustain their resistance effort.[24]

Washington closely followed every Indian War campaign. In the case of the Red River War, the course of the campaign was of particular interest because of the significant ideological positions at stake. Proponents of the

Peace Policy sought evidence that the campaign would fail to result in the subjugation of the Comanches and other southern tribes. With equal ardor, the war camp—which had assisted in the quick political approval of the campaign—sought evidence to show the military operation was an effective tool of subjugation. Continuous reporting on the army's disposition and destruction of the Indians and their supplies provided enough evidence to congressional and executive branch leaders that there was a corresponding relationship between the military operation and the degradation of the tribes' capability and will to resist. Thus the reports produced by the officers, including Pratt and Davidson, leading troops in the field were essential in sustaining the federal government's political will to continue funding continuous military operations, in giving the war camp positive proof that subjugation would be achieved, and in discrediting the proponents of the Peace Policy.

THE RESULTS OF THE CAMPAIGN

The five columns achieved General Sheridan's objective of exhausting the tribes during the Red River War. Although the army and Indian tribes fought less than a dozen skirmishes or engagements, the tribes were kept in relatively constant motion from summer through fall and deep into the winter of 1874. Led by Pratt's Indian scouts, the columns commanded by Davidson, Mackenzie, and Buell accepted the surrender of hundreds of Indians, their weapons, and ponies and destroyed thousands of pounds of food, lodges, clothing, and camp equipment. The Indian scouts kept the army columns in close proximity to the resisting tribes. As a result, the tribes were not afforded the opportunity to stop moving long enough to replenish their provisions.[25]

Colonel Mackenzie, one of the five principal commanders, praised the Tonkawa Indian scouts as indispensable for any campaign in the Texas Panhandle and Indian Territory. What prompted such praise was the effectiveness of the Tonkawas in finding trails of the resisting Indians and guiding Mackenzie's command to them. They gave the colonel the most critical information during the campaign when four Tonkawas found a trail that led to the most significant and arguably the decisive action of the Red River War—the September 28, 1874, attack on the Palo Duro Canyon in the Texas Panhandle. It was Mackenzie's column that broke the resistance of the largest concentration of Indian adversaries through an attack on the combined Kiowa, Cheyenne, and Comanche Indian village in the Palo Duro. The Tonkawa scouts found the village, guided Mackenzie's column to the canyon, and led the attack.[26] Although most

of the Indians escaped from the canyon, they lost virtually all of their possessions, the most important of which being their entire herd of horses.

When exhausted tribes surrendered to Sheridan's soldiers, suspected leaders of the Indian resistance were arrested. It was the final part of Sheridan's
plan to eliminate future defiance of federal authority. In April 1874 after a
somewhat dubious selection process, Sheridan ordered seventy-four of the
prisoners to Fort Marion, Saint Augustine, Florida, for confinement. With
the exception of Quanah Parker's Quahadi Comanche band, which remained
on the Staked Plains until its surrender in July 1875, the departure of the
selected Indian prisoners for Florida marked the final subjugation of the
Southern Plains tribes under federal authority.

CONCLUSION

The successful societal disruption strategy of the Red River War was based on
several factors. Without the skill of the scouts, trained and commanded by
Lieutenant Pratt, this strategy would have been difficult to implement; that
is, commanders would not have been able to locate the hostile tribes quickly
enough to keep them in a state of constant movement. Capturing and destroying resources were predicated on the army's ability to locate and press the tribes
to move repeatedly. In this sense, Lieutenant Pratt's work was pivotal, and the
assessment framework sensibly measured campaign progress. The underlying
understanding of Indian society and its fragile, subsistence-level productivity was crucial for linking the military tasks of tracking and pursuing to the
desired objective of ending the tribes' ability to resist. Observable metrics, such
as the numbers of livestock captured and minor engagements, allowed the
cavalry to track progress toward exhausting the enemy and at the same time
ensure its continued political support.

Pratt's recruitment of more than a hundred Indians for duty during the
Red River War is indicative of how effectively the societal disruption strategy worked. Although Pratt had rapport with and the confidence of several
minority Indians bands, the reality was that until 1874 the members of the
Comanche, Kiowa, and Cheyenne confederation were the undisputed masters of the Southern Plains. The overwhelming response Pratt received to
his requests for scouts indicates the smaller tribes and bands believed the
army would break the power of the confederation. This realization brought
a large number of Indians to Fort Sill even as the threat of hostility arose
from "peaceful" factions of the confederation tribes that remained encamped
nearby Fort Sill throughout the war.[27] That warriors risked intertribal conflict

by choosing to enlist under Pratt's leadership demonstrates that the southern confederation's societal structures were failing because those who volunteered believed they would suffer no consequence for serving the army. Pratt's offer to pay, provision, and arm Indians as scouts provided non-resisting Indians greater opportunities for social advancement through sanctioned war making than anything the resisting Indian tribes could offer. It appears that as the specter of social disruption loomed, the Indians recognized the opportunity to fight with Pratt, who was viewed as a surrogate war chief, as a more legitimate means to advance their social and political standing within their tribal communities.[28]

Another piece of evidence regarding the effectiveness of the societal disruption strategy is found in Pratt's utilization of rations as a reward. Breaking with army regulation, which specified that army rations were to be issued only to soldiers or those directly in the employ of the army, General Sheridan authorized Pratt to issue rations to both the scouts and those men not selected as scouts. This act illustrates the insight with which Pratt understood the Indian dilemma: While issuing the rations directly provided benefits to the Indians (and their families) as a result of their service as scouts, the act simultaneously further separated the resisting tribes from the "friendly" tribes.[29]

The third indicator of the strategy's effectiveness came during the campaign. As each expedition swept through the Red River Valley and up to the Staked Plains, it found more and more villages abandoned. During the first expedition, the capture of the disoriented Indian indicated the army's unexpected maneuver disrupted the connection between one warrior and his camp. During the second expedition, the army columns retained their relative effectiveness while the rising number of abandoned villages indicated the resisting tribes were losing their cohesiveness under the pressure of relentless pursuit. As Pratt and his scouts chased the tribe onto the Staked Plains in the midst of a growing winter storm, it was clear the southern confederation tribes had little hope for retaining the societal rhythms. Their fight was ending.

NOTES

1. Richard Henry Pratt, *Battlefield and Classroom: Four Decades with the American Indian*, ed. Robert M. Utley (Norman: University of Oklahoma Press, 2004), 8, 37, 42–43, 82–84, 257. Also see Richard Henry Pratt, "Drastic Facts about Our Indians and Our Indian System," *Berkeley Gazette*, 1917, 5, 8, 12.
2. The Division of the Missouri was the largest army command and consisted of an area encompassing all US territory between the Mississippi River in the east, the Rocky Mountains in the west, the Mexican border in the south, and the

Canadian border to the north, see Robert Wooster, *The Military and United States Indian Policy, 1865–1903* (Lincoln: University of Nebraska Press, 1988), 17–20; and Edward Stanton, *Annual Report of the Secretary of War* (Washington DC: Government Printing Office, 1869), 6.

3. The white buffalo hunters at Adobe Walls—whites who began the systematic slaughter of buffalo for commercial exploitation of pelts in the early 1870s—represented a relatively new phenomenon to confront the Indians. The white hunters were a direct threat to the survival of the Indian peoples of the Great Plains because the Bureau of Indian Affairs, which by treaty was supposed to issue provisions for the sustenance of the tribes of the Southern Plains, rarely provided anything more than starvation rations.

4. James Haley, *The Buffalo War: The History of the Red River Indian Uprising of 1874* (Norman: University of Oklahoma Press, 1976), 40–44.

5. Ibid., 12. Also see Paul A. Hutton, *Phil Sheridan and His Army* (Lincoln: University of Nebraska Press, 1985); and Robert M. Utley, *Frontier Regulars: The United States Army and the Indian, 1866–1891* (New York: Macmillan, 1973).

6. The model for Sheridan's legal campaign plan came from the Modoc War of 1872–73. For additional information on the Modoc War, see Gregory Michno, *Encyclopedia of the Indian Wars: Western Battles and Skirmishes, 1850–1890* (Missoula MT: Mountain Press, 2003), 260–63, 265–68; Peter Cozzens, ed., *The Wars for the Pacific Northwest*, vol. 2 of *Eyewitness to the Indian Wars, 1865–1890* (Mechanicsburg PA: Stackpole Books, 2002), part 2, "The Modoc War," 98–298; Arthur Quinn, *Hell with the Fire Out: A History of the Modoc War* (Boston: Faber and Faber, 1997); and Edward Hathaway, *The War Nobody Won: The Modoc War from the Army's Point of View* (Show Low AZ: American Eagle, 1995).

7. Regarding Sheridan's request for authority to campaign against the Southern Plains Indians and to operate on the reservations, see Hutton, *Phil Sheridan*, 247–51; Haley, *Buffalo War*, 105–6; and Utley, *Frontier Regulars*, 219, 229–30.

8. Sheridan to Whipple, November 23, 1875, Box 85, Sheridan Papers, quoted in Hutton, *Phil Sheridan*, 261.

9. Robert Utley and Wilcomb Washburn, *The Indian Wars* (New York: American Heritage, 1985), 47–56. See Jill Lepore, *The Name of War* (New York: Knopf, 1998), for a detailed account of the ferocity of the war and its consequences.

10. Robert M. Utley, *The Indian Frontier of the American West: 1846–1890* (Albuquerque: University of New Mexico Press, 1984), 161.

11. Wilbur S. Nye, *Carbine and Lance: The Story of Old Fort Sill* (Norman: University of Oklahoma Press, 1988), 211; and Michael Tate, "Indian Scouting Detachments in the Red River War, 1874–1875," *Red River Valley Historical Review* 3, no. 2, Red River Valley Historical Association, Durant OK (Spring 1978): 215–16.

12. See T. W. Dunlay, *Wolves for the Blue Soldiers: Indian Scouts and Auxiliaries with the United States Army, 1860–90* (Lincoln: University of Nebraska Press, 1982), 43–57, for a detailed discussion of congressional authorization regarding scouts. Also see Fairfax Downey and Jacques Noel Jacobsen Jr., *The Red/Bluecoats: The Indian Scouts, U.S. Army* (Fort Collins CO: Old Army Press, 1973), 11. The Tonkawas were under the command of Lieutenant Pratt between the spring of 1873 and the summer of 1874; see Pratt, *Battlefield and Classroom*, 50–60. See also Don Russell, *The Lives and Legends of Buffalo Bill* (Norman: University of Oklahoma Press, 1960), 80–81.

13. Haley, *Buffalo War*, 104–6; Hutton, *Phil Sheridan*, 248–51; and William H. Leckie, *The Buffalo Soldiers: A Narrative of the Black Cavalry in the West*, rev. ed. (Norman: University of Oklahoma Press, 2003), 113–14.

14. Letter to Anna Pratt, dated August 30, 1874, from Fort Sill, Family Correspondence, Box 18, File 611, Pratt Collection, Series 2, in the Beineck Rare Book and Manuscript Library at Yale University, New Haven CT, http://beinecke.library .yale.edu/collections/highlights/richard-henry-pratt-papers. (Hereafter Beineck Library.) Pratt's papers are also found in the collection at the Archives and Special Collections at Dickinson College, Carlisle PA, http://carlisleindian.dickinson .edu/collections/richard-henry-pratt-papers. Pratt referred to Davidson by his brevet rank of major general of volunteers that he had earned during the Civil War.

15. Dunlay, *Wolves for the Blue Soldiers*, 181.

16. Letter to Anna Pratt, dated September 9, 1874, from Fort Sill, Family Correspondence, Box 18, File 611, Pratt Collection, Series 2, Beineck Library.

17. Pratt, *Battlefield and Classroom*, 69–70. This attack was on the German family. Col. Nelson Miles and his column ultimately secured release of two of the sisters.

18. Ibid., 70. Scouts were paid the same thirteen-dollar monthly salary of a white soldier.

19. Letter to Anna Pratt, dated October 22, 1874, from camp near Old Fort Cobb, Indian Territory, Family Correspondence, Box 18, File 611, Pratt Collection, Series 2, Beineck Library; and Pratt, *Battlefield and Classroom*, 71–72.

20. Letters to Anna Pratt, dated October 25, 1874, from Seventh Cavalry Creek, Indian Territory, and dated November 7, 1874, from Gageby Creek, Indian Territory, Family Correspondence, Box 18, File 611, Pratt Collection, Series 2, Beineck Library; and Homer K. Davidson, *Black Jack Davidson: A Cavalry Commander on the Western Frontier: The Life of General John W. Davidson* (Glendale CA: Arthur H. Clark, 1974), 193–94.

21. Andrew J. Birtle, *U.S. Army Counterinsurgency and Contingency Operations Doctrine, 1860–1941* (Washington DC: Center of Military History, 1998), 65. Also see Don Rickey, *War in the West: The Indian Campaigns* (Crow Agency MT: Custer Battlefield Historical and Museum Association, 1956).

22. Birtle, *U.S. Army Counterinsurgency*, 67–69.

23. Hutton, *Phil Sheridan and His Army*, 249–51.

24. Russell F. Weigley, *The American Way of War: A History of United States Military Strategy and Policy* (Bloomington: Indiana University Press, 1960).

25. Letters to Anna Pratt, dated October 25, 1874, from Seventh Cavalry Creek, Indian Territory, and dated November 7, 1874, from Gageby Creek, Indian Territory, Family Correspondence, Box 18, File 611, Pratt Collection, Series 2, Beineck Library. Also see Davidson, *Black Jack Davidson*, 193–94.

26. Haley, *Buffalo War*, 175–82.

27. The threat of intertribal conflict rose significantly following the attack on Adobe Walls. See ibid., 109.

28. For an introduction to warrior culture, see Bernard Mishkin's *Rank and Warfare among the Plains Indians* (Lincoln: University of Nebraska Press, 1992); Haley, *Buffalo War*; Kingsley Bray, *Crazy Horse: A Lakota Life* (Norman: University of Oklahoma Press, 2006); and Grenville Goodwin, *Western Apache Raiding and Warfare, from the Notes of Grenville Goodwin*, ed. Keith H. Basso, with E. W. Jernigan and W. B. Kessell (Tuscon: University of Arizona Press, 1971).

29. Pratt, *Battlefield and Classroom*, 8, 37, 42–43, 82–84, 257; and Pratt, "Drastic Facts," 5, 8, 12.

8

ASSESSING THE PHILIPPINE WAR

Brian McAllister Linn

THE PHILIPPINE WAR (1899–1902) was fought by an army in transition from nineteenth-century frontier constabulary to a force prepared to wage modern warfare among the Great Powers. Even as American forces suppressed guerrilla resistance in the remote archipelago, Secretary of War Elihu Root (1899–1904) initiated the radical restructuring, or transformation, of the US Army's administrative, educational, and personnel policies. The simultaneous Philippine pacification campaign and Root's reforms created an odd situation. Many of the army's tools of assessment, along with the men expected to use them, were products of the "Old Army." But for the most part, these traditional methods, as practiced by officers in the Philippines, worked adequately, if perhaps more by luck than design. They had some serious weaknesses, particularly in appraising the strategic situation, in planning operations, and in gathering and disseminating intelligence. But against these shortcomings must be set the clarity of analysis and the prioritization of important information that this antiquated system allowed. Indeed, the very inability of headquarters to helicopter in or demand constant briefings and videoconferences empowered local commanders to adapt and to innovate, which were two crucial factors in winning a diverse and localized war. With the end result being a clear military success, the Philippine experience still deserves consideration by students of military assessment.

The US military intervention in the Philippines was largely a matter of tactical success, producing enormous strategic results. When Commodore George Dewey defeated the Spanish naval squadron at the Battle of Manila Bay on May 1, 1898, his victory had no direct impact on a war being fought ostensibly to liberate Cuba. It was, in fact, something of an accident. But based on information that was misleading at best—including Dewey's own idiosyncratic assessments—President William McKinley ordered the War Department (administering the US Army) to dispatch a small expedition to Manila Bay. The expedition's objectives were vague, reflecting McKinley's recognition of a chaotic situation where he had little to gain, and much to lose, by committing either himself or the nation to any firm policy in the archipelago. The war was only a few weeks old, but already the United States had done far better in the Far East than anyone had expected. Why shut off the possibility of further gains?

McKinley demonstrated from the beginning another important strategic gift, an appreciation of what was possible in the chaos of war. He knew he could not exercise anything but general oversight, providing only broad strategic guidance based on the most important data and reports. His willingness to accept imperfect knowledge and the comparative lack of data freed McKinley from many distractions that plagued later presidents and their military staffs. He remained firmly in the strategic realm and, as a result, could see the war from a broad perspective. Nor did he allow minor setbacks to distract him from his strategic objective of a Philippines ruled, at least by his own standards, for the benefit of Filipinos. He never deviated: The mission of the US armed forces was to lay the foundation for colonial government by imposing law and order, restoring the infrastructure, and always behaving in such a way that the civilian population would recognize the benefits of US rule. Furthermore to his great credit, McKinley understood the difficulties his viceroys would face while executing his noble goals, and he supported them against political and media criticism.

McKinley's improvised expedition to the Philippines proceeded with commendable speed and efficiency. The first troops arrived in June, and on August 13 the Americans captured Manila from the Spanish. In the meantime, the Philippines had erupted in a series of local uprisings against Spanish authority, but most of them had no connection to the self-proclaimed president, Emilio Aguinaldo, whose support was in the Tagalog region of south-central Luzon surrounding Manila. While he attempted to put together a government and assert his claim to rule an independent Philippines, his forces remained outside Manila, waiting in the wings and all but besieging the Americans. McKinley's proclamation of December 21, 1898, declared that the United States intended to extend sovereignty throughout the archipelago, with the army serving as the imperial agent of "benevolent assimilation."[1] Dewey and Maj. Gen. Elwell S. Otis, the army commander, viewed benevolent assimilation as a long-term objective. For the present, they wanted explicit permission to defend themselves against Aguinaldo's increasingly belligerent forces.

McKinley's appraisal of the situation was strategically more astute than that of his subordinates in Manila. He had no doubt that US forces could defeat these opponents, but he recognized such a war would be costly and would sacrifice Filipino popular support. Peace worked to the Americans' advantage. It would demonstrate to Filipinos (or at least the elite) the benefits of US rule and weaken Aguinaldo's faction-riven movement. But despite the president's explicit wishes, on the night of February 4, 1899, a minor exchange of gunfire between two patrols prompted a full-scale battle for control of Manila.

In the first months after the fall of Manila, American military leaders obtained much of their strategic information of the situation in the archipelago from that city's educated commercial elites, most of whom had vested interests in collaborating with the United States and were hostile to Aguinaldo. The information the Filipinos provided confirmed American prejudices, helping policymakers, both in Manila and Washington, to misjudge the situation in several ways. First, the Americans dismissed Aguinaldo and his Philippine Republic as an ambitious and tyrannical Tagalog tribal confederacy held together by bribery, intimidation, and ignorance. Second, the Americans assumed that Aguinaldo's supporters were the sole representatives of any Filipino independence movement and, once defeated, that no further resistance would occur in the rest of the archipelago save for sporadic banditry. Third, by repudiating Aguinaldo's government, by ignoring the clear evidence of a breakdown in law and order across the archipelago, and by believing that most Filipinos would welcome US liberation, an imperialist agenda seemed appropriate. In retrospect, none of these assumptions was entirely wrong; in some regions and at some times, each was probably more right than wrong. But each of these beliefs confirmed the other two, making it difficult for American political or military leaders to accept any contradictory data. To do so threatened the entire intellectual construct.

The first ten months of active hostilities saw a series of American campaigns to destroy Aguinaldo's conventional forces and to control the main island of Luzon. The campaigns were fought primarily in central Luzon; it had the only railroad in the archipelago and consequently the only means to support large forces. Although the Americans consistently won on the battlefields, weather, disease, poor communications, and logistical problems allowed Aguinaldo's increasingly disorganized army to escape annihilation. April brought not only the rainy season, with skyrocketing disease rates, but also the demobilization of units whose Spanish-American War obligations had long since expired. Military operations were put on hold. During the summer, the United States rebuilt regiments that had been shattered by disease in Cuba and created a unique volunteer force of thirty-five thousand soldiers to restore order in the archipelago. These new forces allowed Otis to destroy any large organized military forces by early February 1900 and to place dozens of military garrisons in every major town from the top of Luzon to the Sulu Archipelago. Soon afterward Otis declared military operations over. For the task of policing the archipelago, he broke up tactical brigades and divisions, replacing them with administrative organizations to govern the archipelago.

During this conventional war phase of the Philippine War, the assessment process worked imperfectly. For the first months, nearly all information on the situation in the islands came from Commodore Dewey and US consul Oscar F. Williams. Together they reported the archipelago was in a state of violent anarchy and that the Filipinos both needed and desired a strong American presence.[2] Indeed, Dewey would later claim that if he had had five thousand marines he could have pacified the entire archipelago without a war. As soon as possible, McKinley recalled him, dispatching a more cooperative and balanced naval officer, but for the most part the navy provided little information on the situation in the Philippines. The army soon supplanted the navy once the war began, and as McKinley's main source of information, Otis wore two hats—commanding general of land forces in the archipelago and military governor. Otis had to plan, execute, and assess operations against enemy forces while simultaneously building the foundations for colonial rule. He was up to the task. Displaying a virtuosity and gift for improvisation that most modern generals would envy, Otis not only waged a series of successful campaigns, but he also drew up the civil law code, developed a secular education system, recruited several influential Filipino collaborators, and otherwise worked to extend the military government.

If one of the indexes of strategic assessment is how it influences or shapes political policy, Otis ranks as an effective communicator. The extensive record of his telegraphic correspondence contains regular assessments reflecting War Department and presidential priorities. McKinley and the War Department relied on his assessments to develop policy for the Philippines. Yet Otis was sometimes wrong. He underestimated both the military resources and the will of his opponents. He relied on the opinions of collaborators from the Manila or merchant elites, men who stood to gain the most from US rule, to develop his own views on the situation in the archipelago. They were glad to tell Otis what he wanted to hear. Otis was pleased to relay this overoptimistic evaluation to McKinley and the War Department, bolstering the president's view of Filipinos as desiring US rule and attributing all resistance to bandits, terrorists, sectarians, and members of the Tagalog "tribe." From these premises it followed that once the army smashed Aguinaldo's predominantly Tagalog army, it could easily occupy the countryside and restore order to a

grateful Filipino populace. The example of the Visayan Island of Negros—
where at the request of a delegation an American regiment quickly suppressed
a millenarian sect, created a police force, and established a collaborationist
government—further confirmed these strategic premises.

The organizations charged with assessing the achievement of US strategic
objectives were small but efficient. Otis's staff numbered perhaps a dozen;
its senior member, Brig. Gen. Robert P. Hughes, served as both chief of staff
and provost marshal of Manila. Their tools were limited. Otis had telegraph
communications with Washington, but it was expensive and only appropriate
for conveying factual data such as casualties, distances advanced, towns occupied, disease rates, and so forth. More detailed analysis was reserved for the
lengthy annual or biannual reports to the War Department, most of which
were incorporated in the agency's own report to Congress. These reports
followed a similar format: a chronology of combat engagements; statistical
data on manpower, casualties, and dispositions; and extended commentary
on the important developments in the military and civil sphere, concluding
with a short assessment of the immediate future. Otis included reports from
his senior commanders—who often followed his format—and any reports
from regimental or company officers that he judged especially significant.
By including reports of subordinates at a variety of command levels, Otis
provided his readers with differing perspectives and clearly conveyed the
diversity of the situation in the Philippines. One district commander might
report strong guerrilla opposition—and include his subordinates' accounts
of pitched battles—while another district commander detailed little violence
but much success with schools, roads, and local government.

American policymakers had other sources as well. In the first year of the
war, a handful of journalists covered the conflict for American papers. With
one exception, they supported the imperial adventure and the military; their
stories tended to focus on heroism, the difficulties of the terrain and weather,
and the success of campaigns. They all disliked Otis intensely. Not only did he
try to censor their dispatches but also much of their information came from
other generals who blamed Otis for their own failures. The journalists knew
Filipino resistance was stronger and deeper than Otis admitted, and they
caused a minor controversy by accusing him of misrepresenting the situation.
But for the most part their assessment of the war corresponded with that of
the army. Another source of information came from letters that army officers
sent to policy-setting friends in Washington. In this respect, an important
source was Adj. Gen. Henry C. Corbin, who served as McKinley's unofficial chief of staff and corresponded with several officers in the Philippines,
both receiving information from them and passing along the administration's

wishes.[3] Altogether these unofficial reports provided an alternative view of the strategic situation and a view of the problems of pacification from those in the boondocks.

On the operational level, the assessment process was frustrating and often fraught with conflict due to clashing personalities. Otis was the archetypal rear-echelon bureaucrat, pestering his subordinates for reports, questioning their decisions, and generally trying to micromanage events from his office in Manila. His two division commanders, Henry W. Lawton and Arthur MacArthur, were disloyal prima donnas who were quick to complain to sympathetic newsmen and subordinates about "Granny Otis." Both were uneven performers. Lawton, although a charismatic warrior, so lacked any ability to coordinate the movement and supply of large bodies of troops that after two days of any campaign he would exhaust his food, scatter his soldiers, and demand more of both. Dying heroically in a completely unnecessary skirmish gave Lawton a martyr's halo, but his own words convey neither the strategic wisdom nor the benevolent views toward Filipinos that later writers, and many gullible historians, ascribe to him. MacArthur, equally erratic, was a better planner and manager, but his offensives also collapsed from exhaustion, weather, disease, and logistical breakdown. Believing himself a military genius, MacArthur's grandiose pronouncements—based largely on his own intuition—carefully included sufficient qualifications to cover himself should his bombastic predictions proved untrue. He was quick to blame others for his own mistakes. It was inevitable that their warring personalities and the tension between these senior commanders would complicate the assessment process. Otis learned quickly not to trust either man's evaluations. In turn, his generals blamed Otis for preventing them from taking advantage of perceived tactical opportunities. Fortunately for the Americans, their opponents were too disorganized, factionalized, and badly led to exploit these problems. And despite the personality issues, the US campaigns largely succeeded.

The lack of strategic and tactical information made everything more difficult. How could the army assess the situation if it lacked such essential knowledge as its own location, the enemy positions, and the basic geography of the islands? The maps that the Spanish bequeathed were more imaginative than accurate. More than once a well-conceived encircling movement bogged down when a clearly labeled road dwindled to a carabao track. Fortunately West Point still required cadets to learn topography, and the army's topographical engineers were picked from the best. Beginning with line sketches of enemy positions; then tactical maps of roads, towns, mountains, and rivers; and finally detailed maps of provinces and regions, the US Army built up a detailed picture of the archipelago. Mapping was part of an officer's duties, and it was standard operating procedure for every tactical report, even of a quiet patrol to outlying barrios, to include a sketch of barrios and terrain. The detailed and precise maps included in the contemporary operational reports are literal illustrations of the competence and skill of the army topographers.

Another crucial instrument of assessment was intelligence in all its levels: strategic, operational, and tactical. As with mapping, military intelligence in the Philippines began from scratch. The existing Military Information Division (MID) in Washington was next to useless, as its minimal capabilities were fully engrossed in the Cuban campaign. To illustrate MID's incompetence, a top secret report sent to the chief intelligence officer for the Philippine expedition contained only an *Encyclopaedia Britannica* article. So in the early days, military intelligence was virtually indistinguishable from mapping and reconnaissance.

When hostilities with Aguinaldo's forces broke out, Otis created the Bureau of Insurgent Records, charged with translating and analyzing captured records and with providing tactical and strategic information on the insurgents. The rapid capture of Aguinaldo's capital of Malolos and the disarray of his retreat provided a mountain of documentation on his efforts to create a coalition and national government. Public and political pressure from Washington required that Manila demonstrate both Aguinaldo's evil intentions and his responsibility for the war. The fledgling intelligence bureau had to spend so much effort developing a detailed picture of the origins and evolution of the independence movement in south-central Luzon that it had little to devote to on-time tactical or operational intelligence for commanders engaged in conventional operations. From necessity, intelligence gathering and analysis was decentralized. A general's staff might only have three officers, but one would be a topographer and the other an adjutant charged with assessing and evaluating the operational situation.

What would prove one of the most critical tools of assessment was adapted almost as an afterthought. In May 1899 Otis, perhaps influenced by MacArthur, authorized officers to purchase serviceable firearms for thirty pesos each—roughly what a field laborer might earn in two years—as well as the promise of good treatment to any soldier who surrendered with a rifle. The benefits of this policy increased over time, for rifles and ammunition were not only in short supply in the guerrilla ranks but often the only means of intimidating the population. Moreover, this campaign was much cheaper, in both time and lives, than active combat operations and resulted in almost as many weapons. For example, between January and April 1900, one innovative captain captured 177 rifles and purchased 95. The weapons bonus was expanded to include informants, who were instrumental in the capture of weapons, and some commanders used it to both pay and arm their police and auxiliaries. By buying firearms, the army removed both an actual threat to their soldiers' lives and provided the population with more means to resist insurgent demands. And unlike surrenders of personnel, the loss of firearms marked the permanent removal of the guerrillas' military potential in any locale. In most cases, the surrender of rifles and personnel were simultaneous, often because one was used to secure favorable terms for the other. Thus when Juan Cailles, the brilliant but brutal leader of the resistance in Laguna Province surrendered with his six hundred guerrillas, he received more than $5,000 in gold for the 386 rifles and 4,000 rounds of ammunition that his guerrillas turned in. Cailles also negotiated a pardon and an offer to become governor of the province he had so recently terrorized, and he was soon leading paramilitaries against his former comrades and seeking more rifles. In both Manila and the boondocks, officers recognized that the rifle count was a far more effective means of assessing the war's progress in any district than either the body count or social reforms, and operational records reflected this emphasis. In their final reports on the successful pacification of their districts, more than one commander cited as proof that all, or nearly all, of the firearms in the area were accounted for; thus, no resurgence of military resistance was possible.

The US Army applied the assessment system developed during its operations in Luzon to the rest of the archipelago in 1900 and achieved mixed results. Convinced that resistance came only from a few Tagalog malcontents, there was a collective cognitive dissonance when the occupation of non-Tagalog towns provoked strong opposition. In retrospect, the occupiers clearly faced an insurgency, and the long-derided name "Philippine Insurrection" was not simply an imperialist term to "other" the enemy or to justify the deployment of soldiers overseas. American troops occupied towns and provinces to begin the process of benevolent assimilation, and guerrillas, many with little or no connection to Aguinaldo's movement, ambushed their patrols, attacked their logistical lines, and murdered suspected collaborators. Both the nature of the resistance and its timing made assessment difficult. In some areas believed to be naturally pro-American, full-scale revolts and pitched battles took place, and dozens of rebels were killed. Yet two of the areas that would prove the most difficult to subdue—the province of Batangas and the island of Samar—experienced little fighting in the first months. The assessments from American officers in the boondocks illustrate their confusion: They attributed resistance to Tagalogs, *ladrones* (bandits), religious fanatics, the remnants of defeated armies, and so forth. Otis, in Manila, could find no rational pattern to this violence; therefore, he saw no reason to revise his earlier view that the war was over and all that was needed was police work.

Exhausted and ill, he asked McKinley for permission to come home. On the whole, he had done a commendable job in executing McKinley's strategic guidance, defeating all Filipino conventional forces, establishing the foundations of colonial government, and, for the most part, ensuring that soldiers followed the president's humane directives.

Arthur MacArthur, who inherited Otis's dual roles as commanding general and civil governor, had openly criticized his predecessor, not least for his sanguine evaluation of the strategic situation. Yet if Otis erred toward optimism, refusing to accept the scope and dimension of the insurgency, MacArthur was the opposite, being prone to vacillation, contradiction, and gloom. Fortunately he compensated with a greater sensitivity to the depth and diversity of the irregular resistance. Shortly after conventional operations ended, MacArthur warned that the enemy might not be limited to the guerrillas in the field. More likely the enemy was to be found in many army-occupied towns, serving on clandestine councils, quietly collecting taxes, hiding weapons, and sheltering guerrillas posing as peaceful villagers. As he did so often, MacArthur spoiled his perceptive analysis by extrapolation and predicting a spontaneous uprising to massacre all Americans.[4]

Besides his own analytical skills, MacArthur could benefit from the growing experience of his officers, many of whom judiciously ignored or modified Manila's directives, and from the indirect results of McKinley's emphasis on using the army as an instrument of government. Although as a staff officer in Washington he had served in the MID, MacArthur moved slowly to centralize or improve his access to local information. For the most part, intelligence in 1900 remained localized and improvised. Individual officers developed networks of informants: Some were transparent like the police or town mayor; others, clandestine sources who risked a gruesome and slow death if exposed. Some of the best intelligence came from luck or improvisation. In the First District, Department of Northern Luzon, for example, civil affairs duties required post commanders to monitor the conduct of public officials, collect census and tax information, oversee the construction of roads, and organize the police. The officer in charge of coordinating civil affairs also served as the chief of intelligence as he was perfectly placed to build a network of agents and informants through patronage and bribes.

Lt. William T. Johnston's report of May 21, 1900, detailing the guerrilla organization in La Union Province, confirmed MacArthur's suspicions. Johnston, a Harvard-trained lawyer, proved what many had long suspected: In some towns the very people who claimed to be the most loyal were actually helping the local guerrillas. Far from living in large camps in the jungles, most guerrillas lived quite openly in the towns, only gathering to ambush a patrol or kill a suspected collaborator.[5] Johnston's clear and detailed report demonstrated that the towns were the center of gravity and would greatly influence his district's counterinsurgency policies. Unfortunately it was also taken as a template of the general nature of the guerrilla resistance, and its findings were extrapolated from one area in Luzon to the entire archipelago. But in fact, as other reports demonstrated, towns in many areas including La Union were loyal to the Americans and did not have shadow governments.

The McKinley administration's ability to assess the situation in the Philippines also improved as a result of the arrival in June 1900 of the Philippine Commission under William Howard Taft. MacArthur and Taft detested each other on sight and, beyond this point, agreed on little. MacArthur's evaluation of the war became increasingly negative and often mistaken. Instead of understanding the war as a regional insurgency or, more correctly, as a variety of regional insurgencies, he reported the guerrillas and populace as unified in ideology and command. His unwillingness to leave Manila, his failure to establish informal contacts with officers in the boondocks, and his curious mix of egotism and insecurity—all doomed any accurate analysis for Washington. MacArthur often lost sight of where his authority began and ended. He not only ignored McKinley's oft-repeated instructions to facilitate Taft's civil government, but he also offered strategic analysis based on his limited understanding of the political situation in the United States.

In contrast, upon his arrival in the archipelago, Taft spent two months observing the situation in the countryside and cultivating contacts with Filipinos and such outstanding officers as Brig. Gen. J. Franklin Bell. Even after taking up permanent residence in Manila, he and his fellow commissioners often visited the provinces. Taft's creation of the Philippine Constabulary, and its equally rapid creation of its own intelligence agency, gave him a broad appreciation for the situation throughout the archipelago. He recognized the insurgents' increasing use of violence as an indication of their weakness and declining support. To Taft the US military's most important task had been to develop counterinsurgency policies that would overcome this "system of terrorism and assassination and murder" and would allow Filipinos to live peacefully under American authority.[6] He advocated conciliating the majority by turning the government over to civilians and ruthlessly punishing any who continued to resist. Taft quickly established close contacts with Secretary Root and others, and he reported both his assessment and his criticism of MacArthur's policies. However detrimental Taft's backdoor reporting was to the principle of unified command, in practice it proved highly beneficial as it provided a more balanced view of the situation to the political-military leadership in Washington.

In the fall of 1900 the differences between Taft and MacArthur were brought to the fore by an upsurge in guerrilla violence. Supporters of Aguinaldo's Philippine Republic hoped to influence the US presidential election and see McKinley replaced with the anti-imperialist William Jennings Bryan. Others took advantage of the tactical weakness of the local garrisons, which were often ravaged by malaria and dysentery. In some areas, the guerrillas had some brief but spectacular successes. Facing this explosion of violence, MacArthur provided contradictory and overly dark assessments. But with McKinley's reelection and the arrival of reinforcements, who had clear directives to escalate operations, on December 20, 1900, MacArthur issued a proclamation. A telegram to Washington summarized both his assessment of the situation and his solution. While there had been much progress, it had been too slow; moreover, he feared guerrilla war and armed resistance might become a "chronic" condition in the archipelago. A "more rigid policy" striking at several targets was required. From here on, terrorists and assassins would be held to account, a euphemism for more and faster executions.[7] A few prominent captured revolutionaries who continued to advocate resistance would be deported to Guam. Above all MacArthur intended to sever the connections between the towns and the guerrillas, indicating how influential Johnston's report on La Union had become. Anyone living in occupied areas and benefiting from American occupation could no longer claim neutrality. Dismissing the peasantry as ignorant tools, MacArthur went after the elites—landowners, professionals, and merchants—who he believed controlled popular support. From now on, they must irrevocably commit to the American side or face a variety of sanctions: fines, confiscations, arrest, prison, and exile.

Both at the time and later, some debated whether MacArthur's proclamation was strategically accurate. From the reports of officers in the boondocks, they clearly regarded the new policy as a post hoc justification of methods that had been practiced for some time. In some areas, more retaliatory measures would be adopted, but in others commanders urged protection for the local population. A prominent historian has argued that in Batangas Province, MacArthur targeted the rural elites at the very time they were largely swinging their support to the Americans in part due to their fear of peasant rebels. MacArthur had no such qualms. Within a few months, forgetting his equivocal analysis of the fall, he was trumpeting, "Rarely in a war has a single document been so instrumental in influencing ultimate results. The consequences in this instance, however, which lie very near the surface, seem to preclude all possibility of doubt, and also seem to justify the conclusion that the effective pacification of the Archipelago commenced December 20, 1900."[8]

While the credit due MacArthur is debatable, within the first months of 1901 the insurgents were clearly in disarray. The offensives of the fall of 1900 had flushed many into the open, and their failure to win tactical or strategic victories demoralized them. The Americans were more numerous, better supplied, and now able to rely on good roads and communications. By turning the pacified provinces over to Taft's civil government, the army could concentrate troops on the remaining recalcitrants. In 1901 increasing numbers of Filipino allies joined the Americans, and their combined forces far outnumbered the guerrillas. More and more guerrillas surrendered or were captured, including Aguinaldo in April. By the summer of 1901 only a few provinces remained in a state of insurrection.

MacArthur's policies had neglected his intelligence service. Perhaps he finally recognized the profound contrast between the vibrant local networks established by innovative commanders in the boondocks, the increasingly effective secret service in Manila, and the largely ineffectual Bureau of Insurgent Records, which was still largely confined to translating documents. MacArthur created the Division of Military Information (DMI) on December 13, 1900. He expanded its mission from translating captured documents to analyzing and disseminating information both to headquarters and back to the provinces. Under Capt. Ralph Van Deman, an experienced MID officer, the DMI began to coordinate various activities, such as collecting, copying, and drafting maps for distribution in the provinces. He broke down the previously compartmentalized and sometimes rival intelligence agencies in the Manila police and Philippine Constabulary. In March 1901 the DMI ordered each post commander to fill out identity cards not only on guerrilla leaders but also on the most influential people, such as priests, politicians, and police, in their villages and regions. This information, collated at headquarters, could assess the pacification of a province or island. Copies provided to officers in the towns made it easier to secure tactical intelligence and identify suspected guerrillas.

On September 28, 1901, with the war over in all but Batangas and Samar Provinces, MacArthur's successor, Maj. Gen. Adna R. Chaffee, took the logical step of having each post designate an intelligence officer. Benefiting from early lessons, these officers' first priority was to write a report of the topography, roads, economy, and so forth; noting the identity of guerrillas was secondary. Chaffee's orders maintained the existing local networks while providing clear lines of communication with higher headquarters. Ideally information would move from the field to the DMI and back again smoothly and quickly, allowing for rapid and accurate evaluations of the tactical situation.

The initial result of these improvements in intelligence was a grave miscalculation. Chaffee, with little experience in the Philippines and despite reports of generally peaceful conditions, intuited that "in every town there are men plotting against us and using their influence to persuade the masses to remain against us."[9] Although he was not as openly confrontational as MacArthur was, he also disliked Taft and believed the islands should be returned to military rule for some time.[10] At this critical moment, however, his intelligence sources failed him. As would be proven later by his controversial leadership of the American Protective League, Van Deman, Chaffee's chief of military intelligence, was obsessed with the apparent threat from conspiracies and domestic enemies. So despite his field commanders' reporting peaceful conditions and a widespread acceptance of US authority, Van Deman remained convinced that Japanese agents and Filipino nationalists planned a massive uprising.

When Samareño guerrilla leader Eugenio Daza y Salazar successfully attacked the US garrison at the town of Balangiga on September 28, 1901, Van Deman and Chaffee misinterpreted it as the start of an archipelago-wide insurrection. Chaffee told Taft that the Americans "were standing on a volcano" that was ready to explode. Receiving information from his Filipino contacts and the newly created intelligence service in the Philippine Constabulary, Taft disagreed and told Root that the army was "stampeded."[11] He recognized, as did many soldiers on Samar, that Balangiga was one of the guerrillas' rare tactical successes; it was entirely confined to the town and did not reflect general conditions on the island. But Chaffee, panicked by the attack, sent the intemperate and probably demented Brig. Gen. Jacob H. Smith to Samar. Smith lacked any appreciation of the situation; his solution was brutal and destructive warfare, punishing everyone. After issuing orders for an all-out punitive campaign, he soon lost control of his forces, partly because he wandered off on expeditions without informing his staff. Although some American forces, most notably Maj. Littleton W. T. Waller's marine battalion, burned and killed with little discrimination, most US Army units resisted Smith's injunctions. Smith also interfered in neighboring Leyte, which was under civil government. Taft, receiving better information from the constabulary than Chaffee had from Smith, protested. In January Chaffee finally visited Samar and soon relieved Smith, but by this time the media had uncovered widespread evidence of atrocities. The campaign in Samar led to a national scandal, to courts-martial, and to a Senate investigation. It provided ample fodder for the anti-imperialists and later for historians who pilloried the American pacification campaign as little more than a series of massacres. It was, and remains, a graphic example of how a relatively minor tactical setback (the so-called Balangiga Massacre) can confirm the strategic biases of senior leaders and prompt a completely inappropriate tactical response with disastrous short-term and long-term strategic effects.

While Samar marked the low point in American assessment, the Batangas campaign may have been its apex. Brigadier General Bell was the war's most competent commander, and his experience in a variety of assignments—as an intelligence officer, a regimental commander, a district chief, and the provost marshal of Manila—had uniquely equipped him to understand both the tactical and strategic situation. Batangas Province, immediately south of Manila, was considered a hotbed of resistance. Bell spent almost a month analyzing the situation and developing an operational plan, which he disseminated through informal meetings and telegraphed orders. He brought in a corps of counterinsurgency experts, including Lt. William T. Johnston, and targeted particular towns for investigation. Coordinated sweeps cordoned off previously inaccessible areas and destroyed supplies and guerrilla camps. Bell also resettled much of the population into protected zones, further cutting the guerrillas off from shelter and supplies. Perhaps because Bell knew what information to ask for, the DMI could better assist the campaign in Batangas, providing sketches and summaries of key guerrilla leaders, collecting and distributing maps, and providing funds to hire spies and paramilitary militias. Bell monitored the activities of his troops through the telegraph and visits; thus, he knew what was happening in the field, and his commanders understood his wishes. The campaign was a great tactical success, with resistance ending in April. A few months later, President Theodore Roosevelt declared the "insurrection" in the Philippines over.

For the most part, the assessment process during the Philippine War worked better than could be expected. Because of both the distances and the limits of telegraphic correspondence, McKinley provided only the broadest strategic guidance to his military representatives and trusted them to carry out his orders. Senior military commanders reported to Washington regularly on both operational and civil developments. Washington, in turn, provided information and guidance. The chief authors of the strategic assessment— Dewey, Otis, MacArthur, and Chaffee—had significant flaws and biases as individuals that were reflected in their reports. But except for MacArthur, whose antipathy to Taft and objection to the transfer to civil government nearly led him to outright defiance, all did their best to comply with the president's wishes. The telegraph allowed information to flow between Manila and Washington, while the annual reports provided not only the longer-range strategic evaluations but also the alternative views of regional and tactical commanders. Taft's willingness to challenge military assumptions and to provide an alternative view gave Washington a better perspective as well. The main assessment problem at the operational level was the gap between the experience of officers in the boondocks and the perspective of Manila.

MacArthur, in particular, misinterpreted the strength of the resistance and his own role in developing policies to defeat it. The isolation of most US Army garrisons and the very nature of the regional guerrilla war made it difficult for Manila to appreciate the diversity and complexity of the resistance and how local officers were combating it. It proved impossible for "lessons learned" to pass from one area to another unless it was imparted personally when individual officers such as Bell and Johnston were transferred.

Perhaps as a result of its diverse experiences and its comparatively rapid success, the US Army made virtually no effort to study the Philippine campaign after the war. Taft, now serving as secretary of war, actually suppressed the army's official history, and the service made no effort to publish it after he moved on. Nor did it ever write its own operational study. In many respects, the army left it to civilians to assess its most successful counterinsurgency campaign.

NOTES

1. William McKinley to Secretary of War, December 21, 1898, in U.S. Army Adjutant General's Office, *Correspondence Relating to the War with Spain: Including the Insurrection in the Philippine Islands and the China Relief Expedition, April 15, 1898, to July 4, 1902* (1902; repr., Washington DC: Center of Military History, 1993), 2:858–59 (hereafter AG, *CWS*). This volume is an invaluable source for tracing strategy and assessments throughout the Philippine War.

2. Oscar F. Williams to William R. Day, May 12, 1898, in AG, *CWS*, 2:718–19.

3. Samuel B. M. Young to William McKinley, July 4, 1900, Box 3, Samuel B. M. Young Papers, US Army Military History Institute, Carlisle Barracks PA (hereafter MHI); John H. Parker to Theodore Roosevelt, March 11, 1900, Theodore Roosevelt Papers, Series 1, Roll 4, Library of Congress; and [Clarence R. Edwards] to John T. Knight, September 27, 1900, Box 1, Clarence Edwards Papers, Massachusetts Historical Society, Boston. For examples of informal reporting to Adjutant General Corbin, see William R. Shafter to Henry C. Corbin, November 21, 1900; J. Franklin Bell to Henry C. Corbin, May 17, 1901; and "Autobiography"—all in Henry C. Corbin Papers, Library of Congress. On senior officers leaking information unfavorable to Otis, see "The Army and the Correspondents," *Army and Navy Journal* 36 (July 22, 1899): 1121.

4. AAG, Second Division to CO, First Brigade, January 30, 1900, cited in Fred R. Brown, *History of the Ninth U.S. Infantry, 1799–1909* (Chicago: R. R. Donnelley & Sons, 1909), 359–60.

5. William T. Johnston, "Investigation into the Methods Adopted by the Insurgents for Organizing and Maintaining a Guerrilla Force," in War Department,

Annual Reports of the War Department (Washington DC: Government Printing Office, May 21, 1900), vol. 1, pt. 5, 257–65.

6. William H. Taft, Testimony, U.S. Senate, *Affairs in the Philippine Islands: Hearings before the Committee on the Philippines of the United States Senate*, 57th Cong., 1st sess., doc. no. 331, April 1902, 70, 135–36; William H. Taft to Elihu Root, November 30, 1900, Series 21, William H. Taft Papers, Library of Congress; and Dean C. Worcester to Mrs. Henry W. Lawton, December 5, 1900, Box 2, Henry W. Lawton Papers, Library of Congress.

7. MacArthur to AG, Washington, December 25, 1900, in AG, *CWS*, 2:1237–38. "Report of the Secretary of War," in War Department, *Annual Reports of the War Department* (Washington DC: Government Printing Office, 1901), vol. 1, pt. 1, 31.

8. War Department, *Annual Reports* (1900), vol. 1, pt. 4, 93. For perspectives on MacArthur's policies, see John M. Gates, *Schoolbooks and Krags: The United States Army in the Philippines, 1899–1902* (Westport CT: Greenwood Press, 1975); Glenn A. May, *Battle for Batangas: A Philippine Province at War* (Quezon City: New Day Press, 1993); and Glenn A. May, *A Past Recovered* (Manila: New Day Press, 1987).

9. Adna R. Chaffee to Robert P. Hughes, September 30, 1902, in Taft, Testimony, *Affairs in the Philippine Islands*, 1591.

10. Adna R. Chaffee to Henry C. Corbin, September 2, 1901, Box 1; and "Autobiography"—both in Henry C. Corbin Papers, Library of Congress. See also War Department, *Annual Reports* (1901), vol. 1, pt. 7, 10–11.

11. William H. Taft to Elihu Root, 14 October 1900, Box 164, Elihu Root Papers, Library of Congress.

9

PUTTING THE FUSE TO THE POWDER

STRATEGIC ASSESSMENT IN THE FIRST WORLD WAR

D. Scott Stephenson

IN ONE OF HIS FINAL PUBLIC ADDRESSES, Helmuth von Moltke (the Elder) offered a grim prediction. Appearing before the German Reichstag in 1888, he cautioned that the era of limited "cabinet" wars was over. The wars of the future would be wars of peoples. They might be interminable, and they were likely to break nations and empires. The old field marshal concluded, "Woe to him who first puts the fuse to the powder."[1]

Unfortunately a quarter century later, the leaders of Europe had forgotten Moltke's warning. Instead, when war came in 1914, they remembered his dazzling victories and attempted to emulate them in a series of quick and decisive campaigns. When the initial offensives ended in bloody failure and the war plans lay in ruins, those same leaders were forced to consider the alternatives to rapid, decisive victory—total war and attrition. Victory, indeed, meant breaking nations and empires.

Yet how does one "break" a society, especially when it could call on the assistance of powerful allies? And given such circumstances, how does one measure progress? Old metrics such as ground gained and key points captured seemed both unsatisfactory and, on the western front, cost-prohibitive. Should "progress" be measured by the grim calculus of battle deaths inflicted? Or might it be something more subtle but equally sinister, such as the level of calories available for consumption by civilians on the enemy's home front? How does one ensure that the massive outflow of blood and treasure is leading to a desired outcome—that is, the defeat of the enemy coalition, a coalition that is able to call on the resources of modern, industrialized societies? There were few precedents and no formulas for such an assessment in 1914. Nor was there much experience on either side in linking the various national efforts into a unified coalition strategy. It seemed almost an intractable problem, and one concludes that the difficulty of making strategic assessments in the unique circumstances of total, coalition war helps, in part, to explain the tragedy of the Great War.

The war featured myriad attempts—at both the national and coalition levels—to gauge strategic progress and build strategy using a variety of measurements. This chapter concentrates on three of the most fateful assessments conducted during the war. The Germans tested two in the middle years of the war—Falkenhayn's belief that the French Army could be "bled white" at Verdun and the German navy's judgment that Britain could be starved out of the war by a campaign of unrestricted submarine warfare. The final case considers the strategic appreciation that the supreme allied commander made in the last months of the conflict when he concluded that a series of coordinated allied offensives could finally achieve decisive effects. The first two cases describe decision making that led to disastrous results; the last, undertaken after four years of attrition, found strategic conditions—or ways and means—finally aligned with strategic goals.

FALKENHAYN'S JUDGMENT

By the second month of the war, Lt. Gen. Erich von Falkenhayn served as both the minister of war and the newly appointed chief of the Great General Staff. He had replaced Moltke's nephew when both he and the plan he was charged to execute collapsed in ruins on the Marne. In the months after the plan's failure, Falkenhayn attempted to revive Germany's prospects for a quick and decisive victory. First he sought to outflank the Allied line on the western front and then, failing that, bludgeon his way through it in Flanders. The result was bloody failure and a stern reminder of the predominance of defensive firepower on the modern battlefield. The tactical and operational stalemate on the western front along with the prospect of a two-front war demanded that he reevaluate Germany's strategic prospects.

Erich von Falkenhayn's view of Germany's situation in late 1914 suggests he was a realist. As early as the first winter of the war, he believed that Germany was militarily incapable of defeating the Entente. He told Theobald von Bethmann Hollweg, the imperial chancellor, "If Russia, France, and England hold together, we cannot defeat them in such a way as to achieve acceptable peace terms. We are more likely to be slowly exhausted."[2] Falkenhayn knew that, measured by population, the major Entente powers of Britain, France, and Russia outnumbered Germany, Austria-Hungary, and the Turks nearly two to one. What is more, Britain and France had access not only to the vast demographic resources of their empires but also, thanks to geography and naval power, to the economic and financial assets of the entire planet. A pure statistical accounting of Germany's prospects offered bleak results, and stalemate on the fighting fronts suggested that Teutonic military prowess could not overcome overwhelming material disadvantage.

Falkenhayn's views were not popular. By asking the chancellor to seek a negotiated peace with limited annexations, Falkenhayn had aroused the mistrust of Bethmann, who believed that any settlement must include significant territorial gains for Germany. Perhaps more serious, Falkenhayn's insistence that the western front was the decisive theater of the war earned him the bitter enmity of Field Marshal Paul von Hindenburg and General Erich Ludendorff, the leaders of Ober Ost, the German headquarters in the east. The two "Easterners" had become the darlings of the German public after their victories at Tannenberg and Masurian Lakes, and Bethmann found their promises of decisive victory over the Russians more attractive than Falkenhayn's skeptical judgment of Germany's prospects. Throughout the various crises of 1915, Falkenhayn's position was based almost exclusively on the favor of a kaiser who was jealous of the public's adulation of the two demigods in the east.

The crises passed, and the approach of 1916 seemed to offer Falkenhayn opportunities to vindicate his strategic outlook. In the east the Russians were battered after their defeats following the Gorlice-Tarnów campaign. In the west the Germans had inflicted bloody repulses to Marshal Joseph Joffre's offensives in Champagne and Artois. Elsewhere the Austrians had withstood the initial Italian onslaught while the Turks had stopped the British at Gallipoli and Kut. With the help of the Bulgarians, a fall offensive by the Central Powers had crushed the Serbs. The strategic situation seemed to offer Falkenhayn a chance to seek a decision on the critical front in France and Belgium.

The problem appeared to demand a novel solution. A decisive battle of maneuver seemed out of the question. German reserves were limited, and Falkenhayn's own unhappy experience in Flanders in 1914—along with the failure of the Allied offensives of 1915—suggested that an operational breakthrough on the western front was impossible. Falkenhayn judged the alternative was a battle of attrition, a calculated campaign designed to bleed the French Army "white." Though Falkenhayn believed that Great Britain was the most dangerous enemy, British naval strength outmatched Germany's, and the British Army had yet to commit itself to the war in force. Under these circumstances, the French Army served as Britain's "best sword." If the Germans could strike that sword from Britain's hands by forcing the French to a separate peace, then the Central Powers would take a decisive step in dismantling the implacable alliance that threatened to strangle the Reich.

Falkenhayn's incentives seem clear. From a strategic vantage, driving the French out of the war would demonstrate to the British that Germany could not be beaten. Under these circumstances, Germany might be able to negotiate a favorable peace. From a personal perspective, Falkenhayn's conviction that the west was the decisive theater would be vindicated, and his success would overshadow the German public's fascination with Hindenburg and Ludendorff. His place in the kaiser's favor would be confirmed.

At the operational level, Falkenhayn's plan meant forcing the French into a battle they could not avoid in a place where the advantages accrued to the attacker. Falkenhayn considered a variety of sectors and settled on Verdun, a site with historical significance reaching back to Charlemagne and, before the war, one of the most heavily fortified areas on the planet. Falkenhayn believed that Verdun's symbolic value was so great that French military leaders would sacrifice vast quantities of their limited manpower in defending it.

That part of Falkenhayn's concept seems sound; however, the remainder of Falkenhayn's planning for the Verdun operation appears to be a curious mix of professional estimate and premodern hunch. His professional judgment correctly appraised the advantages offered by an attack around Verdun, where the French defended a salient that was poorly served by roads and rail networks and vulnerable to converging German artillery fire. Verdun itself lay at the bottom of a bowl bisected by the Meuse River, and if the Germans could seize the fortified heights northeast of the city, they would force the French to counterattack at a terrible disadvantage. Yet some of Falkenhayn's most critical planning assumptions were based on a less solid foundation. He believed at the tactical level the Germans could win a battle of attrition by imposing a highly favorable exchange ratio of German to French casualties. Beyond the advantages offered by terrain, he felt the inherent tactical superiority of German units would make such an exchange ratio possible. And as the French troops were mauled in Falkenhayn's trap, French national resolve would be eroded to the point that the government in Paris would be forced to seek a negotiated peace. This last assumption was based on Falkenhayn's view that the Gallic national character was "unsound" and less resolute than that of their German opponents. Thus, his final plan was founded on both a solid staff appreciation commingled with wishful thinking and cultural stereotype.

The problems with Falkenhayn's planning did not end there. Crown Prince Wilhelm's Fifth Army would be responsible for the actual conduct of the operation, and the traditional principles of German command suggested that Wilhelm and his staff would work out the details of the attack. However, in seeking to limit the effects of attrition on his own forces, Falkenhayn interfered by narrowing the extent of the original attack sector, by limiting the number of reserves initially available to the Fifth Army, and, later, by restricting the number of fresh units that were fed into the battle. Each of these interventions had a baleful effect on the conduct of the operation. The initial assault on February 21 seemed to go well, but by February 29, as the Germans approached the decisive high ground above Verdun, the advance stalled. The Fifth Army's troops were exhausted and lacked the reserves to push forward against the French reserves that had been rushed into the salient. Moreover, because Falkenhayn had limited the attack to the eastern side of the Meuse, as the Germans advanced, they became vulnerable to flanking fire from the high ground west of the river. By the first week of March, Falkenhayn was ready to extend the attack to the west bank of the Meuse, but as the French had anticipated this move, German progress on both sides of the Meuse became increasingly slow and costly.

As the battle raged into the spring of 1916, the shakiness of Falkenhayn's assumptions about the strength of French morale and operational proficiency was also exposed. Although the French had vindicated one of Falkenhayn's key assumptions through their willingness to defend Verdun at all costs, they confounded his others. The Frenchman appointed to lead the defense, Gen. Henri-Philippe Pétain, was one of the most outstanding military technocrats of the entire war. As well as any general on either side, Pétain understood the dominant role of artillery in trench warfare, and he hemmed in the French defenses with a torrent of fire while his staff worked logistical miracles in providing the mountains of shells such a defense required. Over time the supposed German superiority in tactical expertise yielded an actual casualty exchange ratio of about 1 to 1.1 in favor of the attackers, a ratio not nearly high enough to justify Falkenhayn's hopes for the operation.[3]

To this essential point, Falkenhayn seemed blind. He knew that German losses were heavy, but his intelligence service, the Nachrichtendienst, told him that French casualties were much heavier. His operations officer recalled that, by May, "French losses were estimated at 525,000, ours at 250,000."[4] Unfortunately for Falkenhayn, the German intelligence service proved to be a critical weakness in his plan. Undermanned and overworked, it based its casualty estimates for the battle around Verdun not on hard data but, instead, largely on the reports of French prisoners. Since these prisoners came from many more units than the Germans had committed to the Verdun sector, the intelligence staff assumed that the French were taking much heavier losses. What they missed was that Pétain was cycling French divisions in and out of the cauldron of Verdun at a rapid rate, seeking to avoid the destruction of whole units brought on through heavy casualties and physical exhaustion. Falkenhayn, by contrast, restricted the supply of fresh troops provided to the Fifth Army. His misguided attempt to limit the damage done to the German Army resulted in the German units, left in the line much longer than their French counterparts, being often completely decimated and demoralized before they were relieved.

In spite of heavy German losses, the end of May found Falkenhayn continuing to press the attack. By then Verdun had become as powerful a symbol to the Germans as it was to the French. Breaking off the attack would be an admission of defeat with disastrous consequences for home front morale; thus, Falkenhayn hid the extent of German casualties from the increasingly skeptical Bethmann. Meanwhile, he assured the chancellor that German attacks at Verdun would steadily press the French into a narrow sector, "where the French are forced to send troops against our concentric fire. It is doubtful the French will long persist given their immense losses."[5] Yet, a week later, Falkenhayn saw his plan begin to unravel. On June 4 Gen. Aleksey Brusilov's Russian armies attacked in Galicia, tearing a gigantic hole in the Austrian front and prompting a desperate appeal for German troops to close the breach. A month later, the great Franco-British attack opened on the Somme sector. Falkenhayn had hoped to use his reserves to counterattack the anticipated British onslaught, but when it came, the size of Gen. Douglas Haig's "Big Push" meant the Germans were hard-pressed to hold the positions they had. Even worse the French participation in the Somme attack suggested that France's resources were far from exhausted.

Assailed on every side, by mid-July Falkenhayn despaired of victory. The Romanians provided the final straw to his discomfiture on August 27 when they entered the war on the side of the Allies. The Romanian decision seemed clear judgment on the strategic prospects of the two rival alliances. Thus, two days later, on the second anniversary of the victory at Tannenberg, the kaiser summoned Hindenburg and Ludendorff to take over supreme command and the leadership of the war. The new "Third OHL" (Oberste Heeresleitung), as it became known, sought to shut down the attacks around Verdun as it dealt with the new crises in the east and west.

The fighting on the Somme and around Verdun ground on into November. By the end of the year, the French counterattacks at Verdun had recaptured much of the ground so dearly won by the crown prince's army. The final butcher's bill for the ten-month battle was immense: The German casualties were 281,000; the French, 315,000.[6] The French had been shaken by the "blood mill on the Meuse," but so had the Germans. Their casualties at Verdun combined with an estimated 400,000 German dead, wounded, and missing on the Somme did irreparable damage to the kaiser's army, decimating its pre-war cadres of junior officers and noncommissioned officers and turning it, in Ludendorff's words, into a "militia" army.

Falkenhayn's downfall suggests the difficulty of strategic assessment in total war. His plan foundered on the inability of his staff to offer an accurate appraisal of enemy strength and a realistic measurement of the progress made toward the goal of breaking the French Army. One is reminded that strategic assessments are built on intelligence, and total war demanded new and expanded forms of intelligence gathering. Falkenhayn lacked these abilities. Nevertheless, he earned much of the blame for the failure at Verdun. It starts with his contempt for the French and their ability to react to the German plan. Also blameworthy was his belief that he could pull strings from the OHL and artificially control the attrition of German forces. Moreover, his faith that German troops, as the attackers on a World War I battlefield, could inflict casualties on the defending French at a ratio of two or three to one demonstrated his poor sense of the dynamics of the tactical battlefield.

HOLTZENDORFF'S CALCULATION

Along with the demotion of Falkenhayn and the ascendance of Hindenburg and Ludendorff, the German crisis in the summer of 1916 also rekindled the fiery debate over the prosecution of the U-boat campaign.[7] Just a year before, Germany had backed down from its unrestricted attacks on vessels bound for Britain. Bethmann had taken President Woodrow Wilson's threats of intervention seriously and feared the entry of the United States into the war would make a decisive addition to the long odds that Germany faced.

Not surprising, the German navy was frustrated by the apparent timidity of Germany's civilian leaders in the face of Wilson's threat. The admiralty was forced to switch its operational emphasis to the Mediterranean while submitting to humiliating limitations to its tactics. In the meantime, the debate over whether Germany should resume its unrestricted campaign was prosecuted in both the highest circles of the Reich's leadership as well as the court of German public opinion. And with the land campaigns going badly in the east and west, the urgency of the U-boat question for Germany's future seemed greater than ever.

By the late summer of 1916, the leading naval advocate for the resumption of unrestricted U-boat warfare was Adm. Henning von Holtzendorff, chief of the admiralty staff. Holtzendorff had led the admiralty since September 1915 when the U-boat controversy had brought down his predecessor. Undeterred Holtzendorff pressed his case, and by October, he had the support of Hindenburg and Ludendorff, as well as the backing of the conservative parties in the Reichstag, who believed Germany's fate depended on supporting the OHL in the ruthless prosecution of total war. On December 22, 1916, Holtzendorff sent the kaiser a compelling appeal for unleashing his U-boats. In this new memorandum, Holtzendorff appeared to be making a far more rigorous case than Falkenhayn's proposal for the attack on Verdun. In contrast to Falkenhayn's vague terms about bleeding France white, Holtzendorff could cite targets for the monthly tonnage of enemy vessels his U-boats needed to sink in a new campaign—or 600,000 tons. The number was derived from a wide-ranging research and analysis of British shipping and its vulnerabilities. The German admiralty had assembled an impressive array of academics, bankers, industrialists, and trade experts, and this working group made what seemed to be a comprehensive review of the chokepoints in Britain's wartime economy. They had put special emphasis on the food supply available to British workers, the lumber needed to support British coal production, the impacts of increased insurance rates and food prices, and the chilling effect an unrestricted campaign would have on neutral shipping. Historian Holger Herwig judges that "for the first time in modern German history, a national grand strategy was devised by committee."[8] Moreover, in the patrol reports of his U-boat captains, Holtzendorff had a feedback mechanism that appeared far more reliable than the prisoner interrogations that Falkenhayn's staff used to measure attritional progress. Finally Holtzendorff was able to use his charts and voluminous data to set a firm target date for the renewed U-boat campaign to achieve its decisive effect—five months from the start of a new offensive.

For Germany it was a turning point in the direction of the war. Chancellor Bethmann understood that surrendering to Holtzendorff's argument would effectively end any civilian input to strategy. For his part Holtzendorff believed that a successful U-boat campaign ensured the future for the German navy, which had been very much a junior partner to the army. For Ludendorff, whatever his doubts about the realism of the navy's promise, a victory over Bethmann's reservations would remove one of the last obstacles to prosecuting total war as the army's leadership envisioned it.

The kaiser and the Reich's senior military and civilian leaders gathered to debate the memorandum at Pless on January 9, 1917. By then Wilhelm was vacillating on the issue while Bethmann had become increasingly alone in his warnings of US involvement. Anticipating his objection, Holtzendorff argued that the United States would not continue a war against Germany if Britain was compelled to surrender. Near the end of the memorandum, the admiral concluded, "In spite of the risk of diplomatic rupture with America, unrestricted submarine warfare is nevertheless the correct means to conclude this war victoriously. It is also the only means that will achieve this end."[9] Holtzendorff insisted that the campaign would need to start by February 1 to be decisive before the harvest of 1917. In the face of these arguments, Bethmann's resistance collapsed. The kaiser gave his assent, and on February 1, 1917, the U-boats began their unrestricted attacks on Allied and neutral shipping.

Just as German advances encouraged Falkenhayn in the early stages of the Verdun battle, the initial reports from Germany's U-boat force indicated that their attacks would soon cripple Britain's war effort. Shipping losses mounted from 328,000 tons in January 1917 to 860,000 in April 1917, and euphoria in the German admiralty was matched by near-despair among Britain's naval leaders. Adm. John Jellicoe, the British First Sea Lord, confided to the American rear admiral W. S. Sims, "Yes, it is impossible for us to go on with the war, if losses like this continue."[10] Heavy loss rates did continue into the summer, though the U-boats were unable to match the numbers from April. Yet when August arrived, the British remained unbroken. What had gone wrong?

In the first place, the Germans had violated Sun Tzu's admonition that the strategist must know himself. A prewar study had suggested that the German navy would need approximately 222 U-boats to prosecute an effective, sustained campaign against British shipping; in February 1917, Holtzendorff had less than half that number (and only 82 were deployed around the British Isles).[11] From that number, at any one moment roughly a third of the U-boats were en route or returning from their patrol stations, and another third were refitting in port. The remainder on station was an insufficient number to maintain a stranglehold on the shipping lanes. German production efforts matched losses but could not raise the number of U-boats to a decisive number. Strategic ends demonstrably overmatched means.

Sun Tzu also warned the strategist to know his enemy, and here the Germans had failed as well. A modern, industrial economy such as Britain's proved not only complex but redundant and resilient as well. The British showed themselves willing to ration supplies, reprioritize production, and find work-arounds for the shortages created by shipping losses. For example, as a food shortage loomed, the British Ministry of Food brought thousands of acres of new farmland into production while impressing armies of women, children, disabled men, and prisoners of war to till the new acreage. When Scandinavian timber ran short to prop up their coal mines, the British cut down their own forests to make up the shortfall and delayed the building of new houses. Worse, the German admiralty's calculation of the tonnage available to the enemy proved hopelessly optimistic as it overlooked the captured German vessels and neutral ships the British could bring into service. Finally the Germans' belief that the supposedly poorly disciplined British would not accept rationing proved as ill founded as Falkenhayn's faith in the fragility of French national morale.

The Germans underestimated the effectiveness of Allied naval counter-measures as well, the most important, of course, being the introduction of the convoy system. German planners had hoped that limited dock capacity and manpower would create traffic jams in British ports if convoys were introduced, but, here again, improved British management techniques overcame the challenge. By September the convoy system had helped to drop tonnage losses to 350,000 (and increased U-boat losses to ten vessels in a single month). For the British, the crisis had passed.

As it turned out, the impressive German investment in research and analysis was an illusion; the figures backing up Holtzendorff's memorandum proved, in the words of historian David Stevenson, "much more a work of intuition than it purported to be."[12] The failure of Holtzendorff's offensive against British shipping suggests the same difficulty that the Allied bomber offensive had in attacking Germany in World War II. In the absence of detailed, accurate strategic intelligence, identifying and targeting an enemy economy turns out to be an uncertain business at best.

The consequences of the German failed U-boat campaign were tremendous. The United States entered the war in April 1917, solving many of Britain's financial difficulties, and in the months that followed, raw materials and US-built vessels helped to overcome losses at sea. The overwhelming war potential of the United States was fully demonstrated a year later, in the summer of 1918, when doughboys began disembarking at French ports at a rate of more than a quarter million a month. The bitterest irony for the Germans was that had they waited but a few months more, Falkenhayn's vision of breaking up the Allied coalition might have been realized, for the overthrow of the czar began a sequence of events that would take Russia out of the war. Perhaps even more egregiously, that same spring, the OHL missed the evidence of widespread mutiny in the French Army. Like the other belligerents of the Great War, Germany lacked the sources of strategic intelligence that would have anticipated revolution and mutiny among its opponents.

FOCH'S VISION

The failure of the 1917 U-boat campaign, the advent of the Russian Revolution, and the anticipated arrival of the Americans in force together compelled the OHL to play out its vision for total war with a massive offensive on the western front in the spring of 1918.[13] As with the Moltke-Schlieffen Plan, the Ludendorff offensives proved to be a desperate gamble devoid of genuine political input based on a unified German view of war aims. The gamble resulted in spectacular tactical successes with unfocused and inconclusive operational outcomes. With the perspective of time, we can see the strategic effect on Germany for what it was—namely, a disaster. Between March and July 1918, the German Army took a million casualties from its best units. It was the kind of attrition—compressed in time and crippling in impact—the Allies could not have accomplished on their own. Along with the devastating losses, the failure of the offensives led to a growing collapse in morale for Germany and the other Central Powers.

The spring crisis also proved a turning point in the Allied direction of its war effort on the western front. On March 26 fears that the German Operation Michael would separate British forces from the French led the Allies to agree to empower Gen. Ferdinand Foch to coordinate the efforts of Allied forces in France and Belgium, codified on April 3 as the "strategic direction of Allied operations."[14] Finally the Allies, with a gun held to their heads, had achieved a form of unified command on the decisive front.

It was a fortunate choice. Although in the received view, Foch is remembered as a single-minded "thruster," the truth is more complex. While the man the Allies chose to lead on the western front did have a reputation for having fiery energy and a relentless offensive spirit, he also had a record of organizing interallied operations—first in Flanders in 1914 and 1915, then on the Somme in 1916. Foch had studied the war on the western front from a variety of staff and command positions, and by the summer of 1918, the French general had developed a unique appreciation for operational realities of combat in the trenches of France and Belgium. More important, by the fall, he saw the potential for ending the war before winter brought stalemate and another year of carnage.

Foch's mechanism for defeating the German armies would be a series of offensives coordinated in scale, timing, duration, and location to have the maximum impact on the enemy. As the generalissimo of the Allied forces on the western front, he could not command the British, American, and Belgian national commanders, but he could use the force of his enthusiastic advocacy to encourage the Allies to organize their attacks in a way that exhausted German reserves. These attacks featured tanks, air support, and, above all, the crushing weight of artillery. Foch sought to sequence the various Allied attacks so that when the Germans had contained one offensive, they were forced to rush reserves to a new crisis point. In their direction, the attacks aimed to force the Germans out of their prepared defensive positions while threatening the key transportation nodes supplying the German armies in

France and Belgium. Foch encouraged the national commanders—Haig for the British, Pétain at the head of the French armies, and Gen. John Pershing commanding the American Expeditionary Force—to press each attack to the point of culmination, at which time the offensive pressure moved to another point on the front. An example of Foch's vision is seen in the combined Allied offensives of late September that attacked from the Meuse-Argonne sector to Flanders in a powerful concentric effort. Gen. Henry Rawlinson, commander of the British Fourth Army, observed, "Under Foch's tuition and the lessons of over four years . . . we are really learning and the synchronization of the various attacks had been admirable."[15] Foch's aim was to compel his enemy to respond to an increasing series of crises that would deplete German resources and deepen German despair. In Ludendorff's case, the scheme led to nervous exhaustion.

Along with ground gained and prisoners captured, a revolution in tactical and operational intelligence gave Foch a critical metric for the success for his offensives—that is, the number of fresh divisions in the OHL reserve. By late 1918, using aerial reconnaissance, agent networks in the occupied regions, prisoner interrogations, and increasingly sophisticated order of battle analysis, the Second Bureau of the French Army staff could track this number with a high degree of reliability. In September and October 1918, the number of fresh divisions dwindled, and Foch knew that when it approached zero, the Germans would no longer be able to contain the advancing Allies. The game would be up.

It could not come a moment too soon. Throughout 1918 Allied losses remained heavy, and by the end of the war, only the Americans had manpower to spare. The London government warned Haig that the heavy losses of 1918 had exhausted Britain's resources. Meanwhile, the French government considered an early call-up for the recruit class of 1920 to maintain the strength of French divisions. For both countries, the manpower cupboard was nearly bare. Both the French and British knew that if the war continued into 1919, the Americans would have the largest Allied army on the western front. And if the war ended in 1919, the late-arriving doughboys—not the long-suffering Tommies and *poilus* (soldiers)—might unjustly claim the laurels of victory. Given the sacrifices endured between 1914 and 1918, this outcome seemed nearly intolerable; thus, for Foch, Haig, and their political masters, winning the war in 1918 became an urgent priority, especially once it became clear that the German morale and matériel were exhausted.[16]

As winter approached, Foch pressed the Allied armies to give the Germans no respite. Yet the initial German peace feelers caught the Allies by surprise, another reflection on the woeful state of strategic intelligence even in the last days of the war. As the final arrangements for an armistice were hammered out, Foch was the key player in crafting the conditions to be imposed on Germany. This process required a delicate and intuitive strategic assessment. If the conditions were too lenient, they might allow the Germans to regroup behind the Rhine River, with a view to resuming hostilities. If the conditions were too draconian, the Germans might fight on with the courage of despair. His intuition and his intelligence sources told him the Germans were on the verge of collapse, so Foch recommended a list of harsh demands: The Germans had to vacate France, Belgium, and the west bank of the Rhine in a month, leaving behind five thousand artillery pieces, twenty-five thousand machine guns, five thousand locomotives, and five thousand trucks. The conditions also required the Germans to withdraw from the east bank of the Rhine, thus enabling the Allies to occupy Rhine bridgeheads at Mainz, Cologne, and Koblenz. Such terms ensured the Germans would be incapable of restarting the war after the armistice had ended. When the government of Prince Max of Baden accepted the terms, the war was truly over. Foch's vision was vindicated.

CONCLUSION: ANOTHER WARNING

If the German Army of 1914 was, in Dennis Showalter's words, a "doomsday machine," or a magnificent organization built to solve an impossible problem, then the European arms race before 1914 might be called a doomsday system.[17] It featured two powerful alliances capable of mobilizing and deploying mass armies supported, motivated, and justified by the mass politics of insecurity and nationalism. Such a system ensured that when war came, the conflict would escalate beyond the inadequate efforts of political leaders to limit the violence while making the establishment of ends that matched the vast expansion of ways and means nearly impossible. By the winter of 1914, Europe was well on its way to the kind of total war that few had anticipated.

When the German leaders Falkenhayn and Holtzendorff attempted to solve the problem of total war through attrition, they called on a curious mix of premodern intuition and mathematical calculation to measure the progress of their efforts. It was Germany's tragedy that on the battlefield and at sea, both their intuition and calculations failed. In 1918, by contrast, Foch could use intuition, which was built on four years of battlefield experience, and calculation—in the form of sophisticated order of battle analysis—to push the German Army to the breaking point.

When the peace terms were finally considered at Paris, the world's statesmen sought a lasting peace for all nations. Dealing with a defeated but still powerful Germany was their central problem, and historians still debate whether the terms offered the Germans were too harsh or too lenient. When he saw the terms, Foch made his own strategic assessment, which became another tragically prescient warning: "This is not a peace. This is an Armistice for twenty years."[18]

NOTES

1. Stig Förster, "German Military Leadership and the Images of Future Warfare, 1871–1914," in *Anticipating Total War: The German and American Experiences, 1871–1914*, ed. Manfred F. Boemke, Roger Chickering, and Stig Förster (Cambridge: Cambridge University Press, 1999), 347.

2. Holger Afflerbach, "Planning Total War? Falkenhayn and the Battle of Verdun, 1916," in *Great War, Total War: Combat and Mobilization on the Western Front, 1914–1918*, ed. Roger Chickering and Stig Förster (New York: Cambridge University Press, 2000), 118.

3. This number is based on the analysis found in Hermann Wendt, *Verdun, 1916: Die Angriffe Falkenhayns im Maasgebiet mit Richtung, auf Verdun als strategisches Problem* (Berlin: E. S. Mittler, 1931). Wendt's is still considered the most reliable analysis of relative losses during the battle.

4. Afflerbach, "Planning Total War?," 128.

5. Ibid., 129.

6. Wendt, *Verdun, 1916*, cited in Afflerbach, "Planning Total War?," 256.

7. The background for this section is based primarily on Dirk Steffen, "The Holtzendorff Memorandum of 22 December 1916 and Germany's Declaration of Unrestricted U-boat Warfare," *Journal of Military History* 68 (January 2004): 215–24; David Stevenson, *Cataclysm: The First World War as Political Tragedy* (New York: Basic Books, 2004), 208–14; and especially Holger Herwig, "Total Rhetoric, Limited War: Germany's U-boat Campaign, 1917–1918," in Chickering and Föster, *Great War*, 189–206.

8. Herwig, "Total Rhetoric," in Chickering and Förster, *Great War*, 194.

9. Memorandum quoted in Steffen, "Holtzendorff Memorandum," 223. Hindenburg and Ludendorff were dismissive of US military strength. After all Germany had more than two hundred divisions in the field while, in 1916, the Americans could barely deploy a single makeshift division to chase Pancho Villa across the border into Mexico.

10. Jellicoe quoted by Sims in John Terraine, *The U-boat Wars, 1916–1945* (New York: Holt, 1989), 48.

11. Herwig, "Total Rhetoric," in Chickering and Forster, *Great War*, 204.

12. Stevenson, *Cataclysm*, 213.

13. The analysis in this section is based on Elizabeth Greenhalgh, *Foch in Command: The Forging of a First World War General* (Cambridge: Cambridge University Press, 2011), especially chapters 12–16. I owe a special debt of gratitude to historian William Philpott for his chapter, "Marshal Ferdinand Foch and Allied Victory," in *Leadership in Conflict: 1914–1918*, ed. Matthew Hughes and Matthew Seligmann (Barnsley UK: Leo Cooper, 2000), 38–53; his article, "France's Forgotten Victory," *Journal of Strategic Studies* 34, no. 6 (2011): 6, 911–18; his unpublished conference notes for a talk titled "The Somme: The Primordial Swamp of Operational Art"; and his insights shared through e-mail correspondence in November and December 2013.

14. Stevenson, *Cataclysm*, 335.

15. Rawlinson diary entry of September 28, 1918, quoted in Philpott, "Marshal Ferdinand Foch," in Hughes and Seligmann, *Leadership in Conflict*, 51.

16. Until very late in the war, Foch hedged his bets, encouraging the British to scour their manpower reserves in anticipation of a 1919 campaign while encouraging the Americans to maintain the massive flow of reinforcements for the American Expeditionary Force.

17. Dennis Showalter, "From Deterrent to Doomsday Machine: The German Way of War, 1890–1914," *Journal of Military History* 64, no. 3 (July 2000): 710.

18. W. R. Keylor, "Realism, Idealism, and the Treaty of Versailles," *Diplomatic History* 38, no. 1 (2014): 215.

10

ASSESSMENT IN WORLD WAR II

Gerhard L. Weinberg

DURING WORLD WAR II, the leaders of the major belligerents at times had to make major decisions about current and future operations that were on the one hand governed by their political goals and on the other hand by their understanding of the realities of recent and anticipated actual developments in the fighting. When confronted with the need for a decision, they were generally very much interested in whatever relevant information they could obtain from their staffs and from higher military commanders who were either involved in recent and current operations or expected to play a major role in implementing the new decision under consideration.

The following two examples from opposite sides of the war illustrate this general practice. They examine in what way Adolf Hitler and Winston Churchill each made a decision of great significance for the subsequent course of the war on the basis of assessing how recent, current, and anticipated developments in the conflict affected the choice they felt called on to make in the hope of realizing their objectives in the conflict.

HITLER'S DECISION TO POSTPONE INVASION OF THE SOVIET UNION FROM 1940 TO 1941

This example shows Hitler making a serious effort to assess the situation at a major turning point in World War II, and because of that process, he arrived at a decision he actually and repeatedly said he would have much preferred not to make. He gathered information from his top military advisers and looked very carefully at the way his confident expectation of victory was affected by the realities of interaction between his major objective and the calendar.

Adolf Hitler was always operating under what he considered very serious personal and practical time pressures. The personal one stemmed from his belief that he would not live to be old, and he both preferred to lead the country in war while he was still vigorous and held the opinion that no successor was likely to be as able and willing to initiate wars as he was. He recognized and explained the practical one to his military and political leaders: Because Germany had started a massive rearmament program before those he expected to attack had, the others—when they recognized their danger—would rearm with more recent models of weapons; so Germany had to use its advantage as soon as possible. His preference for war sooner rather than later can be seen in his handling of starting wars even in some minor ways. For instance, in 1939 he still had one day left for negotiations per his own timetable, but he decided to invade Poland on September 1 rather than September 2 when he realized that Britain and France could not be separated from that country. Similarly, shortly after he learned on December 8, 1941, that the Japanese had attacked the United States, Britain, and the Netherlands as he had been insistently urging, he did not want to wait the three or four days that it would take to assemble the German parliament and go through the formal diplomatic procedures to declare war. Upon receiving the news he immediately directed the German navy, whose chief had been urging war with the United States since October 1939, to initiate hostilities against the United States and eight other countries in the Western Hemisphere.[1]

The expectation of war with the Soviet Union to seize living space for Germanic settlers had been in Hitler's long-term planning from the beginning, and it highlights the impact of assessment on the implementation of his strategic timetable. The war against France and Britain was seen as a necessary preliminary to that enterprise because the German Army could not be sent to the Ural Mountains with potential enemy armies a short distance from Germany's main industrial area in the Rhineland. It is in this context that one needs to understand Hitler's original intention of invading the Soviet Union in the fall of 1940 and his assessment of the situation that led to his postponing that step until 1941.

Unlike many contemporaries and subsequent observers who see a German triumph in the Munich agreement of 1938 that allowed Germany to acquire border areas of Czechoslovakia with a population of predominantly German background, Hitler very much regretted having drawn back from his real aim—war—at the last minute and settling for his publicly proclaimed ostensible goal. In his eyes, it was a tragedy, not a triumph. His lesson of

Munich was that he would never make such a mistake again. He was absolutely determined that no one was going to cheat him of war as he believed Neville Chamberlain had done in 1938. His move toward war in 1939 was thus already a year late in his own thinking.

Another important background detail for the way Hitler assessed the issue of timing and reluctantly postponed the invasion of the Soviet Union was his unhappiness at earlier having been obliged to postpone the attack in the west from the late fall of 1939 to the spring of 1940. He had firmly intended to attack in the west in 1939 just as soon as the rapid defeat of Poland seemed to open that possibility. A series of technical issues involving both the objections from within the German military and the need for good weather so that the German air force could play its essential tactical support role had led to a series of postponements. May 1940 was six months after the date Hitler would have very much preferred, and his subsequent decisions need to be seen in the context of these prior personal disappointments in his plans and thinking.

While the attack in the west was under way, Hitler explained to his military assistants that the invasion of the Soviet Union would follow just as quickly as possible.[2] This concept of an immediate operation in the east was also understood to be Hitler's view by the second man in the German Foreign Ministry, who so noted it on May 23, 1940, right after the German thrust through Belgium had reached the Channel and a month before the armistice with France.[3] Hitler personally explained the same expected sequence on June 2 to Gen. Gerd von Rundstedt, the commander of the German Army group that had made the breakthrough.[4] In late May and in June 1940 Germany intended to invade the Soviet Union in the fall of that year.[5] The contemporary evidence suggests that Hitler and Gen. Franz Halder, the chief of staff of the German Army, set a date at the beginning of September as the logical one. They were certain that Germany could successfully carry out the invasion and could completely and victoriously crush the Soviet Union before winter set in that year. The two assumptions at that time supporting this assertion concerned Germany's "peacetime army," as it would be configured at that moment for obvious reasons, and the anticipated early defeat of France.[6] The armistice with France was signed on June 22, and on the day it took effect, June 25, Hitler told the leadership of the High Command of the German Armed Forces: "We have now shown what we are capable of; believe me Keitel, a campaign against Russia is merely a sand table game by comparison."[7]

By July 31, 1940, however, after deciding that the 1940 date was not feasible and that a date in May 1941 would be appropriate, Hitler so informed the top German Army and navy commanders. What had led to this change of plans? During June and July 1940 the Germans began a major transfer of troops from the west to their border with the Soviet Union in the east.[8] In both the German Armed Forces High Command and the headquarters of the German Army, extensive discussions took place regarding the details of a forthcoming campaign against the Soviet Union.[9] The war diary of the High Command of the German Armed Forces for June and July 1940 is unfortunately missing, but that of Chief of Staff General Halder survived and has been published in full in a carefully edited series of volumes.[10] Entries on the planning for the invasion of the Soviet Union may be found in the diary texts throughout the month of July and in other sources referenced in the corresponding notes to these entries. On July 31 Halder's diary reports at length on the conference in which Hitler set the spring of 1941 as the date for the invasion of the Soviet Union. In that conference Hitler also alluded to his earlier preference for an invasion in the fall of 1940, but he explained that he was now convinced it would be better to wait as a halt in the winter—something that they thought would be avoidable—was not possible and could lead to disaster. Therefore, an invasion in May would provide at least five months of good weather to attain a complete victory.

The available evidence shows that the High Command of the Armed Forces had informed Hitler of the time needed to prepare the required local supplies and transportation networks, and it had influenced his decision. The High Command believed it would take several weeks to implement the necessary preparations in the eastern parts of Germany and the German-occupied portion of Poland. Shortly before the July 31 military planning conference, several senior officers in the High Command had been working on this subject and communicated their findings to Hitler.[11] On the basis of these preliminary studies Field Marshal Wilhelm Keitel provided Hitler with a memorandum that pointed to the time factor as not allowing a campaign to be concluded before winter set in.[12] It is entirely consistent with this analysis of the available evidence that the first subsequent German official, secret directive on the actual preparation of the invasion of the Soviet Union was titled "Aufbau Ost [Buildup East]," with a draft ready on August 2.[13] Containing extensive details on the construction or improvement of railways, roads, and supply depots in the eastern areas under German control, the formal order, now slightly revised, was issued on August 9, 1940.[14]

In retrospect one may conclude that the whole project of the German invasion of the Soviet Union not only was poorly planned and prepared but also was based on a preposterous underestimation of the Soviet Union and of the practical needs of an invading force moving into an enormous area with bad roads, a railway system with a different track gauge, and a shortage of spare parts for the vast variety of vehicles that Germany's army used. That view certainly represents the best, most recent analysis of the first stage of the campaign.[15]

What should be noted, however, is that in this particular case, and surely an extremely important one, the German dictator's military advisers assessed the details of needed preparations and convinced him that it would be best to shift the intended invasion from the date he clearly preferred and had tentatively set to one that appeared both to them and to him to be more attractive and less risky.

CHURCHILL'S DECISION TO SHIFT ROYAL AIR FORCE BOMBING FROM INDUSTRIAL AND OTHER SPECIFIC TARGETS TO AREA BOMBING OF CITIES

Few aspects of Allied operations in World War II have attracted as much attention as the campaign of strategic bombing including especially the area bombing of German and Japanese cities. Ironically the decision to move from targeted to area city bombing in Europe was made by Prime Minister Winston Churchill, whose first role in World War II had been that of First Lord of the Admiralty. The Allied disaster in Norway, in which he himself was deeply implicated, had produced the fall of Neville Chamberlain as prime minister and, in view of Lord Halifax's declining to succeed, had led to Churchill's designation to the post, where some of the most significant decisions about the conduct of the war had to be made. One was that of choosing between the continuation of the policy of bombing specific targets—primarily oil, transportation, and other designated facilities—or the shift to a deliberate policy of area bombing of cities. One critical element in facilitating such a choice would be to examine with whatever precision was possible at the time what effects the targeted bombing over prior months had actually accomplished.

At the beginning of World War II, the Royal Air Force (RAF) had strict instructions to bomb military targets, and all of its planning was based on the assumption that this would be its role.[16] On September 1, 1939, the German decision to start what two days later became World War II with an early morning terror attack on the undefended Polish town of Wielun did not alter this concept.[17] Germany's subsequent bombing of Warsaw and other Polish cities and the aerial machine-gunning of their civilians similarly led to no change in British air operations policy. The only project that the RAF newly adopted to assist Poland was the dropping of leaflets on German cities.[18] While the leaflets may well have relieved any German shortage of toilet paper, their texts encouraging the German people to oppose their government had no effect at the time; and in no way did a similar campaign contribute to the people of East Germany overthrowing their government fifty years later. Whether effective or not, the bombing operations of the RAF aimed at German warships and a few industrial installations during the winter of 1939–40 were all intentionally conducted within the restrictions adopted before the war.

The German invasions of two neutral countries, Denmark and Norway, in April 1940 did not produce any change in RAF bombing policy, and neither did the German invasion of three more neutral countries—Holland, Belgium, and Luxembourg—in May 1940. It is certainly likely that these German steps, especially the bombing of the Dutch city of Rotterdam and the machine-gunning of civilians, led to some different thinking on the part of many in the British government, but there was no break in policy. The rapid defeat of France and the immediately following threat of an invasion of England led the RAF for numerous bombing missions to target barges and other facilities necessary for supporting a German invasion. Operations of this type, however, could lead to the deaths of French civilians in the bombed port areas. This kind of consequence, which subsequently came to be called collateral damage, would become a major issue in the Allied debate over bombing policy before the 1944 Normandy invasion; but as far as the record shows, it was not discussed within the British government and RAF leadership at the time.[19] The major issue facing the government in London, beyond the hope of warding off an invasion, was the fundamental one of how to win the war against Germany now that British forces were being driven from the Continent and were unlikely ever to be large enough to attain victory in a continental fight against Germany's obviously powerful armed forces.

In the last days of May and the first days of June 1940, the British government, led by Winston Churchill and including all three political parties, decided to continue fighting under any and all circumstances even including an occupation of the British Isles. It looked forward to an eventual victory over Germany by the pursuit of three measures: to blockade Germany to the extent possible, to carry out a sustained bombing campaign, and to lead an effort to cause uprisings in German-occupied countries, whose populations were sure to become hostile in the face of German policies. Although British forces were then being evacuated from Dunkirk, after they were reorganized and re-equipped, they would eventually land and aid the occupied people's revolts.[20]

Of the three proposed measures that were designed to bring an eventual victory over Germany, only strategic bombing was perceived as potentially having a decisive effect. The blockade involved primarily passive steps taken by the Royal Navy. Furthermore, the British recognized that as long as the Soviet Union provided Germany both with Soviet supplies and with a means of transit across the Soviet Union for supplies from other countries, the blockade was unlikely to hurt Germany as significantly as it was generally believed to have done in the previous war. The establishment of the Special Operations Executive in July 1940, to "set Europe ablaze" as Churchill phrased it, involved a relatively small number of men and women who were secretly infiltrated into German-occupied parts of Europe in an effort looking to support local popular uprisings, but it could hardly be expected to produce major results promptly. Under the circumstances of 1940 and the time immediately following, only bombing would be a significant active operation involving substantial numbers of people and a considerable and hopefully growing quantity of equipment; hence it was the only one capable of producing substantial results. That this aspect of the British war effort thereafter received constant and detailed attention and a large commitment of resources is therefore not surprising.

In the months that followed the decision to continue the war against Germany from Britain and if necessary from Canada, British bombers were sent to targets in Germany and German-occupied Europe. Their instructions were basically unchanged: The targets were military and industrial, especially oil, facilities. Because the bombardiers needed to see whatever targets had been designated for the raid, a major proportion of the attacks were flown in daylight and, as a result, frequently suffered substantial losses of crews and planes. These efforts had only minimal effects during the summer and fall of 1940 and into the winter of 1940–41.[21] It was obvious by late September 1940 that the Germans were not about to invade England, so the RAF concentrated more effort on targets other than the shipping in Channel ports that might be used in an invasion. As more bombers became available, the RAF flew more missions, and the German invasion of the Soviet Union in June 1941 led the German air force to dramatically reduce its bombing of British cities and factories. That change in turn raised the obvious question of what Britain could do to implement in practice its policy of assisting the Soviets in addition to sending weapons and supplies by ship at a time and under circumstances where the country had no force capable of launching a second front in the west as the Soviets wanted. Again the clear answer as seen in London was to bomb Germany. The British bombing effort from the summer of 1940 to the summer of 1941 and any expectations of thereby seriously assisting a Soviet Union fighting for its life raised another question: What actual effect did the bombing have?

There was much optimism and considerable debate in the British Air Staff over the attacks that were launched in the summer and fall of 1941. Several major issues were under review and debate. Could bomber crews find specific targets? Would not nighttime raids be preferable to daytime raids in the face of substantial losses of planes to antiaircraft fire and German fighter planes?[22] This assessment raised the alternative that some had advocated earlier: Bombing should be done at night, and the targets should be cities that could be found and hit with substantial anticipated effects on both German industrial production and morale. The staff discussed two assumptions, which proved to be entirely erroneous: Germany had already undergone a complete economic mobilization and hence would be very vulnerable to whatever damage was done to the economy, and the German public's morale was likelier to crack under air bombardment and not be as resilient as the British had proved to be during the Blitz. A strong case was made that area bombing of cities was the proper way to utilize the available bomber force.[23] In the context of this argument a careful assessment of the effects of the targeted bombing would be ordered and completed.

In the later stages of the war, both the British and US governments established organizations to assess the impact of strategic bombing, and they produced surveys of their findings in the postwar years. Whatever their merits and deficiencies and regardless of their influence on postwar debates and policies, these reports, of course, were by definition unavailable during the conflict. An entirely serious effort at an evaluation, however, was made at the time at the insistence of Lord Cherwell, Churchill's main scientific adviser. He instructed a member of the war cabinet's secretariat, Mr. David B. Butt, to examine as carefully as possible the RAF bomber pilot reports and photographs from the bombing missions flown in June and July 1941. Butt delivered his report on August 18 of that year.[24] The detailed report stated that on the average only about a third of the bombers had gotten within five miles of their targets, with the proportion varying with the distance of the target from Britain, the weather, and the German air defenses. It must be noted that even that figure of bombers reaching within five miles of their targets did not take into account the aborted flights, the bombers that did not reach the target, and those that were shot down or had crashed on return.

It should not be surprising that such a devastating accounting of a bombing effort that had largely failed should arouse so much discussion and criticism within the RAF headquarters and the higher levels of the Air Ministry.[25] The source base of the Butt report was necessarily limited, and other technical criticisms could be and were raised. There was, however, simply no way to dismiss the findings in general, and there is one aspect of them and their impact on Churchill's decision that the relevant literature does not sufficiently explore. Lord Cherwell, who had commissioned and originally received the report, was personally very close to the prime minister, who had always considered the bombing offensive of enormous importance as a major factor in Britain's wartime role. Churchill pushed for more and more and bigger and better bombers partly because the bomber force was one way the island kingdom could have any hope in the dark days of 1940 and partly because in later years it would be able to lay claim to a significant position in the Allied war effort and councils once the Soviet Union and later the United States were on Britain's side. Whatever the debates that had occurred earlier and the criticisms and arguments raised in subsequent months, Churchill would steer the issue in the direction that some in the RAF and the Air Ministry had been pushing since the 1920s.

The alternative to targeted bombing of military, industrial, and transportation objectives—the most prominent categories in the various RAF war plans—and generally doing so in daytime when there was a chance of actually seeing them were instead (1) to bomb cities, which could be located because of their size and where bombs of any size and variety were practically certain to hit something; and (2) to go at night, thus reducing losses from fighters and antiaircraft fire. That such a procedure aimed the effort at civilians in the cities and, at least in the imagination of the British authorities, at the morale of the German population raised a major question in some wartime discussions then and even more so in postwar debates.

Was it right to target what was essentially the noncombat population? This key objection had been raised in World War I when the Germans introduced the concept of bombing cities far from the fighting front by sending first zeppelin airships and later Gotha bombers to bomb British cities. It had been one reason that the 1919 peace treaty prohibited Germany from having any military air force. The Germans had bristled at that provision, had circumvented it with Soviet assistance in the 1920s, and had disregarded it entirely since 1933. Furthermore, they had demonstrated their enthusiasm for the bombing of cities as it started World War II, and certainly no one in Britain was unaware of this German policy. Those in the United Kingdom who had not experienced German bombing raids themselves—unlike the millions in London, Birmingham, Liverpool, Coventry, and numerous other cities who had been the victims of air raids—had read about the raids in the newspapers and heard about them on the radio and from relatives and friends. It had been, ironically, precisely the American correspondents' radio reports from London about the air raids on that city that had helped turn American public opinion ever more in favor of Britain. If the Germans were so certain that bombing cities was the proper way to wage war, it seemed increasingly appropriate to British leaders to accommodate them.

It is in this context that the resolution of the internal debates, which Tami Davis Biddle has carefully recounted and documented, was to make major changes both in the main directive for RAF targeting and in the person designated to implement the new policy.[26] The new directive issued on February

14, 1942, in addition to numerous other details, explicitly stated that "it has been decided that the primary object of your [Bomber Command] operations should now be focused on the morale of the enemy civil population and in particular of the industrial workers."[27] This directive was clearly phrased, and was so understood in Bomber Command, to the effect that the nighttime area bombing of cities would henceforth be the RAF's main task.

Bomber Command had been under the leadership of Sir Richard Peirse since October 1940 when he succeeded Air Marshal Charles Portal as the latter moved up to be chief of the Air Staff. The RAF's bombing record, according to the Butt report, showed Peirse's preference for targeted bombing; and Churchill's general dissatisfaction with what Bomber Command had hitherto accomplished suggested that a change in direction at the top was also indicated. On February 22, 1942, one week after the issuance of the new directive to Bomber Command, Peirse was replaced as head of Bomber Command by Sir Arthur Harris, who would subsequently become air chief marshal. Harris had previously been an advocate of area bombing of cities and would henceforth have the opportunity to implement in practice the strategic concept with which he is identified in history and to which he continued to adhere resolutely into the last days of the war. It is not a coincidence that the change at the top in Bomber Command was made a few days after the new directive was issued to it. Whatever any in the leadership of the RAF may have thought about the subject then and later, the poor assessment of the prior bombing policy's effectiveness had been read as calling for a new approach that would be implemented under a new leader who was known to be convinced that it was the correct one for Britain to follow.[28]

We can see in these two cases that an assessment, as careful as the circumstances allowed, became the basis of major decisions by World War II leaders. In the case of Hitler, this evaluation related to the timing of initiating the invasion of still another country, and in Churchill's case the issue was a possible change in basic policy and procedures that had been followed for more than two years. In both cases the leaders who were in a position to make such critical decisions turned to advisers in whom they had faith to provide a detailed assessment of what those advisers considered the key relevant factors. The decisions that they thereupon made greatly shaped the subsequent development of World War II.

Neither Hitler nor Churchill invariably followed the procedure they adopted in these two cases. At times each acted without carefully assessing the situation, but it was because of the fundamental difference in their positions. On the one hand, Hitler was a dictator who saw himself and was seen by Germany's military leaders as subject to no rules whatsoever. In other instances, therefore, he took major decisions without consulting anyone or even in the face of completely contradictory advice. Churchill, on the other hand, knew he was the leader of a parliamentary coalition and was at all times operating within the possibility of dismissal by the House of Commons. He therefore relied far more frequently on the assessments of the situation by those at the helm of Britain's political and military hierarchy.

NOTES

1. On this see Gerhard L. Weinberg, *Hitler's Foreign Policy, 1933–1939: The Road to World War II* (New York: Enigma Books, 2005), 778; and Gerhard L. Weinberg, "Four Days in December [1941]," *World War II* 27 (November–December 2012): 33–39.
2. Percy Ernst Schramm, ed., *Kriegstagebuch des Oberkommandos der Wehrmacht, 1940–1945* (Frankfurt: Bernard & Graefe, 1961), vol. 4, pt. 2, 1540.
3. Leonidas E. Hill, ed., *Die Weizsäcker-Papiere, 1933–1950* (Frankfurt: Ullstein, 1974), 204. See also Hans-Adolf Jacobsen, ed., *Generaloberst Halder Kriegstagebuch* (Stuttgart: Kohlhammer, 1962), 1:375.
4. See the sources cited in Andreas Hillgruber, *Hitlers Strategie: Politik und Kriegführung, 1940–1941* (Frankfurt: Bernard & Graefe, 1965), 145n4.
5. Andreas Hillgruber, *Die Zerstörung Europas: Beiträge zur Weltkriegsepoche, 1914 bis 1945* (Berlin: Propyläen, 1988), 244–46.
6. There is an early review of the evidence in Gerhard L. Weinberg, *Germany and the Soviet Union, 1939–1941* (Leiden: Brill, 1972), chap. 7. Hillgruber covers it in more detail in *Zerstörung Europas*, 239ff.
7. Albert Speer, *Erinnerungen* (Berlin: Propyläen, 1969), 188. Keitel mentioned in the quotation was Field Marshal Wilhelm Keitel, chief of the OKW.
8. Weinberg, *Germany*, 107–8.
9. Ibid., 109–12; and Hillgruber, *Zerstörung Europas*, 246–49.
10. The entries for this period in Jacobsen, *Generaloberst Halder Kriegstagebuch*, vol. 2, deal mostly in great detail with the planned invasion of England.
11. See the testimony and statements of Gen. Alfred Jodl and Gen. Walter Warlimont cited in Weinberg, *Germany*, chap. 7; and Gerhard L. Weinberg, *A World at Arms: A Global History of World War II*, 2nd ed. (New York: Cambridge University Press, 2005), 179–80.
12. Helmuth Greiner, *Die Oberste Wehrmachtführung, 1939–1943* (Wiesbaden: Limes, 1951), 292–93; Jacobsen, *Generaloberst Halder Kriegstagebuch*, 2:32n9; and see the end of the "August 1, 1940" entry in Schramm, *Kriegstagebuch*, 1:5.
13. Greiner, *Die Oberste Wehrmachtführung*, 293.
14. Weinberg, *Germany*, 119.

15. David Stahel, *Operation Barbarossa and Germany's Defeat in the East* (Cambridge: Cambridge University Press, 2009).

16. Sir Charles Webster and Noble Frankland, *The Strategic Air Offensive against Germany, 1939–1945* (London: Her Majesty's Stationery Office, 1961), 1:94ff.

17. Jochen Böhler, *"Grösste Härte . . ."*: *Verbrechen der Wehrmacht in Polen September/ Oktober 1939* (Hamburg: Gründeldruck, 2005), 16.

18. Webster and Frankland, *Strategic Air Offensive*, 1:105–6.

19. Walt W. Rostow's *Pre-Invasion Bombing Strategy: General Eisenhower's Decision of March 25, 1944* (Austin: University Press of Texas, 1981) is a helpful early review of the issues at the time.

20. The relevant documentary evidence is summarized and cited in Weinberg, *A World at Arms*, 142–43.

21. Webster and Frankland, *Strategic Air Offensive*, 1:chap. 3–4; Max Hastings, *Bomber Command* (London: Pan Books, 1981), 7–124; Denis Richards, *The Hardest Victory: RAF Bomber Command in the Second World War* (New York: Norton, 1995), chap. 1–8; and Robin Neillands, *The Bomber War: The Allied Air Offensive against Nazi Germany* (Woodstock NY: Overlook Press, 2001), chap. 2–4.

22. There is a fine survey in Edward B. Westermann, *Flak: German Anti-Aircraft Defenses, 1914–1945* (Lawrence: University Press of Kansas, 2001), chap. 4–5.

23. Tami Davis Biddle, *Rhetoric and Reality in Air Warfare: The Evolution of British and American Ideas about Strategic Bombing, 1914–1945* (Princeton NJ: Princeton University Press, 2002), 187–94.

24. Webster and Frankland, *Strategic Air Offensive*, 1:178–79; Robert S. Ehlers Jr., *Targeting the Third Reich: Air Intelligence and the Allied Bombing Campaigns* (Lawrence: University Press of Kansas, 2009), 116; and Neillands, *Bomber War*, 57–60. The full text of the Butt report is printed in Webster and Frankland, *Strategic Air Offensive*, 4:205–13. Richard Overy, in *The Bombers and the Bombed: Allied Air War over Europe, 1940–1945* (New York: Viking, 2014), 68–69, argues that the Butt report was not as important as generally held, but it certainly provided a very substantial argument for those who argued in favor of the shift in bombing strategy.

25. See the books cited in note 24.

26. Biddle, *Rhetoric and Reality*, 194–97.

27. The full text is in Webster and Frankland, *Strategic Air Offensive*, 4:143–45. The quoted passage is on page 144. The heading of the relevant part of the official history is "The Opening of the Offensive and the Transition to Area Bombing," in Webster and Frankland, *Strategic Air Offensive*, 1:ix.

28. Biddle, *Rhetoric and Reality*, 197–200. See also Ehlers, *Targeting*, 117–20; Neillands, *Bomber War*, chap. 5; and Richards, *Hardest Victory*, chap. 9.

11

MEASURING GAINS ON THE BATTLEFIELD AND AT THE PEACE TABLE

SHIFTING ASSESSMENTS DURING THE KOREAN WAR

Conrad C. Crane

THE SEEDS OF THE KOREAN WAR were planted during a botched American occupation after World War II. While US military preparations for governing Germany, Italy, Japan, and the Philippines had begun as early as 1942, Korea was neglected along with most other remnants of the Japanese empire. When Japan capitulated, the Americans and the Soviets agreed to split the Korean Peninsula to accept the surrender of forces there. Two army colonels looking at a map in Washington selected the thirty-eighth parallel as the dividing line between the areas of national responsibility. That soon became an international border between two very different states. While the Soviets nurtured a new Communist Democratic People's Republic of Korea and strengthened its army with T-34 tanks, an American military governor struggled to unite divergent South Korean factions enough to allow a speedy withdrawal of his troops. With the creation of the Republic of Korea (ROK) in 1948, the United States began pulling out its forces, leaving behind a small advisory group for an army kept purposefully weak so it would not be tempted to try to reconquer the north. The ROK Army was equipped primarily to deal with Communist rebels battling in the new country's interior. When the main American forces departed, they left behind a weak South Korean government rent by factional strife and fighting a growing insurgency. The fledgling state was a tempting target for an aggressive neighbor.[1]

The war began because North Korean leader Kim Il Sung saw an opportunity to reunify the peninsula under his rule and persuaded his sponsors in the Soviet Union and China to back him. Faulty assessments on both sides contributed to the beginning of hostilities. A key precondition for Soviet support was no American intervention. The rhetoric of American leaders reinforced perceptions in Beijing, Moscow, and Pyongyang that Korea was not a defense priority, and reduced US forces in the theater were not expected to be able to respond to a North Korean attack in time to have any effect anyway. Leaders in Washington were more concerned about cutting defense spending than bolstering a defense perimeter, and none thought the Soviets or the satellites they controlled would risk an attack anywhere that might bring nuclear retaliation. Both evaluations were wrong.[2]

The conflict can be roughly divided into five phases. The first began on June 25, 1950, when the North Korean People's Army (NKPA) overwhelmed poorly prepared ROK forces and swarmed southward over the thirty-eighth parallel. American leaders were wary, wondering whether it was just the opening gambit of a wider war planned by the Soviets. Reinforcements were rushed to Europe and the Far East. The United States and its UN allies rallied to South Korea's defense, with an initial war objective of stopping the aggression and preserving the noncommunist nation. But overconfident American units deployed from Japan were driven back, and UN forces were soon bottled up in a perimeter, defending the key port of Pusan. However, the NKPA's lines of communication were overextended, and it had suffered tremendous attrition from constant combat. It was therefore very vulnerable to counterattack.

The war's second phase began on September 15, when Gen. Douglas MacArthur landed a strong force at Inchon in the enemy rear, and the besieged US Eighth Army broke out of the Pusan perimeter along with South Korean forces. The NKPA collapsed. The quick turn of events forced decision makers on both sides to make strategic decisions of great importance on short notice. Now US and UN war objectives expanded to include conquering the whole peninsula while the Soviets and Chinese were faced with increasing their involvement to preserve a suddenly beleaguered ally. American leaders gave MacArthur permission to cross the thirty-eighth parallel and reunite the two Koreas, and as UN forces headed for the Yalu River, it was their turn to become vulnerable and overextended.

The war turned again as a massive Chinese intervention in late November caught the US Eighth Army, X Corps, and their allies in North Korea by surprise, and they were lucky to escape without even heavier losses. The Chinese armies rolled over the thirty-eighth parallel to recapture the South Korean capital of Seoul, and for a while Mao Zedong also had a vision of permanently removing American influence from the peninsula. However, because of long supply lines, harsh weather, and growing UN resistance, Communist forces reached their culminating point in early 1951. Then an Eighth Army rejuvenated by the dynamic leadership of Matthew Ridgway spearheaded a counteroffensive that could not be stopped by large Chinese attacks or even by President Harry Truman's relief of MacArthur in April for insubordination. By June UN forces and firepower had recaptured Seoul and restored the battle line to the vicinity of the thirty-eighth parallel.

Once the Chinese had intervened in force, the Truman administration and the United Nations had scaled back their war objectives to a negotiated settlement to restore the status quo. Ridgway's combination of controlled offensives and firepower rolled inexorably northward, prodding the Soviets to ask the United Nations for a cease-fire and armistice. It appeared that both sides now agreed on how the conflict should end, but for the next two years the war settled down to a stalemate in the mountainous Korean terrain and at the peace table. It must be noted also that neither North Korea nor South Korea favored any resolution of the war short of unification, creating bargaining tensions within as well as between the negotiating parties.

As Ridgway feared, Communist forces used the respite gained from the cease-fire to create elaborate defensive positions. With neither side willing to pay the high price of trying to gain military victory on this newly fortified battlefield, both focused on achieving some sort of success in negotiations. Americans were comfortable with judging success by ground gained and enemies killed. But trying to produce results in negotiations with a carefully calibrated combination of coercion and concessions was something new. After much sparring and posturing, a suspension of the discussions at Kaesong in August, and a limited UN ground offensive in September, talks resumed in October 1951 at Panmunjom. While agreement was achieved fairly quickly on items such as fixing a military demarcation line and a supervisory organization for the armistice, some issues were more intractable. Though the rotation and replenishment of military forces after the armistice remained a sticking point for a while, the major disagreement that would prolong the war involved the repatriation of prisoners of war (POWs).

Of the tens of thousands of prisoners herded into UN POW camps after the NKPA offensive collapsed, many were South Koreans who had been impressed into service to replace NKPA losses on its drive down the peninsula. Among the Chinese prisoners a large number claimed to be Nationalists who were forced to serve under the "Reds." Neither group wanted to return to their former military masters. Not only did UN leaders see forced repatriation of these soldiers as being immoral but also the propaganda value of so many refusing to return to Communist rule was apparent to both sides. When the Communists insisted that all their prisoners had to be returned to them, the talks bogged down.

In his book *How Wars End*, Gideon Rose is very critical of American and UN leaders for not assessing the possible costs of standing firm on the issue of repatriation.[3] That judgment, however, could only be made in retrospect. No one questioned that position at the time. When the Communists appeared intractable about the issue, the considered UN responses were always to break off talks or to escalate the war to force concessions but never whether to abandon the prisoners. Basic values are not assessed in wartime. They cannot be bargained away. While preserving the right of prisoners to make their own choices did allow a certain sense of victory in a limited war, jettisoning that freedom would have been viewed as a significant defeat, a denial of the core value that UN forces were defending against perceived totalitarian Communist expansion.

American assessments throughout the war were shaped by a Cold War mind-set that always saw the combat in Korea as part of a wider conflict that was centrally controlled from Moscow and sometimes from Beijing. There was little consideration of independent North Korean action. At the first meeting of the president and his advisers after the war began, besides ordering MacArthur to find out conditions in Korea, Truman directed the Air Force to develop plans to destroy Soviet air bases in the Far East. He also instructed the State and Defense Departments to calculate where the Soviets would strike next.[4]

Because of the realization that the Communist bloc had big advantages in proximity and manpower in the theater, assessments about the possible escalation of the war with nuclear weapons began early and would be conducted periodically whenever expanding the conflict was considered. During a meeting of the Joint Chiefs of Staff (JCS) on July 9, 1950, discussing a request from MacArthur for support, JCS chairman Gen. Omar Bradley remarked that the JCS might want to examine whether A-bombs should be made available to Far East Command (FEC). However, the consensus was against the proposal at that time. Bradley was probably responding to prodding from Gen. Dwight Eisenhower to use one or two of the weapons to resolve the conflict quickly.[5]

During the month US Army and Air Force staffs examined the feasibility of employing nuclear weapons in Korea. The Air Force's Psychological Warfare Division saw no benefit in bombing North Korean targets as the Soviet Union really supplied and controlled the war. Using atomic weapons on tactical targets would probably be ineffective, demonstrating US impotence and cruelty while doing substantial damage to South Korean territory. The psychological warfare study recommended instead that the United States capitalize on its decision not to use the bomb in an extensive propaganda campaign that would include leaflet warnings for civilians of any conventional attacks on North Korean cities. The army study by the G-3 Plans Division also concluded: "At the present time, the use of atomic bombs in Korea is unwarranted from the military point of view, and questionable from the political and psychological point of view." However, it considered that employing the weapon might be necessary "to avert impending disaster" and recommended that preparations should be made for that eventuality.[6]

The "disaster" envisioned was one in which the US Army faced a catastrophic defeat and evacuation through Pusan. During the movement phases of the war, assessments of the situation on the battlefield were very straightforward, basically obtainable by looking at the battle lines on a map, and supplemented by intelligence reports of enemy strength and casualties. Though the hesitance to use atomic bombs except in the most dire circumstances remained, some more scares after July prompted a reexamination of that position.

The first came after the failure of the US assessment process to predict the entry of Communist China into the war. Buoyed by promises of Soviet matériel support, Chinese leaders were confident they could destroy an army that the North Koreans had shown to be vulnerable despite its firepower. Force commander Peng Dehuai persuasively argued that the United States did not have the manpower to wage full war in Asia, nor could its capitalist economy bear the strain.[7] Both the Chinese and North Koreans told their troops that the United States would not use the atomic bomb in Korea for various reasons including a lack of targets, its fear of Soviet retaliation, and its humanitarian impulses.[8]

However, the massive Chinese intervention motivated both the State and Defense Departments to reexamine their stance on using atomic weapons in November. State Department policy planners thought the military benefits of their use were uncertain while political fallout would be considerable. The army G-3 thought that the military situation was more favorable for employment of atomic bombs than it had been in July and persuaded Chief of Staff Gen. J. Lawton Collins to submit a memorandum to the JCS mentioning that "in the event of an all-out effort by the Chinese Communists, the use of atomic bombs against troops and materiel concentrations might be the decisive factor in enabling UN forces to hold a defensive position or to effect the early drive to the Manchurian border." He asked that a study be made to "determine the conditions under which the employment of atomic bombs would be indicated," the most suitable targets to be hit, and what additional policy and operational preparations were necessary "to insure our ability to use this bomb if and when we deem it appropriate." The JCS concurred and referred the memorandum to the Joint Strategic Survey Committee for the preparation of "comments and recommendations" on Collins's questions.[9]

At the first National Security Council meeting after the extent of Chinese involvement became evident in late November, concerns about a surprise Communist air attack dominated the discussion. General Bradley briefed that the enemy had three hundred aircraft in Manchuria, including two hundred twin-engined bombers with the range to strike crowded UN airfields. Retreating road convoys were also very vulnerable. In reply to a question from the president, Air Force chief of staff Gen. Hoyt Vandenberg stated that the only effective defense against the new threat would be either to bomb the enemy airfields or to withdraw UN planes to Japan. Adm. Forrest Sherman discussed similar threats to the navy and agreed that in the event of enemy air attack US forces would have to not only pull back down the peninsula but also hit back. Shortly thereafter, Assistant Secretary of State for Far Eastern Affairs Dean Rusk advised the ambassadors of those nations providing military aid to the UN effort that "if the Chinese concentrate air power in Manchurian air fields and use it in Korea, it will be necessary for us to bomb the bases in Manchuria." The JCS did not necessarily agree, however, because of fears such action might bring in the Russians. In that eventuality, Collins saw no alternative but to consider the use of the A-bomb. One of Rusk's subordinates even proposed, if the situation became very grave, using nuclear weapons to destroy hydroelectric power installations in North Korea as a "heavy blow" against the Communist economy. This option was seconded in the most vehement recommendation for escalating the war, a memorandum by Col. Noel Parrish, the assistant secretary of the Air Staff, who argued that the United States should quit trying "to fight World War II over again." He also advocated conventional raids on Manchurian industry, the leaking of news that we had developed "secret atomic radiation booby traps" to poison strips of territory, and the instigation and support of "murderous subversion" in Russia and Eastern Europe.[10]

Collins made an emergency trip to see MacArthur the first week of December. The commander in chief, Far East (CINCFE) believed if the all-out Chinese Communist attack continued, restrictions on air and naval action against China were not lifted, and significant ground reinforcements were not received, then UN forces would have to withdraw from Korea. However, if MacArthur was allowed to begin a naval blockade and aerial bombardment of Communist China, make maximum use of Nationalist troops, and possibly deploy atomic bombs, then he was confident that his forces "should continue to hold the best possible positions in Korea." Though Collins concurred with MacArthur's conclusions, he promised no reinforcements and returned to Washington to discuss the military situation in the Far East with his JCS colleagues.[11]

They remained reluctant to expand the war unless the enemy did so first. Eventually contingency plans were cleared through the Department of Defense, the Department of State, and the president that were based on the premise that if the Communists did mount a major air offensive from Manchuria or the Shantung Peninsula against UN forces, Far East Air Forces (FEAF) would immediately attack those air bases. Final authority to put the plans into effect remained with the highest levels of government, but in an emergency where obtaining such approval would be difficult, the JCS was authorized to act on its best judgment.[12]

The next great flurry of activity concerning atomic weapons occurred in April 1951. There was much anxiety in the United States. Opinion polls showed that a third of the American public favored a general war with Communist China, and a majority advocated air attacks on Manchuria. Signs of Chinese air and ground preparations for a spring fifth-phase offensive and a corresponding buildup of Soviet forces in the Far East alarmed the president enough that he ordered nuclear weapons and more Strategic Air Command (SAC) bombers to Okinawa on April 6. Vandenberg had begun requesting the transfer of atomic bombs from the Atomic Energy Commission to the Air Force in March, when it became apparent that Russian troops were massing in Manchuria and that more than seventy submarines had assembled at Vladivostok and Sakhalin. Intelligence reports that month also revealed Joseph Stalin had told Foreign Minister V. M. Molotov "to handle matters in Asia," and a reliable high-ranking Polish defector revealed that "Soviet Far East Command has been instructed that rendering of necessary assistance to insure success of offensive takes precedence over avoidance of third World War." Vandenberg and Bradley convinced Truman that the Chinese and Russians might be prepared to do anything to push the United States out of Korea, including invading Japan. It would mean the beginning of global war, and the Air Force needed to be able to respond quickly. On April 11 the JCS issued Gen. Curtis LeMay, commander of SAC, a directive to prepare plans "against targets listed and targets of opportunity in the Far East." After his bombers deployed to Guam with the nuclear cores to complete nine bombs, LeMay sent his deputy, Gen. Thomas Power, to the Far East to coordinate with General Ridgway, the new CINCFE, and direct any atomic operations. Though SAC's nuclear-capable B-29s, and sometimes B-50s (an improved version of the Superfortress), never moved to Okinawa, their deployment to Guam continued until the end of the war.[13]

Inspired by a series of alarming messages warning of possible Soviet reaction to the approaching completion of a US-Japan peace treaty and bolstered by his new agreements with SAC, Ridgway requested atomic weapons himself in May 1951. Two resulting army staff studies complained that SAC only considered the strategic use of the bomb and displayed no appreciation of tactical capabilities. Planning, intelligence, command relationships, and training in SAC and the Far East Command were inadequate to support Ridgway's ground operations with nuclear weapons. In discussing one of these studies in August, the JCS directed the FEC to test atomic delivery procedures by conducting simulated strikes in Korea with the coordination of SAC and the commander in chief, Pacific, for the navy also had some carrier-based nuclear capability. At the same time Ridgway was asking for just such support to be available to him in addition to atomic artillery. The JCS action resulted in the exercise Operation Hudson Harbor, with SAC conducting four practice missions on tactical targets chosen by the FEC. For security the operations were presented as conventional strikes in support of frontline troops and would have appeared that way to observers where the ordnance was delivered, but they actually were conducted as close to actual nuclear procedures as possible, including the wait of three and a half hours for simulated presidential permission to release the weapons for a first strike. Hudson Harbor demonstrated that the evaluation of potential tactical atomic targets was inadequate and the delay between selection and delivery was too long. In addition CINCFE and SAC disagreed on the best way to pick objectives. Ridgway wanted to base choices on each unique battlefield situation while LeMay favored standard "yardsticks." As far as the Air Staff was concerned, the exercise failed to establish any suitable targets for nuclear weapons in Korea, and it reinforced the reluctance of the JCS to employ A-bombs there.[14]

Once the front settled down in the summer of 1951 and the possibility of major ground offensives dwindled, so did fears of the possible need for nuclear escalation. But the calculations suitable for assessment in mobile warfare did not necessarily apply at the peace table. Military commanders had relied heavily upon casualty counts to show progress, and even the State Department bragged to UN ambassadors in May 1951 that their combined forces had caused more than a million Communist casualties. Such data, however, did not translate into any apparent leverage at Panmunjom.[15]

MacArthur's relief sparked hearings by the Senate's Committee on Armed Services and Committee on Foreign Relations to examine the military situation in the Far East, and they produced a brutal public assessment of the stalemate in Korea. The hearings were generally inconclusive on issues of past tactics and strategy, but they did reveal a great amount of shared uncertainty about the future.[16]

Meanwhile the CINCFE wrestled with the dilemma of applying military force to coerce concessions at the peace table without expanding the war in unacceptable ways or giving the Communists excuses to break off the talks. Both sides used that threat often and sometimes exercised it. While assessments were being made in Washington and other Allied capitals about the war's progress, responsibility for conducting the actual peacemaking process belonged to the leader of the UN Command in Korea. Agreeing quickly to an armistice line and to ratcheting down ground operations was probably a mistake by UN leaders that lessened pressure on the Communists. Ridgway decided to use airpower as his coercive military tool. He bombed the North Korean capital of Pyongyang and executed a campaign of air interdiction to strangle troops at the front. While the enemy forces' consumption of supplies was very low during the armistice negotiations, and they had a large supply of labor to maintain communications, FEAF had too few aircraft for its many tasks, and the US Air Force lacked the technology for effective interdiction at night. Ridgway had high hopes that his airmen could prevent the enemy from building up supplies for another offensive, but that proved impossible. As a result he became increasingly suspicious of Air Force claims. He once told his air commanders, "If all the enemy trucks you report as having destroyed during the past ten days or so were actually kills, then there would not be a truck left in all of Asia." In his postwar memoirs he gave the Air Force credit for saving UN forces from disaster and providing essential support for his ground operations, but he also warned against expecting "miracles of interdiction" in future conflicts.[17]

Part of the problem with interpreting the results of interdiction lay with the lack of joint doctrine. There was no agreed-upon definition for the term, thus contributing to the differing opinions concerning its success, and no common standards for assessment. Ground commanders considered the continuing enemy offensives as a sign of the failure of interdiction. Even during lulls in the action, Ridgway complained about the increasing artillery fire falling on his troops. Airmen admitted that their efforts were not decisive but argued that they had achieved great success in harassing and limiting the Communist buildup. Mission reports cited statistics about bridges downed, vehicles destroyed, and rail lines cut to demonstrate operational effectiveness.[18]

Ridgway's initial determination to influence negotiations with airpower eventually was tempered by his disappointment in the interdiction campaign's results and his battles with the JCS about bombing Pyongyang. He also became more hesitant to risk anything that might cause the Communists to break off the peace talks. They had already used UN air attacks on the negotiating site as an excuse to halt them twice—once based on apparently faked evidence and another time because of an actual UN bombing error. Their tactic was effective in restraining Ridgway's actions. When he left the

Far East to become supreme commander in Europe in May 1952, Ridgway took along a strong skepticism about the utility of airpower.[19]

The Communists tried to influence the negotiations in other ways besides threatening to suspend them. They primarily involved influencing international perceptions through adroit information campaigns. In early 1952 North Korean and Chinese leaders accused the United States of carrying on biological warfare (BW) against them. In May they released confessions coerced from American airmen, who admitted they had dropped "germ bombs" as part of an extensive BW campaign against China and Korea. Eventually thirty-eight fliers would confess to such attacks. Besides the obvious propaganda value of the accusations, they also were designed to discredit the US airpower that was punishing Communist forces and facilities. While the United States investigated the confessions and actively worked to counter the charges in the United Nations and public opinion, the Communists' propaganda campaign had the ironic effect of spurring American efforts to develop the actual BW means to carry out such attacks. Leaders wanted a retaliatory capability because they assessed that the Communists were making the accusations to provide an excuse to launch their own BW operations. However, the Americans were not able to develop a viable BW system before the war ended, and when the post-Stalin government in Moscow found evidence that the Chinese and North Koreans were fabricating the BW claims in the spring of 1953, the Soviets stopped the accusations.[20]

Another information campaign was aimed more directly at the POW issue. The Communists had carefully prepared some officers to surrender, and they took advantage of the overcrowded conditions in prison camps on the island of Koje-do to organize resistance there. Close connections were maintained between the North Korean delegates at Panmunjom and their agents in the camps through a complex network of refugees, civilians, and local guerrillas. In May 1952 the prisoners actually lured Brig. Gen. Francis Dodd, the American commander, into the compound and captured him. Then they coerced Brig. Gen. Charles Colson to sign a pledge to stop a list of alleged prison atrocities to obtain Dodd's release. This statement appeared to be an admission of guilt, and it was reprinted throughout the world press. The Communists hoped that embarrassment over abuses at Koje-do could break the UN position on POWs at the peace talks. The camps threatened to get out of control until a few battalions of combat infantry restored order and broke up the Communist cells in June. Afterward the UN forces kept better control of their POW facilities and effectively countered continuing accusations of abuse.[21]

Koje-do did complicate the mission of the UN negotiating team, as the members argued among themselves whether a tougher stance was required with their obstinate adversaries. However, during a brief period of optimism in July 1952, every article of a draft armistice was agreed to, except Article 51 dealing with POWs. A decline in propaganda attacks appeared to indicate that the Communists were indeed serious about reaching an agreement, but they refused to accept any proposal except total repatriation. Breaking the deadlock appeared hopeless. By October the plenary sessions were suspended, and only liaison officers talked directly.[22]

Ridgway's successor, Gen. Mark Clark, had recent experience negotiating with the Soviets as the American high commissioner for Austria and described that duty as "two years of head-knocking with the Russians to teach me what it is that Communists respect: Force."[23] When FEAF commander Gen. Otto Weyland approached Clark with a proposal for a new "Air Pressure" campaign designed to increase coercion with expanded target sets, Clark proved an eager listener. As the truce talks continued through 1952, the stalemate on the ground and the ineffectiveness of air interdiction inspired Brig. Gen. Jacob Smart, FEAF deputy commander for operations, to look for a better way to apply his resources. He directed two members of his staff, Col. R. L. Randolph and Lt. Col. B. I. Mayo, "to devise ways and means of exerting maximum pressure on the Communist Forces in North Korea through optimum application of FEAF effort." Smart was frustrated by the lack of progress in ending the war, and his subordinates' mission was "truly a search for new ideas." Randolph and Mayo began examining the course and results of the interdiction campaign, which had focused on enemy railroads since August 1951. Its objective remained to cut rail lines at selected points and force the enemy to use roads as the primary channel of supply. Planners then hoped that FEAF aircraft could destroy enough enemy trucks so frontline armies could not be supplied. That had not occurred, despite making more than fifteen thousand rail cuts and at least partially destroying 199 bridges. Enemy repair efforts, night movement, and MiG-15 jet fighter attacks had foiled FEAF efforts to close transportation routes. Randolph and Mayo also pointed out that the enemy's daily mortar shell requirement could be carried by only one truck or a hundred coolies with A-frames, and it would be virtually impossible for interdiction to stop all such traffic. In addition, FEAF losses had been heavy. The campaign had cost 243 aircraft destroyed and 290 heavily damaged, and only 131 replacements had been received. The two staff officers looked for a way to reapply American airpower to coerce the Communists to conclude an armistice.[24]

Their staff study was finished on April 12, 1952. It recommended that any air resources beyond those required to maintain air superiority "be employed toward accomplishing the maximum amount of selected destruction, thus making the Korean conflict as costly as possible to the enemy in terms of equipment, supplies, and personnel." Targets were prioritized based on the effect their destruction would have on the enemy, their vulnerability to available weapons, and the probable cost to FEAF of attacking them. Suggested objectives included hydroelectric plants (if they were cleared for attack by the JCS), locomotives and vehicles, stored supplies, and even buildings in cities and villages, especially in areas "active in support of enemy forces." Based on the study, Smart planned to de-emphasize interdiction to concentrate on the new target systems, aiming to "bring about defeat of the enemy as expeditiously as possible" rather than "allowing him to languish in comparative quiescence while we expand our efforts beating up supply routes." He knew the well-dug-in enemy was under no real pressure on the front line and that the enemy needed very few supplies anyway to sustain operations during the stalemate. Smart also believed attacks should be scheduled "against targets of military significance so situated that their destruction will have a deleterious effect upon the morale of the civilian population actively engaged in the logistic support of the enemy forces." He knew that the selection of proper targets to influence enemy decision makers would be difficult, not only for operational reasons, but also because of uncertainty about just who those key decision makers were, how their minds worked, and whether they were in the Soviet Union, China, or North Korea.[25]

Clark speedily approved the plan and obtained clearance to attack North Korean hydroelectric facilities, a target that Ridgway had considered off-limits because of its dual use by civilians as well as the military, in China and North Korea. Air attacks in late June 1952 destroyed 90 percent of North Korea's electric power potential. That had many repercussions besides reducing Manchurian industrial production. The impact on North Korea was apparent to American POWs, who never saw the end of any of the propaganda films they were exposed to that summer because the electricity always failed. But the most apparent effect of the new bombing program was not felt in Moscow, Beijing, or Pyongyang but in London. Always fearful of American escalation, in Parliament the British Labour Party members denounced the bombings as a provocation that could lead to World War III, and only Prime Minister Winston Churchill's announcement that he was appointing a British deputy for the UN Command in Korea mollified them. Secretary of Defense Robert Lovett publicly endorsed this addition to Clark's staff while also providing the misleading explanation to the press that the JCS had given special permission to allow the raids on the hydroelectric plants based only on military considerations. American newspapers were not fooled and speculated that the attacks were the start of a tougher policy to break the stalemate at the peace talks. Some congressmen even questioned why the plants had not been bombed earlier. Both Churchill and Lovett denied that the attacks signified any change in UN policies, though indeed that was the case.[26]

Clark and his subordinates continued to grapple with how best to execute this new concept of "employing air forces as the single strategic offensive in a war" by seeking additional targets, eventually decimating eighteen of twenty-two major North Korean cities. The JCS supported these efforts, and except for delaying one attack on a major supply complex because of a nearby prisoner exchange, it approved all of Clark's target requests, including more bombing of hydroelectric plants. The JCS, however, did prohibit any public statements announcing the operations' intent to pressure the Communists into an agreement, fearing that if their prestige became "seriously engaged" they would find it difficult to accept any armistice. High-level statements had to treat the air attacks as routine operations "based upon solely military grounds." Ironically, as the raids were directed more and more at achieving a political settlement, the less this could be admitted in public as justification for them.[27]

After the suspension of the peace talks, Clark also developed Operations Plan 8-52. This scheme to expand the war if negotiations collapsed included the deployment of additional forces mobilized in the United States and the widespread use of atomic weapons to drive the battle line to the narrowest part of the peninsula. Much else was going on. Neutral nations presented initiatives in the United Nations to end the war. Communist agents incited more trouble at POW camps. Fears of Communist air buildups in Manchuria prompted Clark to ask for authority to attack those airfields, but it was refused. As 1953 opened, Dwight Eisenhower's new administration talked a harder line for the Far East. Then in early March, Stalin died. There were immediate signs of thawing Soviet-European relations, and then on March 28, the Chinese and North Koreans responded positively to Clark's request to exchange sick and wounded prisoners. Operation Little Switch was executed in April, and later that month, full plenary sessions resumed at Panmunjom.[28]

By late May the Communists had dropped their insistence on full repatriation, and an armistice seemed imminent. South Korean president Synghman Rhee, who still desired reunification, was alarmed. Demonstrations erupted throughout South Korea, and in mid-June ROK Army guards released twenty-five thousand prisoners from their camps. Enraged American officials feared the peace talks would be endangered and worked to restrain their recalcitrant ally. Chinese forces did launch some punishing attacks on ROK Army positions, but negotiations continued. UN forces also conducted some military operations, with FEAF attacking the last target set on its Air Pressure list, North Korean irrigation dams, but their primary focus remained on Panmunjom. The final armistice was signed on July 27. Until the end Eisenhower and his advisers remained suspicious of Communist intentions and prepared to execute Operation Plan 8-52 if talks collapsed or signing the armistice proved to be a ruse.[29]

Though no evidence indicates Eisenhower's warnings that the United States was prepared to lift restrictions on nuclear weapons ever reached leaders in the Soviet Union or China, plenty of obvious signs showed US patience was wearing thin and that the war might expand if it continued. Even if notice about the increased possibility of the use of US atomic bombs was never transmitted through diplomatic channels, rumors about Eisenhower's threat to escalate military operations unless a cease-fire was negotiated were rampant throughout Korea, and the Communists would have picked them up from spies or POWs. Many other factors besides military pressure were involved in the Communists' decision to sign the armistice and give up their demand for forced repatriation of all POWs. The death of Stalin and continuing instability in the Kremlin combined with riots in Eastern Europe gave the Soviet Union plenty of incentive to disengage from Korea. Mao had a war in Indochina to support and another to plan against Formosa, as well as delayed economic development to pursue at home. Late gains on the ground against ROK troops allowed the Communists to save face while making concessions for the armistice. Further delays, though, might also have allowed South Korea's unpredictable Rhee to disrupt peace efforts. Even Kim Il Sung was ready to end the fighting, confident that he had consolidated his power in the decimated north and that he would still be able to eventually gain the south without fighting.[30]

Another key component of wartime assessment is interpreting failure and success to shape future policy. Historian William Stueck argues that the conflict in Korea made both sides in the Cold War reluctant to engage in another major conventional confrontation, thus avoiding wars over contended zones such as Yugoslavia that would have been much harder to control.[31] Asian specialist Selig Harrison posits that the North Koreans' programs to develop missiles and weapons of mass destruction have been motivated to a large extent by the desire to deter any future applications of US "air pressure" such as the one that so devastated their country.[32] Perceptions of the war's outcome had an especially profound impact on the United States. The successful effort to preserve South Korea reinforced the logic of containment policies, especially the military aspects, which were now globalized to cover parts of the world not considered in initial concepts. The war speeded the rearmament and development of the North Atlantic Treaty Organization, part of a burgeoning free world system of collective, forward defense that drew the United States into mutual security agreements with many Asian nations as well, and led the United States to increase its support for the French war in Indochina. Assessments of the Korean War would figure heavily in American decision making about entering combat in Vietnam.[33] Unlike after previous American wars, no massive drawdown of the armed forces occurred in 1953. Cold War military expenditures continued to rise, and force levels remained relatively high until after both the collapse of the Soviet Union and the conclusion of Operation Desert Storm. Americans learned to accept the existence of a permanently strong security establishment.

Eisenhower eventually became convinced that his nuclear threats had been the main reason the Communists had finally signed the armistice agreement.[34] That belief helped reinforce his emphasis on such weapons for his administration's New Look policy. The various services also scrambled to increase atomic capabilities. SAC dominated the Air Force, and even its Tactical Air Command came to focus primarily on delivering nuclear weapons with its fighter-bombers. The navy fought for its own piece of the atomic pie, developing larger aircraft carriers and nuclear submarines. Even the army succumbed to the trend, pursuing atomic cannons and the pentomic division. When American advisers began to work with a new ally in Vietnam, they would use the ROK Army as their model, developing a force designed to resist a conventional invasion with firepower on a linear battlefield. And soon another cycle of wartime assessment would begin again in yet another Asian conflict to contain communism.

NOTES

1. For the period leading up to the war, see Allan R. Millett, *The War for Korea, 1945–1950: A House Burning* (Lawrence: University Press of Kansas, 2005).

2. Allan R. Millett, *The War for Korea, 1950–1951: They Came from the North* (Lawrence: University Press of Kansas, 2010), 18–66.

3. Gideon Rose, *How Wars End: Why We Always Fight the Last Battle*, 2nd ed. (New York: Simon & Schuster, 2011).

4. Memorandum of Conversation, by the Ambassador at Large, June 25, 1950, in US Department of State, *Foreign Relations of the United States (FRUS), 1950*, vol. 7, *Korea* (Washington DC: Government Printing Office, 1976), 157–61 (hereafter cited as *FRUS, 1950*).

5. Entries for June 28 and July 9, 1950, Folder, Historical Record Jan–Jul 50, Box 16, Matthew B. Ridgway Papers, US Army Military History Institute, Carlisle Barracks PA (hereafter MHI).

6. Stefan Possony to Col. Walter Putnam, Memorandum, Subject: The Use of Atomic Bombs in Korea, July 27, 1950, with August 2 and August 7, 1950,

transmittal memos by Col. O. L. Grover, File 385.2 Korea (28 Jul 50), Box 906, Record Group (RG) 341, Records of Headquarters, U.S. Air Force (HQ USAF); and Joint War Plans Branch, G-3, summary sheet and attached report, "Employment of Atomic Bombs in Korea," July 14, 1950, General Decimal File, 1950–1951, 091 Korea, Box 34-A, RG 319, Army Operations, National Archives II, College Park MD (hereafter NA II).

7. For the best coverage of both sides' assessments at this time, see Millett, *War for Korea, 1950–1951*, 291–320.

8. H. Goldhamer, "Communist Reaction in Korea to American Possession of the A-Bomb and Its Significance for U.S. Political and Psychological Warfare," Research Memorandum 903 (Santa Monica: RAND, August 1, 1952).

9. Memorandums by the Director of the Policy Planning Staff, November 4, 1950, and by the Planning Adviser, Bureau of Far Eastern Affairs, November 8, 1950, in *FRUS, 1950*, 7:1041–42, 1098–1100; and JCS 2173, Note by the Secretaries to the JCS on Possible Employment of Atomic Bombs in Korea, November 21, 1950, and Memo, G-3 to Chief of Staff, U.S. Army, Subject: Possible Employment of Atomic Bombs in Korea, November 16, 1950, General Decimal File, 1950–1951, 091 Korea, Box 34-A, RG 319, Army Operations, NA II.

10. *FRUS, 1950*, 7:1242–48, 1263–64, 1276–81, 1291–95; Memorandum, Col. Noel Parrish to General McKee, December 5, 1950, OPD 381 Korea (May 9, 1947), Section 12, Box 894, RG 341, Records of Headquarters, USAF, NA II. In reality American intelligence had overestimated the number of bombers available to Communist forces in Manchuria and did not know that Stalin had given strict orders to all Soviet bomber and ground-attack units to stay out of Korean airspace. See Mark A. O'Neill, "The Other Side of the Yalu: Soviet Pilots in the Korean War, Phase One, 1 November 1950–12 April 1951" (PhD diss., Florida State University, 1996), 125–26.

11. Memorandum, Gen. J. Lawton Collins to the JCS, Subject: Report on Visit to FECOM and Korea, December 4–7, 1950, and December 8, 1950, on Reel 9 of the microfilm collection *Records of the Joint Chiefs of Staff*, part 2, *1946–53, the Far East* (Washington DC: University Publications of America, 1979).

12. Gen. Omar N. Bradley, Memoranda of Activities Leading up to the Relief of General Douglas MacArthur, April 24, 1951, with handwritten corrections, Papers Declassified in June 1981, Omar N. Bradley Papers, MHI.

13. O'Neill, "Other Side," 273–74n7; Roger Dingman, "Atomic Diplomacy during the Korean War," *International Security* 13 (Winter 1988–89): 69–79n5; Roger M. Anders, "The Atomic Bomb and the Korean War: Gordon Dean and the Issue of Civilian Control," *Military Affairs*, January 1988, 1–3; Phillip S. Meilinger, *Hoyt S. Vandenberg: The Life of a General* (Bloomington: Indiana University Press, 1989), 175; Msg, C-58676, CINCFE to CG ARMY EIGHT,

March 27, 1951, Records of General Headquarters, FEC, SCAP, and UNC, Office of the Chief of Staff, Chief of Staff Subject File 1945–52, TS Personal File for 1949–1952, Box 3, Records of US Army Commands, 1942–, RG 338, NA II. See also entries for April 24 and May 7–9, 1951, LeMay Diary #3, Box 103; Letter, LeMay to Stratemeyer, November 27, 1951, File B14692, Box B198; and Letter, BG Richard Carmichael to CG FEAF, June 25, 1953, File B28370, Box B203, Papers of Curtis LeMay, Library of Congress. Also see Lt. Col. Crocker, Operations Division, "Action to Conclude Operations in Korea," July 5, 1951, General Decimal File, 1950–51, 091 Korea, Box 38-A, RG 319, NA II; HQ USAF, Staff Study on Use of Atomic Weapons in Korea, May 23, 1952, File 385.2 Korea (28 July 50), Section 2, Box 907, RG 341, NA II; and Interview of Lt. Gen. James T. Stewart by Col. Charles Andrean, 1986, James T. Stewart Papers, MHI.

14. Msg, SAC X-RAY to SAC, May 2, 1951, File B-10856 along with Files B-10951, B-10952, and B-10953, Box B197; Letter, Ridgway to LeMay, November 7, 1951, File B-14389, Box B198; and entries for August 28 and 31 and September 12–14, 1951, LeMay Diary #3, Box 103, LeMay Papers, Library of Congress. See also in NA II: Lt. Col. Crocker, Operations Division, "Action to Conclude Operations in Korea," July 5, 1951, General Decimal File, 1950–51, 091 Korea, Box 38-A, RG 319; Memo for Vandenberg by Maj. Gen. Joseph Smith, Subject: CINCFE Exercise "Hudson Harbor" (JCS 2173/9), September 21, 1951; Msg, DOSPC 0289, CGSAC to CGUSAF, September 27, 1951; Memorandum for Record by Col. J. S. Samuel, October 5, 1951; and Memo, MG Ramey to Director of Plans, Subject: (Top Secret) Use of Atomic Weapons in Korea, May 20, 1952, File 385.2 Korea (28 July 50), Section 2, Box 907, RG 341. There is no indication that these operations were designed to send any message to the enemy, and it seems unlikely from the cover story and flight paths that the Communists could have presumed the missions' intent.

15. Scott Sigmund Gartner and Marissa Edson Myers, "Body Counts and 'Success' in the Vietnam and Korean Wars," *The Journal of Interdisciplinary History* 25, no. 3 (Winter 1995): 377–95; and Memorandum of Conversation by Windsor G. Hackler of the Bureau for Far Eastern Affairs, May 25, 1951, in US Department of State, *Foreign Relations of the United States (FRUS), 1951*, vol. 7, *Korea and China* (Washington DC: Government Printing Office, 1983), part 1, 455–57.

16. US Senate, 82d Cong., 1st sess., *Military Situation in the Far East: Hearings before the Committee on Armed Services and the Committee on Foreign Relations* (Washington DC: Government Printing Office, 1951). The eight reels of microfilm transcripts of the hearings (Washington DC: University Publications of America, 1977) include sections that were deleted from the published record for security reasons.

17. Eduard Mark, *Aerial Interdiction: Air Power and the Land Battle in Three American Wars: A Historical Analysis* (Washington DC: Center for Air Force History, 1994), 289–319; Letter, M. B. Ridgway to Col. Paul Carter, December 15, 1976, Folder C, 1964–1983, Post Retirement A-G, Box 34B, Ridgway Papers, MHI; and Matthew B. Ridgway, *The Korean War* (1967; repr., New York: Da Capo, 1986), 191, 244.

18. Richard H. Kohn and Joseph P. Harahan, eds., *Air Interdiction in World War II, Korea, and Vietnam* (Washington DC: Office of Air Force History, 1986), 15–16, 51; and Ridgway, *The Korean War*, 192, 217–18.

19. Ibid., 200, 202, 244. Portions of this paragraph previously appeared in Conrad C. Crane, "Searching for Lucrative Targets in North Korea," in Coalition Air Warfare in the Korean War, 1950–1953, eds. Jacob Neufeld and George M. Watson Jr. Proceedings, Air Force Historical Foundation Symposium, Andrews AFB, Maryland, May 7–8, 2002, pp. 159–60.

20. Conrad C. Crane, *American Airpower Strategy in Korea, 1950–1953* (Lawrence: University Press of Kansas, 2000), 143–54.

21. Walter G. Hermes, *Truce Tent and Fighting Front* (Washington DC: Government Printing Office, 1966), 233–62.

22. Ibid., 263–82.

23. Gen. Mark W. Clark, *From the Danube to the Yalu* (Blue Ridge Summit PA: TAB Books, 1988), 3.

24. Interview of Gen. Jacob Smart (Ret.) by Conrad C. Crane, November 2, 1997, Arlington VA, with changes provided by letter from General Smart on November 29, 1997; Col. R. L. Randolph and Lt. Col. B. I. Mayo, Staff Study for Deputy for Operations, FEAF, "The Application of FEAF Effort in Korea," April 12, 1952, in FEAF Historical Division, FEAF Operations Policy, Korea, Mid-1952, March 1955, File K720.01, 1952 (addendum), Air Force Historical Research Agency (AFHRA), Maxwell Air Force Base (AFB) AL. Portions of this paragraph previously appeared in Crane, "Searching for Lucrative Targets."

25. Ibid. Portions of this paragraph previously appeared in Crane, "Searching for Lucrative Targets."

26. Maj. Gen. William F. Dean, *General Dean's Story* (New York: Viking Press, 1954), 263; "Labor Protests at Bombing on the Yalu River: Mr. Churchill Denies Change of Policy," *Times* (London), June 25, 1952, 2; also see continued coverage of parliamentary debates the next day in *Times* (London); "Speculation Links Raid to Truce Talks" and "New Initiative in Korea," *New York Times*, June 24, 1952, 3, 28; and Austin Stevens, "Lovett Says the Joint Chiefs Authorized Air Blow at Yalu," *New York Times*, June 25, 1952, 1, 3. Portions of this paragraph previously appeared in Crane, "Searching for Lucrative Targets."

27. "Staff Study of Intelligence Requirements by Cdr, FEAF for the Present and the Future," *History of the Far East Air Forces, January–December 1953*, vol. 3, pt. 1, 5, File K720.01, AFHRA, Maxwell AFB AL; and Msg, JCS 915579, JCS to CINCFE, August 8, 1952, Geographic File, 1951–53, 383.21 Korea (3–19–45), Section 109, Box 40, RG 218, NA II.

28. Crane, *American Airpower*, 157–59; and Hermes, *Truce Tent*, 401–20.

29. Hermes, *Truce Tent*, 436–90; and Crane, *American Airpower*, 159–64.

30. William Stueck, *The Korean War: An International History* (Princeton NJ: Princeton University Press, 1995), 326–30, 341–42; letter to author from Brig. Gen. Theo. C. Mataxis, May 12, 1998; and Millett, *War for Korea, 1950–1951*, 15–16.

31. Stueck, *Korean War*, 348–53.

32. Selig Harrison, "The Missiles of North Korea: How Real a Threat?," *World Policy Journal* 17 (Fall 2000): 13–24.

33. Yuen Foong Khong, *Analogies at War: Korea, Munich, Dien Bien Phu, and the Vietnam Decisions of 1965* (Princeton NJ: Princeton University Press, 1992).

34. In early 1965 President Lyndon Johnson discussed the growing problem in Vietnam with Eisenhower, and the general remarked that he had ended the war in Korea by having the word passed through three different channels, "telling the Chinese that they must agree to an armistice quickly, since he had decided to remove the restrictions of area and weapons if the war had to be continued." Notes by Andrew Goodpaster of a meeting between Johnson and Eisenhower, February 17, 1965, from the LBJ Library, Austin TX, and copy furnished by Charles F. Brower IV.

12

CHOOSING PROGRESS

EVALUATING THE "SALESMANSHIP" OF THE VIETNAM WAR IN 1967

Gregory A. Daddis

THE WEATHER IN DALLAS, TEXAS, on November 19, 1967, was a pleasant 55 degrees, ideal for a National Football League game. Under a strong performance by quarterback Sonny Jurgensen, who threw four touchdown passes, the Washington Redskins held off a late comeback by the rival Cowboys, winning 27–20. Far from the Cotton Bowl stadium that Sunday, the US ambassador to South Vietnam and the top American military commander there appeared on NBC's *Meet the Press*. In the Redskins' hometown, the two senior officials offered their assessment of a war apparently mired in stalemate. Ambassador Ellsworth Bunker, contesting such notions, believed his South Vietnamese allies were making "excellent progress" toward democracy while his uniformed counterpart, Gen. William C. Westmoreland, found "an attitude of confidence and growing optimism" wherever he traveled throughout the war-torn country. "We are making progress," the general affirmed. Asked about the possibility of a reduced American presence given such developments, Westmoreland foresaw "within two years or less that we will be able to phase-down the level of our military effort, which means that we could reduce the number of people involved." Viewers that Sunday morning likely would have concluded the war was being won.[1]

Less than three months later, countrywide attacks by the combined forces of the North Vietnamese Army and the National Liberation Front swept across South Vietnam. The Tet Offensive, launched in late January 1968, not only ravaged the southern population but also brought sharp condemnation from the American press. Westmoreland and Bunker were painted as accomplices in a year-long campaign, run by the White House, to sell the war at home. Though allied forces thwarted the offensive, Tet exposed a yawning credibility gap that seemingly turned most Americans, even respected CBS correspondent Walter Cronkite, against the war. Either senior officials in Vietnam were "truly blind" to the circumstances facing them or, worse, they had been purposefully misleading the public. Journalist David Halberstam believed "the American military apparatus in Vietnam became a vast lying machine, telling Washington what Washington wanted to hear and insisted upon hearing. The purpose of this lying machine was to propagandize our alleged progress in the war and to convince Congress and the American public to support the war."[2]

Yet were these senior war managers acting unethically by publicly highlighting the positive aspects of American strategy in Vietnam to minimize the war's political costs? Were they violating the public trust? Based on numerous assessment metrics, one could legitimately portray progress in South Vietnam: The enemy was stalemated on the battlefield, at least from a military standpoint; economic and social development programs were growing in scope and emphasis; the Army of the Republic of Vietnam was increasingly supporting rural pacification plans; and nation-building efforts were ongoing.[3] Certainly the US Military Assistance Command, Vietnam (MACV) needed to assess more than just attrition of enemy forces given Westmoreland's mission of helping build a viable, independent, and noncommunist South Vietnam. In a war without front lines, demonstrating progress proved daunting. Chairman of the Joint Chiefs of Staff Earle G. Wheeler concluded in early 1967 that the Lyndon Johnson administration "should be doing everything possible now to gain the support of U.S. and international public opinion for our position in Vietnam." Thus, to serve the nation's interests, Wheeler and others—including the president—focused public attention on American accomplishments in Vietnam while simultaneously cautioning the war was far from over.[4]

The confidential, back-channel messages between senior officials in 1967, however, proved more forthcoming than their public pronouncements. Perhaps this disparity between public and private comments, what *New York Times* reporter James Reston called a conversation gap, should not surprise.[5] If wartime assessments appeared contradictory in the uncertain mosaic of Vietnam, was it wrong to accentuate the positive in public when private messages were less sanguine? How Johnson administration officials transmitted information and to whom seemed vital for maintaining domestic support in a war where vital national interests were not clearly at stake. Moreover, by 1967 the media had become the "primary battlefield," according to one foreign correspondent. In that critical year, discerning the truth preoccupied nearly all participants of the American war: the Johnson White House, the Pentagon and MACV headquarters, and major media outlets. At the center of this search for truth stood domestic public opinion. As the president and his war managers increasingly saw Vietnam as a "race between accomplishment and patience," publicizing progress became an integral part of the war.[6] Yet far from a unique case of bureaucratic dishonesty, the 1967 salesmanship campaign demonstrates the reality, even necessity, of conversation gaps when one is assessing progress in wars where the military struggle abroad matters less than the political one at home.

THE WHITE HOUSE AT WAR

By early 1967 senior officials reviewing the war in Vietnam offered a measured outlook for the coming year. Assistant Secretary of State William Bundy believed the prognosis for 1967 "was not comforting." One general officer judged the enemy to be "hurting" but did not think "we're anywhere near the mopping-up stage." (American deaths in the year's first half averaged more than eight hundred per month, validating such claims.)[7] Even Lyndon Baines Johnson (LBJ), hoping to extol American progress in Vietnam for an increasingly skeptical home front, found little to applaud during his State of the Union speech on January 10. "I wish I could report to you that the conflict is almost over," the president remarked. "This I cannot do. We have more cost, more loss, and more agony. For the end is not yet. I cannot promise you that it will come this year—or come next year." For a president less than candid about the war's expanding costs, the speech struck a somber tone. While Johnson spoke of the need to keep sustained pressure on the enemy, he asked Americans for their patience, "a great deal of patience."[8]

Patience, however, seemed to be running out. In January *Time* reported growing doubts that "America's vital interests are sufficiently threatened in Viet Nam to necessitate the growing commitment there."[9] One month later, Senator Robert F. Kennedy (D-NY) broke with Johnson over Vietnam policy, and in March, civil rights champion Martin Luther King Jr. joined the antiwar movement. Even a personal note to Ho Chi Minh and a halt to US bombing of North Vietnam merely left LBJ with sinking approval ratings. In short, the costs of war, now running $20 billion annually, were threatening not only the president's Great Society programs but his political authority as well.[10] Johnson had to plug the dike before a flood of antiwar sentiment upended what had become the centerpiece of US foreign policy. Senior officials consequently required fresh assessments to sustain their case for continuing the American-dominated conflict and, ostensibly, upholding the country's prestige and honor abroad. Making the case for progress—and continued patience and sacrifice—thus focused increasingly on manufacturing domestic support.

Unquestionably the White House placed pressure on military officers to help generate this support. These same officers, however, recognized the importance of public opinion. Adm. Ulysses Sharp, head of US Pacific Command, wrote the Joint Chiefs in December 1966 that the "American people can become aroused either for or against this war. . . . It's up to us to convince our people that there is an end in sight and that it is clearly defeat for Hanoi."[11] Despite pressures to feed into this public relations campaign, Westmoreland, copied on Sharp's message, offered a subdued assessment two months later. In February 1967 the MACV commander summarized Hanoi's strategy as "a practical and clever one designed to continue a protracted war, inflict unacceptable casualties on our forces," and to "establish a favorable political posture." In March the general admitted, "Military success alone will not achieve the U.S. objectives in Vietnam."[12] Little in these official messages, meant only for Westmoreland's superiors, suggested victory was near. Certainly the general was in a conflicted position. He had to show progress for maintaining support of an increasingly contentious war, but he also realized this "conflict of strategic political attrition" would not be concluded quickly. Westmoreland thus had to justify America's investment in Vietnam while admitting the United States was in for a long war.[13]

Translating official reports for public consumption became ever more important to Johnson, whose approval ratings on Vietnam were slipping. In late March the president flew to Guam to confer with Westmoreland, Bunker, and South Vietnamese leaders. Johnson highlighted advances in pacification and revolutionary development programs, declaring upon his arrival that the allies were meeting "in a time of progress."[14] In private meetings with the president, however, Westmoreland struck a sober tone. He noted "serious problems" in the area around Saigon, the continuing infiltration of North Vietnamese forces into the south, and Hanoi's unbroken will. As the general recalled, he indicated it was possible the "war could go on indefinitely."[15] Asking for an "optimum" reinforcement of 200,000 troops, Westmoreland stressed the difficulties ahead. Johnson thus softened his rhetoric before departing Guam. "I think we have a difficult, serious, long, drawn-out, agonizing problem that we do not yet have the answer for," the president noted. "We think that our military situation is considerably strengthened."

The day after Johnson's remarks, the *Los Angeles Times* seemed unconvinced: "The prospects, in sum, are for more of the same."[16]

For proof of a strengthened military position, LBJ called Westmoreland home in April for the first of several public appearances in 1967. Against the backdrop of an antiwar Spring Mobilization march scheduled for mid-month, MACV's commander pressed Johnson in closed-door meetings for more troops. "With the troops now in country, we are not going to lose," Westmoreland argued, "but progress will be slowed down. This is not an encouraging outlook, but it is a realistic one." Sustaining public support drove the general's concerns. Westmoreland feared that in this protracted conflict, attrition of political will at home mattered just as much as attrition of enemy forces in Vietnam.[17] Speaking at the Associated Press's annual meeting in late April, he acknowledged that he did "not see any end to the war in sight," yet as long as Americans remained determined, the war still could be won. While the *Washington Post* hailed the "admirably forthright report," critics latched onto Westmoreland's contention that the enemy saw "protest as evidence of crumbling morale and diminishing resolve" at home. By disparaging legitimate dissent, Senator Thruston B. Morton (KY-R) argued, the general was only adding to the controversy. Johnson's plan to silence critics by bringing MACV's commander home had backfired.[18]

Westmoreland generated further debate when addressing a joint session of Congress on April 28. Carefully avoiding the word "victory," he cited heavy enemy combat losses, an increasing number of defectors rallying to Saigon's South Vietnamese government (GVN), and progress within the South Vietnamese Army ranks as evidence of forward momentum. Though the speech was "warmly received," according to the *Washington Post*, Westmoreland "made no converts to the policies he is carrying out in Vietnam."[19] In fact, critics pointed to the general's unprecedented call home to endorse an ongoing war as proof that Johnson's Vietnam policy was plagued with inconsistencies. Senator George McGovern (D-SD), believing Westmoreland's visit aimed to stifle criticism, proclaimed that deepening US involvement in Vietnam represented "the most tragic diplomatic and moral failure in our national experience." Senator J. William Fulbright (D-AR), chairman of the Senate Foreign Relations Committee, thought from a military standpoint Westmoreland's speech was fine. But he disagreed with Westmoreland, remarking that "the point is the policy that put our boys over there." While numerous congressional leaders and editorial writers sided with Westmoreland in the following days, Johnson's aim of mobilizing domestic support was coming up short.[20]

Moreover, concerns among the president's inner circle over reinforcements and a potentially expanding war surfaced in mid-May. For more than a year,

Secretary of Defense Robert McNamara had been privately questioning American strategy in Vietnam. In February he openly described the limitations of the US bombing campaign against North Vietnam. Then on May 19 he drafted Johnson an honest, if not anguished, critique of Vietnam policy. There was "rot in the fabric" of South Vietnamese society, McNamara opined. Pacification efforts were faltering, corruption was widespread, and the population remained apathetic to the war's outcome. Hanoi's resolve, meanwhile, was far from broken. Challenging Westmoreland's request for additional troops, McNamara argued the "war in Vietnam is acquiring a momentum of its own and that must be stopped."[21] In short with unresolved GVN deficiencies, Americans would achieve nothing more than a stalemate. As McNamara asked long after the war, "If the South Vietnamese government, such as it was, could not gain and keep its people's support and defeat the insurgents, could we do it for them?"[22]

While claims Saigon was not shouldering enough of the burden were unfair—anticommunist South Vietnamese had been fighting since Indochina's partition in 1954—contemporary assessments for President Johnson candidly depicted the political and military struggles inside South Vietnam. These faithfully presented reports rested on solid evidence, at least from their authors' perspectives. Even under pressure from LBJ, Westmoreland, McNamara, and other senior officials privately gave the president their honest appraisal of the war. The White House, though, still contended with flagging domestic support. Thus, when Westmoreland returned home in July for his mother's funeral, Johnson called a hasty news conference with Westmoreland, McNamara, and Joint Chiefs chairman Wheeler. While the president described both the successes and shortcomings in Vietnam, he was generally pleased with the progress being made. "We are very sure that we are on the right track." Taking a few questions, LBJ turned to Westmoreland and asked if he could briefly "touch on this 'stalemate' creature." In front of reporters, the general replied dutifully, "The statement that we are in a stalemate is complete fiction. It is completely unrealistic."[23]

BACK CHANNELS

Without question Westmoreland proved more candid with his confidential assessments and military advice. This private narrative demonstrated not only the war's complexity but also the general's concerns over a prolonged conflict. His concept of operations for 1967 highlighted MACV's primary mission to "support the Vietnamese government and its armed forces and coalesce the military efforts (and civilian efforts as appropriate) of the GVN and Free World Military Assistance Forces in defeating the Communist insurgents and aggressors from the North, expanding security in populated and productive areas, and encouraging and supporting all aspects of nation building."[24] Here was an immense task. When National Security Adviser Walt Rostow forwarded Westmoreland's concept to the president in January, he underlined several "unresolved problems" in the general's report. Among MACV's greatest concerns, none ranked more important than expanding security so pacification efforts could succeed. While acknowledging enemy difficulties, the general thought Hanoi probably would "continue his protracted war" well into 1967. No surprise then that at a high-level conference of GVN and American leaders in Guam, Westmoreland suggested, "As things stand now it may take ten years."[25]

MACV's chief problem remained one of accurately evaluating the war's progress to make such claims. Even assessing conventional operations such as Cedar Falls and Junction City proved nettlesome. Both campaigns, intended to destroy Communist forces and infrastructure, amassed high numbers of enemy killed and supplies captured. Four months after these operations ended, Ambassador Bunker reported that the "enemy has been badly hurt, has been kept off balance, and his time schedule has been disrupted." Westmoreland, though, tempered such optimism, informing Johnson that enemy forces had not been reduced because "heavy infiltration and continuing recruitment in the South were making up for battle casualties."[26] Body counts told only part of the story. Left unanswered was how these operations were impacting the enemy's political infrastructure and, as important, the civilian population. Correspondent Jonathan Schell, reporting on allied troops abusing civilians during Cedar Falls, questioned how an operation could be deemed successful when it had displaced nearly six thousand refugees from the local population.[27]

Equally difficult to ascertain was the willpower of Hanoi's leadership, ostensibly a key target of US military power in Southeast Asia. Relying on captured documents and prisoner interrogations, Westmoreland could only guess at Hanoi's intentions for 1967. MACV believed the enemy would seek a battlefield victory, "not with the intent to hold ground permanently, but rather to create a psychological shock designed to affect U.S. public opinion against continuation of the war, to bolster his own morale, or to improve his position for negotiation or further combat."[28] In truth Hanoi's Politburo heatedly debated its strategic options during 1967. While some party members advocated a diplomatic solution given the war's increasing costs, First Secretary Le Duan insisted upon seeking a decisive battlefield victory. Though the 1968 Tet Offensive would prove Westmoreland's earlier concerns prescient, he was unaware of any dissension within the enemy's camp.[29]

On the American side, debate over strategy proved more public and often centered on what critics perceived as an omission of essential facts on the war's progress. By early July newspapers were openly contesting official reports on Vietnam. Erwin Canham of the *Christian Science Monitor* supposed that "the American people have never been more discouraged about Vietnam than they are now," while Drew Pearson of the *Los Angeles Times* wrote of a "standstill in Vietnam."[30] As MACV officials reasoned they "must convince Washington that there is something more than stalemate in prospect," key questions remained. Who was the audience for public progress reports? Were they generated to provide political support for the White House? Did Westmoreland feel the need to be a public advocate for his own soldiers or to buoy morale inside South Vietnam and generate support for the Saigon government? Certainly airing doubts about the GVN and its armed forces called into question the war itself. Journalist Joseph Kraft, for instance, claimed that "in blaming the continuing war on American public opinion," MACV was covering up "the true failure in Vietnam," the South Vietnamese Army.[31]

Westmoreland was all too cognizant of the faltering public support, yet there is little evidence to suggest he changed his assessments, either publicly or privately, to help sell the war. When Wheeler asked the general in March to report on the bombing campaign's positive results, Westmoreland declined because he found scant evidence supporting a bright assessment.[32] This is not to say MACV was mired in pessimism as 1967 wore on. It was not. Monthly evaluations spoke of measured progress even if the enemy's determination remained unbroken. While MACV's June report admitted "little direct progress was achieved" in meeting the year's campaign plan goals, it otherwise hit an upbeat tone. Reporting on operations in July, Westmoreland spoke of increased enemy losses, progress in revolutionary development programs, and how units of the Army of the Republic of Vietnam were "continuing to improve in all areas." The general's civilian counterparts agreed. Ambassador Robert Komer, head of MACV's civil operations branch, wrote the president in July that "at long last we are slowly but surely winning [the] war of attrition in [the] South."[33]

Of course, optimism had purpose. As foreign policy experts Leslie Gelb and Richard Betts have argued, positive news "was seen as a job well done; bad news represented failure. Moreover, optimism bred optimism so that it was difficult not to continue it."[34] Whether cultural—Americans generally value performance—or organizational, senior military leaders were hesitant to share their personal doubts in public. Westmoreland, for example, was serving not only as the chief advocate for his president's war in Southeast Asia but also as the head of a military organization expected to defeat a Third

World country's military forces. Yet the general also knew full well that over-optimism destroyed the credibility of his predecessor, Gen. Paul Harkins. Thus, Westmoreland approached the press carefully. As journalist Ward Just recalled, MACV's commander "never predicted when the war would end, nor would he forecast the end of the beginning or the beginning of the end, or when the corner would be turned or if, indeed, there was a corner."[35] As such, the very definition of "winning" seemed perpetually open to interrogation.

Making matters worse, the question "How are we doing?" remained a mystery in 1967. Staffs from multiple agencies—MACV, the Central Intelligence Agency (CIA), the US Agency for International Development—counted hundreds of metrics but never achieved consensus on the vector of progress. Was it moving in a positive, upward direction or not? The sheer complexity of tasks required by Westmoreland's comprehensive strategy made any assessment difficult. MACV's concept involved denying enemy infiltration into South Vietnam, securing the population, opening roads and waterways, fighting the enemy's main forces, blocking an invasion, and supporting revolutionary development programs.[36] These tasks were related, yet progress in one area did not guarantee progress elsewhere. A successful search-and-destroy operation, for instance, might create refugees, an outcome that undermined pacification efforts. One CIA report suggested the "ideal would be a single 'Dow Jones' index of how the war is going, but such an index is not currently feasible." No wonder reporters in late summer began speaking of the "ever-widening gap" between the assessments of senior officials and lower-echelon field commanders.[37] The war's interactive, and thus fluid, nature between Washington, Hanoi, and Saigon meant few could agree on the war's true rate of progress.

Senior Washington officials certainly received mixed messages from Saigon. Even during John F. Kennedy's administration, single reports contained internal contradictions on the political and military struggle inside South Vietnam. Little had changed by 1967. Conflicting views flooded the White House, some from individual advisers. The secretary of defense noted "substantial progress" in military operations, yet he conceded there was "not equivalent progress in the pacification program."[38] In fact, McNamara was a prime example of publicly communicating a positive picture while expressing deep-seated concerns in private. In July the secretary proclaimed, "More progress had been made in the Vietnam war in the last nine months than in the previous six years." Yet to the president, McNamara advised that "continuation of our current course of action in Southeast Asia would be dangerous, costly, and unsatisfactory to our people." By late summer, however, Johnson felt incapable of changing course. Rather than reconcile the competing interpretations of what many believed was a stalemated war, LBJ decided upon a more forceful public relations campaign to convince Americans the war was being won.[39]

Ambiguous evidence, however, failed to support such claims. The so-called order of battle controversy, coming to a head in mid-1967, demonstrated the problems of gaining consensus on the evolving war.[40] In open view of the administration, the CIA and MACV bitterly debated including "irregulars"—local self-defense units—in the overall number of enemy forces. Deputy MACV commander Creighton Abrams believed incorporating these figures "in an estimate of military capabilities is highly questionable. These forces contain a sizeable number of women and old people. They operate entirely in their own hamlets." If Abrams missed the potential for such irregulars contributing to the war effort, he clearly understood the risks of adding these figures into official estimates. The general argued that MACV had been "projecting an image of success over the recent months, and properly so."[41] If irregular forces were included in the enemy's order of battle, the press reaction would be potentially damaging, Abrams maintained. Though an honest disagreement with the CIA, rather than press concerns, drove MACV estimates, the controversy clearly revealed the obstacles to gaining consensus on the question "how are we doing?"

In reality deliberations unfolding in backchannel messages, often beyond public view, suggested the impenetrability of what largely, if not exclusively, was a Vietnamese problem. In the end the entire US mission in Vietnam rested on how well the Americans were supporting the development of a legitimate, stable GVN. In this crucial aspect of strategy, Westmoreland and others expressed their deepest concerns. Field commanders found it difficult to gain the trust of the population while Johnson's advisers believed "most Vietnamese are politically inert."[42] A congressional trip report insisted the concept of pacification was "based on the dubious premise that Government control results in political loyalty," and thus "reports of progress in pacification continue to be misleading." Even Robert Komer, a perpetual optimist, recalled the destabilizing presence of US forces: "If we pushed too hard, we would end up collapsing the very structure we were trying to shore up."[43] For a president believing his Vietnam policy under siege, there seemed little choice but to push hard from a public relations standpoint. And push hard he did.

MANAGING THE MESSAGE

As the summer of 1967 wore on, disparate assessments of the war seemed the new norm. The American public read some news reports hailing progress as other journalists used words such as "quagmire" to describe Vietnam. A late July Gallup poll found 52 percent of the nation disapproved of Johnson's handling of the war, yet earlier in the year, the number of Americans favoring a "total military victory" rose by more than 10 percent. The president might argue his critics were misinformed, but LBJ stood partly to blame. As special counsel to the president Harry McPherson recalled, Johnson "sent out confusing signals to the public. We must win; but 'victory' was not our goal. The men of Hanoi were the enemies of freedom and democracy . . . but our ultimate purpose was to make peace with them."[44] Thus, not only did the goals appear contradictory but the momentum toward achieving them did as well. How could Westmoreland, for instance, be making progress yet requesting reinforcements? Though senior military leaders railed against "immature, naïve, and hostile" correspondents in Vietnam, journalists more often reflected, rather than constructed, the concerns of perplexed Americans.[45] At best the United States was making only incremental progress in Vietnam, clearly not enough to bolster domestic support.

Worse for Johnson, those following the war increasingly considered the administration's official assessments misleading. MACV was partially at fault. Leaders such as Westmoreland were unable to articulate, based on the mosaic of Vietnam, what success looked like in 1967. As Komer wrote the president: "The whole trouble with analyzing this peculiar war is that it is so fragmented—so much a matter of little things happening everywhere—that the results are barely visible to the untrained eye."[46] Perhaps unsurprising the Joint Chiefs chairman wrote Westmoreland in early August about his concerns regarding the war. Wheeler thought MACV should "prepare a precise, factual, non-generalized case to explain why we are making progress rather than facing a stalemate in Vietnam." Westmoreland responded by accusing "a vocal segment of the news profession" of "equating a lack of major combat operations such as Cedar Falls and Junction City with a stalemate at best, or a loss of the initiative on our part at worst. Nothing could be farther from the truth." Rather than censor the press—the command would pay "a terrible price for it"—Westmoreland instead increased his number of news conferences and strove "to talk personally with more newsmen and to take as many as possible on field trips with us."[47]

The message, however, seemed only to sour. On August 7 the *New York Times* printed R. W. Apple's story, "Vietnam: Signs of Stalemate." (Of note, the same day US Army chief of staff Harold K. Johnson sensed a "smell of success" in every major area of the war.) Apple doubted progress because the president, the week before, had authorized an additional forty-five thousand to fifty thousand men to be sent to Vietnam. "Victory is not close at hand," the journalist claimed. "It may be beyond reach."[48] Apple's article immediately attracted the Joint Chiefs' attention, with Wheeler writing Westmoreland of his disappointment that senior MACV officers had been "disloyal" by feeding the story with pessimistic evaluations.[49] The White House also took note. Though not directly responding to the *New York Times* piece, the administration established a Vietnam Information Group in August to better coordinate the information campaign. This quick reaction team would seize opportunities to "strike a positive note" and break out of the "siege mentality" overshadowing public relations. Still two weeks after Apple's story ran, the president was fielding questions on whether the United States had reached a stalemate in Vietnam. LBJ dismissed the charge as "nothing more than propaganda."[50]

Clearly, though, accusations of stalemate had rattled the administration. On September 27, Rostow cabled Westmoreland, Bunker, and Komer and urgently requested "sound evidence of progress." Senior military officials, however, were already complying. In mid-August, upon returning from South Vietnam, US Army chief of staff Johnson held a news conference in which he declared "significant progress being made" everywhere he went. Less than a month later, the general gave an interview to *U.S. News & World Report*. "From the Army's No. 1 officer comes one of the most encouraging appraisals yet on the Vietnam war," the news magazine exclaimed. In the interview, Johnson lauded the "forward movement everywhere" in South Vietnam. "We are very definitely winning," the general professed.[51] Internal reports from Westmoreland seemed to bolster such claims even if they hedged on the propinquity of overall victory. MACV evaluations highlighted the enemy losses, the nationwide elections held September 3, and the "emergence of an effective Vietnamese ground force." Though noting "limited progress in pacification programs," Westmoreland enumerated significant objectives being accomplished that fed the public relations campaign.[52]

Even if MACV's upbeat assessments rested on sound evidence—senior military officials believed so—the overall message gained little traction at home. Though Maj. Gen. Winant Sidle, Westmorland's information chief, blamed the media for an "inaccurate and often misleading picture of the U.S. war effort," few news stories in 1967 reflected journalists' personal biases either for or against the war.[53] Accepting the administration's positive messages, however, grew increasingly difficult, especially as draft increases brought the war to more homes. And though most voters steered a middle course on the topic of Vietnam, those leading public discourse had progressively taken sides. In the process, the president struggled to satisfy either side of the debate. While "hawks" demanded greater action to end the "crisis of indecision," the October 21 march on the Pentagon, organized by the National Mobilization

Committee to End the War in Vietnam, laid bare the antiwar movement's growing influence. Despite the White House publicity campaign, Americans increasingly found it difficult to reconcile requests for sacrifice abroad to support a war that seemed stalemated at best, unjust at worst.[54]

By November LBJ's inner circle grasped the full weight of public opinion burdening US foreign policy in Southeast Asia. Walt Rostow reported McNamara's concerns that any advances over the next fifteen months would neither lead to peace nor "convince our people that major progress has been made and there is light at the end of the tunnel." Undersecretary of State Nicholas Katzenbach wrote Johnson on the crucial element of time: "Can the tortoise of progress in Viet-Nam stay ahead of the hare of dissent at home?" The undersecretary even suggested the possibility of losing the war in the United States.[55] Still when Johnson convened the "Wise Men," a group of elder statesmen, early that month, he heard few dissenting voices. Gen. Omar Bradley felt the "need to raise patriotism." Career ambassador Robert Murphy urged the White House to orchestrate a "hate complex directed at Ho Chi Minh similar to Hitler." Rostow reiterated his theme of "guiding the press to show light at the end of the tunnel." As the meeting concluded, the advisers almost unanimously recommended staying the course in Vietnam.[56]

Johnson then called Westmoreland and Bunker home to offer yet another progress report. Senior officers in Saigon realized the president's motives. Lt. Gen. Bruce Palmer Jr. recalled, "It was obvious Westmoreland was being used for political purposes."[57] Two days after his appearance on *Meet the Press*, MACV's commander gave his most important public remarks of the year at the National Press Club in Washington. Dutifully conforming to the president's wishes, Westmoreland offered a laundry list of indexes denoting progress, all of which rested on a truthful accounting of allied accomplishments. The press, however, latched onto fourteen words: "We have reached an important point when the end begins to come into view." Westmoreland defended the statement, saying it was conceivable within two years to turn over more of the war to Vietnamese armed forces.[58] But critics saw the speech as little more than performance art supporting the president's hard sell on Vietnam. Even Westmoreland predicted that the final phase of his strategy "will probably last several years."[59] Such qualifications did little to convince doubters the stalemate had been broken.

As Westmoreland returned to Saigon, the chief doubter within the administration broke ties with Johnson. On November 29 Robert McNamara, secretary of defense since early 1961, accepted the presidency of the World Bank. McNamara's pessimism only grew as the war dragged on. In truth as early as November 1965, in the aftermath of the first US battles inside the

Central Highlands' Ia Drang Valley, the secretary's confidence in helping transform South Vietnamese society had been gradually evaporating. As the White House ramped up its public relations campaign in 1967, the defense secretary dissented increasingly with his commander in chief. "I had come to the conclusion," McNamara recalled, "that we could not achieve our objective in Vietnam through any reasonable military means, and we therefore should seek a lesser political objective through negotiations."[60] Although Johnson's own doubts grew as well, the public relations campaign seemed finally to be yielding limited results. Despite most Americans still disapproving of LBJ's handling of the war by a large margin, a Harris poll at year's end found that 63 percent of those asked "favored escalation over curtailment of the military effort."[61] Low approval ratings and McNamara's departure may have shaken the president but not enough to derail his plans to continue the war.

As 1967 drew to a close, the "conversation gap" seemed as wide as ever. David Halberstam offered a gloomy outlook in *Harper's* magazine, depicting Vietnamese society as "rotten, tired, and numb." Official pronouncements proved more cheerful. At the Association of the US Army's annual meeting in December, Harold K. Johnson offered "clear and concrete evidence of progress": the improving morale and performance of South Vietnamese forces, the prevention of a major enemy offensive across the demilitarized zone, and the food shortages within the enemy camp. Westmoreland called 1967 a year of "great progress," though once more he qualified the good news by admitting he saw no evidence the enemy strategy would change in the coming year.[62] Internal MACV assessments struck a similarly confident tone yet equally acknowledged the limits of US advances. For instance, MACV reported only a 3 percent increase of population under GVN control for the entire year. Westmoreland conceded that the insurgency's political infrastructure "persists as a significant influence over portions of the population." Inadequate South Vietnamese leadership, in both quality and quantity, remained a problem.[63] Few of these concerns, however, surfaced in public. In retrospect, the year's final pronouncements of progress offered the American home front only selective evidence to continue supporting the Johnson administration's policies in Vietnam.

CONCLUSION: EXPECTING A CONVERSATION GAP?

When the Tet Offensive broke in late January 1968, the conversation gap transformed suddenly into a visible credibility gap. As one member of the House Committee on Foreign Affairs asked, "How . . . could the Tet offensive have occurred if things were going so well?"[64] In part the answer could be found in President Johnson's need to maintain support for Vietnam, thus setting a kind of moral trap for senior military leaders given the tradition of American civil-military relations. Westmoreland never acted out of dishonest motives even if he was not completely forthcoming in public. As he recalled in his memoirs, he would have been "out of bounds" if he sought to alter policy through his public statements.[65] Thus, the larger national commitment to South Vietnam became *the* rationale for accentuating the positive. Yet as signs of progress became less compelling, the White House's—and to a large extent, Westmoreland's—conversation about the war became less convincing as the country became more polarized. As the war persisted, the problem of strategic assessment and the pressure to demonstrate progress became more acute. In the process, critical observers wondered aloud if there was some bureaucratic veil behind which the real truth lay.

It seems plausible that senior leaders such as Westmoreland were not simply concealing bad news but may also have been struggling to understand, even make sense of, larger trends in the war. This all raises important questions. What are our expectations of senior civilian and military leaders being candid in wartime? Veteran correspondent Malcolm Browne believed few: "Honest reporting is the last thing most people want when the subject is war."[66] Thus, should we expect those in high office, along with their military commanders, to acknowledge assessment problems, to be somewhat ambiguous, especially in limited wars like Vietnam? Should we expect a conversation gap? As historian George Herring has remarked, the "central problem of waging limited war is to *maintain* public support without *arousing* public emotion" (italics in original). Clearly Johnson had failed at this delicate balancing act. By the end of 1967, with the US troop presence in Vietnam nearing a half million and with American soldiers killed in action surpassing nine thousand, few among the intended audience believed the war was being won. Perhaps the perceived justness of their cause deluded Johnson's war managers into accepting their own optimistic assessments.[67] Nonetheless, there remained a thread of honesty within the larger quilt of wishful thinking.

All humans, of course, are subject to self-deception, and one cannot dismiss the primacy of politics in war. Is it inevitable, though, that public persons shade the truth? If so, is it possible to do so while maintaining one's moral compass? Officers such as William Westmoreland and Harold K. Johnson no doubt withheld the *full* truth because they believed it would prevent some future harm to the war's overriding objective of creating an independent, noncommunist South Vietnam. But politics as they were in the Johnson administration tended to create these ethical dilemmas. In a modern war without front lines, it was difficult, if not impossible, for military leaders to inoculate themselves sufficiently against political pressures to sell their president's war.[68] Thus, they felt compelled to help shape the changing reality of what was an exceedingly complex war. By remaining obedient to political authority, uniformed leaders had to construct a reality, based on selective interpretation of the facts, that justified continued sacrifices in a protracted political-military struggle.

In a large sense, there is a timelessness to this dilemma of the serving officer who must speak to multiple audiences about the progress of a less than existential war without visible decision points and identifiable conventional campaigns. In the Vietnam War the rhetoric of strategic assessment often blurred the reality of back-channel appraisals. It seems important then to appreciate the vague, if not imprecise, language used to publicly assess the progress of protracted wars. Such language arguably requires the public to question the relation of truth to any larger wartime assessment. The problems posed by the murky situation in Vietnam also illustrate the dangers of overselling progress in wartime assessment. The credibility of a government, and its senior civilian and military officials, is a precious commodity that is difficult to restore once it begins to slip. A lack of confidence in higher officials' statements leads, almost inexorably, to a lack of faith in a nation's military power itself. Perhaps this is the true dilemma of strategic assessment in complex wars without front lines. Unlike football, it isn't always clear who is winning and losing.[69]

NOTES

1. The most accessible transcript of the full *Meet the Press* episode, November 19, 1967, can be found at "Different General, Different War, Same Words: Westmoreland on Vietnam, Petraeus on Iraq," *Salon*, September 13, 2007, http://www.salon.com/2007/09/13/westmoreland_petraeus/.

2. Cincinnatus, *Self-Destruction: The Disintegration and Decay of the United States Army during the Vietnam Era* (New York: W. W. Norton, 1981), 111. See also Affidavit of David Halberstam, April 20, 1984, B-210, Folder 42, Box 01, Larry Berman Collection (*Westmoreland v. CBS*), Vietnam Archive, Texas Tech University, Lubbock (hereafter cited as TTUVA).

3. Headquarters, US Military Assistance Command, Vietnam (USMACV), Monthly Evaluation Reports: January 1967, 3, 12; February 1967, 5; March 1967, 3, US Army Military History Institute, Carlisle Barracks PA (hereafter cited as MHI). See also Lyndon Baines Johnson, *The Vantage Point: Perspectives on the Presidency, 1963–1969* (New York: Holt, Rinehart and Winston, 1971), 257–58; and Scott Sigmund Gartner, *Strategic Assessment in War* (New Haven: Yale University Press, 1997), 137.

4. Wheeler to McNamara, February 27, 1967, in US Department of State, *Foreign Relations of the United States*, vol. 5, *Vietnam, 1967* (Washington DC: Government Printing Office, 1996), 207 (hereafter cited as *FRUS*). See also Lawrence R. Jacobs and Robert Y. Shapiro, "Lyndon Johnson, Vietnam, and Public Opinion: Rethinking Realist Theory of Leadership," *Presidential Studies Quarterly* 29, no. 3 (September 1999): 599–601.

5. James Reston, "Washington: The Conversation Gap on Vietnam," *New York Times*, July 14, 1967.

6. Robert Elegant, "How to Lose a War: Reflections of a Foreign Correspondent," *Encounter* 57, no. 2 (August 1981): 73; and Don Oberdorfer, *Tet!* (Garden City NY: Doubleday, 1971), 78.

7. Bundy in William Conrad Gibbons, *The U.S. Government and the Vietnam War: Executive and Legislative Roles and Relationships*, part 4, *July 1965–January 1968* (Washington DC: Government Printing Office, 1994), 527; the general quoted in Jack Foisie, "Outlook in Vietnam: Slow, Costly Progress," *Los Angeles Times*, January 8, 1967; and Gerard J. DeGroot, *A Noble Cause? America and the Vietnam War* (Harlow, Essex: Longman, 2000), 157.

8. Lyndon B. Johnson, *Public Papers of the President of the United States* (Washington DC: Government Printing Office, 1968), 1:12. See also George C. Herring, *LBJ and Vietnam: A Different Kind of War* (Austin: University of Texas Press, 1994), 139; and Robert Dallek, *Flawed Giant: Lyndon Johnson and His Times* (New York: Oxford University Press, 1998), 449.

9. "Youth Questions the War," *Time*, January 6, 1967, 22; and Brandon Rottinghaus, "Following the 'Mail Hawks': Alternative Measures of Public Opinion on Vietnam in the Johnson White House," *Public Opinion Quarterly* 71, no. 3 (Autumn 2007): 367–91.

10. Melvin Small, *Antiwarriors: The Vietnam War and the Battle for America's Hearts and Minds* (Wilmington DE: Scholarly Resources, 2002), 58–59; Robert Mann, *A Grand Delusion: America's Descent into Vietnam* (New York: Basic Books, 2001), 531; Johnson, *Vantage Point*, 252–53; and Oberdorfer, *Tet!*, 81.

11. Sharp to Wheeler and Westmoreland, December 24, 1966, Folder 8, Box 4, Official Correspondence, Series I, W. C. Westmoreland Collection, MHI.

12. Assessment of the Enemy Situation, February 23, 1967, Box 6, Paul L. Miles Papers, MHI; and Westmoreland to Sharp, March 18, 1967, *FRUS*, 255.

13. Gibbons, *U.S. Government*, 530; and Affidavit of David Halberstam, April 20, 1984, B-219, TTUVA.

14. Johnson, *Public Papers*, 1:127; Larry Berman, *Lyndon Johnson's War: The Road to Stalemate in Vietnam* (New York: W. W. Norton, 1989), 33–34; and Frank L. Jones, *Blowtorch: Robert Komer, Vietnam, and American Cold War Strategy* (Annapolis: Naval Institute Press, 2013), 124–25.

15. William C. Westmoreland, *A Soldier Reports* (Garden City NY: Doubleday, 1976), 260; Working Notes on US Delegation Session of Guam Conference, March 21, 1967, *FRUS*, 274–77; and "The Other War in Vietnam—a Progress Report," March 24, 1967, Box 7, Robert M. Montague Papers, MHI.

16. Johnson, *Public Papers*, 1:132; "The Guam Meeting and After," *Los Angeles Times*, March 22, 1967; and Lloyd C. Gardner, *Pay Any Price: Lyndon Johnson and the Wars for Vietnam* (Chicago: Ivan R. Dee, 1995), 358.

17. Notes on Discussions with President Johnson, April 27, 1967, *FRUS*, 350; Charles DeBenedetti, *An American Ordeal: The Antiwar Movement of the Vietnam Era*, with Charles Chatfield (Syracuse: Syracuse University Press, 1990), 163; Berman, *Lyndon Johnson's War*, 34–35; and Charles F. Brower IV, "Strategic Reassessment in Vietnam: The Westmoreland 'Alternate Strategy' of 1967–1968," *Naval War College Review* 44, no. 2 (Spring 1991): 28.

18. David S. Broder, "Westmoreland Says Protests Encourage Enemy in Vietnam," *Washington Post*, April 25, 1967; "No End in Sight," *Washington Post*, April 25, 1967; Morton quoted in Westmoreland, *A Soldier Reports*, 274; Robert J. Donovan, "Westmoreland Visit Backfires on President, Arouses Critics," *Los Angeles Times*, April 28, 1967; and John Prados, *Vietnam: The History of an Unwinnable War, 1945–1975* (Lawrence: University Press of Kansas, 2009), 189.

19. Richard L. Lyons, "Westmoreland Is Warmly Received, Makes No Converts," *Washington Post*, April 29, 1967; Tom Wicker, "Westmoreland Tells Congress U.S. Will Prevail," *New York Times*, April 29, 1967; and "Illogic of Escalation," *New York Times*, April 29, 1967.

20. McGovern quoted in Mann, *Grand Delusion*, 537; Samuel Zaffiri, *Westmoreland: A Biography of General William C. Westmoreland* (New York: William Morrow, 1994), 195; Fulbright in Westmoreland, *A Soldier Reports*, 278; and William M. Hammond, *Reporting Vietnam: Media and Military at War* (Lawrence: University Press of Kansas, 1998), 100.

21. McNamara to Johnson, May 19, 1967, *FRUS*, 437; Berman, *Lyndon Johnson's War*, 45; Dallek, *Flawed Giant*, 458; Gibbons, *U.S. Government*, 626–27; and MACV Commander's Conference, May 21, 1967, Box 5, Paul L. Miles Papers, MHI.

22. Robert S. McNamara, *In Retrospect: The Tragedy and Lessons of Vietnam* (New York: Times Books, 1995), 275.

23. Joint News Conference, July 17, 1967, Folder 10, Box 08, Douglas Pike Collection: Unit 01—Assessment and Strategy, TTUVA; "A Program against the VC Infrastructure," July 27, 1967, Box 4, Richard M. Lee Papers, MHI; and General Westmoreland's Military Assessment for July, August 11, 1967, Folder 14, Box 07, Larry Berman Collection, TTUVA.

24. Westmoreland to Sharp, Strategy and Concept of Operations for 1967, 8, Historian's Files, US Army Center of Military History, Fort McNair, Washington

DC (hereafter cited as CMH). See also Gregory A. Daddis, *No Sure Victory: Measuring U.S. Army Effectiveness and Progress in the Vietnam War* (New York: Oxford University Press, 2011), 109.

25. Rostow to Johnson, January 26, 1967, *FRUS*, 62; Westmoreland to Sharp, January 2, 1967, *FRUS*, 8; and Gardner, *Pay Any Price*, 358.

26. Bunker to Johnson, June 21, 1967, 3, Folder 23, Box 01, Veteran Members of the 109th Quartermaster Company Collection, TTUVA; Westmoreland in Johnson, *Vantage Point*, 259; and Westmoreland to Sharp and Wheeler, February 17, 1967, Historian's Files, CMH.

27. Schell in Hammond, *Reporting Vietnam*, 84; Gibbons, *U.S. Government*, 542; and Robert Buzzanco, *Masters of War: Military Dissent and Politics in the Vietnam Era* (New York: Cambridge University Press, 1996), 279.

28. COMUSMACV to JCS and CINCPAC, Assessment of the Enemy Situation, February 23, 1967, 2, Historian's Files, CMH.

29. Lien-Hang T. Nguyen, *Hanoi's War: An International History of the War for Peace in Vietnam* (Chapel Hill: University of North Carolina Press, 2012), 76, 81, 90.

30. Erwin D. Canham, "Summer of Discouragement," *Christian Science Monitor*, July 11, 1967; and Drew Pearson, "The Standstill in Vietnam," *Los Angeles Times*, July 20, 1967. Robert J. Donovan also reported on the "gloomy mood about the war" in Washington. See "Pessimism over Vietnam War Outcome Rises in Washington," *Los Angeles Times*, July 9, 1967.

31. Komer to Westmoreland, June 19, 1967, *FRUS*, 524; and Joseph Kraft, "The Organization General," *Washington Post*, May 3, 1967. See also Jonathan Randal, "Vietnam's Army: Sometimes It Only Seems to Fight," *New York Times*, June 11, 1967; Hammond, *Reporting Vietnam*, 87–88; and Heintges to Westmoreland, April 21, 1967, Box 6, Paul L. Miles Papers, MHI.

32. Hammond, *Reporting Vietnam*, 97; Brower, "Strategic Reassessment in Vietnam," 26; and Westmoreland, *A Soldier Reports*, 273.

33. Komer in Graham A. Cosmas, *MACV: The Joint Command in the Years of Escalation, 1962–1967* (Washington DC: Center of Military History, 2006), 439; and Headquarters, USMACV, Monthly Evaluation Report, June 1967, 3, MHI. See also COMUSMACV Monthly Assessment, August 11, 1967, in Robert E. Lester, ed., *The War in Vietnam: The Papers of William C. Westmoreland* (Bethesda MD: University Publications of America, 1993), History File I, Folder 20, Reel 10 (hereafter cited as WCWP).

34. Leslie H. Gelb with Richard K. Betts, *The Irony of Vietnam: The System Worked* (Washington DC: Brookings Institution, 1979), 309.

35. Ward Just, *To What End: Report from Vietnam* (1968; repr., New York: Public Affairs, 2000), 77; Cosmas, *MACV*, 443; and Loren Baritz, *Backfire: A History of*

How American Culture Led Us into Vietnam and Made Us Fight the Way We Did (Baltimore: Johns Hopkins University Press, 1985), 51.

36. Westmoreland to Wheeler, October 30, 1967, Policy/Strategy File, Box 6, Paul L. Miles Papers, MHI; and Richard H. Moorsteen, Trip Report (April 25–May 6): The Big Picture, Folder 96, State of the War: September 1967 Assessment, Thomas Thayer Papers, CMH.

37. CIA Preliminary Report of Data Task Force, October 26, 1967, Folder 86, War Indicators SVN, Thomas Thayer Papers, CMH; and Hal Humphrey, "Different Picture of Vietnam War," *Los Angeles Times*, August 28, 1967.

38. Robert S. McNamara remarks, July 5, 1967, Folder 07, Box 07, Larry Berman Collection (Presidential Archives Research), TTUVA; and Gelb and Betts, *Irony of Vietnam*, 300.

39. Bruce Piggott, "McNamara Sees Surge in Viet War's Progress," *Washington Post*, July 10, 1967; Johnson, *Vantage Point*, 372; Gibbons, *U.S. Government*, 843; Gartner, *Strategic Assessment in War*, 141; and Edward J. Drea, *McNamara, Clifford, and the Burdens of Vietnam, 1965–1969* (Washington DC: Historical Office of the Secretary of Defense, 2011), 214–17.

40. Sam Adams, "Vietnam Cover-Up: Playing War with Numbers," *Harper's* 250, no. 1500 (May 1975): 41–73; James J. Wirtz, "Intelligence to Please? The Order of Battle Controversy during the Vietnam War," *Political Science Quarterly* 106, no. 2 (Summer 1991): 239–63; Cosmas, *MACV*, 446–61; and Daniel O. Graham, *Confessions of a Cold Warrior* (Fairfax VA: Preview Press, 1995), 54.

41. Abrams to Wheeler, Sharp, and Westmoreland, August 20, 1967, Folder 3, Box 6, Official Correspondence, Series I, W. C. Westmoreland Collection, MHI. For the CIA's views, see Carver to Helms, September 11, 1967, *FRUS*, 772–74. See also McNamara, *In Retrospect*, 240–42.

42. Brig. Gen. Frank Linnell, interview, October 25, 1967, VNIT Folder 104, CMH; and McPherson to Johnson, June 13, 1967, *FRUS*, 494.

43. R. W. Komer, *Bureaucracy Does Its Thing: Institutional Constraints on U.S.-GVN Performance in Vietnam* (Santa Monica: RAND, 1972), 32; and John V. Tunney, *Measuring Hamlet Security in Vietnam: Report of a Special Study Mission* (Washington DC: Government Printing Office, 1969), 2.

44. Harry McPherson, *A Political Education: A Washington Memoir* (Boston: Houghton Mifflin, 1988), 394; Dallek, *Flawed Giant*, 452, 474; William L. Lunch and Peter W. Sperlich, "American Public Opinion and the War in Vietnam," *Western Political Quarterly* 32, no. 1 (March 1979): 25, 30; and Johnson, *Public Papers of the President*, 1:311.

45. Notes on Meeting with the President, July 13, 1967, *FRUS*, 613.

46. Komer to Johnson, October 4, 1967, *FRUS*, 861; William Tuohy, "There Are No Certainties in Vietnam," *Los Angeles Times*, January 8, 1967; and Walter

Lippman, "Gen. Westmoreland's Task: Explaining the Viet War," *Los Angeles Times*, April 30, 1967.

47. Wheeler to Westmoreland, Johnson, August 2, 1967, Folder 1, Box 6, Official Correspondence, Series I, W. C. Westmoreland Collection, MHI; Westmoreland to Wheeler, August 2, 1967, Folder 29, Box 01, Veteran Members of the 109th Quartermaster Company Collection, TTUVA; and Notes on Meeting with the President, July 13, 1967, *FRUS*, 613.

48. R. W. Apple Jr., "Vietnam: Signs of Stalemate," *New York Times*, August 7, 1967; "U.S. Army Chief Finds 'Smell of Success,'" *New York Times*, August 7, 1967; and Rostow to Johnson, August 1, 1967, *FRUS*, 653.

49. Wheeler to Westmoreland, August 8, 1967, Folder 32, Box 01, Larry Berman Collection (*Westmoreland v. CBS*), TTUVA.

50. Herring, *LBJ and Vietnam*, 143; and Johnson, *Public Papers of the President*, 2:358.

51. Rostow to Bunker, September 27, 1967, Folder 07, Box 22, Larry Berman Collection (Presidential Archives Research), TTUVA; Wheeler to Westmoreland, Johnson, and Sharp, August 11, 1967, Folder 29, Box 01, Veteran Members of the 109th Quartermaster Company Collection, TTUVA; Harold K. Johnson, Report on Vietnam, August 12, 1967, in *Weekly Compilation of Presidential Documents* 3, no. 1 (Washington DC: Government Printing Office, 1967), 1141–44; "End of Vietnam War in Sight?," *U.S. News & World Report*, September 11, 1967, 44–48; and Berman, *Lyndon Johnson's War*, 86.

52. Westmoreland to Wheeler, August 25, 1967, Folder 6, Box 21, Series I Official Correspondence, W. C. Westmoreland Collection, MHI; Achievement of Objectives, August 29, 1967, History File July 6–August 3, 1967, Folder 19, Reel 10, WCWP; and Bunker to Johnson, October 10, 1967, Folder 03, Box 02, Veteran Members of the 109th Quartermaster Company Collection, TTUVA.

53. Sidle in Gibbons, *U.S. Government*, 845; Daniel C. Hallin, "The Media, the War in Vietnam, and Political Support: A Critique of the Thesis of an Oppositional Media," *Journal of Politics* 46, no. 1 (February 1984): 12, 19; and Daniel C. Hallin, *The "Uncensored War": The Media and Vietnam* (New York: Oxford University Press, 1986), 140–41.

54. Small, *Antiwarriors*, 75–76; and Robert Shaplen, "Viet Nam: Crisis of Indecision," *Foreign Affairs* 46, no. 1 (October 1967): 110.

55. Rostow to Johnson, November 2, 1967, *FRUS*, 971; and Katzenbach to Johnson, November 16, 1967, Folder 19, Box 02, Veteran Members of the 109th Quartermaster Company Collection, TTUVA.

56. Berman, *Lyndon Johnson's War*, 97–101; and Hanson W. Baldwin, "Vietnam War Evaluation Being Made for Johnson," *New York Times*, November 15, 1967.

57. Bruce Palmer Jr., *The 25-Year War: America's Military Role in Vietnam* (Lexington: University Press of Kentucky, 1984), 75.

58. William C. Westmoreland, Progress Report, November 21, 1967, National Press Club, Washington DC, Speech File Service, WCWP; Westmoreland, *A Soldier Reports*, 284–85; and Zaffiri, *Westmoreland*, 246–47.

59. Westmoreland quoted in George C. Wilson, "War's End in View—Westmoreland," *Washington Post*, November 22, 1967; Ward Just, "President's Hard-Sell on Vietnam," *Washington Post*, November 26, 1967; and "Optimists Have Their Say," *New York Times*, November 26, 1967.

60. McNamara, *In Retrospect*, 313; and Prados, *Vietnam*, 207, 215.

61. Mann, *Grand Delusion*, 568; and Herbert Y. Schandler, *The Unmaking of a President: Lyndon Johnson and Vietnam* (Princeton NJ: Princeton University Press, 1977), 59.

62. David Halberstam, "Return to Vietnam," *Harper's* 235, no. 1411 (December 1967): 49; "Vietnam—Progress or Stalemate?" *Army Digest* 22, no. 12 (December 1967): 7; "Westmoreland Calls 1967 Year of Progress," *Los Angeles Times*, December 27, 1967; and Lewis Sorley, *Honorable Warrior: General Harold K. Johnson and the Ethics of Command* (Lawrence: University Press of Kansas, 1998), 270.

63. USMACV Quarterly Evaluation Report, December 1967, 4–6, MHI; and Westmoreland's 1967 End of Year Report, Folder 95, Thomas C. Thayer Papers, CMH.

64. Tunney, *Measuring Hamlet Security*, 1.

65. Westmoreland, *A Soldier Reports*, 273.

66. Browne quoted in Susan A. Brewer, *Why America Fights: Patriotism and War Propaganda from the Philippines to Iraq* (New York: Oxford University Press, 2009), 228.

67. George C. Herring, "'Cold Blood': LBJ's Conduct of Limited War in Vietnam," in *An American Dilemma: Vietnam, 1964–1973,* ed. Dennis E. Showalter and John G. Albert (Chicago: Imprint Publications, 1993), 72; Stanley Karnow, *Vietnam: A History* (New York: Viking Press, 1983), 512; Jacobs and Shapiro, "Lyndon Johnson," 606; and Dallek, *Flawed Giant*, 456.

68. Brower, "Strategic Reassessment in Vietnam," 35.

69. My thanks to David Frey, Richard H. Kohn, Paul Miles, and Alex Roland for their invaluable comments on these concluding paragraphs.

PART III: CURRENT CASES

13

ASSESSING COUNTERINSURGENCY

THE IRAQ WAR, 2004–5

William C. Hix and Kalev I. Sepp

FROM ITS ESTABLISHMENT IN 2004, the US-led Multinational Force in Iraq fought a counterinsurgency campaign shaped by an expanding series of independent yet complementary political and military assessments and personally directed by the general in charge of the campaign. After the invasion in the spring of 2003 had concluded and the occupation had been established, an insurgency grew. An unexpected battle for control of Iraq had started. Gen. John Abizaid, the senior American military commander in the Middle East, considered how to best organize and direct the Coalition forces to deal with the increasingly violent Iraqi resistance to the presence of foreign troops. As the beleaguered Combined Joint Task Force–7, headed by a lieutenant general, transitioned into the new Multinational Force–Iraq (MNF-I), Abizaid decided that he needed a four-star theater commander in Iraq who could do what a three-star general and a corps headquarters could not.

On May 20, 2004, the chief of staff of the US Army surprised his deputy, Gen. George W. Casey Jr., with the news that the president of the United States had personally chosen him to command the new MNF-I.[1] Casey was to take charge of the force on July 1, which was only forty-two days away. He immediately began his preparation by studying the most crucial documents to frame the objectives and processes he would assess to measure progress and success. They included United Nations Security Council Resolution (UNSCR) 1546, approved on June 8, 2004; the US National

Security Presidential Directive of May 11, 2004; and President George W. Bush's Army War College speech of May 24, 2004.[2]

In addition Casey interviewed officials in all the major departments and agencies of the US national government, particularly the Departments of Defense and State, and in the intelligence community. He reviewed letters exchanged between Secretary of State Colin Powell and United Nations secretary-general Kofi Annan. These letters and UNSCR 1546 established a UN-approved timeline for implementing agreed-on activities in Iraq and provided the basis of the desired political end state for Iraq.

Also important, Casey and John Negroponte, the incoming US ambassador to Iraq, consulted each other on their shared way ahead before they departed separately for Baghdad. Just before assuming command of MNF-I on July 1, Casey spoke directly to President Bush and his advisers by video teleconference from Baghdad. He told the president that in thirty days, he would report his assessment of the situation in Iraq and his initial plans. Casey enunciated four priorities:

1. "develop an integrated counterinsurgency plan,"
2. "develop a plan for the formation of ISF [Iraqi Security Forces],"
3. "build the consultative and coordinating mechanisms with the IIG [Iraqi Interim Government]," and
4. "complete the transition of military support from the Coalition Provisional Authority to the Embassy."[3]

Immediately after taking command, Casey received direct guidance from General Abizaid, who was also overseeing the theater of combat operations in Afghanistan. Casey then toured Iraq for a month to interview the military chiefs who reported to him and to visit the units in his force. The MNF-I then comprised 162,000 troops from thirty-three countries, principally in US Army, US Marine, British, and Polish divisions.[4]

In close cooperation with Negroponte, Casey formulated an initial assessment of the situation in Iraq that included their mutual views of the insurgents, the capacity of the US and Coalition militaries, and the viability of the new Iraqi government and security forces. At an early commanders' conference, Casey announced his initial assessment-based decisions. First, the ongoing campaign planning, begun before his arrival, would continue. Second, he and Negroponte agreed to create a Red Team of American and British military, intelligence, and diplomatic corps members.[5] This team was to help unify the Coalition's understanding of its mission and to independently evaluate the emerging campaign plan. Casey gave the team thirty days to accomplish this task.[6]

The Red Team completed its assessment in early August 2004, providing Casey and Negroponte a picture of a dangerous and growing Sunni rejectionist insurgency. It also furnished the basis for a joint mission statement for both the MNF-I and the US Embassy and their common objective: "To help the Iraqi people build a new Iraq, at peace with its neighbors . . . and deny Iraq as a safe haven for terrorists."[7] The political, security, and economic tasks that would be necessary to achieve this goal required delineation and integration. Casey turned to his MNF-I staff and the Red Team, which was vetting the campaign plan, to direct and coordinate all his subordinate organizations toward this end.

Beginning earlier in the summer of 2004, while Combined Joint Task Force–7 was still managing operations in Iraq, British Army Col. Andrew Sharpe worked to deliver a campaign plan for the Coalition forces to counter what was now unmistakably an insurgency. The US Central Command's staff augmented the Red Team's contributions with the results of a war game conducted at the forward headquarters at Camp As Sayliyah near Doha, Qatar. Casey, who closely studied each page of the plan, ordered its issue on August 5, 2004. This campaign plan focused on countering a multifaceted insurgency and for the first time provided a coherent vision for setting the conditions necessary to achieve the objectives of the Coalition and the United Nations as outlined in UNSCR 1546. The plan addressed four major activities, doctrinally named lines of operation: security, governance, economic development, and communications. It informed the structure of all operations, placing them in a framework where their purpose was driven not by reaction to the enemy but by objectives defined by the Coalition and aimed at realizing strategic purposes that were focused on the Iraqi people and key political outcomes.

Even as elements of the MNF-I began to implement Casey's directive, Muqtada al-Sadr's Shia Mahdi Army in Najaf was violently challenging both the new MNF-I command and the Iraqi Interim Government. Casey concurrently ordered a critical assessment of the campaign plan he had just approved. Asking, "Where is my COIN guy?" ("COIN" being the spoken acronym for counterinsurgency), Casey sought to more fully develop the counterinsurgency components of the campaign to accomplish the MNF-I's objectives in Iraq. Among these goals, of immediate and principal importance was preparing the disorganized Iraqi army and police to provide security at the balloting stations during their national elections, scheduled for January 2005, to ensure widespread voter participation.[8] This task would shortly fall to a new staff section designed to conduct assessments.

Even though Negroponte had joined Casey in assessing post-invasion Iraq, writing a joint mission statement, and endorsing the new campaign plan, the

MNF-I and embassy staffs did not subsequently work to synchronize their efforts. They differed significantly on resource allocation, economic development priorities, and engagement with the disaffected Sunni population. Coincidentally the first major operational test of the re-formed Iraqi armed forces came when intense fighting broke out in the city of Najaf. For three weeks in August 2004, US Army and Marine units, along with Iraqi army troops, fought house to house until they forced al-Sadr's Shia rebels to surrender their weapons and abandon the town. However, the rapid and successful reconstruction effort in Najaf, effected through contracts with Iraqi construction companies, could not be repeated after subsequent urban battles. Strictly interpreting legislated restrictions on expenditures of Iraq Relief and Reconstruction Funds, US Embassy staffers set obstructive constraints on the use of relief monies intended to rebuild Iraq's devastated infrastructure. It drove senior military commanders to personally knock on doors in the Republican Palace–*cum*–US Embassy in Baghdad and lobby State Department officers for funds for civic projects.

These intramural frictions added to Casey's press for a new look at the initial campaign plan, and this time he focused on the conduct of operations to suppress the Iraqi insurgents. He split the Strategic Political-Military Division of his headquarters staff in two—a new "Pol-Mil" directorate to work directly with the US Embassy and another designated as the deputy chief of staff for strategy, plans, and assessment (DCS-SPA). Maj. Gen. Steve Sargeant (USAF) headed "the Spa," as it was universally called. Known informally as the "Keeper of the Campaign Plan," Sargeant was already assembling a group of strategists, drawn principally from the faculty of the US Air Force Academy in Colorado Springs.[9] Sargeant's strategy section was soon headed by Col. William C. Hix (USA), a recent member of the Operation Iraqi Freedom Joint Lessons Learned team. To supplement his own counterinsurgency expertise, gained during a Special Forces assignment in Asia, Hix recruited Dr. Kalev I. Sepp, a former Special Forces officer and professor of defense analysis at the Naval Postgraduate School in Monterey, California. Regardless of their individual assignments in the SPA, all of the officers—an economist, a psychologist, a mathematician, a historian, and political scientists—would engage in the next round of assessments.

The DCS-SPA assessments proceeded separately from and parallel but not subordinate to the new Commander's Assessment and Synchronization Board, established by the initial campaign plan and intended to both assess and oversee the plan's execution. The board initially met each month, but to ease the staff's workload, the meetings were later held once every two months.[10] Both efforts applied metrics to the ongoing military campaign, in terms of progress and failures, while also polling the Iraqi population for opinions on events and tracking levels of violence. At the outset, these endeavors did not provide viable data for assessment. American and European polling techniques were alien and uncomfortable to Iraqis, and they had to be extensively amended to garner responses. Reporting on violence from the multiplicity of Coalition military units was irregular and inconsistent. Some battle-hardened patrol leaders used their personal sense of what constituted a significant combat action and wouldn't report some shootings or bombings. In other cases, untrained or undermanned staffs simply failed to gather and report the information.

It was apparent to Casey this effort to understand the fundamental requirements for a successful counterinsurgency effort in Iraq required a better assessment process. By the autumn of 2004, he had a well-qualified interdisciplinary assessment team in his Strategy Division. Hix led the team in laying out an assessment framework, including key metrics for success derived from a study of previous counterinsurgencies. To this end, he also consulted Dr. Stephen T. Hosmer and Dr. Bruce Hoffman of the RAND Corporation, both well-regarded experts in analytical methods, particularly in terrorism and insurgency studies. At the beginning of large-scale US military involvement in the Vietnam War, Hosmer had chaired RAND's landmark 1962 Symposium on Counterinsurgency that evaluated recent insurrections in Malaya, Algeria, South Vietnam, Kenya, and the Philippines, among others. Several of the best-known practitioners of this kind of warfare were present, including Charles Bohannan, Napoleon Valeriano, Frank Kitson, David Galula, Edward Lansdale, and Sam Wilson.[11] Hix now asked the same questions Hosmer had raised to the symposium members forty-two years before: "How do you measure whether or not you are winning a counterguerrilla struggle? What are the precise factors to be included in a yardstick? What weight would you give, for example, to numbers of casualties or to the incident rate of terrorism and guerrilla attacks? What are the most significant measurements?"[12] Forty-two years later, Hix found these questions were still valid.

Hix saw it was necessary to determine first what tasks had to be done to prosecute a successful counterinsurgency and, second, what metrics should be employed to assess how well the responsible units carried out those tasks. To delineate the tasks, Sepp developed a historical analysis of as many counterinsurgencies as he could reference to derive what Hix, using a business school term, called "best practices in counterinsurgency."[13] Hix then turned to Hosmer for selecting the measurements of success and failure in counterinsurgency operations. Based on the historical assessment and consultations with Hosmer, among others, Hix initially settled on five: violence, information, propaganda and politics, casualties, and popular opinion.

- Violence—Was armed violence increasing or decreasing? Was the violence principally acts of random terrorism and uncoordinated attacks? Were there indicators of more organized operations? Was the object of the violence aligned with the insurgents' declared charter for the violence? More sophisticated strikes would seem to signal growing confidence among insurgents and increasing popular support for them. However, terrorism focused on the population would not necessarily reflect a lack of insurgent capacity or organization.

- Information—Was the population freely giving information on insurgents and their activities to the army and police? If so, it would indicate popular confidence in the Coalition forces and, more important, in the Iraqi security forces to protect them and to win the contest for control.

- Propaganda and politics—What was the response or compliance of the local population to insurgent propaganda? Did insurgent propaganda influence popular behavior toward the Iraqi government and Coalition, or did it manipulate the outcomes of political events, such as elections? It would suggest whether political choices offered to various political and demographic groups, including pro-government and antigovernment constituencies, were aligned either with the insurgents or with the Iraqi government and the associated campaign plan's objectives. Also the forecasted outcomes could be evaluated against the capabilities and preparations of security forces to respond to them as necessary.

- Casualties—Did the enemy have the ability to control its losses? That is, did the insurgents incur casualties in operations they chose to conduct—for example, ambushes, attacks on police stations, suicide bombings—or did they lose fighters as a result of operations initiated by the Coalition and Iraqi security forces? If the insurgents' losses were due to government and Coalition reactions to operations the insurgents undertook, it would indicate that they were taking the initiative and could plan for and recruit replacements for their anticipated casualties. If government and Coalition attacks caused their losses, it would mean they had been forced onto the defensive, or into a position of physical, political, and psychological disadvantage. It would concurrently indicate that the population was providing more information to the government than to the insurgents, leaving them with insufficient intelligence to take the initiative. It could also show if the ratios of security personnel to the population are effective.

- Popular opinion—What was the Iraqi population's view of the new government? It would reveal whether government support and security were being provided to the people and whether the population both required and desired to fulfill that role.

These best practices, measures of success, and resulting patterns of operation would frame much of the analysis conducted outside of the Commander's Assessment and Synchronization Board. Together they would offer a necessary and useful alternative perspective.

As this COIN-focused analysis developed, it was complemented by two other endeavors. First, the SPA recognized that the outcomes of the January 2005 election would influence the conduct of the Coalition's operations throughout that year. Maj. Tom Mowle (USAF), who holds a PhD in political science, led the effort to assess the upcoming election. He used interest-based political models to project possible election outcomes and to assess their impact on Coalition operations and the accomplishment of the UNSCR 1546 objectives.[14] As this effort matured, Casey heard its projections and directed that 2005 planning had to account for all the potential election outcomes and had to be structured to succeed whatever the elections produced.

Using demographic projections, Mowle foresaw the importance of securing the Sunni minority's participation in the election; however, this engagement was unsuccessful. Moreover, even given a successful election process, Iraqi political and operational momentum would almost certainly slow for three to four months as Iraqi political and sectarian groups struggled to form a government. This loss of political momentum, and the limited capacity of the resultant government, figured into the 2005 planning scheme. Other planning considerations included estimating the ability of the Iraqi Transitional Government to deliver security, to draft a constitution, and to hold both a constitutional referendum and a national election. Related issues included fostering reconciliation with armed opposition members and determining how soon the new government would be able to accept full governing responsibility in accordance with UNSCR 1546. This assessment informed the several requests to extend the UNSCR authorities beyond December 2005, and the United Nations eventually granted them.

In the second complementary endeavor, the SPA team assessed the conditions under which Coalition forces could begin to transition security responsibilities to the Iraqi government's military and police units. The political and institutional capacity of local and national Iraqi government leaders and their agencies counted as heavily as the abilities of the Iraqi armed forces. Reviewing the performance of Iraqi leaders and troops across the country, including the experience of the August 2004 battle for Najaf and the November combat in Fallujah, this assessment pointed to the importance of embedded advisers with the Iraqis and the potential to progressively transition from Coalition to Iraqi dominance in security operations.

As Casey approached his sixth month in command, he presented the initial summary of this ongoing counterinsurgency campaign assessment at his monthly commanders' conference. The staff used the COIN best practices, patterns of counterinsurgency, and metrics to provide an in-stride assessment of the effects of the campaign on the insurgency, to identify areas of risk, and to establish where to concentrate its efforts in preparation for the Iraqi election. The staff cited shortcomings, including limited Iraqi government capacity and economic progress, inadequate ratios of Coalition and Iraqi troops to the population, and varying security effects. Also of concern were the ability of the insurgents to replenish their ranks despite significant losses; uneven, sometimes ill-informed, and counterproductive engagements with the Iraqi population; and enduring popular dissatisfaction. The staff revealed that information garnered from the population and the nature of enemy losses were two areas inadequately assessed during much of the campaign to that point, but these measures potentially could provide the most accurate indications of operational success and failure. The SPA staff routinely updated this new assessment over the coming months and used it to frame planning options and decisions.

Casey decided to further complement the personal assessments he provided each month to the White House and Defense Department with yet another evaluation of the situation in Iraq. This mission fell in the DCS-SPA office to Col. Sandy Storrie, a British Army officer with extensive service in Northern Ireland and Africa. Casey deliberately chose a Brit for the job to ensure an assessment free of American command influence. Designated the campaign plan manager, Storrie set out to appraise the state of the ongoing campaign. Storrie interviewed civilian and military personnel across the Coalition and the Iraqi government and armed forces. He sought to discern where the MNF-I stood in the process of executing the campaign plan: what was known and not known, what was being done and left undone, and what was working and what was not. All this research was to inform a consideration of possible changes to the existing plan.

Storrie turned in a sharply candid assessment, which was distributed to senior US government and Coalition leaders. He voiced serious concern about the feeble Iraqi economy, bitter political rivalries debilitating Iraqi governance, and the disjointed Coalition efforts to rebuild the damaged and derelict Iraqi infrastructure. Storrie pointedly noted the shortcomings of the government support teams, holdovers from the since-disestablished Coalition Provisional Authority that had been managed by Ambassador Paul Bremer. These teams were supposedly crucial to reconstruction and were ostensibly a shared US State Department–Defense Department undertaking. Negroponte's US Mission staff had instead reduced their manning and had failed to fund and resource them adequately.

On the one hand, Storrie foresaw a strong turnout by Shia Iraqis in the upcoming January 2005 national elections; and on the other hand, he predicted the now-dispossessed Sunnis would sit out the ballot. It would occur, he felt, despite the increasingly successful suppression of the insurgents' resistance to the elections. In November and December 2004, two US Marine regiments, a US Army brigade, a British battalion, and several Iraqi battalions battled and defeated Sunni rebels in the Second Battle of Fallujah. This closed the city as a sanctuary and base for Sunni insurgents and, for the near term, broke their ability to disrupt the elections in Fallujah by armed attacks.

Storrie's assessment proved correct. While the elections proceeded with an unexpectedly high degree of calm, great voter participation, and Iraqi security force's presence, Sunnis eschewed the opportunity to help choose their new government. The success of the election process exposed their avoidance of political engagement as foolish, and paradoxically it made selecting a new chief executive for Iraq very difficult. The resultant internecine squabbling, posturing, and maneuvering ensured there was no coherent Iraqi political activity until May 2005, when Ibrahim al-Eshaiker al-Jaafari won the intramural contest for the prime ministry of the Iraqi Transitional Government.

Concurrently senior US and allied military commanders modified an MNF-I staff proposal to extend the tours of three US brigades until spring. They requested an additional brigade as a security hedge, to ensure the Iraqi political process could fully mature in the interim. Ultimately the entire proposal was disapproved. This lull in Coalition military action, while the Iraqi polity was distracted with wrangling over who would be in charge, allowed the three major insurgent groups—Shia, Sunni, and al-Qaeda—to recover. The ongoing MNF-I assessment processes anticipated the rise in violence during those months, and the increase in killings of Iraqi civilians in towns and cities signified the terrorists were establishing themselves there.

Informed by the COIN assessments and hard-won operational experience, Casey began building support for the establishment of an embedded adviser program. His intent was to improve the quality and effectiveness of Iraqi forces and to support them with Coalition intelligence assets and airpower. This effort formalized a variety of actions across the MNF-I and extended beyond the Iraqi army to include local, provincial, and national Iraqi police forces. As revealed in the best practices analysis, a functioning police force was a key factor to gaining stability. The MNF-I staff recognized the Iraqis' political sensitivity regarding their police and their presence in all Iraqi neighborhoods, and it led to a formal MNF-I agreement with the Iraqi government to create the Police Partnership Program.

By the spring of 2005, Casey perceived the principal enemy threat in Iraq was shifting from former regime members and Ba'ath Party diehards to more radical groups associated with the al-Qaeda terrorists. He based this observation on the assessment indicators he regularly followed, his frequent visits to his field commanders across Iraq, and his regular meetings with the leadership of the Joint Special Operations Command. This shift was also evidenced after the election by some 170 attacks employing car bombs and suicide bombers, the signature weapons of al-Qaeda and its partners. Casey stepped up operations, dubbed the Western Euphrates River Valley Campaign, along the Syrian border. They included moving the Third Armored Cavalry Regiment into western Nineveh Province, pushing Joint Special Operations Command and US Army forces into northern and western Anbar Province to counter al-Qaeda infiltration, and authorizing Special Forces and supporting agencies to expand their engagement of the Sunni tribes in western Iraq. When Casey first met with Prime Minister Jaafari after he assumed office, the general pressed him to take immediate action to protect Baghdad against this rising threat because of the city's central political, geographical, and cultural status in Iraqi society. Jaafari accepted Casey's counsel and ordered Iraqi forces to reinforce the capital.

About the same time, Casey directed a mid-year assessment of the campaign plan consistent with the work Storrie had done in December 2004. British Brig. Bill Kingdon, recently assigned as the new campaign manager, followed a similar pattern to Storrie's and consulted with Hix to ensure continuity. Kingdon's frank assessment noted several successes: There were no insurgent safe havens for the January elections, the development of Iraqi security forces was on schedule, and transition teams had enhanced the Iraqi security forces' capabilities. But he also noted several problems, including rising insurgent violence, lagging political inertia caused by the four-month-long delay in forming the Jaafari government, increasing threats to Baghdad, and growing Sunni disaffection. Moreover, they faced a very tight timeline for meeting UN-mandated Iraqi political goals. Given these factors, Kingdon's assessment set out four major objectives to attain by the end of 2005: contain insurgent violence, develop a constitution agreeable to the various factions, hold a constitutional referendum, and conduct elections in December 2005 and form a constitutional government. This assessment, as equally candid as Storrie's December 2004 report, was also submitted to the White House, the secretary of defense, and the Joint Chiefs of Staff without any modification by Casey or members of his MNF-I staff.

The Iraqi government assumed formal control of its army, numbering more than 110 battalions, in a ceremony on Iraq's Army Day. Casey wanted to place as much of the obligation for security as possible on those units and on the Iraqi political leadership. His goal was to have the Iraqis embrace the responsibility for their own country while simultaneously unburdening the MNF-I forces. Time was short. That summer veteran US and allied units were departing Iraq, and new units were arriving to replace them. Meanwhile, the Iraqis had to draft a new constitution over the summer of 2005, and they had to ratify it by a nationwide referendum that fall, only a few months away. Then the next round of national elections to choose a new prime minister for the post-interim government was to be held three months later, in December 2005.

To assess both the readiness of the MNF-I to support the electoral timeline and the state of the Iraqi units they were training, Casey resolved to examine all the division and brigade counterinsurgency operations across the entire Coalition. In similar fashion to his previous selection of a single officer for the campaign plan assessment, Casey chose two members of his staff—Hix and Sepp—to conduct a survey of his entire force.[15] The objective, he told them, was to gauge the ability of all units to conduct counterinsurgency operations. He charged his survey team, simply and clearly, to determine whether we were doing the right things and doing them well.

The two-person survey team had to first make a plan to gather evidence for the assessment they would eventually make. They asked each other, what do we measure? What will we and won't we assess and evaluate? What analytical tools do we use: a model, direct and/or indirect observation, or deductive reasoning? What are the aids and impediments to this sort of assessment, including political and bureaucratic considerations? What conceptual framework do we employ: theoretical (how to do counterinsurgency), practice (how is counterinsurgency executed), or assessment (how should counterinsurgency be done)? In terms of command guidance, Hix understood how Casey saw policy and political objectives, strategy, and assessments. To prepare his assessment questions, Hix consulted again with RAND's Hosmer. Sepp based his interview questions on his historical analysis of best practices in counterinsurgency, and Hix incorporated it into the latest campaign plan as an unclassified annex.[16] Also important, they would solicit the assessments of US and Coalition unit leaders on the state of training and readiness of the Iraqi units under their advisership.

For a full month that summer, beginning in July and into August 2005, Hix and Sepp gathered evidence for their report by visiting thirty-one brigades and battalions, as well as all headquarters in the borders of Iraq. Sandstorms and enemy action only briefly delayed their travels. From the metrics-based standpoint they developed, Hix and Sepp gauged the relative counterinsurgency performance of British, Polish, Salvadoran, US Army, and US Marine

Corps regular and reserve units, including the Army National Guard, and both conventional and special operations forces. To expedite the delivery of their report, Hix and Sepp continuously compared and integrated their evaluations as they traveled. Hix wrote out the key findings that emerged from each set of interviews, adding to and editing the analysis with each visit. Thus Hix was able to present the completed report to Casey within two days of the team's return to Baghdad.

The assessment, simply titled the "COIN Survey," made several striking observations. Chief among them was American units that had fought in Iraq in 2003 and 2004 and rotated out to their home bases in the United States were returning to Iraq without a clear understanding of how the MNF-I mission had changed. Instead of training for dispersed, small-unit security operations in cooperation with Iraqi forces to protect civilians, they had prepared for the same battle they had been fighting when they left more than a year earlier—that is, large-unit sweeps to clear urban areas and indiscriminately arrest all Iraqi males they encountered. Of the commanders and staffs visited, only about 20 percent had a firm intellectual and operational grasp on the effective conduct of a counterinsurgency campaign. A large middle group, about 60 percent, had varying degrees of understanding of the requirements this kind of warfare demanded, and they struggled to improve themselves. The operations of the remaining 20 percent of the units—Hix felt it may have been significantly more—were actually counterproductive to the MNF-I mission.

Broadly many units held avoidance of casualties as their leading priority, skewing a proper execution of the COIN fight, which sought to protect the Iraqi population from the emergent terrorist threat. Hix and Sepp found disconcertingly that almost all American commanders throughout the country confidently asserted that the Iraqi troops they advised would be fully trained and combat ready in six months, coincidental with the departure of their respective units. The American units before theirs had repeatedly made these same estimates and had been almost entirely wrong. This finding reflected a tendency on the part of almost all Coalition units to plan to the end of their tour rather than beyond their tour with an eye toward achieving long-range MNF-I objectives in their zones of operation.

In its conclusions, the COIN Survey also revealed a serious shortcoming in the development of Iraqi self-governance. Coalition commanders reported to Hix and Sepp that they had not been educated and prepared to provide assistance to the Iraqis to create and increase governing capability, which was essential to establishing a viable Iraqi state. Nor were the commanders provided specialized personnel and appropriate resources to help reconstitute Iraqi civil society in accordance with the UNSCR 1546 mandate. This pointed to the disconnection in purpose and cooperation in Baghdad between the MNF-I and the US Mission in the embassy. Among other issues, field commanders reported that regional security officers prohibited State Department personnel on the provincial reconstruction teams (PRTs) from leaving their fortified encampments to engage with the Iraqis. The regional security officers cited the bureaucratic rationale that the contract for private security companies to guard PRT members had expired, but they would not accept the protection offered by the same Coalition military units that the PRTs supported. At several executive levels, both civilian and military leaders did not comprehend the strategic centrality of establishing functional governance and the essential activities of civil society in Iraq. These factors would be key determinants in whether the MNF-I campaign plan would succeed in the long term. The COIN Survey concluded that Iraq would struggle with an armed insurgency for possibly ten years to come and would continue to require significant US assistance.

When the team returned to Baghdad at the end of August 2005, Hix presented the findings to Casey. He listened closely, taking in the mixed review of the force charged with carrying out his MNF-I campaign. Clearly many areas required attention, but of particular importance was the need to build functional governance. When Hix concluded his presentation, Casey reflected for a moment and then characteristically sought a second opinion. He turned to Sepp and asked, "What do you think? What would you do?" Recalling the Vietnam War–era Civil Operations and Revolutionary Development Support program, Sepp reinforced the idea that an imbalance favoring military operations over civil government would continue to feed the dissatisfaction that kept most Iraqis "on the fence." Further it was allowing the various insurgencies to survive, grow, and operate with little hindrance.

Within the MNF-I the assessments offered by the COIN Survey helped inform Casey's thinking on the next iteration of his campaign plan. Most notably he directed the formation of a counterinsurgency school for arriving Coalition units to educate them about the plan, their specific mission (often different from what they had been told by their stateside commanders), and right and wrong counterinsurgency tactics. Established at the Taji airfield, twenty miles north of Baghdad, and named the COIN Academy, the weeklong leaders' school for all officers and senior sergeants functioned under the directorship of a US Army Special Forces colonel, with a cadre of instructors. Casey was regularly the first speaker at each iteration of the COIN Academy's courses, so he could give the new unit members their mission orders personally.[17] Arriving in Baghdad in June 2005, the new American ambassador, Zalmay Khalilzad, found the COIN Survey reinforced the lessons of his

recent experience as ambassador to Afghanistan. It also matched the conclusions of another Red Team study that an independent civilian-military group
conducted to inform consultations between the ambassador and Casey as they
mapped out their updated mutual way ahead. Khalilzad understood the necessity of building the Iraqi capacity for governance at local levels, and he worked
with Casey to improve the operations of the provincial reconstruction teams.

In August 2005, Casey flew with his survey team to Camp As Sayliyah,
Qatar, where Hix presented a summary directly to General Abizaid and his
US Central Command senior staff. Many of Hix's insights did not surprise
Abizaid, but he remarked at length on the impact of insurgent violence on
the Iraqi population and Coalition forces, and the striking absence of viable
governance. The ensuing discussion raised the topic of initiating a program
in Iraq that was similar to the one used in Vietnam. Hix also pointed out
the increasing presence in Iraq of Iranian advisers and weapons—especially
advanced types of roadside bombs—supporting almost all insurgent factions.
Casey later mentioned the results of the COIN Survey during his congressional testimony in Washington, DC, declaring he could not meet all the objectives set down in the UNSCR 1546 that he was charged with accomplishing
in 2005. He engaged with senior officials in the Department of State and the
United Nations to have the dates extended, for the assessment affirmed that
it was unlikely his MNF-I could gain the required level of internal security
by the end of the year.

For all that effort, the COIN Survey seemed to have little impact outside
of Iraq. The assessment evaluated tactical and operational military matters
and pointed to the underpinnings of political success: an improving economy, a functioning government, and a stable civil society. These aspects of
counterinsurgency needed attention as much as the training of local police
and proper intelligence-gathering techniques; moreover, they required the
attention of the US government and that of the international partners of the
Coalition as well.

The COIN Survey was the last assessment presented to Casey in his first
year leading the war against the armed insurgency in Iraq. He had established
how much he valued and relied on assessments in making his decisions. How
he approached the assessment process was now evident to his staff. Casey
sought both formal and informal inputs. He often had several teams and individuals working on similar questions; sometimes they worked collaboratively,
but often they strove competitively. Hix observed that when their assessments
coincided, Casey took it as a strong indicator of necessary action. He set this
pattern in July 2004, with the cross-functional ad hoc Red Team assessing the
draft campaign plan along with the MNF-I joint and combined staff. After

approving the first campaign plan, he assessed it by employing a creation of the same plan, the Commander's Assessment and Synchronization Board, and Colonel Storrie's independent evaluation. The August 2005 COIN Survey was later compared to political and economic assessments made in the following months.

In the aftermath of the COIN Survey assessment, Casey tasked Hix to assess how long it would take to completely defeat the Iraqi insurgency. Hix amalgamated the results of more than a year of assessments and his more than two years of personal experience in the Iraq War. Once he returned to the United States, he added the benefit of perspective. He compiled a comprehensive assessment and forward projection of what was required to fully succeed. For this final assessment, he defined *defeat of the Iraqi insurgency* as an Iraqi population intolerant of violence perpetrated by insurgent, terrorist, and criminal groups. The people would cooperate with legitimate Iraqi authorities in ways that prevented those malign groups from using violence to disrupt daily life and to undermine the credibility and effectiveness of the Iraqi government. Those authorities in turn would maintain popular support by creating and sustaining conditions that allowed the Iraqi people to go about their normal lives—that is, by meeting popular expectations for security, well-being, independence, and economic opportunity.

Examining Iraq by means of best practices, measures of success, and patterns of COIN operations, along with evidence such as the World Bank's metrics of instability, Hix's final 2005 assessment concluded it would take another five to seven years to defeat the Iraqi insurgency and perhaps several years more. He factored in the insurgents' ability to sustain and escalate violence, the time needed to develop Iraqi capabilities, and the time required to mitigate issues that fueled ethno-religious factionalism and violence. The assessment considered inputs—that is, the level of effort to address the challenges facing Iraq—and outcomes, or the time required for those efforts to actually have an effect. Too often, inputs were measured and treated as progress, but the effort to achieve the defeat of the Iraqi insurgency had to be predominantly political with an appropriate security component, not the other way around. To make that defeat permanent, in Hix's assessment, would require an additional three to eight years of continued military, social, economic, and political engagement and investment to ensure Iraq was viable, stable, and productive. It was a tall order.

The conduct of the MNF-I campaign was informed by a series of independent but complementary political, military, and comprehensive assessments. In addition to Casey's personal assessments, he drew on a simultaneous stream of assessments from the staff of his subordinate Multinational Corps–Iraq and the Assessment Division of his DCS-SPA. For all the progress he managed in the first year of the war, Casey would later judge that his hardest year as commander in Iraq would begin in 2006–7, a full year after his assessment process had been functioning to his liking. As stated in his memoir of the war,

> I found that getting the assessment process to yield meaningful results—ones the Ambassador and I could act on—took a great deal of my personal effort. The tendency of a staff is to track the things that are most easily measured, not necessarily what is most critical. I finally found that if I forced the staff to answer the following three questions about each effect, I came closer to getting what I needed: What are we trying to accomplish? What will tell us if we are accomplishing it? How do we measure that? It took a year of trial and error before I was satisfied with the assessment process.[18]

Ten years after Gen. George Casey began assessing the war in Iraq, internecine violence—compounded by the intervention of powerful neighbors, criminal syndicates, and stateless terrorists—still wracked the country. At one time a thorough assessment process seems to have positively aided the senior military commander in the country in his decision making toward the objective of ending all the conflicts in Iraq. It remains to distinguish what factors and events confounded the attainment of that long-sought goal.

NOTES

The authors' personal notes are the sources for much of the information presented herein.

1. George W. Casey, *Strategic Reflections: Operation* Iraqi Freedom, *July 2004– February 2007* (Washington DC: National Defense University Press, October 2012), 5.
2. Ibid., 6.
3. Ibid., 20.
4. Ukraine, Australia, Portugal, Slovakia, El Salvador, Dominican Republic, and Honduras also had units in Iraq. Spain withdrew its brigade in April and May 2004.
5. At the start of 2004, Brig. Gen. Barbara Fast, the J-2 intelligence chief for CJTF-7, appointed Dr. Derek Harvey to lead a Red Cell to assess how the various resistance and insurgent elements operated against the Coalition. Thomas Mowle, ed., *Hope Is Not a Plan: The War in Iraq from Inside the Green Zone* (Westport CT: Praeger Security International, 2007), 65. Harvey's Red Cell continued its

work in the new MNF-I C-2 (Intelligence) section, providing analyses of the evolving threats.

6. Although the Red Team consulted Iraqis in its work, no Iraqis were on the Red Team itself. Casey, *Strategic Reflections*, 23.

7. Ibid., 27.

8. Ibid., 32.

9. Mowle, *Hope Is Not a Plan*, 8. The group's PhD-holding officers were nicknamed the Doctors Without Orders, a play on the name of the aid organization Doctors Without Borders. They were Col. Joyce Adkins, Col. Mike Davis, Lt. Col. Mike Fiedler, Col. Darrall Henderson, Maj. Mike Lewis, Maj. Tom Mowle, Lt. Col. Neal Rappaport, Lt. Col. Tom Ruby, and Dr. Kalev I. Sepp. All were US Air Force officers, save Henderson, who was from the US Army, and Sepp, a Department of the Navy civilian.

10. Casey, *Strategic Reflections*, 32.

11. Stephen T. Hosmer and Sibylle O. Crane, *Counterinsurgency: A Symposium, April 16–20, 1962* (1963; repr., Santa Monica: RAND, 2006), xi.

12. Ibid., 141.

13. Robert Kaplan, *The Insurgents: David Petraeus and the Plot to Change the American Way of Wars* (New York: Simon & Schuster, 2013), 104.

14. Maj. Tom Mowle, who specialized in the study of elections while on the faculty of the US Air Force Academy, predicted the results of the January 2005 Iraqi general elections sooner and more accurately than the MNF-I intelligence staff and its associated intelligence organizations did. His work highlighted the value of dedicated specialists in the assessment process.

15. In the event, two additional officers accompanied Hix and Sepp during part of their survey as observers. One was from the MNF-I C-2 section, and the other was from the Multinational Corps–Iraq headquarters.

16. With General Casey's permission, the US Army journal *Military Review* published Sepp's analysis, which was later translated into Arabic, Spanish, and Portuguese. Kalev I. Sepp, "Best Practices in Counterinsurgency," *Military Review* 85, no. 3 (May–June 2005): 8–12.

17. The Coalition command in Afghanistan subsequently created a counterinsurgency school of its own, using the Taji COIN Academy as its model.

18. Casey, *Strategic Reflections*, 32–33.

14

CIRCULAR LOGIC AND CONSTANT PROGRESS

IW ASSESSMENTS IN AFGHANISTAN

Alejandro S. Hernandez, Julian Ouellet,
and Christopher J. Nannini

AND IT OUGHT TO BE REMEMBERED that there is nothing more difficult to take in hand, more perilous to conduct, or more uncertain in its success, than to take the lead in the introduction of a new order of things. Because the innovator has for enemies all those who have done well under the old conditions, and lukewarm defenders in those who may do well under the new. This coolness arises partly from fear of the opponents, who have the laws on their side, and partly from the incredulity of men, who do not readily believe in new things until they have had a long experience of them.

Machiavelli

Terrorist safe havens, insurgencies, violent popular movements, and their ilk are symptoms of the failure of legitimate authority. In the modern international system, recognized states are expected to assert authority over their territory.[1] Where that ability is absent, the United States will sometimes get involved.[2] In the national security community, these symptomatic failures call for a set of specific policy options that generally fall under the umbrella of irregular warfare (IW).[3] When we assess IW campaigns, we acknowledge that improving legitimacy is a key goal. However, this can mean many different things. An emphasis on legitimacy may lead to a focus on building and enhancing democratic institutions, improving government administration, decreasing corruption, refining the criminal justice system, building schools, increasing access to food and water, and so on. Indeed, over the last decade-plus of war in Afghanistan and Iraq, these efforts have consumed hundreds of billions of dollars.[4] Hotly debated is whether the investment has been worth it, and directly related is the question of winning. Are we winning? What does winning look like? Is there a connection between improved government legitimacy and winning?

In 2009, facing an increasingly dire situation in Afghanistan, President Barack Obama undertook a strategy review and laid out principles for defining success: "Our overarching goal remains the same: to disrupt, dismantle, and defeat al Qaeda in Afghanistan and Pakistan, and to prevent its capacity to threaten America and our allies in the future. To meet that goal, we will pursue the following objectives within Afghanistan. We must deny al Qaeda a safe haven. We must reverse the Taliban's momentum and deny it the ability to overthrow the government. And we must strengthen the capacity of Afghanistan's security forces and government so that they can take lead responsibility for Afghanistan's future."[5]

These goals and objectives have remained relatively constant throughout the Obama presidency. At roughly the same time, and not coincidentally, the commander of the International Security Assistance Force (ISAF) determined that his force's assessment frameworks were inadequate and ordered a broad effort to improve assessments.[6] Since 2009 these strategic assessments have evolved and arguably improved. However, the same experts tasked with improving the assessments noted in a separate, independent report to Congress in 2014 that the Afghans will need a larger force than estimated and require Coalition assistance through at least 2018.[7] On the surface, it would appear that, given an ending mission and an enduring requirement for US efforts, assessments have improved while overall strategy has failed. At the very least, it would appear that success was not achievable in the time allotted.

Better assessments from the outset may have improved the chances of success, but it is just as likely that success on the scale desired was not possible in the first place. As one recent RAND Corporation's report states: "[G]iven the duration of most contemporary insurgencies and the length of time it typically takes to build state capacity or institutionalize mechanisms of political inclusion, the United States should enter into partnerships with the expectation that they will be long-term and have relatively low odds of success in the short-to-medium term."[8]

Put another way, the larger effort of building a stable and legitimate state falls outside the bounds of warfare as conventionally understood, and thus it likely exceeds our will to commit to the effort.[9] The RAND report's focus on state capacity and political inclusivity puts insurgencies squarely within the larger phenomenon of economic and political development; this is not a common approach within the assessment literature. More frequently assessment critiques focus on past wars, insurgencies, and assessments.[10]

We can critique strategic assessments in Afghanistan from two points of view. First, critiques of strategic assessments more frequently occur within the context of other IW assessments. Assessments are measured against each other. Second, less frequently, assessments are critiqued by fitting the conflict within the larger literature of economic and political development. Many well-researched articles have taken the first approach; this chapter focuses on the second.[11] In so doing, we hope to show that properly included in the planning process, assessments can inform a commander not only of a campaign's progress but also of what outcomes can reasonably be expected. This approach provides a more realistic sense of progress for all involved and improves the efficiency and effectiveness of data collection and analysis.

The next section briefly examines irregular warfare and existing doctrine on military end states. The subsequent section will review how the larger social, economic, and political development literature can inform our understanding of these end states. Next this chapter reviews some assessment models used in Afghanistan and concludes with recommendations to improve the strategic assessment process.

CONCEPTUAL UNDERPINNINGS

The struggles in Afghanistan and Iraq from 2002 to 2006 caused a broad rethinking of American strategy. A small group of military thinkers advocated new ideas about counterinsurgency, and concepts and doctrine began to evolve, leading most notably to the publication of Field Manual (FM) 3-24, *Counterinsurgency*, and the development of a broader joint operating concept for IW and a multitude of other concepts, doctrines, and directives.[12] The IW concept—under which counterinsurgency, counterterrorism, stability operations, unconventional warfare, and foreign internal defense all fall—emphasizes that IW is a fundamentally different form of conflict insofar as it is population centric and primarily concerned with indirect approaches. IW may emphasize elements of national power—such as diplomacy, economics, and information—more than traditional military power. The theoretical work of this period precipitated changes in approach on the battlefields and at headquarters, and some leading IW proponents went on to become the commanders of ISAF forces.

At the same time that population-centric warfare was becoming the dominant paradigm for our current conflicts, new technology facilitated an explosion in data collection and the requirement for analysis. Standard battlefield metrics were augmented with data collected from human terrain teams, public opinion surveys, new spatial statistics, social network analysis, and other advanced methods that had not been previously available.[13] These developments followed from the central organizing logic of IW, as espoused in "Irregular Warfare: Countering Irregular Threats, Joint Operating Concept, Version 2.0": "Since irregular warfare is a contest for legitimacy and influence over the relevant populations, the populations carry particular weight as both the battleground and object of the conflict."[14] But while twenty-first-century technological advances allowed massive data collection to measure progress in Afghanistan, they did not appreciably change the underlying ideas driving the collection and analysis of data. New analytical techniques were often radically divorced from the social science literature from which they were developed; thus assessments relied on new techniques and analysis in the service of old ideas.

As others have shown, many of the statistics now generated in great depth were also collected for other wars.[15] Similarly many of the ideas behind IW are lessons relearned from Vietnam and other conflicts, and new data did not necessarily improve efficacy or understanding. By the time Gen. John R. Allen took over as commander of ISAF, a drive to reduce the data flowing into strategic assessments was under way simply because of the possibility that the quantity of the data could create noise without much signal. In other words, aside from the quality and validity of the message produced, the effort required to obtain it was often overwhelming, and the staff found it difficult and time consuming, even in the best circumstances, to provide meaningful analysis for a commander's critical assessment of the campaign. However, while improvements in the assessment process significantly enhanced the quality of the information reaching the commander, these analytical products did not fundamentally affect the campaign. As Jonathan Schroden and others note, "Whether or not the assessment team has been involved in campaign or operations planning, the requirement to assess the plan's objectives remains."[16] While the revised assessment framework applied assessment standards, it did so without the context in which it could properly be judged. In a sense by judging war as a phenomenon unto itself, it graded the campaign on a curve. Success was judged outside the context of whether success was possible. The value of treating war as a social phenomenon is that a healthy body of social science literature exists to inform decision makers about what is or is not feasible in conflict resolution and political and economic development.

A curious puzzle emerged: Why did military leaders who had learned the lessons of past insurgencies and thoughtfully sought to improve and diversify the data they received continue to make assessments that overrepresented campaign progress? The answer reflects two key failings in the assessment process. First, in existing concepts and doctrine, the logic of IW is inherently tautological. In conventional war two parties in conflict eventually establish a new status quo, where, except in the case of annexation, the relationship is primarily structured upon the anarchic nature of the international system. In irregular war the parties in conflict must return to some system of governance. The object of the conflict is to decide the structure of the government. The population merely consents to one form of domination or another. To claim that the population is the object of the conflict either omits the centrality of government or presupposes democratic governance. The latter claim flies in the face of what most political scientists agree on regarding the likely stability of democratic governance in weak states; the former suggests that the IW concept never made complete sense in the first place.[17]

Second, the techniques for analyzing this human dimension were divorced from the body of knowledge that created them. During this period, military leaders recognized that the social sciences might be helpful to the war effort and thus went about hiring social scientists to support it. There was no corresponding effort, however, to understand how to usefully employ these experts, leading to reductive approaches focused on "hearts and minds" and "money as a weapon system." Where conventional war is linear and physics based, irregular war was considered complex and irreducible to simple physical approaches. This basic assumption, which has the virtue of being both wrong and widely accepted, has led to a continuing bifurcation of social science methods (seen as useful) from social science theory and epistemology (seen as academic and irrelevant). In practice this means that the use of surveys and survey research techniques has proliferated but with little regard to context, meaning, or how previous studies of civil conflict and economic development might inform efforts and expenditures in Afghanistan. Qualitative and quantitative social network analysis has been used to identify high-value targets, but there has been little understanding of the high levels of uncertainty involved or the limited impact these targets might have on a network. Meanwhile, significant improvements in education and health outcomes have not corresponded with widespread popular rejection of the Taliban.[18] Social scientists could have predicted that, but the fact continues to confound our campaign assessments.[19]

The goal in this chapter is not to tear down these assessments, which have improved over time, or to poke holes in a set of doctrines that military planners follow only loosely, although these too continue to improve. Instead, we argue that assessments have been poorly integrated with the planning process, and we suggest improvements. At the same time, we discuss how treating war as a social phenomenon separate from broader social development, particularly in cases of civil conflict, leads to a poor understanding of what can be achieved, controlled, and ultimately measured and assessed. The analysis community has the responsibility to continuously inform commanders and planners about what has been done and what can be done before, during, and after a conflict.

THE ROAD TO IW ASSESSMENTS IN AFGHANISTAN

Many decision-analysis and assessment methods have been used to support decision making in Operation Enduring Freedom–Afghanistan. Research analysts and social scientists have provided direct support to commanders in the field and "reach-back" analytical support from the continental United States.[20] In a recent study, RAND found that assessment efforts in Afghanistan support four primary categories: force protection, logistics, force structuring, and campaign assessments.[21] While the first three predominantly concern tactical and operational considerations, the last one centers on assessing progress toward mission objectives.

The primary purpose of campaign assessments is to evaluate progress against operational and strategic objectives. Their iterative process is designed to measure and explain progress, shift resources to evolving requirements, and inform changes to operations and strategy. While the operational analysis methods developed over the last several decades work well for applications such as models for predicting attrition among conventional forces, using them to quantify what "peace" looks like in an IW environment has been a much more challenging endeavor. In Afghanistan, assessments directed at monitoring campaign success have been plagued with poorly defined problem statements, insufficient data, and untested methodologies.[22]

Campaign and strategic assessments in Afghanistan may be classified into two categories. First, theater commanders may make assessments based on their knowledge and intuition, forged over years of training and combat experience. Senior leaders assimilate insights from their subordinate commanders, allowing them to make timely and informed decisions, develop and modify plans, and adapt to the ever-changing, complex environment of IW. This instinctual level of decision making does not require equations or mathematical models, yet it often demonstrates profound understanding and accuracy. A second way in which assessments are made in Afghanistan is through formal analytical approaches. These techniques often employ tools for data collection, quantitative and qualitative evaluation methods, and textual and graphical descriptions of data and results in an attempt to monitor the progress of tactical and operational activities. Using analytical approaches to inform defense and national security issues is not a new enterprise; World War II ushered in this revolutionary approach.[23]

During World War II, operations researchers and systems engineers were called upon to leverage mathematical models and statistics to help with the development, fielding, and employment of radar systems and advanced weaponry.[24] Over the next four decades, the United States expended more than $15 trillion (in 2014 purchasing power) for real military acquisitions as it competed with the Soviet Union during the Cold War arms race.[25] During this time both nations employed operations analysis to help inform defense acquisition programs.[26] At the end of the Cold War, operations research analysts used computer simulations to model the Iraqi air defense system, to estimate attrition among Iraqi air defense units, and to assess the efficiency of proposed air-refueling operations in preparation for Operation Desert Storm.[27] For more than a half century leading up to the global war on terrorism, military analysts employed advanced analytical approaches to inform national security decisions. The assessments informed by these analyses primarily focused on evaluating the effectiveness of military operations and matériel solutions by attempting to find causal links between capability and performance factors and intended mission outcomes.

During the first few years of the global war on terrorism, military analysts focused on force protection and optimizing resource allocations.[28] In many instances, self-motivated analysts developed analytical products to help provide context to observed outcomes rather than monitor the progress of defined strategic priorities. Many theater-level staff members interviewed by RAND researchers in the 2014 study reportedly spent much of their time managing data feeds, data processing, and developing graphical presentations (i.e., generating charts and longitudinal plots).[29] These military and contractor analysts were typically trained in various statistical software suites, programming and scripting languages, and advanced computer database management and spreadsheet applications. They became highly proficient at database management, systematization, and automation—essential skills for large-scale, day-to-day data collection, summarization, and presentation. While these theater-wide efforts highlighted the exceptional skills and initiative of the analysts, they also uncovered a failure to link data requirements and metrics (measures of performance and effectiveness) to critical issues that would support the monitoring and assessment of strategic and theater-level campaign objectives. In fact, it wasn't uncommon for an analyst team to select metrics based on the type of data already being collected and perceived (by the analyst) as indicators of commander priorities.[30] While some of the deployed analysts were heavily engaged in data collection and summarization, others performed correlation analysis to help determine campaign progress.[31]

CAMPAIGN ASSESSMENTS: THREE EXAMPLES

In 2009 ISAF created the ISAF Joint Command (IJC) to command and control the operational and tactical war.[32] At the time the ISAF strategic campaign plan consisted of several lines of effort (LOEs) concentrated in security, governance, development, and neutralization of malign actor networks.[33] Each LOE contained many sub-measures, reported by district, of commanders' subjective ratings and objective measures (e.g., the number of improvised explosive device detonations.)[34] The IJC developed a process to monitor campaign progress by assessing key terrain districts across Afghanistan.[35] The assessment methodology incorporated five colors —gray, red, orange, yellow, and green—in a coded scale to represent stability and status.[36] Each district was evaluated and assessed with a color across LOEs. Analysts linked multiple data elements collected within the districts to sub-measures and their respective LOEs. The data elements included polling results, surveys, focus groups, subjective ratings, and data points (some consisting of single events and others recurring regularly).[37]

The IJC assessment effort improved over time and attempted to link data elements to measures that supported LOEs aligned with strategic campaign objectives. This process is similar to the convention used by the defense acquisition community for operational test and evaluation plans. Operational test plans link data requirements, measures of performance, measures of effectiveness, and critical operational issues to systematically evaluate the effectiveness and suitability of combat systems.

In 2010 ISAF requested aid in developing, improving, and implementing a new data-collection and management plan for the North Atlantic Treaty Organization (NATO), ISAF, and the government of the Islamic Republic of Afghanistan during the implementation of the integral plan (or the transition to Afghan lead).[38] The System Analysis and Studies Panel of the NATO Research and Technology Organization created a team to assist this initiative. In a paper published by the National Defense University's Center for Technology and National Security Policy, Michael Baranick and his colleagues recommend that Coalition partners and the government of the Islamic Republic of Afghanistan clearly communicate strategic elements necessary to support the transition process.[39] In addition, they propose a comprehensive data support plan to be linked to metrics for monitoring capacity development and national ownership.[40] These recommendations are consistent with the 2012 direction that the

ISAF commanding general, John Allen, provided concerning the creation of a theater-level assessment process. Subsequent improvements in the process have streamlined data collection but have not fundamentally altered the lines of operations–based approach used for campaign planning through late 2011.

After assuming command in July 2011 General Allen directed the ISAF Afghan Assessment Group to develop a theater-level assessment process for campaign and strategic plans.[41] These campaign plans fall under the purview of the ISAF commander, whereas NATO is responsible for directing strategic plans for the Afghanistan-Pakistan region. The subordinate functional commands (e.g., the IJC) are responsible for campaign assessments while ISAF staff prepares the strategic assessments. Both assessments include narrative reports. Commanders provide subjective numerical evaluations to describe progress, and contextualized quantitative data in the narrative reports are optional.[42] By combining quantitative data with qualitative assessments from subordinate commanders, General Allen hoped to gain a holistic understanding of campaign successes and failures that was not anchored to isolated lines of operation or tied to deceptive quantitative metrics.

In 2013 Gen. Joseph Dunford, Allen's successor as commander of ISAF, pushed this approach further, relying on strategic narratives with heavy input directly from subordinate commanders to assess campaign progress. We are now confronted with a second curious puzzle: While tools for campaign assessment are improving, we find successive commanders driven toward more qualitative, narrative-driven campaign assessments. What lessons can we take from this experience?

ASSESSMENT THINKING IN THE PLANNING PROCESS

> Comprehensive assessment of the US-led intervention in Afghanistan will necessarily wait until the undertaking ends.
> Todd R. Greentree, "A War Examined: Afghanistan"[43]

The importance of understanding the progress made toward strategic objectives *during* a conflict cannot be overstated. Thus Greentree's sentiment is not only disheartening for commanders in the heat of conflict but also unacceptable; therefore, it must be remedied. We offer a reengineered conceptual construct for this purpose.

As the war in Afghanistan evolved, so did its assessment paradigm. The suite of available analytical tools has changed as the conflict has progressed, and it is likely to so do again in the future. If there is a lesson to be learned from the

ISAF experience in Afghanistan, it is not about which assessment framework to use or which tools to apply—they will also change in future conflicts—but about how to integrate assessments into the overall structure of planning and execution. Assessment must be integral to planning; in the past, it has often been an afterthought, to the detriment of the campaign. The stated objectives of IW pose an enormous challenge in measuring the success of these objectives.[44] We consider two basic tenets from David Kilcullen—"have a game plan" and "take stock regularly"—for they may be scaled to a strategic level.[45] While not the focal point of our thesis, they illuminate the critical concept that assessments should not simply be planned for in the planning process; instead, they should inform the plan itself.

BASICS OF PLAN DEVELOPMENT

The deliberate planning process (DPP) consists of five formal phases that culminate in an executable plan. Central to the process is the concept development phase (see figure 14.1), which yields the commander's strategic concept.[46] This concept of operations defines how the commander expects to achieve the mission and drives the subsequent planning phases. As a critical first step, it requires review and approval from the chairman of the Joint Chiefs of Staff (CJCS), with the support of the Joint Planning and Execution Community. If the Joint Planning and Execution Community relies on and plans for analysis and assessment at this phase, positive effects will accrue and persist throughout strategic development. The introduction of analytical ideas at this level, with the major players taking responsibility for their planning and execution, is crucial. This approach provides some certainty that the elements of assessment will be embedded in the prosecution of the overall strategy. Perhaps more important, it enables analysis of civil conflict and social development to help shape the end state and the resulting strategy.

Mission analysis, the first of six steps in concept development, results in a mission statement that provides focus for the remaining steps.[47] Mission analysis is followed by the most important output in this phase—namely, the commander's *planning guidance*, which defines his intent and the envisioned end state of the campaign.

We adapt this second step of concept development to incorporate a review of the planning guidance with an analytical agenda in mind. This does not suggest that we can condense war into a single, quantifiable mathematical formula to assess it.[48] Nor does it suggest that a proper analytical plan would somehow have better, more precise, and more quantifiable metrics of success.

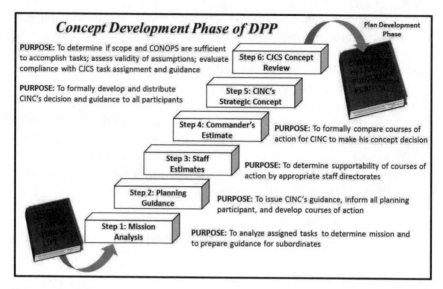

Figure 14.1. The six steps of the concept development phase in the deliberate planning process

Note: CONOPS is concept of operations; CINC, commander in chief.

Source: Joint Forces Staff College, *JFSC Pub 1: Joint Staff Officer's Guide* (Norfolk VA: National Defense University, Joint Forces Staff College, 2000), 4-34.

Rather, we simply maintain that at this strategic level of plan development, adjusting the commander's guidance with better analysis can amount to a slight but significant redirection of war efforts. That analysis can lead to actionable results if it frames IW in consistent, measurable terms informed by prior conflicts and existing social science research. Analysts must be prepared to perform dynamic analyses at each juncture of the war.[49] Each new development can result in a new trajectory of actions that requires a new set of assessment methods. By focusing on the strategic aims of the campaign and developing consistent measures, the actual tracking of progress can become a more manageable effort.

DENDRITIC ANALYSIS

Our approach is to systematically deconstruct the planning guidance. We develop a dendritic (i.e., branching, tree-like) diagram, where each element of guidance branches out into more refined and specific descriptions. From these basic components, we gain a greater understanding of the inherent limits, restrictions, and constraints on measuring progress toward the proposed end state. The dendritic process begins with rephrasing the envisioned end state as multiple objective questions. Each major question is further parsed into more detailed questions.[50] At each juncture, the analyst and the staff determine if the objective can be answered with quantifiable and collectable data.[51] If quantifiable and collectable data elements cannot be identified for a question, it is further deconstructed into more detailed questions or sub-objectives.

For instance, if a major element in the desired end state is the return of a legitimate government, the rephrased objective question may be, is the re-formed government legitimate? A more detailed question deriving from this objective is, does the population trust the government? It is followed by the query, what proportion of the population believes that government actions serve the people? At this point, we would expect a discussion to ensue on the collectability of data. While the data is certainly quantifiable, data that could be considered representative of the total population is difficult to collect in countries such as Afghanistan. Survey research is valuable for understanding a population's sentiments; indeed, Afghanistan, despite its low level of development, is one of the most surveyed war zones in history. But access to conflict zones, precisely where we might be most interested in public opinion, is difficult, and gaining a complete profile of the environment is challenging and highly dynamic. The lag time in capturing the mood of the people is often weeks and months, while a change in attitude may be instantaneous.[52] Furthermore, new developments often occur between data collections. Similarly, while human-terrain teams are plentiful in Afghanistan, no evidence suggests that they have had a strategic impact on the campaign; instead, all evidence of their success is tactical.

To continue the example, the planning debate that follows from the mission analysis may lead to a reexamination of whether establishing government "legitimacy" is a truly feasible end state. As a result, a modified end state might be adopted to replace the original desideratum of "a democratically elected government."[53] This refined end state may be more amenable to evaluations and identification of incremental or radical improvements at different phases in the campaign. Now quantifiable data to support election tallies at all levels of government can indicate what percentage of the eligible population voted and the percentage of votes that each candidate received. Along with the major staff sections, analysts also confer with the commander's advisory group, which is often seen as the command's brain trust. A thorough discussion of recommended changes to the planning guidance informs the commander of the proposed end state's feasibility and allows progress of the overall strategy to be assessed.

Once the planning guidance is issued, the main activities for planning the campaign begin. Course-of-action (COA) development and analysis based on staff estimates is a vigorous and disciplined drill of crafting plans that manifest the commander's planning guidance. The validity of each COA is tested using several factors—suitability (whether it can achieve the mission), feasibility (availability of resources), acceptability (cost of execution), distinguishability (degree of difference from other COAs), and completeness (information on who, what, where, when, and how)—followed by staff estimates.[54] In this step of concept development, an iterative examination of the COA through an assessment lens must begin.

ASSESSMENT CONCEPT: LINES OF ANALYSIS IN CAMPAIGN PLANNING

Evaluating COAs shapes the analysis that supports them while staying within the bounds of strategic assessment. The analyst recognizes the mutating nature of IW in the context of the COA under review and the planning guidance (perhaps modified after the dendritic process). An *assessment concept* for each COA should be developed parallel to the development of the plan. Specifically, each COA should have a corresponding assessment concept. The following example presents an alternative scenario that can be troubling.

Within the first few months of taking command, General Allen issued a directive to find innovative approaches to perform campaign and strategic assessments. The Afghanistan Assessment Group responded with forty pages of metrics and a detailed data collection effort. The group was an experienced team that quickly saw the difficulties of assessing the turbulent nature of IW. The hundreds of measures it produced attempted to account for the various branches that the campaign might follow. In response, the commander determined that the proposal was too complex for the theater.[55]

The relevant point is not whether a new assessment approach was eventually developed and implemented but that the call for a new approach occurred after the campaign had been initiated. It may be that perhaps a new strategy came into effect. If so, new planning guidance should have followed, one that activated the previously discussed dendritic process. Consequently, new COAs for the strategy should have been developed, generating the recommended practice of embedding a supporting assessment concept in each COA. The development of an assessment concept for each campaign should begin concurrently with COA development and analysis.

A *staff estimate* is a methodical examination of each COA by the major staff sections in a military command.[56] Each staff estimate involves an in-depth review of the COAs. Volume 1 of the *Joint Operational Planning and Execution System* outlines procedures for crafting these estimates.[57] The director of joint strategic plans and policies (J5) can play a major role in staff estimates by reviewing each COA for the presence of an assessment concept. It may be further advocated that an assessment concept should be considered in the decision matrix. The absence of an assessment concept would initiate its development.

The analysis team and staff members develop assessment concepts after studying COAs and their desired outcomes. As in the review of planning guidance, this evaluation determines whether the outcomes can be measured and the degree to which they can inform the strategic assessment. Many techniques and frameworks for analyzing IW have been applied in Afghanistan. They join the emerging literature on IW analysis to produce a rich library of modeling and simulation, social network analysis, and spiral designs.[58] These capabilities may align to shape an assessment concept for a COA.

The corresponding assessment concept accompanies the COA chosen in the concept development phase. When the CJCS accepts the COA as the commander's strategic concept, plan development begins. The assessment concept is fully developed as a supporting plan in the DPP's last phase. In this last step, the analysis team develops an assessment action plan (AAP) for the COA. The AAP defines a set of *lines of analysis* (LOA) to support the COA.[59] LOAs are the methods and techniques that the assessment team applies to execute the assessment concept, corresponding with the lines of operations / lines of effort (LOO/LOE) in the COA. At this stage, the cache of tools, techniques, and procedures that US and Coalition forces have developed in the past decades become the key components in supporting the assessment concept.

Building on the example of a newly approved strategic end state of establishing a democratically elected government, a COA for implementing the strategy might contain a LOO/LOE to build infrastructure for secure elections. A desired outcome of this LOO/LOE may be to provide easy public access to election sites. Consistent with dendritic analysis, the outcome is transformed into the objective question, was the public provided easy access to election sites? A cascade of secondary or supporting objectives may eventually pose the question, what percentage of voters used a form of public transportation? Some semblance of this question might be asked at the voting booth, in which case the LOA would use survey techniques. In addition, the LOA could specify the employment of reach-back capabilities to agencies with greater access to computational and modeling and simulation tools and data than what is available to the theater assessment team. This reach back could help develop the expected demographics of the voting population as compared to the groups that actually voted, and the combined data could establish how effective the new infrastructure was in enticing reticent voters. The assessment concept would contain one LOA for each LOO/LOE in the COA and, as a result, be synchronized with the given COA. Furthermore, information from an LOA supports measurements for the strategic end state. If the commander selects the COA, then the assessment concept would be completely developed as a supporting plan. The final supporting plan for the assessment concept is designated as the AAP, which contains both the research design and the data collection and analysis plan.

We have outlined two critical areas of plan development where assessment thinking could be imposed to strengthen the analytical framework for measuring strategic progress in an IW campaign. Growing the connective tissue for campaign and strategic assessments begins with an iterative review of the planning guidance and comes to fruition when the assessment concept and its supporting LOAs are created as an AAP for the approved plan. Building assessment thinking into the deliberate planning process reduces or eliminates the need to develop procedures for campaign analysis after operations have already begun. The assessment concept within the overall plan becomes valuable to the commander as a decision support system that is consistent with overall strategy and, from a practical perspective, makes the task of linking campaign and strategic assessments more manageable.

CONCLUSION

This chapter examines the development and adapting of assessment plans in Afghanistan to suggest improvements for assessing future IW campaigns. It does not offer a broad critique of analytic tools. As technology improves, tools may change. The optimal use of any analytic tool is to inform a decision-making process.

Second, well-informed analysis improves the efficiency and effectiveness of data collection, and the specific details of any conflict environment require the planners and analysts to adapt. Better data is not a silver bullet; better analysis may be. New data is often treated as additional data for collection and not as different data. A data-centric focus to IW assessments can quickly overwhelm other parts of the planning process.

Third, assessment frameworks are highly idiosyncratic and reflect the personality, experience, and preferences of the commander using them. Better assessment frameworks will always rely on a well-structured data collection and analysis process that is informed by the appropriate methods and acted on by the military leaders in theater using their best judgment.

Ultimately it is essential to integrate the assessment methodology for a campaign into the initial planning process so that a commander can receive useful assessments from the start. Two parallel efforts are envisioned. First, at the strategic level, the analytic community, grounded in a solid understanding of existing research, advises the commander about the requirements for achieving the campaign's end state. The goal is not simply to inform a commander of the critical facts in a particular region but to ensure that the pertinent lessons from other times and places are integrated into the planning process as well.

The analytic community next uses the end state to progressively deconstruct the problem set into its most parsimonious form. This deconstruction will result in a manageable set of measures and a collectable set of data. A constrained and modest approach toward data collection and analysis ensures that the assessments that reach the commander are timely and valuable. Irregular warfare will always be fraught with social complexity, but that is no excuse to avoid data and analysis or, conversely, to drown a campaign in data and analysis. War is highly dynamic, and assessments and analyses must be as well. Better integration of assessment and analysis into the initial planning process will support winning wars.

NOTES

For the epigraph, Machiavelli, *The Prince*, trans. W. K. Marriott, Project Gutenberg (updated November 5, 2012), https://www.gutenberg.org/files/1232/1232-h/1232-h.htm#link2HCH0006.

1. Stephen Krasner, *Sovereignty: Organized Hypocrisy* (Princeton NJ: Princeton University Press, 1999).
2. In the presence of that authority, the United States will accept gross violations of human rights, violence, and terror against citizens in those states (e.g., see North Korea). Lacking that authority, in the best of circumstances, the United States will remain neutral to moral claims of the contending parties, but the evidence for this is mixed. In the world in general, the default preference appears to be toward existing states and institutions regardless of their human rights track record or their ability to govern (e.g., Syria). Ibid.
3. IW in this context is defined as "a violent struggle among state and non-state actors for legitimacy and influence over the relevant population(s)." US Department of Defense, "Joint Publication 1-02: Department of Defense Dictionary of Military and Associated Terms," November 8, 2010 (updated monthly), http://www.dtic.mil/doctrine/new_pubs/jp1_02.pdf.

4. Joseph E. Stiglitz and Linda J. Bilmes, "The True Cost of the Iraq War: $3 Trillion and Beyond," *Washington Post*, September 5, 2010, http://www.washingtonpost.com/wp-dyn/content/article/2010/09/03/AR2010090302200.html.

5. Barack Obama, "Remarks by the President in Address to the Nation on the Way Forward in Afghanistan and Pakistan," US Military Academy at West Point, New York, December 1, 2009, http://www.whitehouse.gov/the-press-office/remarks-president-address-nation-way-forward-afghanistan-and-pakistan.

6. Jonathan Schroden et al., "A New Paradigm for Assessment in Counterinsurgency," *Military Operations Research* 18 (2013): 5–20.

7. Jonathan Schroden et al., *Independent Assessment of the Afghan National Security Force* (Arlington VA: Center for Naval Analyses, 2014).

8. Steven Watts et al., *Countering Others' Insurgencies: Understanding U.S. Small-Footprint Interventions in Local Context* (Santa Monica: RAND, 2014), xviii.

9. Indeed the most recent Quadrennial Defense Review notes, "Although our forces will no longer be sized to conduct large-scale prolonged stability operations, we will preserve the expertise gained during the past ten years of counterinsurgency and stability operations in Iraq and Afghanistan. We will also protect the ability to regenerate capabilities that might be needed to meet future demands." US Department of Defense, *Quadrennial Defense Review 2014*, March 2014, vii, http://www.defense.gov/pubs/2014_Quadrennial_Defense_Review.pdf.

10. For an example see Ben Connable, "Learning from Vietnam-Era Strategic Assessment Failure," in *Innovation in Operational Assessments: Recent Developments in Measuring Results in Conflict Environments*, ed. Andrew Williams et al. (The Hague: NATO Communication and Information Agency, 2014), 16–36.

11. Schroden et al., "New Paradigm"; and Connable, "Learning," in Williams et al., *Innovation*, 2014.

12. Schroden et al., "New Paradigm," 8.

13. Ben Connable, *Embracing the Fog of War: Assessments and Metrics in Counterinsurgency* (Santa Monica: RAND, 2012), http://www.rand.org/content/dam/rand/pubs/monographs/2012/RAND_MG1086.pdf.

14. US Department of Defense, "Irregular Warfare: Countering Irregular Threats; Joint Operating Concept," version 2.0, May 17, 2010, 13, http://www.dtic.mil/doctrine/concepts/joint_concepts/joc_iw_v2.pdf.

15. Connable, *Embracing*.

16. Schroden et al., "New Paradigm."

17. Torsten Persson and Guido Tabellini, "Democracy and Development: The Devil in the Details," NBER Working Paper 11993 (Cambridge MA: National Bureau of Economic Research, 2006), http://www.nber.org/papers/w11993.pdf?new_window=1; and Adam Przeworski, "The Mechanics of Regime Instability in Latin America," *Journal of Politics in Latin America* 1 (2009): 5–36.

18. Zachary Laub, "The Taliban in Afghanistan" (Washington DC: Council on Foreign Relations, July 4, 2014), http://www.cfr.org/afghanistan/taliban-afghanistan/p10551?cid=rss-fullfeed-the_taliban_in_afghanistan-080613.

19. Przeworski, "Mechanics of Regime Instability," 2009.

20. Christopher J. Lamb et al., *Human Terrain Teams: An Organizational Innovation for Sociocultural Knowledge in Irregular Warfare* (Washington DC: Institute of World Politics Press, 2013); and Ben Connable et al., *Modeling, Simulation, and Operations Analysis in Afghanistan and Iraq: Operational Vignettes, Lessons Learned, and a Survey of Selected Efforts*, 76 (Santa Monica, CA: RAND, 2014), 2.

21. Connable et al., *Modeling*, 12.

22. Ibid., 71.

23. Michael Fortun and Silvan S. Schweber, "Scientists and the Legacy of World War II: The Case of Operations Research (OR)," *Social Studies of Science* 23, no. 4 (1993): 595–642.

24. Ibid.

25. Robert Higgs, "US Military Spending in the Cold War Era: Opportunity Costs, Foreign Crises, and Domestic Constraints," *Policy Analysis* 114 (Washington DC: CATO Institute, 1988).

26. Fortun and Schweber, "Scientists," 1993.

27. Frederic T. Case, Christopher W. Hines, and Steven N. Satchwell, "Analysis of Air Operations during DESERT SHIELD and DESERT STORM," *Naval Research Logistics (NRL)* 42, no. 4 (1995): 715–36.

28. Connable et al., *Modeling*, 76.

29. Ibid., 77–80.

30. Ibid., 79.

31. Ibid., 82–86.

32. David Hudak, *Improving Assessments for Strategic Decision-Making in Counter Insurgency Operations* (Carlisle Barracks PA: Army War College, Center for Strategic Leadership, 2012), 8.

33. Jan L. Rueschhoff and Jonathan P. Dunne, "Centers of Gravity from the Inside Out," *Joint Force Quarterly* 60 (2011): 120–26.

34. Ibid., 9.

35. Connable et al., *Modeling*, 82.

36. William P. Upshur, Jonathan W. Roginski, and David J. Kilcullen, "Recognizing Systems in Afghanistan," *Prism* 3, no. 3 (2012): 89.

37. Hudak, *Improving Assessments*, 9–10.

38. Michael Baranick et al., *Elevating the Role of Socioeconomic Strategy in Afghanistan Transition* (Washington DC: National Defense University, Center for Technology and National Security Policy, 2011), iii.

39. Ibid., 21–22.

40. Ibid., 22.
41. Connable et al., *Modeling*, 86.
42. Ibid., 86.
43. Todd R. Greentree, "A War Examined: Afghanistan," *Parameters* 43, no. 3 (Autumn 2013): 87.
44. Here we mean the general objectives of IW as stated by IW JOC 2.0 (cite) Eric V. Larson et al., *Assessing Irregular Warfare: A Framework for Intelligence Analysis* (Santa Monica: RAND, 2008), 16–20.
45. David Kilcullen, "Twenty-eight Articles, Fundamentals of Company-level Counterinsurgency," *IOSphere*, Summer 2006, 4–7, http://www.au.af.mil/info-ops/iosphere/iosphere_summer06_kilcullen.pdf.
46. For details on the deliberate planning process, see Joint Forces Staff College, *JFSC Pub 1: Joint Staff Officer's Guide* (Norfolk VA: National Defense University, Joint Forces Staff College, 2000), 4-26, http://www.uscg.mil/directives/cim/3000-3999/cim_3020_15d.pdf.
47. Ibid., 4-34.
48. Barry D. Watts, in *Clausewitzian Friction and Future War*, McNair Paper 52 (Washington DC: Institute for National Strategic Studies, National Defense University, 1996), 22, cites Henry Humphrey Evans Boyd and Dietrich Adam Heinrich von Bulow regarding their early attempt to develop absolute formulas for war.
49. Larson et al., *Assessing*, 23–29, explain dynamic analyses as an adaptive analytic framework to respond to tactical and operational scenarios.
50. Roger T. Stevens, *Operational Test and Evaluation: A Systems Engineering Process* (New York: John Wiley and Sons, 1979), 50–56.
51. Richard L. Scheaffer et al., *Elementary Survey Sampling*, 5th ed. (Belmont CA: Duxbury Press, 1996), discuss that most data are just counts, including responses to open-ended questionnaires (8–24, 64–65).
52. Col. Alejandro Hernandez was the director of analysis and assessments, US Joint Forces–Iraq, 2009–10, where his organization oversaw the polling efforts for the theater.
53. Changing or modifying political or policy goals, or end states, must be coordinated with and ultimately approved by the president of the United States.
54. Joint Forces Staff College, *JFSC Pub 1*, 4-42.
55. Connable et al., *Modeling*, 111, 2014.
56. Joint Forces Staff College, *JFSC Pub 1*, 4-43–4-46.
57. Chairman, Joint Chiefs of Staff, *Joint Pub 5-03.1: Joint Operational Planning and Execution System*, vol. 1 *(Planning Policies and Procedures)*, (Washington DC: Joint Staff, Pentagon, August 4, 1993), explains the application of different systems to perform the deliberate planning process.
58. Larson et al., *Assessing*; and Connable et al., *Modeling*, 2014.

59. Hernandez, in 2009–10, first termed "lines of analysis" as a set of mutually supporting analytic methods and techniques that the assessment team may employ to study a strategic objective. He coined a 360-degree approach for measuring improvements in Iraq, in which the team used polling, media, and kinetic data, along with subject matter expertise from cultural and operational advisers.

15

MONITORING FROM AFAR

HOW AL-QAEDA ASSESSES ITS PROGRESS

Mark Stout

THE MEMBERS OF THE JIHADIST MOVEMENT centered on al-Qaeda exist along a continuum of commitment to instrumental action. At one end are warriors who see participation in violent jihad purely as an expression of identity and faith. For these expressive warriors the question of victory is remote. Their concept of war is oriented around issues such as showing their Islamic faith, maintaining solidarity with their friends, demonstrating bravery, and getting martyred. At the other end of the spectrum are soldiers or strategists who see participation in violent jihad as an instrumental act that can bring a desired end state closer. While they too see engagement in jihad as an expressive act, they also feel themselves obligated to attempt to bring about victory, which entails reforming Islam to what they view as its pure roots and restoring a caliphate or at the very least creating Islamic emirates that might someday be part of the caliphate. They believe, in fact, that God has promised them victory though they may suffer setbacks along the way.[1] While assessments of their progress are scarcely relevant to the expressive warriors, the soldiers and strategists have definite ideas about what constitutes progress toward their desired end state.

However, just because many members of al-Qaeda think instrumentally about using violence and therefore as individuals must assess their progress toward at least tactical goals, it is not necessarily clear that al-Qaeda as such does the same. In short, it is easy to ask the question, how does al-Qaeda assess its progress in its jihad? However, that question begs several others: Does al-Qaeda have goals toward which progress can be measured? Is al-Qaeda an entity capable of making assessments on more than the individual level? Does al-Qaeda actually assess its progress toward its goals?

Unfortunately the sources available to help answer these questions are rather thin. Ideally we would have access to the internal records of al-Qaeda. In fact, American and Coalition forces have captured immense quantities of these records. Unfortunately only a tiny fraction, perhaps a few hundred, has been made public. In themselves, the files are remarkably valuable; however, they are probably not a representative sample and typically lack any significant archival context. Furthermore, with the exception of just a few dozen, these documents date to the pre-2001 period. In addition to captured records, a great deal of open source material is available from the jihadists including books, postings on jihadist forums, videos, and audio materials. These sources can be valuable; however, not surprising, the elites within the al-Qaeda movement seldom publicly give specific or sensitive details. In addition, of course, the movement's public pronouncements often serve an exhortatory purpose that sharply limits their utility in understanding how al-Qaeda assesses its progress. Nevertheless, these open source materials can not only help us identify key measures of merit but also provide insights into assessments when they step out of form and reveal what al-Qaeda would consider bad news.

With those considerations in mind, we consider each of the previously mentioned questions in turn. Then having answered them with a qualified affirmative, we examine the standards by which al-Qaeda assesses its success.

DOES AL-QAEDA HAVE GOALS TOWARD WHICH PROGRESS CAN BE MEASURED?

Captured documents show that al-Qaeda's goals have always been clear: "the victory of the mighty religion of Allah, the establishment of an Islamic regime and the restoration of the Islamic Caliphate, God willing," as its constitutional charter says.[2] The charter goes on to say that it expects this work to be "international and in gradual stages, depending on Al Qaeda's policies."[3]

In particular, a core component of the al-Qaeda ideology is that it is a vanguard movement that will awaken the conscience of the people and make them aware of the need for action.[4] This was a key idea in the writings of Sayyid Qutb, al-Qaeda's ideological godfather.[5] In the 1980s Abdullah Azzam, the organizational grandfather of al-Qaeda, wrote in a famous essay called "The Solid Base" that "every principle must be supported by a vanguard, which clears a path for itself toward society, at the price of vast efforts and sacrifices. . . . The vanguard has a long and difficult path to travel before it can implant this dogma in real life . . . the vanguard represents the solid base of the society we hope to create."[6] Similarly Ayman al-Zawahiri used the term in reference to al-Qaeda in his book *Knights under the Prophet's Banner*, which was written around the time of the September 11, 2001, attacks on the United States.[7]

As we shall see, from its founding and up until the early weeks of Operation Enduring Freedom, which was launched after September 11, al-Qaeda had a highly bureaucratized structure. (We shall call this group al-Qaeda 1.0.) Further information about its subsidiary goals can be gleaned from the charter of the various committees that administered the group. Hence, the Military Committee's tasks included the "recruitment of individuals for enlistment in al-Qaida," followed, of course, by their training. For its part, the Information Committee was to engage in the "calling and instigation of Muslims to the jihad in the word of God . . . and spreading and embracing concepts and general rules of the Sunnis and the community in all legal affairs of the jihad."[8] Al-Qaeda 1.0 never strayed from these goals after it first enunciated them. Al-Qaeda 2.0, the group that existed after the launching of Operation Enduring Freedom, also retained these goals.

Other al-Qaeda affiliates and similar groups may have more local or regional aspirations. For instance, the various groups tend to focus on establishing an Islamic regime in their own part of the world and growing to the caliphate from there.[9] Nevertheless, they all share al-Qaeda's overall goals and the implied subsidiary goals.

IS AL-QAEDA CAPABLE OF MAKING ASSESSMENTS?

The answer to this question depends on the period in question and the definition of "al-Qaeda." With regard to al-Qaeda 1.0, it is reasonable to speak of a unitary organization capable of making assessments. Al-Qaeda was formed in 1988 and from its early years had a hierarchical structure and committees to oversee its various activities (see figure 15.1).[10]

The reality of any organization will differ from the procedures laid out in its bylaws. Captured records make clear, however, that al-Qaeda 1.0 was a highly bureaucratized hierarchical organization capable of making assessments.[11]

During this time, al-Qaeda existed alongside a variety of jihadist groups with similar ideological orientations. One of these groups, Ayman al-Zawahiri's Egyptian Islamic Jihad, later merged with Al Qaeda. Other groups such as the Taliban, the Egyptian Islamic Group, the Arab mujahideen in Chechnya, and Jemaah Islamiyah in Southeast Asia had connections with al-Qaeda but

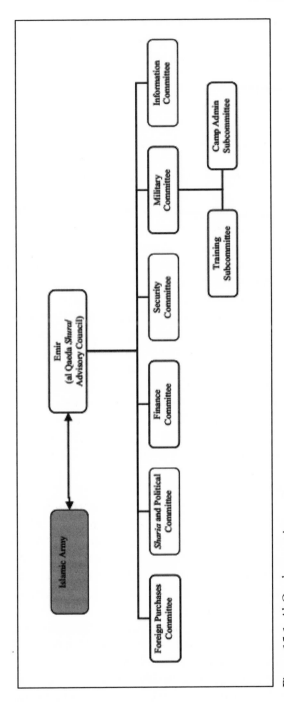

Figure 15.1. Al-Qaeda committee structure

Source: 9/11 Commission, "Overview of the Enemy," Staff Statement No. 15, http://govinfo.library.unt.edu/911/staff_statements/staff_state
ment_15.pdf. See also Combating Terrorism Center, "Al-Qa'ida Goals and Structure (English Translation)," West Point NY, https://www.ctc.usma
.edu/posts/al-qaida-goals-and-structure-english-translation-2.

remained independent.[12] Not surprising, most of them were objects of Coalition operations under the rubric of the global war on terrorism. However, before 2001, they were not part of the al-Qaeda organization or subordinated to it. Accordingly, this chapter ignores these groups during this period.

After the launching of Operation Enduring Freedom, the situation became more complicated. Coalition military, intelligence, and law enforcement operations did enormous damage to al-Qaeda 1.0, forcing it to dismantle most of its structure and to take refuge largely in Pakistan and Iran, thus making meetings and communication among its members difficult. All this severely reduced al-Qaeda's ability to mount terrorist operations and led it to restructure the group.

Despite its travails, the new al-Qaeda 2.0 and Osama bin Laden retained enormous authority in the jihadist world. In addition al-Qaeda retained at least a semblance of its old bureaucratic ways and thus the ability to make assessments. Bin Laden (and later Zawahiri) surrounded himself virtually, though perhaps not physically, with senior subordinates. In particular, the group had a succession of operations chiefs, or "general managers," who were responsible for coordinating both informational and military operations and for maintaining relations with the regional affiliates. The general manager had under him a first deputy and a second deputy who served for fixed but renewable terms, as well as a military commander.[13]

The affiliates with which al-Qaeda's general manager maintained contact were a phenomenon of the post-9/11 period. During this time, many of the same jihadist groups that had existed alongside al-Qaeda continued to operate, and more were born. However, a few swore allegiance to al-Qaeda and some even took the name of al-Qaeda. These groups included al-Qaeda in the Arabian Peninsula (AQAP), al-Qaeda in Iraq (AQI), al-Shabaab, al-Qaeda in the Islamic Maghreb (AQIM), and Jabhat al-Nusra in Syria.[14] In 2014 al-Qaeda announced the formation of a new affiliate, al-Qaeda in the Indian Subcontinent.

In theory, al-Qaeda Central could issue orders to these affiliates, an arrangement underlined by the naming in 2013 of Nasir al-Wuhayshi, the emir of al-Qaeda in the Arabian Peninsula, to be concurrently al-Qaeda Central's latest general manager.[15] As a practical matter, al-Qaeda's ability to command and control the affiliates was sharply limited. Communication between the groups was always difficult. Though some electronic communication was possible, contact was maintained largely through couriers.[16] In addition formal affiliates could be overtly rebellious as AQI was under Abu Musab al-Zarqawi. While al-Qaeda and its affiliate in Iraq patched up their relations after Zarqawi's death in 2006, the situation deteriorated again, and in early 2014 al-Qaeda Central disavowed the Islamic State of Iraq and Syria, as AQI had become known.[17]

In essence, then, al-Qaeda 2.0 exists at the center of a fractious coalition with only the barest of coordination.[18] This situation suggests that whatever assessment processes exist are likely to be rudimentary.

DOES AL-QAEDA ACTUALLY ASSESS ITS PROGRESS TOWARD ITS GOALS?

The various incarnations of al-Qaeda and its coalition have and do conduct assessments of their struggle albeit imperfectly. In al-Qaeda 1.0, bin Laden and the Shura Advisory Council were responsible for assessment as a part of their leadership functions.[19] In addition several of the group's committees might have had a role in assessment. However, the Sharia and Political Committee was probably the nexus of such work on a day-to-day basis. It was explicitly charged with "preparing political reports and the needed studies for work." The context of this charge appears to cover not only studies of the work of the Political Committee itself but of al-Qaeda as a whole.[20]

More generally the topic of assessment shows up in various ways in captured documents from the period. While details are mostly lacking on what the assessment processes were, clearly al-Qaeda's leadership was aware of the topic. To begin with, al-Qaeda 1.0 gathered strategic intelligence especially by dispatching trusted agents to report on the situation in particular regions of interest and by reading open source materials.[21] For example, bin Laden's bodyguard reports that in the 1990s bin Laden listened to several international radio stations, was "kept up to the minute" by reports from the al-Qaeda media center in Kandahar, and received a weekly press review drawing from French, German, Russian, English, Spanish, and Pashto sources.[22]

In addition several documents have been captured from al-Qaeda facilities in Afghanistan describing strategic intelligence processes that would have been useful in making assessments. One was an undated document found at the house of Mohammed Atef, al-Qaeda's military chief until his death in late 2001. Prepared by the Egyptian Islamic Group, this work contained a sophisticated explanation of the relationship between intelligence and policy and illustrated it in the diagram shown in figure 15.2.[23] A portion of this diagram can be recognized as what Americans call the intelligence cycle. The presence of this document among Atef's possessions suggests relevance to al-Qaeda 1.0's own processes.

Al-Qaeda records captured in Afghanistan include an example of the sorts of assessments that may have come out of this system; it is hard to say for certain given the lack of information about the document's provenance. A 1996 study titled "Political Gaps in Algeria: Rhetoric and Incitements" described

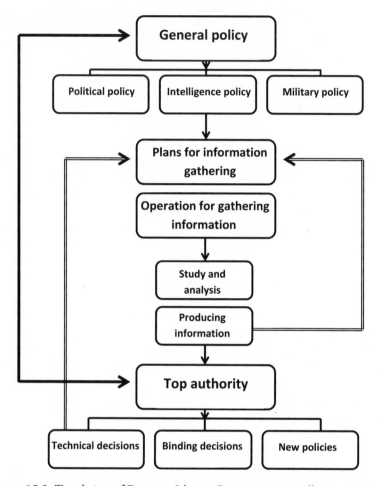

Figure 15.2. Translation of Egyptian Islamic Group text on intelligence recovered from al-Qaeda facility in Kandahar

Source: Reproduction of "'Security and Intelligence Gathering,' prepared and published by the Egyptian Islamic Group (al-Gamaa al-Islamiya), unknown date (prior to 2003)," AQ-INSE-D-000–033, Conflict Records Research Center, Fort McNair, Washington DC.

the military situation in that country as favorable but warned that the political situation there was "alarming" due to the shortcomings of the Armed Islamic Group's leadership. As a result, total defeat in Algeria was assessed to be a real possibility.[24]

Other surviving records hint at shortcomings in the assessment processes. For instance, in 2000 a man known only as Abu Huthayfa gave bin Laden his views on the importance of assessment: "For any movement to achieve its publicized goal it requires actual premises upon which it builds its strategy. Between now and then the movement needs to reevaluate its status quo accurately and to live this status quo and know in which direction it is heading. Inasmuch as the evaluation is actual and accurate, the action based on this evaluation will be sound, especially in establishing the strategy for action. Any wrong evaluation of the status quo will certainly result in equally wrong action."[25]

Abu Huthayfa even urged the creation of an assessment infrastructure: "We emphasize the importance of having a special mechanism within the movement to fill in this sensitive aspect by producing a huge database of actual data to measure the standing of the people of all classes. The leadership of the movement should be updated of these huge amount[s] of real data that will enable it to manage [the] struggle cleverly. This is what states endeavor to do by establishing strategic research centers."[26]

Al-Qaeda 2.0 appears to do assessments as well. Certainly the leadership continues to make use of open source materials about the strategic situation. For instance, late in his life, bin Laden asked Adam Gadahn to translate for him a piece apparently titled "The Most Important Things about Al Qaeda" written by Robert Fisk, and in 2011 bin Laden was aware of comments Secretary of State Hillary Clinton made about the situation in Yemen.[27] Furthermore, informal assessments emerge from general correspondence among the elites in the group. For example, in a January 2011 letter, Adam Gadahn advised bin Laden how to craft a video release in light of the present American political and media scene. He went on to describe the movement's strategically counterproductive actions especially by the affiliate in Iraq. He warned that al-Qaeda's "reputation will be damaged more and more as a result of the acts and statements of this group." Later in the letter he listed further atrocities inflicted on innocent Muslims by al-Qaeda affiliates, and he lamented, "I have no doubt that what is happening to the Jihadi movement in these countries is not misfortune, but punishment by God on us because of our sins and injustices."[28]

In a further indication of an inclination to ensure that operations are appropriate to the situation, bin Laden in 2010 asked Atiyatullah al-Libi to obtain an independent opinion on the media efforts of al-Qaeda and its affiliates.

> We are in need of an advisory reading, with constructive criticism to our entire policy and publications at the center and in the regions. . . . From abroad, . . . achieve a contact with one of the knowledge seekers so long as he is credible and trusted; inform him that we are in a new phase of amendment and development and require an advisory reading and development of our entire policy and publication at the center and in the regions. The purpose is to amend our mistakes and develop our jihadist work according to their suggestions and opinions, especially in corresponding with the masses of the nation.[29]

There is some evidence that the al-Qaeda-led coalition conducts assessment also. Certainly there is communication among al-Qaeda and its affiliates that allows for a degree of assessment. For instance, in his letter to Atiyatullah, bin Laden emphasized the importance of deliberative processes within the coalition regarding strategy that probably at least implicitly included assessment.[30]

In the same letter, bin Laden indicated that he expected the leadership council of each affiliate to provide its emir with "recommendations" and an "annual report" describing the "progress of the local Emir in his activity and his dealings with the *mujahideen*." This information was to be sent to al-Qaeda Central.[31] Bin Laden also asked Atiyatullah to solicit separate reports from Nasir al-Wuhayshi, the head of AQAP; Anwar al-Awlaki; and another member of AQAP about the situation in Yemen "so that it is feasible for us . . . to make the most appropriate decision to either escalate or calm down."[32] In 2011 bin Laden asked for a report from "the brothers in Somalia" about the "economic situations in the states they control."[33] There is at least one known example of AQI preparing such a document in about 2007, though it is unclear whether al-Qaeda Central received it.[34]

On at least two occasions documents of this type have been disseminated laterally among the affiliates (or sent to al-Qaeda Central and then redistributed outward).[35] On another occasion Zawahiri asked Zarqawi in Iraq to establish contact with jihadists in Algeria (who were not yet formally affiliated with al-Qaeda) on his behalf to gather information from them.[36] The possibility of correspondence among all the members of the al-Qaeda coalition raises the likelihood of informal assessments emerging organically, though there is no evidence to confirm that they happen.

If the affiliates are to provide situation reports to al-Qaeda Central, then they must conduct assessments of their own. We know little about such efforts, though we have at least one example of such work. Sometime around July 2012, Abdelmalek Droukdel, the emir of al-Qaeda in the Islamic Maghreb, assessed his group's situation in Mali. It is not clear if his assessment amounts to a rebuke to his lieutenants. He noted that the mujahideen were "isolated in society," largely as a result of the "extreme speed with which [they] applied *shariah*, not taking into consideration the gradual evolution that should be applied in an environment that is ignorant of religion." Furthermore, "the great powers . . . despite their weakness and their retreat caused by military exhaustion and the financial crisis, still have many cards to play that enable them to prevent the creation of an Islamic state." In fact, it was "very probable . . . that a military intervention will occur . . . or that a complete economic, political and military blockade will be imposed . . . which in the end will either force us to retreat to our rear bases or will provoke the people against . . . or will enflame the conflict between us and the other armed political movements in the region." In any event, "administration of the region and standing up to the international, foreign and regional challenge is a large duty that exceeds our military and financial and structural capability for the time being." Accordingly Droukdel advised building a broad coalition of the peoples of Mali so as to deal with immediate governance problems and maximize the chances of repelling foreign aggression. Finally he believed that in the likely case of a coming defeat, such a strategy would have planted the seeds for a future resurgence.[37]

Beyond all these formal efforts, for most of al-Qaeda's existence, the work of what might be called jihadist public intellectuals has offered an additional informal way to make assessments. These individuals may or may not be members of an al-Qaeda-linked jihadist group, but they have connections with the jihadist world and their views circulate within it. The most prominent among these public intellectuals both before and after 2001 has been Abu Musab al-Suri. Though not a member, this al-Qaeda sympathizer at times worked closely with the group but was also very willing to criticize its leadership and its operations.[38] Al-Suri has been prolific in his work. In, apparently, 1998 he released a lengthy assessment of the situation in Afghanistan called "Afghanistan, the Taliban and the Battle of Islam Today."[39] Its primary purpose was to determine whether jihadists should rally to the defense of the Taliban in Afghanistan. In 1999 he assessed Central Asia as fertile ground for jihadist activity in part because of the population's many grievances and its members' high level of military expertise and bravery.[40] At about this time he began work on a scathing assessment of the jihad conducted by the Armed Islamic Group in Algeria.[41] His magnum opus was a late 2004 book titled *Call to Global Islamic Resistance*. It assessed the efforts of jihadist movements throughout history, culminating with an appraisal of the work of al-Qaeda, its affiliates, and sympathetic groups.

WHAT MEASURES DOES AL-QAEDA USE TO ASSESS ITS PROGRESS?

Given the spotty nature of available information and, at least since the destruction of al-Qaeda 1.0, the few formal mechanisms for assessment that have been uncovered, it is not surprising that there is no definitive answer for what measures of merit factor into al-Qaeda's assessments. Nevertheless, it is possible to identify several measures of merit to which the strategic elites often refer during the period in question and whose connection to al-Qaeda's goals seems clear and direct.

THE DEGREE TO WHICH MUSLIMS EXPRESS DISCONTENT
WITH THEIR SITUATION AND SYMPATHY TOWARD AL-QAEDA

Al-Suri wrote in *Call to Global Islamic Resistance* that that there are three levels of resistance. The first is "Islamic religious sentiment," and the second, "the will to fight," entails religious sentiment and the awareness of the "enemy's hostile works." The final one involves possessing "the jihadist creed" and actually participating in jihad.[42]

For our purposes, we shall condense al-Suri's three steps to two. The first is simply awakening the people to the unacceptability of their situation and making them aware that al-Qaeda shares their concerns. A few internal records from the al-Qaeda movement speak to this point. For instance, Zawahiri wrote to Zarqawi in 2005 that "the strongest weapon which the *mujahedeen* enjoy . . . is popular support from the Muslim masses in Iraq, and the surrounding Muslim countries. So, we must maintain this support as best we can, and we should strive to increase it."[43] Bin Laden wrote to Atiyatullah in 2010 that "the purpose is for the *mujahideen* publications to be a good potential for the competition and to gain the crowds. The main goal is to spread awareness amongst the people of the nation." He went on to say that the absence of popular support would cause al-Qaeda to be "crushed in the shadows."[44] Similarly a strategy document from al-Qaeda in the Islamic Maghreb calls for "building bridges" to the people of Mali, and a trove of audiocassette tapes from the early years of al-Qaeda contains discussions of how attacks against American and Jewish interests can win support from Muslims.[45]

This imperative to awaken the people shows up also in many public pronouncements from senior figures in the jihadist movement. As Ayman al-Zawahiri put it in his September 2013 statement, a "basic task" must be "creating awareness within the masses, inciting them, and exerting efforts to mobilize them so that they revolt against their rulers and join the side of Islam and those working for its cause."[46] That the goal of awakening and educating the people is a good thing in itself helps explain why some ideological leaders within the jihadist movement have even come around to accepting the Arab Spring as a modest improvement even though the new governments fall short of their definition of being properly Islamic.[47]

THE NUMBER OF JIHADISTS IN THE FIGHT

Ultimately al-Qaeda's project is to bring all the world's Muslims back to the allegedly correct understanding of the faith. This understanding entails a commitment to participation in or support of violent jihad. The small number of people in the movement, however, seems to be disappointing to some elites.

Al-Suri characterized the size of this movement in the 1990s as a tiny fraction of 1 percent of the Muslims in the world.[48] In his eyes, the situation did not get much better after September 11. He noted that the "'war on terror' has led to the near extinction of the *mujahideen*" and lamented that "the size of the elite resisting the invading enemies is a frighteningly small segment of the ummah [Islamic community]."[49] Similarly bin Laden privately complained in 2010 about "the alienation of most of the [Islamic] nation from the *mujahidin*."[50]

Also in 2010 Doku Umarov, the head of the Caucasus Emirate—an al-Qaeda-aligned group but not an affiliate—lamented in 2010 that "every day I spend in this world brings disappointment with those Muslims who because of their slumber, because of their sleep, hypnosis that they have had thrust on them, lost the greatness of Islam."[51] The next year he said, "We see in what disastrous state our Ummah is. Today, the Ummah is 1.5 billion in numbers, and we know that even .05% of these numbers of this Ummah do not wage the jihad."[52]

THE DEGREE TO WHICH JIHADIST GROUPS OPERATE FREELY

The movement's elites realize that they cannot advance their cause if they cannot operate; hence, they worry a good deal about the degree to which their operations are impeded. Bin Laden expressed this general thought in a 2010 letter to Mukhtar Abu al-Zubayr, the head of al-Shabaab, in which he urged al-Shabaab to stay below the radar so as to avoid having "the enemies escalate their anger and mobilize against you."[53]

In general al-Qaeda finds that it is unable to operate effectively if governments put up a serious fight. Historically the "apostate" security services have been a nearly insurmountable impediment, often playing a major role in inducing jihadists to leave their home countries and conduct their jihad elsewhere.[54] Not only are these governments effective at crushing jihadist groups but also the very knowledge that they are watching can have effects. Abu Muhammad al-Maqdisi acknowledged this fact with an essay on how paranoia about electronic surveillance can needlessly paralyze jihadists.[55] More recently a new problem has arisen—drones. Jihadists from bin Laden to a senior commander in al-Qaeda in the Arabian Peninsula to a low-level foot soldier put on trial in the United Kingdom for going to the camps in Pakistan have commented on the impediments that American drone operations have caused.[56]

Beyond American drones specifically, the al-Qaeda coalition has developed a healthy respect for the capabilities of modern Western militaries. For instance, a document found in 2013 from Abdelmalek Droukdel, the leader of AQIM, noted the dire consequences of provoking military intervention from "the great powers" even "despite their weakness and their retreat caused by military exhaustion and the financial crisis." He wrote that a military intervention or a blockade "will either force us to retreat to our rear bases or will provoke the people against us because of starvation or the cutting of supplies and salaries, or will enflame the conflict between us and the other armed political movements in the region."[57]

Of course, the ease of movement and operation also depends on the degree to which the population provides at least passive support. That support depends not only on the population's political awareness but also on the degree to which the local regime detects and punishes support to the mujahideen, as noted in an internal assessment of al-Qaeda in Iraq from about 2007.[58] Al-Qaeda has discovered that its ability to operate can also depend on the degree to which it can figure out how to operate within the existing social structures, such as the tribal systems of Iraq and Somalia.[59]

THE GAIN OR LOSS OF TERRITORY

The al-Qaeda movement seeks to liberate territory within which true Islam (as the group sees it) will prevail. Hence, in his 2010 letter to Mukhtar Abu al-Zubayr, bin Laden highlighted the importance of the creation of an Islamic emirate.[60] Victories, both tactical and strategic, are celebrated. For instance, in 2012, not long before being named al-Qaeda's general manager, Nasir al-Wuhayshi congratulated the leader of AQIM: "Allah has crowned your jihad with victories [in Mali] and put the country in your hands."[61] Meanwhile, losses are lamented, whether at the Battle of Jalalabad in 1989 or the overthrow of the Taliban regime in Afghanistan.[62] For his part, al-Suri in the 1990s did a lessons learned project that dissected the failures of jihadists in numerous countries going back to the 1960s.[63]

THE PROBLEM OF SELF-INFLICTED WOUNDS

The al-Qaeda movement has a serious problem with self-inflicted wounds. These issues could be called a measure of negative merit. Just as unfortunate or ill-considered actions by junior American military personnel can have negative strategic consequences, so too can such actions when committed by jihadists.[64] Indeed, elites in the jihadist movement routinely complain about reckless tactical operations conducted by the expressive warriors who kill innocent or protected people or who give a negative impression of the movement and thereby negatively affect all of the previously mentioned strategic measures of merit.

Self-inflicted wounds were a particular point of contention between al-Qaeda Central and Abu Musab al-Zarqawi in Iraq, notably when

Atiyatullah wrote a letter of admonition to Zarqawi in 2005 telling him that his violence against Sunnis was reducing al-Qaeda's ability to win "the hearts of the people."[65] However, the problem predated Zarqawi and has outlasted him. For instance, one of the reasons that Fadil Harun, al-Qaeda's confidential secretary, wrote his memoirs was to denounce the many unlawful acts being undertaken in the group's name.[66] Similarly, bin Laden's 2010 letter to Atiyatullah blamed al-Qaeda's alienation from most Muslims on the harm they believe that al-Qaeda has inflicted on them. Indeed, he wrote, "It is apparent . . . that most people in Yemen, if given a choice between a government formed by al-Qaeda or a government formed . . . by any of the Gulf States . . . they will choose the government that is formed by the Gulf States."[67]

CONCLUSION

A few conclusions emerge. First, it is clear that al-Qaeda in all its incarnations assesses (and has assessed) its progress in its global jihad.

Second, the measures of merit that al-Qaeda's elites prioritize are consistent with a Maoist view of insurgency. This observation should not be surprising, given that Maoist military thought has greatly influenced the writings of jihadist strategists.[68] Like the jihadists, Mao Zedong emphasized in his military writings the importance of being one with the people so that guerrillas could attract them to the cause and swim in their "sea." Mao's construct of the three stages of guerrilla warfare also talks about the progressive liberation of territory as the guerrillas move into stage 2 and then stage 3 of their struggle.

Finally, however, al-Qaeda's assessment processes have not been robust since at least since 2001 and possibly were not before then, either. They depend too much both on acquiring information through uncertain channels that is seldom timely and on reporting from affiliates that are likely to put a positive spin on their local situations. Furthermore, it is reasonable to speculate that the sources of information and the assessors themselves suffer from motivated bias. This information would suggest that al-Qaeda's assessments are likely to only very imperfectly reflect the world as it is.

NOTES

1. Mark E. Stout, Jessica M. Huckabey, and John R. Schindler, *The Terrorist Perspectives Project: Strategic and Operational Views of al Qaida and Associated Movements* (Annapolis: Naval Institute Press, 2008), 38–39.

2. "Al Qa'ida Constitutional Charter (English Translation)," Combating Terrorism Center, West Point NY (hereafter CTC), https://www.ctc.usma.edu/posts/al-qaida-constitutional-charter-english-translation-2. Ayman al-Zawahiri also discusses the establishment of a caliphate in Office of the Director of National Intelligence, "Letter from al-Zawahiri to al-Zarqawi," October 11, 2005, ODNI News Release no. 2-05, Washington DC; and "f," n.d., attached to ODNI New Release no 2-50.

3. CTC, "Al Qa'ida Constitutional Charter."

4. Stout et al., *Terrorist Perspectives Project*, 39–41.

5. Michael W. S. Ryan, *Decoding al-Qaeda's Strategy: The Deep Battle against America* (New York: Columbia University Press, 2013), 38.

6. Abdullah Azzam, "The Solid Base," in *Al Qaeda in Its Own Words*, ed. Gilles Kepel and Jean-Pierre Milelli (Cambridge MA: Belknap Press of Harvard University, 2008), 140.

7. Ryan, *Decoding Al-Qaeda's Strategy*, 77, 79, quoting Ayman al-Zawahiri.

8. "Al-Qa'ida Goals and Structure (English Translation)," CTC, https://www.ctc.usma.edu/posts/al-qaida-goals-and-structure-english-translation-2.

9. See, e.g., Geoff D. Porter, "AQIM's Objectives in North Africa," *CTC Sentinel* 4, no. 2 (February 1, 2011).

10. Notes of its founding meeting are available at "Date of Al Qaeda's Founding," Intelwire.com, February 24, 2009, http://intelwire.egoplex.com/2009_02_24_blogarchive.html. See also Peter Bergen and Paul Cruickshank, "Revisiting the Early Al Qaeda: An Updated Account of Its Formative Years," *Studies in Conflict & Terrorism* 35, no. 1 (2012): 3–7.

11. See, e.g., Allan Cullison, "Inside Al Qaeda's Hard Drive," *The Atlantic*, September 1, 2004, http://www.theatlantic.com/magazine/archive/2004/09/inside-al-qaeda-s-hard-drive/303428/. See also Fadil Harun quoted in Nelly Lahoud, *Beware of Imitators: Al-Qaida through the Lens of Its Confidential Secretary* (West Point: Combating Terrorism Center, 2012), 24–25, for a description of al-Qaeda's bureaucratic structures as they stood in 1998.

12. Bergen and Cruickshank, "Revisiting the Early Al Qaeda," 17–20 and 24–25.

13. "Letter from UBL to 'Atiyatullah al-Libi 3 (English Translation)," October 21, 2010, CTC, https://www.ctc.usma.edu/posts/letter-from-ubl-to-atiyatullah-al-libi-3-english-translation-2; and "Letter from UBL to 'Atiyatullah al-Libi 4 (English Translation)," May 2010, CTC, https://www.ctc.usma.edu/posts/letter-from-ubl-to-atiyatullah-al-libi-4-english-translation-2. See also Thomas Joscelyn and Bill Roggio, "AQAP's Emir Also Serves as al Qaeda's General Manager," *Long War Journal*, August 6, 2013, http://www.longwarjournal.org/archives/2013/08/aqap_emir_also_serve.php.

14. Aymenn Jawad al-Tamimi, "GUEST POST: Jabhat al-Nusra's Relations with Other Rebels after the Bay'ah to Zawahiri," *Jihadology*, May 14, 2013, http:// jihadology.net/2013/05/14/guest-post-jabhat-al-nusras-relations-with-other -rebels-after-the-bayah-to-zawahiri/.

15. Joscelyn and Roggio, "AQAP's Emir." For a 2010 view from bin Laden of the kind of control he expected al-Qaeda Central to exert, see CTC, "Letter from UBL to 'Atiyatullah al-Libi 4."

16. Eli Lake and Josh Rogin, "Exclusive: Courier Led U.S. to al Qaeda Internet Conference," *Daily Beast*, August 20, 2013, http://www.thedailybeast.com/ articles/2013/08/20/exclusive-courier-led-u-s-to-al-qaeda-internet-conference .html.

17. Whitney Eulich, "Al Qaeda Disavowal of ISIS Opens Door to Other Jihadist Groups," *Christian Science Monitor*, February 4, 2014, http://www.cs monitor.com/World/Security-Watch/terrorism-security/2014/0204/Al-Qaeda -disavowal-of-ISIS-opens-door-to-other-jihadist-groups.

18. Lahoud, *Beware of Imitators*, 5.

19. Nasser al-Bahri, *Guarding bin Laden: My Life in al-Qaeda* (London: Thin Man Press, 2013), 104.

20. CTC, "Al-Qa'ida Goals and Structure."

21. See, e.g., "Letters on al-Qa'ida's Operations in Africa," CTC, https://www.ctc .usma.edu/posts/letters-on-al-qaidas-operations-in-africa-english-translation-2; and Stout et al., *Terrorist Perspectives Project*, 67, 75–78.

22. Al-Bahri, *Guarding bin Laden*, 90–91.

23. "'Security and Intelligence Gathering,' Prepared and Published by the Egyptian Islamic Group (al-Gamaa al-Islamiya), unknown date (prior to 2003)," AQ-INSE-D-000–033, Conflict Records Research Center, Fort McNair, Washington DC; and Stout et al., *Terrorist Perspectives Project*, 66.

24. Jessica M. Huckabey, "Jihads in Decline: What the Captured Records Tell Us," in *9/11, Ten Years Later: Insights on al-Qaeda's Past & Future through Captured Records*, ed. Lorry M. Fenner, Mark E. Stout, and Jessica L. Goldings (Washington: Johns Hopkins University Center for Advanced Governmental Studies, 2012), 78–79.

25. Abu Huthayfa, "A Memo to Sheikh Abu 'Abdullah (English Translation)," CTC, https://www.ctc.usma.edu/posts/a-memo-to-sheikh-abu-abdullah-english-trans lation-2.

26. Ibid.

27. CTC, "Letter from UBL to 'Atiyatullah al-Libi 3"; and "Letter from UBL to 'Atiyatullah al-Libi 2 (English Translation)," April 26, 2011, CTC, https://www.ctc .usma.edu/posts/letter-from-ubl-to-atiyatullah-al-libi-2-english-translation-2.

28. CTC, "Letter from Adam Gadahn (English Translation)," January 2011, https://www.ctc.usma.edu/posts/letter-from-adam-gadahn-english-translation-2.

29. CTC, "Letter from UBL to 'Atiyatullah al-Libi 4."

30. Ibid.

31. Ibid.

32. Ibid.

33. CTC, "Letter from UBL to 'Atiyatullah al-Libi 2."

34. CTC, "Analysis of the State of ISI (English Translation)," https://www.ctc.usma.edu/posts/analysis-of-the-state-of-isi-english-translation-2.

35. Rukmini Callimachi, "Al-Qaida Tip Sheet on Avoiding Drones Found in Mali," Associated Press, February 21, 2013, http://bigstory.ap.org/article/al-qaida-tip sheet-avoiding-drones-found-mali; Rukmini Callimachi, "Yemen Terror Boss Left Blueprint for Waging Jihad," August 9, 2013, http://bigstory.ap.org/article/yemen-terror-boss-left-blueprint-waging-jihad; and Associated Press, "Al-Qaida Papers: First Letter from Abu Basir to Emir of al-Qaida in the Islamic Maghreb," May 21, 2012, http://www.longwarjournal.org/images/al-qaida-papers-how-to-run-a-state.pdf.

36. "f," n.d., attached to ODNI New Release no 2-50.

37. Associated Press, "Mali-Al-Qaida's Sahara Playbook," http://hosted.ap.org/specials/interactives/_international/_pdfs/al-qaida-manifesto.pdf.

38. The standard work on al-Suri is Brynjar Lia, *Architect of Global Jihad: The Life of Al-Qaeda Strategist Abu Mus'ab Al-Suri* (New York: Columbia University Press, 2009). See also James Lacey, ed., *A Terrorist's Call to Global Jihad: Deciphering Abu Musab al-Suri's Islamic Jihad Manifesto* (Annapolis: Naval Institute Press, 2008).

39. 'Umar 'Abd-al-Hakim, "Afghanistan, the Taliban, and the Battle for Islam Today (English Translation)," CTC, https://www.ctc.usma.edu/posts/afghanistan-the-taliban-and-the-battle-for-islam-today-english-translation-2.

40. Abu Mus'ab al-Suri, "The Muslims in Central Asia and the Upcoming Battle of Islam (Original Language)," 1999, CTC, https://www.ctc.usma.edu/posts/the-muslims-in-central-asia-and-the-upcoming-battle-of-islam-original-language-2; and Huckabey, "Jihads in Decline," 79–80.

41. Ryan, *Decoding al-Qaeda's Strategy*, 214–15, 218–20.

42. Lacey, *A Terrorist's Call*, 8–10.

43. "f," n.d., attached to ODNI New Release no 2-50.

44. CTC, "Letter from UBL to 'Atiyatullah Al-Libi 4."

45. Associated Press, "Mali al-Qaida's Sahara Playbook"; and Flagg Miller, "Insights from Bin Laden's Audiocassette Library in Kandahar," *CTC Sentinel*, October 31, 2011, https://www.ctc.usma.edu/posts/insights-from-bin-ladin%E2%80%99s-audiocassette-library-in-kandahar.

46. Ayman al-Zawahiri, "General Guidelines for Jihad [A.H.] 1434," *Jihadology*, September 2013, https://azelin.files.wordpress.com/2013/09/dr-ayman-al-e1ba 93awc481hirc4ab-22general-guidelines-for-the-work-of-a-jihc481dc4ab22-en.pdf.

47. Joas Wagemakers, "Al-Qaida Advises the Arab Spring: Al-Maqdisi," *Jihadica*, August 23, 2013, http://www.jihadica.com/al-qaida-advises-the-arab-spring-al -maqdisi/; and Joas Wagemakers, "Al-Qaida Advises the Arab Spring: Egypt," April 22, 2012, http://www.jihadica.com/al-qaida-advises-the-arab-spring-egypt/.

48. Lacey, *A Terrorist's Call*, 10.

49. M. W. Zackie, "An Analysis of Abu Mus'ab al-Suri's 'Call to Global Islamic Resistance,'" *Journal of Strategic Security* 6, no. 1 (2013): 12; and al-Suri is quoted in Lacey, *A Terrorist's Call*, 5.

50. CTC, "Letter from UBL to 'Atiyatullah Al-Libi 4."

51. "Dokku (Dokka) Umarov, Leader of the Islamic Emirate of the Caucasus: Thousands of 'Mujahideen' in the Region," *Views from the Occident*, March 8, 2010, http://occident2.blogspot.com/2010/03/dokku-dokka-umarov-leader-of-islamic .html.

52. Kavkaz Center, "Appeal by Emir Dokku Abu Usman to Muslims of Caucasus and Russia: 'Fight Enemies Wherever Your Hand Reaches Them!,'" *Kavkazcenter.com*, March 3, 2011, http://www.kavkazcenter.com/eng/content/2011/03/03/13715 .shtml.

53. "Letter from Usama Bin Laden to Mukhtar Abu al-Zubayr (English Translation)," August 7, 2010, CTC, https://www.ctc.usma.edu/posts/letter-from-usama-bin -laden-to-mukhtar-abu-al-zubayr-english-translation-2.

54. Jessica M. Huckabey and Mark E. Stout, "Al Qaida's Views of Authoritarian Intelligence Services in the Middle East," *Intelligence and National Security* 25, no. 3 (2010): 327–49.

55. Abu Muhammad Asim al-Maqdisi, "Precaution, Secrecy and Concealment: Balancing between Negligence and Paranoia," At-Tibyan Publications, n.d., https:// azelin.files.wordpress.com/2010/08/precaution-secrecy-and-concealment -balancing-between-negligence-and-paranoia.pdf.

56. CTC, "Letter from UBL to 'Atiyatullah Al-Libi 3"; Associated Press, "The Al-Qaida Papers—Drones," June 17, 2011, http://hosted.ap.org/specials/inter actives/_international/_pdfs/al-qaida-papers-drones.pdf; and Paul Cruickshank, "UK Trial Reveals New Al Qaeda Strategy to Hit West," *CNN.com*, February 21 2013, http://security.blogs.cnn.com/2013/02/21/uk-trial-reveals-new -al-qaeda-strategy-to-hit-west/.

57. Associated Press, "Mali al-Qaida's Sahara Playbook"; Rukmini Callimachi, "In Timbuktu, al-Qaida Left behind a Manifesto," Associated Press, February 14, 2013, http://bigstory.ap.org/article/timbuktu-al-qaida-left-behind-strategic-plans; and Associated Press, "Mali-Al-Qaida's Sahara Playbook."

58. CTC, "Analysis of the State of ISI."

59. Ibid.; and Clint Watts, Jacob Shapiro, and Vahid Brown, *Al Qa'ida's (Mis)Adventures in the Horn of Africa*, Harmony Project (West Point NY: Combating Terrorism Center, July 2007).

60. CTC, "Letter from Usama Bin Laden to Mukhtar Abu al-Zubayr."

61. Callimachi, "Yemen Terror Boss"; and Associated Press, "Al-Qaida Papers: First Letter from Abus Basir."

62. "Mustafa Hamid's Analysis of Mujahidin Activities (English Translation)," CTC, https://www.ctc.usma.edu/posts/mustafa-hamids-analysis-of-mujahidin-activities-english-translation-2.

63. Stout et al., *Terrorist Perspectives Project*, 122–23.

64. Ibid., 52–55.

65. "'Atiyah's Letter to Zarqawi (English Translation)," 2005, CTC, https://www.ctc.usma.edu/posts/atiyahs-letter-to-zarqawi-english-translation-2; and CTC, "Letter from Adam Gadahn."

66. Lahoud, *Beware of Imitators*, 12.

67. CTC, "Letter from UBL to 'Atiyatullah Al-Libi 4."

68. Ryan, *Decoding al-Qaeda's Strategy*; and Stout et al., *Terrorist Perspectives Project*, 126–28.

PART IV: ALTERNATIVE DIMENSIONS OF ASSESSMENT

16

ASSESSMENT, PROPORTIONALITY, AND JUSTICE IN WAR

Bradley J. Strawser and Russell Muirhead

THE ANALYSES IN THIS VOLUME ILLUMINATE the metrics that are used to assess whether going to war is worthwhile and how successfully (or unsuccessfully) wars are going as they are being fought. These metrics constitute the most elemental aspect of assessing war; yet, as the chapters of this book reveal, generating clear, accurate, and usable metrics is not easy. Indeed, such metrics have often eluded both civilian and military leaders. The metrics many leaders have relied on have proven woefully erroneous, with grave consequences not only for the probability that wars will be prosecuted successfully but also for our ability to morally assess wars.

The uncertainty, confusion, misapprehension, and ignorance that arise as a result of shifting and inadequate metrics imperil our ability to invoke what is one of the most fundamental and central standards for assessing the justice of war—proportionality. A uniquely important standard, proportionality is the only standard of just war that is directly relevant to and applied within both *jus ad bellum* (the moral criteria governing the justice of waging a war) and *jus in bello* (the moral criteria governing the justice of the way in which war is waged). Many have followed Michael Walzer's seminal argument in *Just and Unjust Wars* that *jus ad bellum* and *jus in bello* are independent standards of moral assessment. Put briefly, it holds that one can fight unjustly even in a just cause or, vice versa and more controversially, that one's behavior in war can still be just even if the cause for which it is fought is not.[1] But even those recent so-called revisionist just war theorists who claim the two streams of analysis are connected (perhaps holding that one cannot fight justly in an unjust cause) agree that different considerations inform the two kinds of questions of whether the cause of war is just and whether the war is fought justly.[2]

The exception is with respect to proportionality, which matters in both kinds of analysis. The ubiquity of proportionality reflects the fact that it is a worldly, commonsense standard that does not invoke the often more subtle considerations only accessible to those practiced in the moral assessment of war. It simply asks whether a given war (or the tactics used in a war) is "worth it" given the amount of harm the war (or the tactics used in the war) will bring about in the world. This harm is usually taken to be the anticipated number of innocent people who will die, but it can, and often is, also taken to include the total military casualties that either side in a given war will suffer or even the total destruction to infrastructure, and so forth. Proportionality prevents the justice of war from becoming too rarified, too formal. Even in cases when there is a just cause and the other traditional requirements for *jus ad bellum* are met—that is, the war is waged as a last resort and for the right intention, the probability of success is high, and the war is decided on by a proper authority—still the war may be unjust if it imposes great costs in return for trivial gains.[3] Countries may have a right to go to war, for instance, when their territory is violated, but they may not invade, bomb, and occupy a neighboring country merely to answer a small cross-border incursion by a few soldiers. Occasionally countries are criticized for violating proportionality even when the other standards of *jus ad bellum* are in place. For instance, some international institutions and countries criticized Israel's invasion of Lebanon on this basis in 2006.[4] Proportionality may be a commonsense standard, but it is not without teeth or controversy.

To clarify an oft-confused point, proportionality is not a crude tit-for-tat standard that holds if one side in a conflict imposes X amount of harm, the other side is only behaving proportionately if they respond with a similar X amount of harm. Rather, it is that for any given harm—either the overall, total harm unleashed by a war (on the *jus ad bellum* metric) or the specific harm unleashed by a particular operation (on the *jus in bello* metric)—the harm done must be worth, or proportionate to, the good to be gained by such harm. The good to be attained in the *jus ad bellum* proportionality determination is accomplishing the just cause; the good to be attained in the *jus in bello* proportionality determination is the success of a given mission or operation and its contribution to overall victory in the war.[5]

Another way in which proportionality assessments should be used in our moral reasoning about war is in our decisions on when to end a war once it has begun. This relatively new part of just war theory analysis—when it is right to end a war—has been dubbed *jus ex bello*.[6] The proportionality question for *jus ex bello* is when, all things considered, the good to be attained by the *continuance* of an already ongoing war no longer outweighs the harms that are now predicted to result in attaining victory. That is, at what point (if ever) does a war, initially deemed just at the start (it met the *jus ad bellum* conditions, including initial proportionality assessments), become no longer just to continue because our newly revised assessments tell us that the costs of continuing the war would simply be too high?

However they are deployed as a standard of analysis, proportionality assessments have always implicitly *assumed* that we can in fact estimate the number of deaths and grievous injuries that innocent people or soldiers will suffer as a consequence of going to war. They assume, in short, that in going to war we can reliably estimate the "cost"—more concretely, the deaths and grievous injuries—of what we are getting into. The analyses in this volume cast serious doubt on that basic proposition; indeed, there is ample reason to believe that we lack the ability to accurately assess the costs of war before a war begins. Moreover, the absence of solid metrics for assessing the progress of wars suggests that once a war has commenced, we lack the ability to accurately assess the costs that will be incurred to achieve a successful outcome.

Consider, for instance, some of the examples in this volume. Brooks Simpson argues that Abraham Lincoln and his advisers believed that secessionist fervor would quickly subside in 1861, and their systematic underestimation of the enemy's determination and resilience led to mistaken strategies and miscalculating the costs of the war. Brian Linn shows us that during the Philippine War, American military leaders in Manila restricted their sources of local information in ways that caused them to vastly underestimate the intensity of Philippine resistance. Scott Stephenson demonstrates how in World War I the German military leadership's exaggeration of the chances of success was "desperately unrealistic and devoid of political context."

This persistent inability to accurately gauge the costs of war is not restricted to the historical record; it continues to distort both political and strategic decision making about war. In late February 2003, testifying to the Senate Armed Services Committee, US Army chief of staff Gen. Eric K. Shinseki said that an invasion of Iraq would require "something on the order of several hundred thousand soldiers." Two days later, testifying to the House Budget Committee, Deputy Defense Secretary Paul Wolfowitz called Shinseki's estimate "wildly off the mark." The defense secretary himself, Donald Rumsfeld, said, "The idea that it would take several hundred thousand U.S. forces I think is far off the mark." Both Wolfowitz and Rumsfeld denied that it was possible to estimate the monetary costs of such a war. "We have no idea what we will need until we get there on the ground," Wolfowitz said.[7]

Wolfowitz and Rumsfeld, of course, had a political reason to contradict the general: They wanted to generate public support for the invasion and thus had an interest in minimizing the invasion's anticipated costs. Any public official who supports a war has a similar interest, and we should expect that advocates of war will always bias estimates of a war's human and monetary costs downward. But it is not clear that Wolfowitz and Rumsfeld—or the various political and military leaders discussed in other chapters of this volume— were trying to deceive the political leadership or the public about the costs of war. From Lincoln to Rumsfeld, leaders seem to have authentically believed their own subsequently disproven estimates of the cost of war. Perhaps they deluded themselves; in any case, in the end they were simply mistaken. Given the absence of concrete and workable metrics—the situation that this volume has taken on to repair—such mistakes should not be surprising.

Of course, the mistakes all tend in the same direction: They *underestimate* the costs of war. Without any method of generating accurate forecasts, and in the presence of powerful psychological and political pressures to maximize the probability of success (by minimizing the anticipated costs), such understatement is also understandable. We should expect, in general, that estimates of the costs of war will be discounted, often massively, in comparison with the true costs.

The tendency to understate the costs of war in turn has a fundamental consequence for the way we think about proportionality in *jus ad bellum*. Generally it means that the benefits must not merely be proportional to the costs but should vastly *exceed* the estimated costs of military engagements if wars are to pass the proportionality test. In the extreme, one might argue that the uncertainty that afflicts estimates of military costs and casualties is so severe that we cannot make estimates of proportionality at all; therefore, the only wars that can be justified are those where the benefits are so extreme they would justify *any* cost.[8] But the uncertainty around prewar casualty estimates is probably not so vast as to warrant such a conclusion, or so one would hope. What the cases in this volume suggest is that the costs of war are systematically underestimated and might be corrected by introducing an error factor into cost estimates. We could, for instance, multiply the estimated cost by some factor and then hold that the criterion of proportionality is not satisfied unless the anticipated benefits of war exceed two (or three) times the estimated costs. What the error factor should be will certainly be a bit contrived, but introducing any error factor will make analyses of proportionality more accurate and more morally coherent given the rampant historical underestimating of wars' costs. The consequence, in the end, is that fewer wars will satisfy the moral criteria of just war. Such a conclusion is quite plausible given that many wars certainly appear to be unjust once they are in the rear-view mirror of history—that is, only after it has been regretfully discovered that the war's costs were so much higher than initially predicted.

All of this discussion is analytically straightforward. Things get far more complicated, however, when we consider how analyses of proportionality are used *after* wars commence. We do not mean here to refer to the way proportionality is used in considerations of *jus in bello*, or the justifications of the methods and tactics in the ways wars are fought. We mean rather the application of proportionality to questions of *jus ex bello*, as discussed earlier. One way to understand *jus ex bello* in this regard is to think of it as the reiterated asking of the moral question that arises before a war commences: Is the war just? The criteria that inform the answer to this question often change as a war is being fought. The cause of a war, for instance, may shift during the course of fighting. A war to prevent secession becomes a war to end slavery (in the case of the US Civil War), a war to contain the threat posed by weapons of mass destruction becomes a war to establish a representative government that is accountable to the people (in the case of the US war in Iraq), and a war to defeat al-Qaeda becomes a war to establish a rights-respecting regime (in the case of the US war in Afghanistan). As the cause of war transforms during a war, so the moral analysis of whether the war is justified must be reengaged. Wars that might be justified initially (before they commence) may become unjust to continue, and wars that might not have been justified in their initial stages might become just wars as their defining purposes shift.

A similar reiteration of the proportionality standard in our *jus ex bello* analysis should occur as we learn more about the costs of war during the course of fighting. As cost estimates become more accurate in the course of a war, the proportionality standard must be reengaged. But exactly how this reengagement should work is an open—and quite difficult—question. In the initial analysis, the way proportionality works is simple and intuitive: Prior to the start of a war, the higher its estimated cost, the more difficult it is to satisfy the *jus ad bellum* proportionality standard. Thus, as estimated costs go up, the anticipated benefits of a successful outcome must also be greater if the costs and benefits are to be proportional.

But it is not clear that proportionality works in the same way during the course of fighting. If, for instance, we learn during the course of fighting that the costs of a war are higher than was believed initially (measured in the number of soldiers and noncombatants killed, perhaps), then, by using the analysis the same way *during* a war as is done *prior* to the start of a war, it would become more difficult to justify continuing with the war if we hold the anticipated benefits constant (as they presumably are if the cause for the war has not shifted). If the aims and the expected benefits of a war are constant and if the estimated costs of attaining success increase, in principle it should be the case that the war that was justified initially becomes unjust during the course of fighting. In the view of Darrel Moellendorf, once the costs initially deemed to be proportionate for a given war are exceeded, then the war becomes unjust to continue fighting.[9] We note that this may be a central reason why the goals of a war tend to expand during the course of fighting. By expanding the goods that will be attained in a successful outcome, the (increased, initially unanticipated) costs of a war remain proportionate.

However, some argue that as estimates of the costs of a war increase, it becomes, in fact, easier to justify the war. This unintuitive development depends on entertaining a new kind of goal, one that almost necessarily arises during the course of fighting—that is, ensuring that those who have been killed have not died in vain for a failed cause. While this point may sound initially superficial, upon reflection it can carry some significant moral weight. If one imagines being called upon by his or her state to fight in a just war and dying in that war, surely one would rather have his or her death be part of a successful just war effort than a failed one. Jeff McMahan has argued that this "redemptive value" for soldiers' sacrifices made on behalf of a just cause should be taken seriously and can impact our thinking about the good to be attained in a given war.[10] McMahan writes,

> Soldiers are often willing to risk and sometimes even to sacrifice their lives for the achievement of a just cause. It matters to them, however, that the just cause actually be achieved. They may be willing to give their lives to achieve a noble end, but few are willing to die for what they can know will be a failed attempt that will achieve nothing. Thus, whether the just cause of a war is actually achieved can affect, albeit retroactively, the meaning and significance of the deaths of those who lost their lives in its pursuit. If the just war in which they fought ends in victory, they will have died while contributing to the achievement of a just and perhaps noble aim. But if it ends in defeat, their sacrifices will have had less significance.[11]

And if such moral reasoning matters to those who die waging a war, it should matter to the decision makers deciding whether to continue fighting a war or to end it. Note, importantly, this line of reasoning is not claiming that the *value* of a soldier's life (or death) is dependent upon the attainment of a just cause; a soldier's death is a tragedy regardless. However, the success of a just cause adds a new moral good of redeeming the loss of a soldier within our proportionality calculus, for the soldier's death helped attain this good rather than serving no greater good. Thus, the redemptive force the success of the cause can generate is *added* to the good to be attained by victory, affecting the proportionality calculus from the other side of the scale. As McMahan writes, "It is not, therefore, that a soldier's loss is diminished if the just cause for which he risked his life is achieved. It is, rather, that his loss is partially *redeemed*."[12]

There is still another way one could approach the question of proportionality assessments as a war goes along. One could hold that for any given decision one must make in the present regarding proportionality concerns, all one should rightly weigh are those costs that one can predict to occur going *forward*. David Rodin has argued for such a view.[13] He contends that past costs should be discounted at every new reiteration point of a proportionality decision to continue forward with a given cause. This is because the proportionality decision at time t_2 is not over whether the costs going forward from t_2 plus the previously incurred costs from time t_1 are worth a continuance of the war effort. Rather, all proportionality considerations are simply questions at the given present time over whether the future predicted costs are worth the future predicted gains. Otherwise, we risk getting caught in a "sunk costs problem." We must look instead, Rodin insists, afresh at the predicted costs with each new iteration of a proportionality assessment. Otherwise, we will become stuck in a sunk costs problem wherein the costs of an ongoing war will become so large as the war continues that there will be no way the good to be achieved could ever be worth the costs, even if only minor further costs were necessary to achieve the goal. Or, in the least, Rodin argues, we should heavily discount the past losses so as to avoid such sunk costs problems. But, Rodin notes, such thinking, while rational, can get us caught its own kind of particularly sticky war trap, as we shall discuss later.

So we have three views on how to handle proportionality assessments *jus ex bello*. Consider a simplistic example to better explain the views. In the first view, as expressed by Moellendorf, we must apply a reiteration of the initial *jus ad bellum* proportionality assessment continuously as a war goes along to gain ever-new (and hopefully better) cost assessments. In this view, we should hold the initial cost barrier (the proportionality cost ceiling) constant, even as cost totals and estimates change, and make our decisions to continue or end the war by staying true to our initial threshold.

Imagine that we initially predict that a given war would result in 1,000 casualties and that this also represents the cost ceiling—that is, the limit of the costs proportionate to the good to be attained by waging this war. If we initially assess that the war would result in 1,100 casualties, then we would hold that the good to be attained is not worth waging war and we would not enter it. But suppose we do enter the war and, after incurring some unpredicted high losses in a few battles, sustain 1,000 casualties. Should our new war assessment inform our decision makers that we can attain victory at the cost of (only) another predicted 150 casualties, on this first view of proportionality *jus ex bello*, we must stop waging the war. It has become disproportionate to our initial standard of what we have concluded is proportionate to the good to be attained by victory; therefore it is wrong to continue. We arrive at this conclusion because the estimated losses would now total 1,150, or greater than the ceiling of proportionate harm we originally concluded the war is worth.

In the second view of proportionality assessment *jus ex bello*, the assessment is different for such a case. In this view, as expressed by McMahan, the good to be attained by victory includes not only the original good, which is the cause for war to be attained in the first place, but also the redeeming factor that the 1,000 lives lost will not have been in vain were we to continue fighting the war and achieve victory. That is, the 1,000 lives lost at this point in the war must be *added* to the good that could potentially be attained by victory; thus, the redemption of those deaths becomes itself a further cause to continue fighting. It is unclear in this view how much good the redemption value of winning the war adds to the overall good attained by victory, but, presumably, it would be significant enough that in some cases, such as this example, it would be proportionate to continue fighting.

In the third view of proportionality assessment *jus ex bello,* things are different still. In this view, as expressed by Rodin, the costs under consideration must be weighed differently as the war goes along; that is, we must only consider future costs to be had for any decision we are currently making about a future good to be achieved. So at time t_1, before the war begins, we deem the costs of 1,000 lives lost proportionate to the good to be attained by victory. But now at time t_2, we have to decide whether the good to be attained by victory is worth 150 lives. In this view, clearly the answer is yes, because we originally decided that that same good was worth 1,000; so clearly it is worth 150 lives now in making our decision at time t_2. Moellendorf here would object and argue that in fact it is not whether 150 lives is worth the good to be attained but whether 150 *more* lives—that is, 1,000 plus the 150—is worthwhile. But Rodin insists that the decision before us at time t_2 is whether now, *going forward*, we think it is worth 150 lives to attain the same good we initially said was worth 1,000. And clearly it is.

But, of course, as Rodin laments, this kind of thinking, while it may be rational at time t_2, can result in a perplexing war trap for our proportionality assessments. This trap occurs because this kind of decision can, in theory, continue indefinitely. That is, with each new assessment, the prediction can be that with "just a few more losses," we will have victory.[14] In such a scenario, Rodin is seemingly correct: it would be irrational to not try to attain victory and a substantial good with only (relatively) minor costs to be incurred. But precisely because war assessments are so notoriously unreliable—as this volume has shown—this kind of rational decision at any given particular point (t_1, t_2, t_3, and so on) can become irrational *on the whole* because it can result in never-ending wars.

A similar war trap may arise from McMahan's analysis. McMahan is right to focus attention on the obligations of those who are willing to bear the greatest risks of war, but the logic of these obligations directs us away from proportionality. From the soldiers' point of view, if a cause is worth dying for, it is worth winning at almost any cost. If once soldiers start dying in a war we have a moral duty to make good on their sacrifice, then proportionality matters far less. Indeed, it may not matter at all.

This problem is only compounded further if we combine the second and third views here on proportionality. That is, if we add in McMahan's claim that the good to be attained is itself increased as losses rack up because of the possibility of those past losses being redeemed in a successful war effort, the war trap becomes almost insurmountable on any proportionality calculus. And this entire problem, notice, is exacerbated by the unreliability of accurate wartime assessments either before a war has begun or once the war is under way. Were we better able to make accurate wartime assessments before a war ever began, then we would not face such profound and perhaps morally inscrutable problems of which is the right way to evaluate proportionality. On the one hand, perhaps the first view expressed by Moellendorf is right, and when we hit our prewar assessment ceiling of what costs are disproportionate, we must simply stop fighting. But that thinking results in cases where that decision clearly seems irrational, especially if the goal is close at hand with only minimal further cost. Yet if we take either or both of the competing views, we end up in equally irrational war traps of the kind described here—that is, we find ourselves stuck in a quagmire of perpetual war, far outstripping the value we originally believed it had. Hence, precisely *because* of the problems endemic to deriving accurate and reliable assessments, the critical moral concept of proportionality—a central pillar for just war theory—is made moot.

Without metrics, the most elemental standard of just war theory is nearly impossible to deploy. So long as roughly accurate forecasts elude us, so long as metrics of a war's success are impossible to forge, the doctrine of proportionality is likely to lead to a war trap in which fighting and more fighting always seems justified, if not required. It might not be an exaggeration to say that without metrics that allow us to forecast costs, the very enterprise of just war theory must be relegated to a purely intellectual exercise. Just war theory is philosophic, but it is not unworldly; it is not as if the justice of wars can be decided in a manner independent of the worldly costs that war is likely to impose, often on perfectly innocent persons. For just war theory to guide and constrain the use of military force, it must rely on elemental estimates about the costs of war. There is ample reason to believe that such estimates have not been accurate—not principally because some have an interest in distorting them but, more devastatingly, because we simply do not know how to produce them. This volume is an emphatic step in the right direction. Unless efforts like this one succeed, the urgent enterprise of assessing the justice of war will be consigned to academic debates, not the realm of decision makers.

NOTES

1. Michael Walzer, *Just and Unjust Wars: A Moral Argument with Historical Illustrations* (New York: Basic Books, 1977).

2. Those in the revisionist camp include McMahan, Rodin, Fabre, and one of the authors of this article. See Jeff McMahan, *Killing in War* (New York: Oxford University Press, 2009); David Rodin, *War and Self-defense* (New York: Oxford University Press, 2003); Cécile Fabre, *Cosmopolitan War* (Oxford: Oxford University Press, 2012); and Bradley J. Strawser, "Walking the Tightrope of Just War," *Analysis* 71 (July 2011): 533–44.

3. Brian Orend, "War," *Stanford Encyclopedia of Philosophy*, section 2.1, February 4, 2000, substantive revision July 28, 2005, available at http://plato.stanford.edu/entries/war/#2.1.

4. Enzo Cannizzaro, "Contextualizing Proportionality: Jus as Bellum and Jus in Bello in the Lebanese War," *International Review of the Red Cross* 88, no. 864 (December 2006): 779–92.

5. Under revisionist just war theory, following the principle of proportionality *in bello* becomes particularly difficult to reconcile for a side that has not met the conditions of *jus ad bellum* (that is, a side that is fighting for an unjust cause). It is hard to see what the "good" is that any given military operation is trying to attain for an unjust side, because, presumably, victory for the unjust cause would not be a good. If that is correct, then there is no good to be attained that counterbalances the harm the unjust side unleashes in its war efforts. As such, revisionist just war theorists claim that those fighting for an unjust cause cannot meet the principle of proportionality, *in principle*.

6. See Darrel Moellendorf, "Jus Ex Bello," *Journal of Political Philosophy* 16, no. 2 (June 2008): 123–36. Also see David Rodin, "Two Emerging Issues of Jus Post

Bellum: War Termination and the Liability of Soldiers for Crimes of Aggression," in *Jus Post Bellum: Reflections on a Law of Transition from Conflict to Peace*, ed. Jane Kleffner and Carsten Stahn (The Hague: T. M. C. Asser Press, 2008). Note that Rodin refers to this area of moral analysis of war as *jus terminatio*.

7. Eric Schmitt, "Threats and Responses: Military Spending; Pentagon Contradicts General on Iraq Occupation Force's Size," *New York Times*, February 28, 2003, A14, accessed at http://www.nytimes.com/2003/02/28/us/threats-responses -military-spending-pentagon-contradicts-general-iraq-occupation.html.

8. Many might hold this view for wars of an "existential threat," for example.

9. See Darrel Moellendorf, "Two Doctrines of Jus Ex Bello," *Ethics* 125, no. 3 (April 2015): 653–73.

10. See Jeff McMahan, "Proportionality and Time," *Ethics* 125, no. 3 (April 2015): 696–719.

11. Ibid., 13.

12. Ibid., 14.

13. See David Rodin, "The War Trap: Dilemmas of *jus terminatio*," *Ethics* 125, no. 3 (April 2015): 674–95.

14. Consider how often we see this public discourse over a war's continuance. In the US war in Iraq, for example, Bush administration officials often expressed that the resistance was in its "last throes" and just a bit more work needed to be done to quell the insurgency. See, for instance, "Iraq Insurgency in Its 'Last Throes,' Cheney Says," cnn.com, June 20, 2015, available at http://www.cnn.com/2005/ US/05/30/cheney.iraq/.

17

ASSESSING CYBER WAR

Dorothy E. Denning

THIS CHAPTER INTRODUCES A FRAMEWORK for assessing cyber war. The framework can be used to assess a war that takes place exclusively in cyberspace or to assess the cyber component of a war that cuts across multiple domains—for example, land, air, and cyber. It is written from the perspective of one country, say the United States, which is engaged in a cyber war with an adversary.

The framework provides for two types of assessments. The first, cyber battle damage assessment, is used to evaluate the effects of cyber operations to determine whether operational goals and benchmarks are met. The second, cyber strength, is used to determine the relative strength of our own cyber forces against those of the adversary so that we can estimate the likely success of planned and future cyber operations by ourselves and the adversary.

Although the framework might be applicable to all types of cyber operations, the focus here is on *cyber attacks*, defined by the National Institute of Standards and Technology (NIST) as attacks "via cyberspace, targeting an enterprise's use of cyberspace for the purpose of disrupting, disabling, destroying, or maliciously controlling a computing environment/infrastructure; or destroying the integrity of the data or stealing controlled information."[1] Note that under this definition, cyber espionage and intelligence collection, or what the US Department of Defense calls exploitations, are considered to be cyber attacks. However, the definition excludes influence and information operations that do not affect cyber resources.

The framework uses as its foundation risk assessment, which is an assessment of the risks to cyber systems, operations, and organizations from cyber attacks. The chapter describes the elements of risk assessment, using the NIST model as its basis. It then shows how risk assessment can be applied to assess cyber war. With the framework in place, the chapter then discusses some of the difficult issues and challenges that arise in cyber war assessment.

RISK ASSESSMENT

Risk assessment is the process of identifying, estimating, and prioritizing risks that arise from the operation of cyber systems. These risks can jeopardize cyber systems, individuals and organizations, and a nation as a whole.

Cyber risks are identified and evaluated in terms of threats, vulnerabilities, impacts, and likelihoods. *Threats* are events that can cause harm. Sources of threats can be either adversarial or non-adversarial, with the latter covering accidents and natural disasters. Here we are concerned primarily with adversarial sources, which can be individuals, groups, organizations, and nation-states and are characterized by capability, intent, and targeting. Cyber threats from adversarial sources correspond to events associated with cyber attacks. Threat events are described by the tactics, techniques, and procedures used—for example, cracking passwords to gain unauthorized access, sending links to malware in deceptive e-mail messages, exfiltrating data from a compromised computer to a drop site, or flooding a site with packets in a denial-of-service (DoS) attack.

Vulnerabilities are weaknesses that can be exploited by an adversary. They include flaws in technology (both hardware and software), the configuration and operation of cyber systems (e.g., failing to change default system passwords), user practices (e.g., clicking on malicious links), and business practices (e.g., failing to plan for contingencies and ensure continuity of services). They are examined in the context of predisposing conditions, including system architecture and cyber defenses in place.

Impacts are the effects or harms produced by threat events. They include harms that can result from unauthorized disclosure or theft of data from cyber systems and from tampering with or denying access to cyber systems. They include both effects to cyber systems (e.g., data deleted or systems down or corrupted) and effects to those who depend on them (e.g., inability to perform functions of organization).

Likelihoods are the chances that threats will be realized (attacks will be initiated and then succeed) and that harms will occur. Once threats, vulnerabilities, impacts, and likelihoods have been identified and evaluated, they are combined to determine risk. The result is an appraisal of the ability of the cyber systems and organizations under review to resist and withstand the identified cyber threats.

Risk assessment can be quantitative, qualitative, or something in between. With quantitative assessment, individual factors are given numerical values, say on a scale from 1 (lowest) to 10 (highest). With qualitative assessment, they are given categorical values, say ranging from very low to very high. An approach in between might assign numeric ranges to categories such as 1–2 to very low, 3–4 to low, 5–6 to medium, 7–8 to high, and 9–10 to very high.

The NIST's *Guide for Conducting Risk Assessments* (Special Publication 800–30) offers a model and guidance for conducting risk assessments.[2] The processes and approach described therein are intended to be consistent with the risk assessment standards of the International Organization for Standardization and the International Electrotechnical Commission. The NIST guidance includes sample tables for identifying and qualitatively assessing each of the individual risk factors. The table for adversarial threat events, for example, includes descriptions for more than eighty sample events associated with cyber attacks. In addition, the guidance offers a sample adversarial risk table for combining the factors to determine risk (see table 17.1). Each row of the table corresponds to a threat event in a potential cyber attack. The columns of the table describe the threat event; possible sources of the threat and an assessment of their capability, intent, and targeting; the relevance of the event; the vulnerabilities that could be exploited by the threat and an assessment of their severity; the likelihood of one or more sources initiating the cyber attack and then succeeding; the level of impact from the threat event; and finally risk as a combination of likelihood and impact.

The NIST risk assessment methodology can be applied across three levels: Tier 1, or the organizational level; Tier 2, or the mission-business process level; and Tier 3, the cyber systems level. The levels correspond roughly to strategic, operational, and tactical risks, respectively.

CYBER WAR ASSESSMENT

To assess cyber war, we need to be able to assess two things. First, we need to assess cyber battle damages—namely, the effects of cyber operations—to determine if the United States is meeting its operational goals or benchmarks. Second, we need to assess our relative cyber strength against that of the adversary to determine the likely success of planned and future cyber operations by ourselves and the adversary. The following describes how the concepts and factors used in risk assessment apply to these assessment efforts.

Cyber battle damages are the effects produced by cyber operations conducted by ourselves and our adversary. These effects can be direct or indirect

Table 17.1 Sample adversarial risk table

Column	Heading	Content
1	Threat event	Identify threat event
2	Threat sources	Identify threat sources that could initiate event
3	Capability	Assess threat source capability
4	Intent	Assess threat source intent
5	Targeting	Assess threat source targeting
6	Relevance	Determine relevance of threat event
7	Likelihood of attack initiation	Determine likelihood that a threat source initiates the threat event
8	Vulnerabilities and predisposing conditions	Identify vulnerabilities that could be exploited during threat events and conditions that could increase the likelihood of adverse impacts
9	Severity pervasiveness	Assess severity of vulnerabilities and pervasiveness of predisposing conditions
10	Likelihood initiated attack succeeds	Determine likelihood that an initiated threat event succeeds
11	Overall likelihood	Determine likelihood that threat event is initiated and succeeds
12	Level of impact	Determine adverse impact of threat event
13	Risk	Determine risk of threat event as combination of likelihood and impact

Adapted from table 1-4 of NIST, *Guide for Conducting Risk Assessments*, Special Publication 800–30 (Gaithersburg MD: NIST, September 2012).

and correspond to the impacts used in risk assessment. The difference is that whereas risk assessment is concerned with the effects of *potential* cyber attacks, cyber battle damage assessment is concerned with the effects of *actual* cyber attacks. However, both deal with effects not only to cyber systems but also to the organizations that depend on them.

The effects on cyber systems can be expressed in terms of effects relating to data and effects relating to hardware and software. Effects relating to data include exfiltration of data, corruption and destruction of data, and insertion of false data. They might be measured in terms of bytes, records, files, or media. For example, they could be reported as 100 gigabytes of data exfiltrated, 250,000 customer records taken and posted online, 15 files corrupted, 1 website defaced, or the hard disks of 30,000 machines erased. Effects relating to hardware and software include corruption and destruction of hardware and software, injection of backdoors and other malicious software (malware), system takeovers (i.e., system under control of adversary), and system outages (e.g., system becomes inaccessible because of a DoS attack). They might be measured in terms of the number of systems or components affected or the length of outages or disruptions.

The effects of cyber attacks on organizations can be expressed in terms of operational effects, monetary losses, and reputational effects. Operational effects include the inability to perform certain functions or to provide certain services. In a warfare environment, examples would be the inability to provide logistical support, rely on air defenses, deploy computer-controlled weapons systems, execute command and control, communicate with forward-deployed troops, or access certain intelligence sources. They might be measured in terms of the scope or duration of operations affected.

Monetary losses include direct losses (e.g., from fraudulent money transfers) as well as costs associated with responding to and recovering from cyber attacks (e.g., restoring systems, changing passwords, installing software updates or new security products, and investigating incidents). Monetary losses may be less important to military organizations than losses to operational capability during war, but they are still important as they reduce the funds available for other products and services.

Reputational effects include lost stature, trust, and respect that can undermine military objectives and missions. During war, for example, human intelligence sources might refrain from providing further information after a system compromise exposes them to possible harm, or allied forces might be unwilling to share their intelligence data if they believe it will not be adequately protected. Reputational effects can be enduring, jeopardizing future operations.

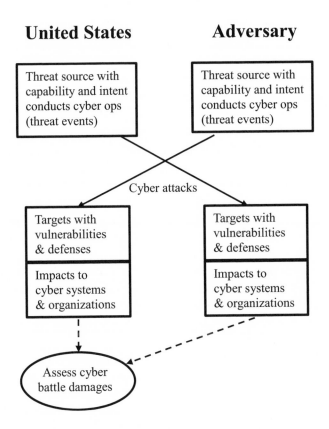

United States   **Adversary**

Figure 17.1. Assessing cyber battle damages from US perspective

Note: Solid lines represent actual cyber attacks; dashed lines represent information flows for battle damage assessments.

We need to assess cyber battle damages inflicted on us as well as those inflicted on the adversary. In general, it will be easier to assess our own damages than those of the adversary, where our situational awareness is likely to be incomplete. However, we need to estimate the effects to their systems and organizations to know if we are meeting our operational goals and benchmarks in the cyber domain. Figure 17.1 illustrates.

Cyber strength refers to our relative advantage over the adversary in cyber war—that is, our ability to affect its cyber systems and operations versus its ability to likewise affect ours. To measure cyber strength, we need to consider more than the cyber capabilities of ourselves and the adversary. We also need to know whether our cyber operations are likely to succeed against the adversary and produce the desired effects, and conversely whether the adversary's operations are likely to succeed against us with their intended effects.

The only way to know if our cyber operations against the adversary will succeed is to factor in the adversary's vulnerabilities and defenses, and the only way to know what effects to expect is to add the impacts and likelihoods of success to the equation. This requires conducting a risk assessment of the adversary's systems while using ourselves as the threat source; that is, we need to consider the risk to the adversary of threat events caused by our cyber attacks. Even if our own capability is high, if the adversary either does not use cyber systems or has well-defended systems for functions we want to affect, our cyber capability will not afford an advantage. Likewise, the only way to know if the adversary's operations against us will succeed is to take into account our vulnerabilities, our defenses, and the impacts and likelihoods of its attacks. This requires conducting a risk assessment of our systems while using the adversary as the threat source. Only after undertaking these risk assessments will we know if our cyber operations and our adversary's are likely to succeed and create the desired effects. Figure 17.2 illustrates the process of assessing (a) their risk from our potential cyber attacks and (b) our risk from their potential cyber attacks.

Our cyber strength (CS) is then expressed as the ratio of the adversary's risk to ours, where its risk is determined using ourselves as a single threat source against it and where our risk is determined by using the adversary as a single threat source against us. Thus, all rows in its adversarial risk table have us as the threat source, and all rows in our table have the adversary as the threat source. If we let risk (to X from Y) denote the risk to X from threat source Y, conceptually we have:

$$CS = \text{risk (to adversary from US)} \,/\, \text{risk (to US from adversary)}.$$

If CS > 1, then the adversary's risk is higher than ours. That means we are in a better position to affect its systems and operations than conversely; in military terms, it is similar to the notion of having air superiority. If CS = 1, we are equally matched. And if CS < 1, we are at a disadvantage; the adversary can harm us more than we can harm it.

Although CS is expressed as the ratio of two risk scores, the risk methodology outlined earlier does not yield a single estimate for risk but rather a risk estimate for each threat event. Further, these estimates could be qualitative rather than quantitative. To produce a single estimate of risk, the risks for the individual threat events must be combined in some way. If the risk estimates are numeric, this might be done by taking their weighted average,

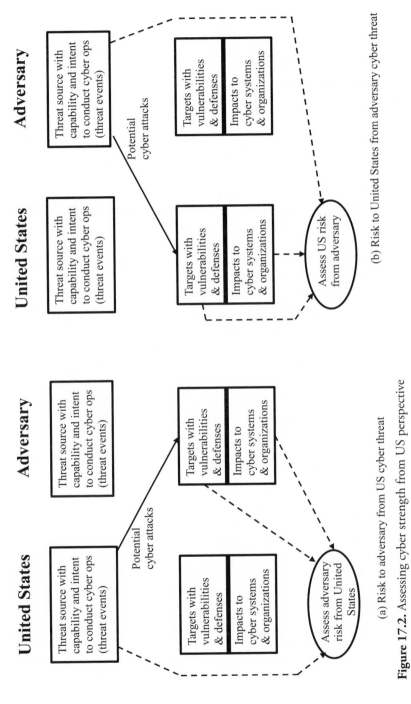

(a) Risk to adversary from US cyber threat

Figure 17.2. Assessing cyber strength from US perspective

Note: Solid lines represent potential cyber attacks; dashed lines represent information flows for risk assessment.

(b) Risk to United States from adversary cyber threat

where the weights reflect the priority of the threat events. If the risk estimates are qualitative, they might be converted to numbers and then used to produce a weighted average. Alternatively, if the threat events for each side are equivalent, rather than reducing each side's risk to a single score, risk could be expressed as a vector of scores. With that approach, we can determine the strength of the United States relative to the adversary for different types of cyber attacks.

While the focus here is on cyber operations, the same reasoning applies to other domains. To assess the strength of any type of military force against an adversary, one needs to consider the adversary's risk relative to these forces. In the domains of land and sea, geography especially is an important factor. Army forces, for example, may be capable of defeating almost any enemy on a conventional battleground, but if the conflict takes place in a highly populated urban environment, they may lack the training and experience to fight effectively in that environment. Similarly otherwise strong naval forces might have little to offer against an adversary that is landlocked.

In performing the risk assessments needed to measure cyber strength, we need to consider every cyber system that could be the target of a cyber operation. In addition to military systems, they might include civilian systems such as those used for communications, electric power distribution, or finance. We will say more about this issue later when we discuss scope.

Although methodologies are available for estimating the impacts and losses from cyber attacks (battle damage assessment) and for conducting risk assessment, they have not been combined in the manner proposed here to assess cyber strength in the context of cyber war. In particular, the idea of conducting a risk assessment of adversary systems while using ourselves as the threat source is novel, as is the idea of looking at the adversary's threat in terms of the risk it poses to our systems and not just in terms of its capabilities and intent.

Assessing capabilities and intent, however, is a large part of the picture, and the approach introduced here can build on earlier efforts to do that. A team at the Naval Postgraduate School developed a methodology for assessing the state threat by examining not only a state's military cyber capabilities but also what is going on more broadly inside the state regarding industry, academia, and hackers. In the process, the methodology was used to assess the cyber threats of Iran and North Korea.[3] While the approach was qualitative and ad hoc, a subsequent effort used the Situational Influence Assessment Module (SIAM) influence modeling tool to create a more quantitative approach. The resulting Cyber Warfare Capability Model uses a four-level, hierarchical model to assess a state's cyber capability.[4] In addition to the Naval Postgraduate School's work, a University of New Hampshire research team, under the direction of Andrew Macpherson, developed a Cyber Threat Calculator to assess both the state and non-state cyber threat in terms of capability and intent.[5] Technolytics published numerical scores of cyber capability and intent for more than sixty countries, but it did not describe the methodology used in its assessments.[6]

ISSUES

While conceptually straightforward, the approach outlined in the previous section for assessing cyber war is complex and difficult. This section discusses some of the issues raised. Although many of these problems pertain to assessments of war in general, others are peculiar to or aggravated by cyber war.

DEALING WITH COMPLEXITY AND UNCERTAINTY

Risk assessment is hard, uncertain, and speculative. It is difficult, if not impossible, to identify and assess all of the factors contributing to risk, including threats, vulnerabilities, impacts, and likelihoods. There are too many unknowns and insufficient data to ground assessments. Knowledge is incomplete and the future uncertain. Security researchers are continually finding new vulnerabilities and methods of attack, and cyber attacks can have cascading effects, owing to dependencies.

Consider the task of assessing our risk from adversarial cyber threats. We need to know the adversary's cyber capability, intent, and targeting strategy along with the types of cyber events that could arise during its cyber attacks. We need to know whether our own systems and operations are vulnerable to these attacks and the likelihood of the attacks succeeding. We need to know the impact of successful attacks, not only to cyber systems, but also to operations, organizations, and the nation. We need to know the likelihood of these impacts being realized. None of these factors are easy to determine.

Each year, thousands of new vulnerabilities in software systems are discovered and reported to vendors and the public. According to the security firm Sourcefire, more than five thousand new software vulnerabilities were reported in 2012 alone.[7] This number does not even cover the cases where security is inadequate because of weak passwords or poor security settings. Although tools are available for locating and fixing software vulnerabilities that are already known, these tools are likely to miss vulnerabilities that have not yet been discovered and disclosed. If the adversary finds and develops an exploit for one of these unknown vulnerabilities, its attack is likely to succeed. Such exploits are called zero-day exploits because the time from the disclosure of the vulnerability to the release of the exploit is zero days. Indeed, it may be the use of the exploit in a cyber attack that brings about the disclosure and subsequent remediation of the vulnerability. Such was the case of Stuxnet, which exploited four previously unpublished vulnerabilities. Most cyber attacks do not employ zero-day exploits; instead, they take advantage of vulnerabilities that have been known for months or years and for which fixes are available but not installed. But even organizations that are diligent about security and installing security updates can still be vulnerable to zero-day attacks.

Zero-day exploits are bought and sold in underground and legitimate markets before they are released, sometimes going for hundreds of thousands of dollars. They provide a lucrative source of income for independent researchers who like to hunt for new vulnerabilities and develop exploits for them. Many companies have "bug bounty" programs to encourage researchers to report vulnerabilities to the companies, which want to fix them, rather than to other parties that may exploit them nefariously; but militaries also develop and purchase zero-day exploits for possible cyber warfare operations. Knowing what zero-day exploits the adversary might have or obtain, and how they could affect our own systems, is obviously problematic.

In addition to knowing about possible zero-day attacks, we need to determine the adversary's other capabilities, including its methods of targeting; penetrating, controlling, and planting backdoors, spyware, and other forms of malicious software (malware) on systems; exfiltrating data; disrupting service; and so forth. We might reasonably assume that the adversary has certain capabilities that are commonly observed in cyber attacks emanating from a variety of threat sources, but we might miss learning about its unique methods that have not yet been observed in actual attacks.

Military operations can depend on many complex and interdependent cyber systems. To fully understand the possible impact of cyber attacks, including their indirect effects on operations and missions, we need to be able to map the dependencies of cyber systems on each other, as well as the dependencies of operations on cyber systems. Doing so for an organization the size of the US military is a daunting task. But without understanding the dependencies and the vulnerabilities they introduce, we may not know that the loss of some logistics or surveillance system, for example, could make deploying troops, executing a particular operation, or achieving mission objectives impossible.

The problem gets even worse when we factor in the civilian systems that the military depends on, including telecommunications and power systems. We will say more about this point later when we discuss scope.

Assessing the risk to the adversary from our cyber attacks is also problematic. While we can reasonably assess ourselves as a threat source to an adversary, we are unlikely to know as much about its systems or its vulnerabilities and dependencies. Consequently, we might think that a proposed cyber attack will succeed, when in fact it will not, or that the attack will cause less collateral damage than it does when executed. Without a complete picture of the adversary's systems and vulnerabilities, we might also miss seeing potential methods of attack. This brings us to the next issue.

SEEING THROUGH THE ADVERSARY'S EYES

In general, it is easier to assess our own strengths and weaknesses than those of another party. Yet to determine where our cyber forces stand relative to those of an adversary, we must be able to evaluate the adversary both as a threat source to us in an assessment of our risk and as a target of our cyber operations in an assessment of its risk. These assessments will only be as good as the data on which they are based, underscoring the need for solid intelligence about the adversary.

Further, to fully appreciate the adversary as a threat source, we need to know not only its capabilities and intents but also how the adversary views us as a target of its operations. If it thinks its cyber operations will succeed (i.e., our risk to its attacks is high), it may be more likely to launch the attacks than if it thinks the attacks will fail to produce the desired effects. This suggests the possibility of presenting our systems in a way that leads the adversary to conclude that the systems are immune to its attacks.

Similarly, it is useful to know how the adversary views us as a threat source. If it thinks we are capable of causing severe harm, it might be less willing to engage us in cyberspace or even in other warfare domains. Conversely, if it thinks its systems are adequately protected from our attacks, it might be more willing to attack ours or less diligent about defending its own.

Battle damage assessment is also more difficult when applied to the adversary than to ourselves. We might not know if certain effects were achieved, especially indirect effects on its operations. We can reduce this potential blindness by integrating a cyber espionage capability into our operations that reports effects, but doing so is unlikely to produce as good a picture as "being there."

CONTROLLING SCOPE

During war valid targets for military operations can include civilian infrastructure such as bridges and electric power systems that serve military objectives when the operations are conducted according to the principles of the law of armed conflict (LOAC). The same would be true of military cyber operations conducted during war. They could potentially target civilian cyber systems, for example, to temporarily disrupt power or telecommunications in a conflict zone. In addition, an adversary might not even abide by LOAC, further broadening the scope of its cyber attacks.

Thus the risk assessments used to determine cyber strength need to take into account risks to potential civilian systems as well as military ones, especially when military systems or operations depend on the civilian systems. For example, if we want to know if the adversary's cyber forces can disrupt or damage our power grid, we need to evaluate the risk those systems operating the grid face from the adversary. Conversely, to determine if our cyber forces can affect the adversary's power systems, we need to assess what risk we pose to its power systems.

However, conducting a risk assessment across our military and our adversary's, or even across segments of two militaries fighting a particular war, is daunting enough without also factoring in risks to civilian systems. As a practical matter, it will be necessary to control the scope of these risk assessments.

One way of controlling scope is to limit the breadth of the assessments— that is, the number of target systems examined. For example, we might only evaluate risks to military systems that are critical to particular operations against the adversary and rely on the general risk assessments performed by the owners of civilian and other military systems as part of their overall cyber security efforts. Although these assessments would not be tailored to a particular adversary during war, they would be better than nothing. Alternatively, we might control scope by limiting the depth, or the level of detail, of the assessments. We could also take a hybrid approach, examining a few critical systems in detail while taking a higher-level approach across a broader set of systems.

RECOGNIZING CYBERSPACE AS A GLOBAL, PERPETUAL CONFLICT ZONE

Cyberspace is constantly under attack by a variety of state and non-state actors, including criminals, spies, protesters, and hackers. It is a perpetual conflict zone, where borders are usually ignored and attacks can be far-reaching and widespread. A single attacker might compromise and control tens of thousands of computers located in dozens of different countries, commanding them to conduct a coordinated, distributed DoS (DDoS) attack against a target across the world. Prolexic, a security firm that specializes in DDoS and network protection, observed more than seven thousand DDoS attacks per day on average in 2013.[8] A single attack can generate tens of gigabits of traffic per second and shut down websites and services.

Of course, systems face more than DDoS attacks. Cyber spies exfiltrate terabytes of data from systems they penetrate, with major operations such as those from China scooping up data from dozens of organizations in multiple countries. Criminals conduct billions of dollars' worth of cyber fraud annually. Protesters such as Anonymous deface or hijack thousands of websites, take over hundreds of Twitter and other accounts, and disclose sensitive personal and organizational information, in addition to being a major source of DDoS attacks. Hardly anyone is immune to cyber attacks, and any device connected to the Internet is likely to be a target, even as it successfully wards off the attacks.

Consequently, when two states (or other political entities) are engaged in warfare, they also have to worry about cyber attacks from actors besides their adversaries. An attack from a third party could impact the state's military capabilities, including, for one, the ability to deploy offensive cyber weapons against the adversary.

This issue could be addressed by including all threat sources in our risk assessments; that is, we could conduct general risk assessments rather than ones tailored to the adversary as a single threat source against us and to our cyber forces as a single threat source against the adversary. However, the result will be more a determination of the relative cyber security posture of us versus the adversary than of the relative cyber strength of us against the adversary. We could get the benefits of both general and tailored risk assessments not only by focusing on ourselves and the adversary as threat sources but also by including other threat sources whose cyber attacks could have serious effects.

DEALING WITH PATRIOTIC HACKERS

In traditional domains of warfare—land, sea, and air—non-state actors tend to leave the fighting to military forces. Indeed, under the international LOAC, they are not supposed to fight except under official state control (e.g., as militias of the state). In cyberspace, however, it is quite common to see patriotic hackers take up cyber arms. During the Russian-Georgian conflict in 2008, for example, pro-Russian hackers conducted many if not most of the attacks in cyberspace. They were recruited on Russian-language web forums such as stopgeorgia.ru and given instructions and tools for attacking Georgian sites. They launched DoS/DDoS attacks, defaced websites, and interrupted Georgia's Internet connections to the rest of the world, seriously impacting Georgia's ability to communicate with its citizens and the international community through cyberspace.[9] More recently, the civil war in Syria has inspired both pro-regime hacking groups, such as the Syrian Electronic Army, and anti-regime groups, such as the Hackers of the Syrian Revolution.[10]

During wartime patriotic hackers effectively add to the cyber forces of the state or non-state entity they support. They increase the entity's threat without introducing any significant risk to it, which is already a legitimate target of the opposition. Even if the patriotic hackers become targets themselves, cyber attacks against them are unlikely to impact the larger entity and its ability to conduct cyber war. In assessing cyber war, therefore, including patriotic hackers as a component of each side's cyber threat seems reasonable. While their capabilities may not be as sophisticated as those of the entity they support, patriotic hackers may be more brazen and nondiscriminatory in their targeting.

DETERMINING ATTRIBUTION

Determining the source of a cyber attack can be difficult. Attackers can hop through intermediary sites, hide their tracks with tools such as The Onion Router, and erase evidence of their attacks. Often what appears to be the source of an attack is just another hacked computer that was compromised and exploited to obscure the identity and location of the attack's true source.

To conduct cyber battle damage assessment against our own systems, we need to know which attacks originated with the adversary and therefore which effects can be attributed to it. Because cyberspace is constantly under attack by many parties and establishing attribution is difficult, it may be hard to distinguish attacks by the adversary from those by others, thus complicating the task of determining damages brought on by the adversary.

Attribution is less of an issue in assessing the effects of our cyber attacks against the adversary. In that case, we know what we did. Even if we observe multiple effects to adversary systems, we might reasonably be able to determine which ones we caused. However, because the main reason for assessing the damages to their systems is to determine whether we are meeting mission and operational objectives, it may matter less whether we produced certain effects as that the effects were achieved.

ABIDING BY THE LAW OF ARMED CONFLICT

For the most part, the preceding discussion assumes that we are already at war, and the question is how to assess the cyber component of that war—namely, the cyber battle damages and the relative strength of our cyber forces against the adversary's. However, another issue arises before the onset of a clearly defined war, and it involves determining the conditions under which a cyber attack could be viewed as an act of force in violation of the LOAC. In particular Article 2(4) of the Charter of the United Nations prohibits states from using force against other states (except for self-defense and under a UN Security Council resolution): "All Members shall refrain in their international relations from the threat or use of force against the territorial integrity or political independence of any state, or in any other manner inconsistent with the Purposes of the United Nations." Although the term "force" is not defined, it is generally understood to include armed attacks from traditional military forces.

Because the UN Charter was written long before cyberspace became a domain of warfare, it does not explicitly address cyber attacks. Nevertheless, a general consensus has emerged that the UN Charter and LOAC more generally apply to cyberspace. Thus, to determine whether a cyber attack violates Article 2(4), we need to know first and foremost whether it constitutes a use of force. While several scholarly works address this issue, the *Tallinn Manual*, which was produced by an international group of experts, is the most thoughtful and thorough treatment of cyber war under LOAC to date.[11] The manual offers nearly a hundred rules for applying LOAC to cyber warfare. Several of the rules pertain directly to Article 2(4), with rules 10, 11, and 12 being especially relevant. Rule 10 prohibits cyber attacks and threats of cyber attacks that constitute force: "A cyber operation that constitutes a threat or use of force against the territorial integrity or political independence of any State, or that is in any other manner inconsistent with the purposes of the United Nations, is unlawful." Rules 11 and 12, respectively, specify the conditions under which a cyber operation constitutes a use of force or threat of force. Rule 11 defines the use of force: "A cyber operation constitutes a use of force when its scale and effects are comparable to non-cyber operations rising to the level of a use of force."[12] Rule 12 addresses the threat of force: "A cyber operation, or threatened cyber operation, constitutes an unlawful threat of force when the threatened action, if carried out, would be an unlawful use of force."[13]

These definitions bring us back to cyber battle damage assessment. To know whether a cyber attack is a use of force, we need to determine first its effects and then whether those effects rise to the level of force in traditional military domains. The *Tallinn Manual* provides guidance for the latter, acknowledging that some cyber operations would not rise to the level of force. The guidance includes criteria first introduced by the manual's editor, Michael Schmitt, that are sometimes referred to as the Schmitt criteria.

Together with other articles of the UN Charter, Article 2(4) falls in the area of LOAC referred to as *jus ad bellum*, or the law of conflict management. LOAC has a second part that is called *jus in bello*, or the law of war. While jus ad bellum is concerned with promoting peace and avoiding hostilities, jus in bello is concerned with fighting ethically and minimizing suffering during war. Jus in bello is often expressed as a set of principles that relate to the distinction of combatants from noncombatants, military necessity, proportionality, indiscriminate weapons, superfluous injury, perfidy, and neutrality. The *Tallinn Manual* also provides guidance in the form of rules for applying the principles of jus in bello to cyber operations. When conducting a battle damage assessment during war, this guidance may be useful for determining whether our cyber operations and those of the adversary are abiding by jus in bello.

Although the *Tallinn Manual* provides helpful guidance for assessing cyber attacks, that guidance is neither definitive nor black and white. Determining whether a particular cyber operation would violate LOAC is still subject to interpretation.

KEEPING UP

Cyberspace is a rapidly evolving domain, with a steady influx of new technologies and applications. One of the challenges in assessing cyber war is simply keeping up with changes in the cyber battlefield—that is, the weapons and systems that may be used or targeted in cyber attacks. New technologies can provide new opportunities for conducting cyber attacks, new vulnerabilities to exploit, and new methods of defense. Even software upgrades for operating systems, networks, and applications can positively or negatively affect risks.

One particularly challenging aspect of this evolving environment is that a cyber weapon can become obsolete after a single use, for releasing the weapon exposes the security flaws that it seeks to exploit and, in turn, can lead those responsible for the flaws to rectify them. No other domain of warfare has such a short life cycle for its weapons. The same type of bomb or missile, for example, can be used again and again, as conventional defenses are much slower to adapt.

Consequently cyber weapons are constantly evolving to get around the latest fixes and updates to the signatures used by antivirus products and intrusion prevention systems. The security firm McAfee, for example, reported seeing 100,000 new malware samples *per day* in 2012.[14] While most of them are variants of existing malware and many pose little threat, the raw numbers reveal the magnitude of the problem of keeping up in this dynamic environment.

CONCLUSIONS

This chapter introduces a framework for assessing cyber war that builds on the elements of risk assessment. The framework can be used to assess both the effects of cyber attacks (battle damage assessment) and the relative cyber strength of our forces against an adversary. Although the focus here has been on cyberspace, the framework might also prove useful for assessing war in other domains where operations are kinetic and their effects physical. It is less clear whether the framework is useful for assessing information and influence operations other than cyber attacks, such as what the Department of Defense once called psychological operations and now calls military information support operations. For those types of operations, it is not clear whether the standard risk variables—namely, threats, vulnerabilities, effects, and likelihoods—even apply.

While perhaps simple and straightforward in principle, risk assessment is complex and difficult in practice. It is highly speculative and fraught with uncertainty. We offer the framework as a way of thinking about cyber war assessment and identifying the variables and issues that need to be considered. Although its application to cyber battle damage assessment seems reasonably straightforward, we leave open whether it could be practically applied to assess cyber strength.

Another limitation of the framework introduced here is that it does not address the dynamics of cyber conflict, including an adversary's responses to cyber attacks and the potential escalatory effects of cyber operations. While important, this topic is left for future study.

NOTES

1. R. J. Kissler, ed., "Glossary of Key Information Security Terms," Revision 2, NISTIR 7298 (Gaithersburg MD: National Institute of Standards and Technology [NIST], May 2013).
2. NIST, *Guide for Conducting Risk Assessments*, Special Publication 800–30 (Gaithersburg MD: National Institute of Standards and Technology, September 2012).
3. Dorothy E. Denning, "Assessing the CNO Threat of Foreign Countries," in *Information Strategy and Warfare*, ed. John Arquilla and Doug Borer (New York: Routledge, 2007), 187–210.
4. Brian D. Cummings and Aric L. McElheny, "Developing a Software Model to Assess a Nation's Capability to Conduct Sustained, Offensive Cyber Warfare" (thesis, Naval Postgraduate School, September 2011), https://www.hsdl.org/?view&did=691268.

5. Lori Wright, "Who Are the Greatest Cyber Attack Threats to the United States?," *University of New Hampshire News*, January 25, 2007, http://www.unh.edu/news/cj_nr/2007/jan/lw25cyber.cfm.
6. Technolytics, *The Cyber Commander's Handbook* (McMurray PA: The Technolytics Institute, 2009), 12–13.
7. Yves Younan, "25 Years of Vulnerabilities: 1988–2012," Sourcefire Vulnerability Research Team, 2013, https://labs.snort.org/blogfiles/Sourcefire-25-Years-of-Vulnerabilities-Research-Report.pdf.
8. Prolexic, "Knowledge Center," http://www.prolexic.com (accessed November 1, 2013).
9. Eneken Tikk, Kadri Kaska, and Liis Vihul, *International Cyber Incidents: Legal Considerations* (Estonia: Cooperative Cyber Defence Centre of Excellence, 2010), https://ccdcoe.org/publications/books/legalconsiderations.pdf.
10. SalamaTech, Syrian Digital Safety Project, "Flash Note: Syria; Syria's Hacker Wars" (Ontario: The SecDev Foundation, October 8, 2013), http://new.secdev-foundation.org/wp-content/uploads/2014/08/Flash-Note-Syria-13-Syrias-Hacker-wars.pdf.
11. Michael N. Schmitt, ed., *Tallinn Manual on the International Law Applicable to Cyber Warfare* (New York: Cambridge University Press, 2013).
12. Ibid., 45.
13. Ibid., 52.
14. McAfee, "Infographic: The State of Malware 2013," McAfee for Business, April 1, 2013, http://www.mcafee.com/us/security-awareness/articles/state-of-malware-2013.aspx.

18

ASSESSING THE WAR OF IDEAS DURING WAR

Robert Reilly

HOW CAN ONE ASSESS STRATEGIC COMMUNICATION—or what is called the war of ideas—during war? What is the role of the war of ideas once the shooting starts, and how can its progress be determined? One cannot measure something—or even know if it is measurable—unless one knows what it is and what it is for. Therefore, we will establish some basic definitions and considerations and, through several examples, try to illustrate the importance of strategic communication and how it functions in conflicts.

One must begin by acknowledging that wars of *ideas* are among the primary causes as well as the primary objectives of conflict. A clash of ideas almost always precedes a clash of arms. In their own minds people are already at war when they prepare for or precipitate armed conflict. In the armory of any combatant is an idea "weapon" that explains why he fights. The combatant fights for a purpose or a cause, usually expressed in ideas grounded in some conception of justice. Of course, the term "justice" has many different definitions, which is one reason why wars of ideas occur in the first place. It is on this stage that the drama is played out. Even tribal war, such as the slaughter between the Hutus and the Tutsis, contains some notion of "right," no matter how parochial.

War's practical objective is to cause one's enemies to give up the ideas that animate their struggle, either by demonstrating the illegitimacy of their ideas or by crushing those who hold them—or more likely using a combination of the two. War's objective is also to convince enemies that further pursuit of their ideas is futile, or no longer worth the effort. "Willingness to kill and die signifies seriousness," writes Professor Angelo Codevilla. Yet the key to victory in the war of ideas is "which side proves that it represents something *worth* killing and dying for" (emphasis added).[1] Determining the worth of the respective causes—or who is truly just—is one of the decisive elements in victory. It is the job of strategic communication to articulate that determination. It cannot be stressed enough that this effort is not a matter of messaging. It consists of putting into words what one really does live and die for. War is not a form of advertising. It sweeps away pretense.

The struggle over justice, therefore, is not simply a component of the war; it *is* the war. It constitutes the struggle. It is at war's center; it is the dynamo. Solutions that do not address the concerns of justice are irrelevant; so too is any information operation or campaign that is not in some way related to it. If you are going to explain your cause in terms of its justice, then you will have to be able to explain *what* justice is. If you cannot do this, you will have already forfeited the moral and spiritual battlefield and conceded the high ground to those whose claims are higher. You will end up speaking *their* language or at least forgetting the one you had spoken when you started. In the end, the winner's conception of justice is what will define the nature of the peace that will follow the war. The character of the order imposed by the victor is defined by what he thinks is "right."

This does not mean that self-interest, greed, pride, hatred, and ambition are absent ingredients in war; in fact, they are almost always present. It means that even these factors require rationalization in the language of higher moral purpose to justify them. One of the most common stratagems in a war of ideas is to unmask the opponent's rationalizations as nothing more than base self-interest and to advance one's own as expressions of the highest good. Samuel Adams, one of America's founding fathers, expressed part of this trenchantly when he said, "It is a good Maxim in Politicks as well as in War to put & keep the Enemy in the Wrong."[2]

Of course, conveying the "rightness" of one's cause does not guarantee victory in war, *but failure to make and support the claim to the right in a convincing manner can fatally undermine one's chances of success.* It can lead not only to the demoralization of the troops, who will not know what they are fighting for, and of those on the home front, who will not know what they are supporting, but also to the loss of allies, who are unlikely to identify with a cause they do not understand. (See the Vietnam War, for example.)

The whole presumption of strategic communication is that the cause for which a war is being fought can be undermined by something other than military defeat or advanced by something other than success at arms. It does not mean that strategic communication can or should operate apart from military operations. The side that is better able to integrate the case for its cause with all the other elements of the conflict, especially the military, is most likely to succeed, as we shall see in the following examples of Sultan al-Malik al-Nāṣir Muḥammad and Abraham Lincoln.

Correct assessment during war requires, first of all, a correct assessment *before* the war begins of the relative strengths and vulnerabilities of the ideas animating the two sides. One needs to know *why* one fights and, just as important, why the enemy fights and for what. Without this knowledge, strategic communication flounders. Needless to say, strategic communication will also be ineffective if the end for which the war is fought is misconceived; in that case, even effective communication of the goal will only spread confusion. As the old advertising adage has it, "nothing kills a bad product faster than good advertising." Bad policy cannot be rescued with excellent communication.

How well or badly one is doing at any given time during a conflict is always hard to fathom due to the fog of war. Assessment requires accurate intelligence about one's enemies: What is their location? What weapons do they have and how will they use them? What are their next moves? Many of these questions can be answered quantitatively because they deal with tangible things. One can count the soldiers, tanks, rounds, aircraft, and rockets on both sides. If one's object is to physically eliminate these items, it is relatively easy to keep score.

It would be nice to have comparable metrics to measure whether one is succeeding in the war for men's minds. We can map geographic territory; we can even map cultural terrain. It is more difficult to map the human soul. It has intangibles that are not quantifiable. Its movements have no ready metrics. As Ayatollah Ruhollah Khomeini famously said, "The revolution is not about the price of melons."[3] Ideas are not commodities. Try to measure them as if they were, and you miss their essence. Yet how, and in what way or in which direction, ideas move is decisive for the war's outcome.

How then can you tell if you are winning the war of ideas? The answer is by the *language* people use, by the way in which they express what is right or "good," and by the way they define what is legitimate and what is not. *Ultimate victory comes when the enemy speaks your language and embraces your idea of what is right, when he accepts your standard of justice and concedes the legitimacy of your cause.* This outcome does not mean simply repeating the same words but embracing the same meaning of those words. Success may have to come from military defeat, as it did for the Japanese in World War II; but as Sun Tzu would argue, it is an even greater victory if such a change comes without it.

One such notable victory came in the Cold War. In 1982 President Ronald Reagan called the Soviet Union an "evil" empire. In 1990 Alexander Yakovlev, the Politburo chief of Soviet ideology, agreed with him when he said publicly that Leninism was based upon class struggle and class hatred and that this was "evil." Yakovlev used Reagan's language and meant the same thing by it. The war of ideas had been won, and the Soviet Union collapsed within a year.[4]

What is at stake in the clash of ideas also helps to determine what kind of conflict it will be and what it may be worth spending to win. In other words, proper appreciation for what is at stake is necessary to judge the proportionality of the response and to formulate a justification for it. Is the war "worth" it? The subject of the dispute defines and limits the struggle over it.

For instance, let us consider a dispute that arises because property markers are being moved in an oil patch at night. The person moving the markers is caught by the owner of the other property. A shooting takes place. One might say at this point that a war has already broken out. Over what? Both sides agree that there should be fence posts; neither is questioning the concept of property rights per se. The fight is over *whose* property it is and where the fence posts belong. Such fights are amenable to settlement, usually in a court of law (but by force if necessary), where each side presents its legal claims in the form of deeds and property surveys. Once those claims are adjudicated and the property line demarked, the dispute is over. The *nature* of justice is not in dispute here, only its application. The shared concept of justice defines the character of the peace following the dispute with everyone being secure in their own property.

What if the struggle is between those who believe in fence posts and those who do not. The latter remove them because they believe that property markers should not exist at all, since private property is the source of oppression. Both fights over the fence posts involve justice, but the second struggle involves *different* conceptions of justice, ultimately based upon conflicting notions of human nature. The second struggle takes place over what the very idea of justice is. The contending sides are fighting from and for different conceptions of reality. For the side fighting for the abolition of private property, the conception of justice defines peace as a classless society in a world without private property.

Obviously the language used in these two kinds of disputes would have to be vastly different to be effective. For instance, if one kept speaking to the disputants in the second conflict only in litigious terms of property rights, one would be speaking past the central issue at hand. Such discourse would be completely ineffective as it does not address the issue at the level at which it exists but at a level at which one is more familiar and comfortable. For instance, those who understood the Soviet Union as just another manifestation of Russian Realpolitik missed the matter's true nature, which was much more effectively addressed by those, like Ronald Reagan, who understood that different conceptions of human nature were at stake. By addressing the *moral* nature of those differences, they were able to win. The contemporary relevance of these analogies becomes clear in the language that the Islamic State in the Middle East uses. Those who are disposed to understand its message only in terms of local grievances miss the significance of its members' statements, such as that of Abu Yusaf, a senior security commander for the Islamic State, who said, "We don't believe in countries . . . breaking and destroying all borders is our aim."[5]

It would be a huge mistake to think about and fight an ideological war as if it were the other sort. One would have a total mismatch of means and ends. One must determine what *kind* of war one is in by the nature of what is at stake in it. For instance, President Harry Truman accurately described World War II as "a victory of one way of life over another."[6] He undoubtedly meant that the war was a struggle over two inimical meanings of human existence. When the meaning of life is at stake, the war is total.

The claim to justice *always* has the highest priority in a war of ideas (whether expressed in public diplomacy, strategic communication, or information operations) and likewise when such wars become kinetic. In a few more current examples, the US invasion of Panama in 1989 was called Operation Just Cause. When a group of sixty prisoners escaped from jail in the Nigerian city of Kano in 2012, the suspected fighters for Boko Haram left a message carved into the cell wall: "What we want is justice in Nigeria." In a December 7, 2001, video, Osama bin Laden claimed, "Our terrorism against America is commendable. It seeks to make the unjust stop making injustice."[7] In 2005 a captured al-Qaeda letter to Abu Musab al-Zarqawi in Iraq admitted that al-Qaeda's chief vulnerability is "a loss of the justice of our cause."[8]

Regarding one's enemies, one most needs to know what constitutes moral legitimacy and justice in their eyes. What are the vulnerabilities of their conception, and how can it be undermined in the minds of the combatants, their families, and their society? As Lawrence Freedman writes, "Measuring the results of a narrative or media battle is much more difficult [than assessing the physical battle]. . . . Audiences are likely to test the message by reference to their own experience and established belief systems. Indeed, success in a narrative battle lies in changing these belief systems. . . . Given the resilience of belief systems this may be no small matter."[9]

The rule here, as stated by Angelo Codevilla, is that we have to "contend with foreigners for the right as we understand it in terms of their own logic."[10] Unless we can explain our purpose, presence, and activities in the terms that the local population uses in *its* concept of justice, strategic communication cannot add to whatever force we may be applying and will most likely detract from it. If the local population finds what we are doing is incomprehensible in terms of justice, we will be opposed.

Most people's concept of justice is not arrived at philosophically but is a product of their culture, which, in turn, is a product of cult. Changing the people's conception of justice, therefore, is often seen as an attempt to change their religion, which is why, for instance, so many Afghans have understood the US military's presence in their country as an attempt to destroy Islam, the foundation of their culture.

Let us now see how the war of ideas influenced the course of several conflicts—that is, how the respective sides used information tools or strategic communication to fight, with what effect, and how that effect was measured. One will note the centrality of the issues of legitimacy and justice in these examples.

When the Mongols thundered through the Middle East in the mid-thirteenth century (capturing Baghdad in AD 1258), the Muslim Mamluk regime in Cairo had no difficulty in justifying its resistance to the invader because the Mongols were infidels who were attempting to encroach upon Muslim territory, the Dar al-Islam. The case for jihad was self-evident. In fact, the Mamluks were the only ones who successfully resisted the Mongol onslaught at that time and, again, in 1281 at the Second Battle of Homs.

However, between 1299 and 1312, the Mongols returned several more times to take Syria, which the Mamluks still held. At that time the Mongols were led by the Ghāzān Khān, leader of the Ilkhanate centered in Persia. Before assuming the throne in 1295, Ghāzān converted to Islam. His action considerably complicated the Mamluks' rationale for resisting him.[11]

Aside from apostasy, the single worst thing a Muslim can do is kill another Muslim. According to the Qur'an Muslim blood is sacrosanct. Ghāzān Khān assumed the title padishah al-Islam (king of Islam) and presented himself as the protector of Islam. To further enhance his credentials, he imposed the *jizya* (poll) tax, from which Christians and Jews had been free since the abolition of the Abbasid caliphate, throughout his territories. He also adopted black banners similar to those flown by the Abbasid caliphs.

Ghāzān Khān further justified his invasion by claiming that "our fervor for Islam has urged us to march against this land with a host of soldiers in order to put this aggression to an end and pull this tyranny away."[12] The aggression to which he referred was the Mamluks' attack on the city of Mardin, located in southern Turkey, where the sultan's soldiers purportedly killed civilians and raped Muslim women. Ghāzān Khān therefore based his case on the requirements of restoring justice as understood in Islamic jurisprudence. He set forth his justification in a declaration (a security assurance called an *amān*) read in the Great Umayyad Mosque in Damascus before his troops entered the city in January 1300. Further, in another public document, Ghāzān Khān stated that "it was the rule of Islam to fight against rebels."[13] Not only were the Mamluks rebels but they also caused disorder, one of the great offenses within Islam. Moreover, argued the Mongols, the khan's noble lineage reached back to Genghis Khan while the Mamluk sultan was the son of a Turkish slave, without any right to rule. Ghāzān Khān also translated the Mongol mandate of heaven into Islamic terms as Allah's appointed ruler.

By what justification, then, could the Mamluks resist him with physical force? In his reply to a letter from Ghāzān Khān, Sultan al-Malik al-Nāṣir Muḥammad complained that many of his best troops believed that Ghāzān's conversion to Islam was sincere and, therefore, refused to fight him. The Mamluk sultan accused Ghāzān Khān of misusing his faith for tactical advantage.[14] Further complicating the situation for the sultan was the fact that some Mamluk emirs had defected to Ghāzān Khān.

In the face of the Mongol's claims, was it legitimate for the Mamluks to wage jihad against Ghāzān Khān? It was not an academic question. In fact, it was a jurisprudential one of great religious significance. Sultan al-Malik needed a positive answer to galvanize his troops and to ensure that they would fight.

To his rescue came Ibn Taymiyya, the famous and highly respected Damascene Sunni jurist, who issued three fatwas on the subject of the Mongols and concluded that the Mongols *must* be fought. His reasoning was that they had infidels and, even worse, apostate Mamluk Muslims in their ranks. They were also under the influence of the Shia, who were also apostates. Moreover the Mongols, despite their profession of Islam, still had to be fought because they were living in a pre-Islamic state of *jahiliyya* (the polytheistic paganism that had preceded Mohammed in Arabia), having retained Genghis Khan's tribal law, or the Yasa code. What, asked Ibn Taymiyya, was the origin of this code? Nothing more than the reasoning of one man, Genghis Khan. In other words, said Ibn Taymiyya, Yasa was not divine law, and it competed with Islamic sharia, which had its divine source in the Qur'an and the Sunna. By ruling according to the Mongol code rather than sharia, Ghāzān Khān was engaged in *bida* (forbidden innovation). Ibn Taymiyya established the principle that a Muslim ruler who failed to apply the sharia became illegitimate.

The case was further spelled out by Ibn Taymiyya's disciple Ibn Kathir, who gave the following exegesis of the Qur'anic verse that "whoso judgeth not according to what God hath revealed, they are transgressors": "[These verses] refer to people who abide by regulations and laws set by men, to fit their own misguided desires and whims, rather than adhering to the Shari'a bestowed upon us by Allah. This was the case with the inhabitants [of Arabia] during the jahiliyya . . . and (today) with the Mongols who follow the *Yasa* code set down by Genghis Khan . . . ; the whole amalgam being given priority over the laws of Allah laid down in the Koran and the Sunna. Those who follow such (man-made) laws are infidels and should be combated until they comply with the laws of God."[15]

This interpretation was the effective case for jihad against the Muslim Mongols and their allies. Ibn Taymiyya not only wrote his three fatwas but also energetically espoused their contents before the Mamluk officials and directly to the Mamluk troops. He served as a kind of combined combatant chaplain and political commissar during the fighting. According to French scholar Denise Aigle, "Ibn Taymīyah took part in this battle [the battle of Shaqḥab in which Ghāzān Khān and his army were defeated], bearing arms and urging the combatants to engage in jihad. During the fighting he issued a fatwa exempting the Mamluk soldiers from the ritual fast during the month of Ramaḍān."[16] Historian Thomas Raff states, "Ibn Taimiya devoted his efforts to inciting the fanaticism of Mamluk troops for the crucial day, i.e. the Battle of Marj as-ṣuffār, by making exhortations to them and even participating in the combat himself."[17]

How would one have assessed the relative situations in the progress of this war regarding strategic communication? Each side was trying to take the high ground in the Muslim version of *jus ad bellum* (justification for war) and to delegitimize its opponent. Both sides were moving within the same universe of meaning; it was a matter of which side had the better claim to jihad. One could have counted the copies of Ibn Taymiyya's fatwas and, likewise, the number of times the khan's letters and declarations were circulated and read in mosques, but the only quantifiable metric that really mattered was whether the troops would fight the jihad to which they were called. They were the principal audience, along with those religious authorities whom they respected—namely, the *qadis* (judges) and mullahs—for the question they faced was ultimately a theological and jurisprudential one. This question was decided by the *substance* of the arguments and not by the means of their dissemination, necessary though they were.

Since war is a life-and-death matter, the soldiers had to be convinced that their participation in it would not imperil their immortal souls but would, rather, lead to paradise. That the Mamluks fought was the measure of Ibn Taymiyya's success because he had given them the moral and religious justification for their participation. He had won the argument. According to the sultan's own words, without Ibn Taymiyya's success, the sultan could not have relied on his own troops. With his keen sense of strategic communication, Sultan al-Malik solicited the work of Ibn Taymiyya and made sure it was spread far and wide. In this way, he achieved a military objective by religious means. He was able to do so because he recognized the religious nature of the dispute. Had he only appealed to his subjects in terms of their self-interest and the defense of their own, he most likely would have failed. They needed to know that what they were defending was just. They needed to be impelled and inspired by what was right as they understood it as Sunni Muslims. Therefore, through Ibn Taymiyya, Sultan al-Malik fought the war of ideas in the language of justice as defined by Sunni Islam. He got the *substance* right. If he had not, the *means* of communication would have meant nothing, and the enemy would have obtained the moral high ground from which to defeat him militarily.

Thanks in large part to Ibn Taymiyya, the Mamluks won. His impact on the war of ideas was so great that it endures to this day. One can argue as to whether his work has been correctly understood, but he is one of the principal sources of inspiration for Islamists today. It is to Ibn Taymiyya's works that they appeal when they declare Muslim rulers apostates for not applying the sharia. For better or for worse, his living legacy demonstrates the decisive power of ideas before wars, during wars, and in their aftermath.

The conflict between the Mamluks and the Mongols gives an example of how a war of ideas affected a conflict on a large scale over a long period (more than a decade) and what the means of assessing the influence of those ideas were through the behavior of the soldiers. On a much smaller scale, the American Revolutionary War provides an example of a well-targeted information campaign designed to affect a segment of the enemy's soldiers. In 1775 King George III signed an agreement with the German prince of Hesse to provide Hessian troops to fight with the British against the American colonists. Through good intelligence work, the Continental Congress obtained a copy of this treaty and used it as an example of the perfidy of the British monarch to send foreign mercenaries against the colonists. In August 1776 Congress set up a committee to create plans to encourage Hessian desertions. Benjamin Franklin advised that "the leading people, among the Germans of Pennsylvania, should likewise be consulted."[18] Congress decided to offer fifty acres of land not only to the Hessians but also the Irish, Scottish, and other deserters from the British forces. Officers would receive hundreds of acres. While the leaflets arrived too late for any effect on the Battle of Long Island in August 1776, American agents eventually succeeded in infiltrating the Hessian ranks to distribute the leaflets. The program worked. Ultimately one in six Hessians deserted. One might claim that this offer was simply bribery, but it would have failed if it had not persuaded the Hessians and others that they were fighting for an unjust cause, one that was not against foreigners but rather against people like themselves, their very own countrymen who had immigrated to America.[19]

A later example from American history, the Civil War, gives an even more dramatic instance of how important the war of ideas is during a war. In 1860 Abraham Lincoln's chief aim was to preserve the Union but not at any price. It mattered very much what kind of union was *worth* preserving. His entire prewar political strategy had been to create the circumstances for slavery's eventual demise by not allowing for its expansion in the western territories. He was willing to tolerate slavery to preserve the Union only if it were understood as a necessary and temporary evil, the ultimate extinction of which would fulfill the founding principle of the United States that "all men are created equal." However, when war came, Lincoln could not win it based upon the moral superiority of the Union side alone. He needed a military victory. But to gain that victory, it was essential to prevent the intervention of European powers in the war and to avert their recognition of the South. Lincoln reported on this danger in his message to Congress in a special session on July 4, 1861: "This illegal organization in the character of confederate States, was already invoking recognition, aid, and intervention, from foreign powers."[20] To prevent it, he used moral means aimed directly and especially at the working classes of Great Britain.

In the early days of the war, Lincoln said in private, "I cannot imagine that any European power would dare to recognize and aid the Southern Confederacy if it becomes clear that the Confederacy stands for slavery and the Union for freedom."[21] At the beginning of the war, however, Lincoln was reluctant to define the conflict in these terms because an antislavery crusade would most likely have alienated the border states of Kentucky and Tennessee, which the Union sorely needed for its survival. It might also have alarmed the European powers, which feared a revolutionary bloodbath in the South akin to what the British had experienced during the Indian Mutiny of 1857–58.[22] Since the war did not go well for the Union in its early days, Secretary of State William Henry Seward also argued that a proclamation freeing the slaves "may be viewed [in Europe] as the last measure of an exhausted government, a cry for help . . . the last *shriek*, on the retreat."[23] Therefore, as we will see, Lincoln needed to perform a delicate balancing act between political pragmatism and moral principle—in this case, retaining the slave states in the Union while holding in reserve a proclamation to free the slaves in the South.

A major international economic issue, with potentially grave political consequences, was also involved. The textile workers in Europe, of which there were almost 1,250,000, depended on raw cotton from the South for a substantial part of their livelihood. The Confederacy first withheld cotton in hopes that the workers would pressure their governments to intervene on the side of the South. Later the Union blockade prevented the cotton from reaching Europe. Though it would have seemed in the British textile workers' self-interest to do whatever was necessary to resume the cotton trade, they were, in fact, deeply against slavery and shared Lincoln's view on the dignity of free labor versus slavery's abasement of labor. Lincoln took every advantage of this situation to make it harder for the British government to consider recognizing the South. He was able to do so not through some act of leger-demain but because he shared the workers' moral substance on this issue and spoke about it in the same moral language.

Though the term "public diplomacy" had not yet been invented, Lincoln engaged in a lively version of it by going over the heads of European govern-ments and appealing directly to their workers. He encouraged their demon-strations, sent public letters to them, covertly sent them funds, and sometimes even secretly drafted their proclamations.[24] In his public letter, dated January 19, 1863, to the workers in Manchester, Lincoln wrote,

> I have understood well that the duty of self-preservation rests solely with the American people. But I have at the same time been aware that favor or disfavor of foreign nations might have a material influence in enlarging and prolonging the struggle with disloyal men in which the country is engaged. I know and deeply deplore the sufferings which the working people of Manchester and in all Europe are called to endure in this crisis. It has been often and studiously represented that the attempt to overthrow this Government which was built on the foundation of human rights, and to substitute for it one which should rest exclusively on the basis of slavery, was likely to obtain the favor of Europe. Through the action of disloyal citizens, the working people of Europe have been subjected to a severe trial for the purpose of forcing their sanction to that attempt. Under the circumstances I cannot but regard your decisive utterances on the question as an instance of sublime Christian heroism which has not been surpassed in any age or in any country. It is indeed an energetic and re-inspiring assurance of the inherent truth and of the ultimate and universal triumph of justice, humanity and freedom.[25]

British workers found this message so inspiring that there remains to this day a statue of Lincoln in Manchester, with an extract from his letter carved on the plinth.

The measure of Lincoln's success was in the number of demonstrations, the size of the crowds, the substance of their declarations, and their impact on the press and, therefore, the politics of England. They are the first metrics of his success.

The Department of the Army's field manual FM *3-13: Inform and Influence Activities* (January 2013) states, "Influence activities typically focus on persuading selected foreign audiences to support US objectives or to persuade those audiences to stop supporting the adversary or enemy. To accomplish operational objectives effectively, commanders may direct efforts to shape, sway, or alter foreign audience behaviors."[26] Lincoln's public diplomacy could serve as a model for such activities. What the field manual neglects to say is that this kind of influence can only be exercised if the same language is spoken with the audience.

After the Battle of Antietam, Lincoln judged the time right for issuing the Emancipation Proclamation, thinking the Union victory would demonstrate that emancipation was not done as an act of desperation but rather that it joined military strength with moral principle. If it appeared that the Union had a good chance of winning the war, no European power would take a chance on joining the losing side. Also Lincoln had now made it abundantly "clear that the Confederacy stands for slavery and the Union for freedom," rendering it politically and morally impossible for a European power to recognize or intervene on behalf of the South. Lincoln correctly assessed the importance of the proclamation, explaining that his decision was "not a question of sentiment or taste, but one of physical force, which may be measured and estimated as horse-power and Steam-power are measured and estimated."[27] He understood how to translate moral power—perhaps more correctly described as political power—into something akin to physical force. What were the standards by which to measure the success of his approach? Very simply the European powers stayed out of the conflict and did not extend recognition to the South. If a power can control what its enemies or potential adversaries are allowed to say about it, then that power has already won the war of ideas. With this masterstroke, Lincoln achieved his objective. He made it impossible for the Europeans to be against the Union without being pro-slavery. This too was a metric of success. Of course, as stated by Professor Harry V. Jaffa, Lincoln's "greatest contribution to the final result was his ability to articulate the purposes of the war and to persuade those making terrible sacrifices why those sacrifices were worth making."[28]

Two contemporary examples teach not from success but from failure. In Afghanistan and Iraq, the United States was confused about what it was attempting to achieve. It failed in its prewar assessment, which led to failed assessments during the wars. How would we know when the ends were achieved when we were uncertain as to the ends themselves? It seemed at times that the ends were adjusted to fit the assessments. How well were we doing the wrong things? There is no room here to go into the specifics of the respective failures regarding strategic communication in these wars.[29]

However, it is worth noting a few points. Articulating an end incompatible with the history or wishes of the Afghan people was sure to provoke opposition and threaten failure. The goal of a highly centralized, Western-style government at the expense of local autonomy was certainly going to fail to attract the majority of Afghans. Speaking to Afghans as if they were Americans only produced confusion at best and disillusionment at worst. Arturo Munoz, in *US Military Information Operations in Afghanistan: Effectiveness of Psychological Operations, 2001–2012*, concluded, "If the overall [information operation] IO mission in Afghanistan is defined as convincing most residents of contested areas to side decisively with the Afghan government and its foreign allies against the Taliban insurgency, this has not been achieved."[30] We were not speaking the same language.

In fact, we did not understand the language that we or our allies needed to speak to have an effect on the war of ideas, of which the war in Afghanistan was an expression. On April 4, 1996, Mullah Mohammed Omar wrapped himself in the reputed cloak of Mohammed, paraded around the rooftop of a building in central Kandahar as the rapturous crowd below greeted him as "Amir-al-Mumineen, the Leader of the Faithful," and thereby claimed leadership of all Muslims.[31] His assumption of this title was every bit as audacious as Ghāzān Khān's self-assumed title of padishah al-Islam. This early episode with Mullah Omar should have revealed that the Afghan Taliban presented a theological and jurisprudential problem for those who challenged them. The Taliban, however, were hardly invulnerable. They had violated both the tribal code of Pashtunwali and the folk Islam of Afghanistan.

Yet the United States failed to take advantage of the Taliban's failings because it was not tribally literate and because it did not understand the religious and jurisprudential issues in Islam. When the Taliban declared jihad against the US forces in Afghanistan, the United States and its allies had no Ibn Taymiyya to declare a counter-jihad against the Taliban. Unfamiliar with the jurisprudence of jihad, the United States conceded the religious and theological field to the Taliban and helped create a theological safe haven for the group.[32] We failed to talk in a language of justice in terms that were comprehensible to the Afghan population. Their reference for justice is not based on individual rights or religious freedom, two notions outside of the sphere of their version of Islam. Their language was religious, but we were the illiterates who chose to remain illiterate. Thus, we were unable either to delegitimize the enemy or to legitimize our escalation efforts.

Afghan Pashtunwali and Islam would order their lives, as they always have. The cultural renovation of the Afghan people to make them suitable for modern constitutional government was a goal formed by either ignorance or hubris. In either case, the United States did not possess the cultural literacy or the means to accomplish it. Predicating success on Afghan cultural transformation more or less guaranteed failure. Dr. Steve Tatham, a British military veteran of several deployments in Afghanistan, states that the United States tried "to sell to Afghans a 'vision' of the country that fails to connect utterly with the reality of their lives."[33] In other words, we got the *substance* wrong.

In the conflict in Iraq, meanwhile, the ends kept shifting, and the means were not congruent with them. The United States and its allies went in to liberate a country without realizing what liberation would mean either to the ethnically and religiously disparate peoples of Iraq or to Iraq's neighbors. Then we switched gears to occupation, a task for which we were not prepared or equipped and, most important, one repugnant to the Iraqi people. One of the leaders of the General Military Council for Iraqi Revolutionaries, which was attempting to overthrow the Nouri al-Maliki government, said, "We consider the Iraqi government illegitimate because it is a result of the US occupation."[34] We failed to understand the sources of legitimacy in Iraq. No amount of superb strategic communication could overcome a strategic blunder of this magnitude. We were assessing the wrong things because we had established mistaken ends.

Conducting war correctly requires matching sufficient means with the right ends. The *expression* of those ends is one of the most powerful means to their achievement—both in motivating one's own forces and in demoralizing one's opponents. Progress in this endeavor can be assessed in terms of changes in the language of justice respectively employed by each side. He who wins the argument about justice wins the battle of ideas, which is crucial to winning the war and assuring that the "right" for which it was fought prevails in its aftermath.

NOTES

1. Angelo Codevilla, *Advice to War Presidents: A Remedial Course in Statecraft* (New York: Basic Books, 2009), 56.
2. Quoted in J. Michael Waller, "The American Way of Propaganda: Lessons from the Founding Fathers," *Public Diplomacy White Paper No. 1* (Washington DC: Institute of World Politics, January 18, 2006), 3.
3. Ray Takeyh, "Islamism: R.I.P." (Washington DC: Council on Foreign Relations, April 1, 2001), http://www.cfr.org/world/islamism-rp/p7375.

4. Robert R. Reilly, *Ideas Matter: Restoring the Content of Public Diplomacy* (Washington DC: Heritage Foundation, 2009), 22.

5. Anthony Faiola and Souad Mekhennet, "In Turkey, a Late About-face on Islamic Fighters," *Washington Post*, August 13, 2014, A8.

6. Harry S. Truman, as printed in "Radio Report to the American People on the Potsdam Conference (August 9, 1945)," Miller Center at the University of Virginia, Charlottesville, http://millercenter.org/president/speeches/speech-3821.

7. Josh Pollack, "Full Text of bin Laden Videotape in Translation (from Al -Jazirah Satellite Channel Television [in Arabic])," December 27, 2001, in Yahoo! Groups, MidEast Web News Service, https://groups.yahoo.com/neo/groups/MewNews/conversations/topics/4339.

8. Captured letter, "'Atiyah's Letter to Zarqawi (English Translation," 2005, Combating Terrorism Center, West Point NY, https://www.ctc.usma.edu/posts/atiyahs-letter-to-zarqawi-english-translation-2.

9. Lawrence Freedman, "The Transformation in Strategic Affairs," The Adelphi Papers 45, no. 379 (New York: Routledge for International Institute of Strategic Studies, 2006),78.

10. Codevilla, *Advice to War Presidents*, 274.

11. Nazeer Ahmed, "Ghazan the Great: The Conversion of Ghazan the Great," *History of Islam: An Encyclopedia of Islamic History*, http://historyofislam.com/contents/the-post-mongol-period/ghazan-the-great/.

12. Denise Aigle, "The Mongol Invasions of Bilād al-Shām by Ghāzān Khān and Ibn Taymīyah's Three 'Anti-Mongol' Fatwas," *Mamlūk Studies Review* 11, no. 2 (2007): 109.

13. Ibid., 111.

14. Ibid., 97.

15. Quoted in Emmanuel Sivan, *Radical Islam: Medieval Theology and Modern Politics* (New Haven CT: Yale University Press, 1990), 97–98.

16. Quoted in Aigle, "Mongol Invasions," 105.

17. Ibid., 95.

18. Waller, "American Way," 9.

19. Ibid.

20. Quoted in Harry Jaffa, *A New Birth of Freedom: Abraham Lincoln and the Coming of the Civil War* (Lanham MD: Rowman & Littlefield, 2000), 359.

21. Kevin Peraino, *Lincoln in the World: The Making of a Statesmen and the Dawn of American Power* (New York: Crown, 2013), 192.

22. Ibid., 195.

23. Ibid., 199.

24. Ibid., 217.

25. Ibid., 218.

26. Department of the Army, *FM 3-13: Inform and Influence Activities* (Washington DC: Government Printing Office, January 2013), 1-2.
27. Peraino, *Lincoln in the World*, 222.
28. Ibid., 358.
29. I have dealt with this issue in two separate chapters: "Strategic Communications," in *The Three Circles of War: Understanding the Dynamics of Conflict in Iraq*, ed. Heather S. Gregg, Hy Rothstein, and John Arquilla (Washington DC: Potomac Books, 2010), and "Shaping Strategic Communication," in *Afghan Endgames: Strategy and Policy Choices for America's Longest War*, ed. Hy Rothstein and John Arquilla (Washington DC: Georgetown University Press, 2012).
30. Arturo Munoz, *U.S. Military Information Operations in Afghanistan: Effectiveness of Psychological Operations, 2001–2010* (Santa Monica: RAND, 2012), xv–xvi.
31. Steve Coll, "Looking for Mullah Omar: Will the United States Be Able to Negotiate with a Man It Has Hunted for a Decade?," *New Yorker*, January 23, 2012, http://www.newyorker.com/magazine/2012/01/23/looking-for-mullah-omar.
32. Robert Andrews, conversation with the author, 2009.
33. Steve Tatham, *U.S. Governmental Information Operations and Strategic Communications: A Discredited Tool for User Failure? Implications for Future Conflict* (Carlisle Barracks PA: Strategic Studies Institute and U.S. Army War College Press, December 2013), 4.
34. Jane Arraf, "A Revolution Brews among Some Iraqi Sunni Leaders," *Washington Post*, March 13, 2014, A6.

19

ASSESSING ECONOMIC OUTCOMES IN NATION-BUILDING OPERATIONS

Aric P. Shafran

FOLLOWING THE OVERTHROW OF THE TALIBAN in 2001, the United States has engaged in an extended nation-building operation in Afghanistan in an attempt to build a stable government and make Americans safer through the permanent defeat of the Taliban and the elimination of Afghanistan as a safe haven for al-Qaeda. In fact, the last half century has seen a dramatic shift in US military operations from traditional combat against other states to counterinsurgency in conjunction with nation building. Although the primary focus of counterinsurgency operations is to defeat insurgents, establish an effective democratic government, and provide basic security, economic development and stabilization is recognized as an important goal for successful nation-building operations.[1] As such, the ability to assess economic outcomes in war-torn countries is an integral aspect of any attempt to assess a nation-building operation as a whole.

As the United States reduces its presence in Afghanistan and the nation-building effort draws to a close, it is natural to pose two questions regarding the effectiveness of the US operation on the Afghan economy. First, how has the Afghan economy fared, and are the people of Afghanistan better off? Second, if there have been improvements in quality of life, are these improvements sustainable following the exit of US forces and aid, or will welfare stagnate or decline? These questions, while posed from the perspective of welfare economics, are important for the broader goals of the nation-building mission, as the improved welfare of Afghans is critical for ensuring the stability of the new government and defeating the insurgency.

The United States and its allies implemented more than eighty thousand development projects since 2002 in areas such as agriculture, education, infrastructure, and health, and Afghanistan has experienced large real gross domestic product (GDP) growth of more than 9 percent annually since 2004.[2] Both are encouraging indicators that US operations have improved the quality of life for the average Afghan. However, these indicators, while commonly reported to assess operational progress, may in fact overstate the true benefits of US aid, both by missing key elements of quality of life today and by ignoring the question of sustainability. For example, social indicators such as the health component of the United Nations Human Development Index (HDI) grew only 1 percent per year from 2005 to 2012, and consumption, the part of GDP most closely related to quality of life, grew at only 2.5 percent per year from 2004 to 2012. Furthermore many infrastructure projects remain underutilized or incomplete. For example, schools and other facilities were built but never used, or the structures were completed but never furnished or wired for electricity.[3] Figure 19.1 shows the trend for selected economic and social indicators in Afghanistan between 2005 and 2012. GDP growth is high, but other metrics—household consumption, access to improved sanitation, non-income components of the HDI, the percentage of irrigated land, and the percentage of permanent cropland—exhibit much slower growth. These facts highlight the potential pitfalls in assessing economic outcomes through traditional metrics like GDP or expenditures.

The purpose of this chapter is to review the metrics that economists typically use to evaluate economic performance while noting specific issues related to developing nations and to nations in the midst of armed conflict. We consider a variety of alternate metrics to use in evaluating economic outcomes with a focus on answering the two questions regarding operational effectiveness and accurately assessing the prospect for long-term economic improvements that benefit the entire population. Then we contrast metrics that look at current economic conditions with metrics that take into account the long-term prospects for stable economic growth after the nation-building operation is complete and US forces leave the country. We also consider long-term economic stability to be of greater importance than short-term economic growth and propose several metrics to assess economic outcomes that take this view into account.

It is also important to emphasize that the choice of metrics in assessing nation-building operations can affect the actions that the military and policymakers take. This change of incentives can exacerbate the problems arising from using a poor metric. Not only will policymakers be uninformed about the true state of the operation, but they may also make poor choices that are

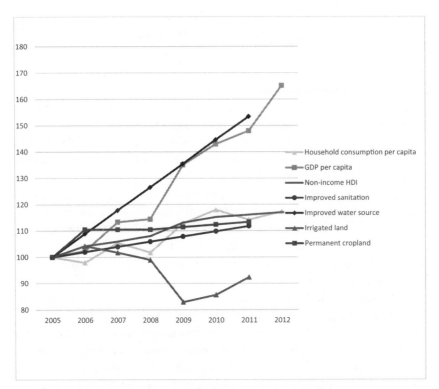

Figure 19.1. Selected economic and social indicators, Afghanistan, 2005–12

Note: All values are normalized so that 2005 value = 100. All $ values expressed in 2005 US $.

Source: World Bank, *World Development Indicators*, 2013, data.worldbank.org.

based on increasing the metric rather than on improving the population's welfare. For example, using GDP as a metric for economic well-being may lead policymakers to take actions that are perceived to increase GDP even if they do not actually benefit the country's citizens. The choice of good assessment tools to evaluate the economic well-being of citizens in war-torn countries is thus of great importance in selecting smart policies that improve welfare.

The remainder of this chapter is organized as follows. The first section defines GDP and explains the drawbacks of using GDP as a welfare measure, and the second section presents alternatives that, like GDP, assess the current state of the economy but not its long-term stability. The following section uses the tools of game theory to gain insight into how to achieve long-term stability following nation-building operations. The final section presents several alternative metrics to assess the prospects for long-run economic stability after a nation-building operation concludes.

GDP AND ITS LIMITATIONS

Despite some well-known limitations, gross domestic product is the most commonly used measure of the economic well-being of a country's citizens. For example, economists and the popular media commonly use the US GDP growth rate as a barometer of the American economy, and per capita GDP numbers are used to make cross-country comparisons of the relative standard of living of many countries. GDP is also used to measure economic outcomes in a nation-building setting. Ellyn Creasey, Ahmed S. Rahman, and Katherine A. Smith examine the effect of nation-building operations on GDP growth rate while Paul Collier and Anke Hoeffler examine the effect of aid and policy on GDP growth.[4] James Dobbins and his colleagues use GDP growth as a way to assess the economic effect of nation-building operations.[5] The Department of Defense also focuses on GDP and GDP growth as a measure of economic development.[6]

GDP measures the total market value of all final goods and services produced in a country. One of the main advantages of GDP is that it is relatively easy to compute, and there are well-defined international standards regarding the computation of GDP that ensure some degree of consistency. For the purposes of measuring economic well-being, we typically use per capita GDP, or the total GDP divided by the population. This measure is approximately equal to the average income in a country. The growth rate of GDP is a useful metric to assess welfare improvements in a war-torn country because a country that produces more and engages in more economic activity will usually experience rising living standards.

However, GDP as a measure of well-being has key limitations that are worth considering. In this chapter, we focus on several specific limitations of GDP that are of particular importance in assessing nation-building operations. These issues are briefly summarized in figure 19.2. We also suggest modifications or alternatives to GDP to address these limitations.

First, GDP includes all production within a country even if foreigners are responsible for that production. Thus, if the returns to production for a large part of GDP go to foreigners, then GDP will overstate the welfare of the domestic population. A classic example presented by Joseph E. Stiglitz, Amartya Sen, and Jean-Paul Fitoussi is Ireland.[7] Beginning in the mid-1990s, profits earned by foreign firms investing in Ireland fueled GDP growth. It led to large increases in GDP relative to household income, so the high GDP growth in the next two decades probably overstated the increases in welfare that the average citizen of Ireland felt.

• Includes profits earned by foreigners
• Includes production that does not directly make individuals better off, such as defensive expenditures
• Values government services based on expenditures instead of benefits provided
• Does not take into account inequality of income or consumption
• Includes benefits of foreign aid, which may not be sustainable after nation-building operation ends

Figure 19.2. Problems with GDP as a welfare measure in nation-building operations

This issue has relevance in developing countries as well. For example, consider the mining industry in Afghanistan. Richard Hogg and his colleagues predict that mining is a potentially significant growth sector for Afghanistan with the potential to generate $1 billion in revenue per year through 2031, or about 5 percent of current GDP. Although mining represented only 0.6 percent of Afghanistan's GDP in 2011, it could be a major factor in GDP growth in the coming decades.[8] Chinese, Indian, and Canadian firms have secured rights to various mineral basins in Afghanistan.[9] While foreign investment is necessary to provide the technical knowledge necessary for extraction, these firms will capture the profits earned from extraction minus royalties paid to Afghanistan. The value of resources mined and exported by these firms will count as part of Afghanistan's GDP, but only a fraction of this value—the royalties paid to the Afghan government and the labor income paid to Afghan workers—actually will benefit the Afghan people. Hogg and his colleagues note that "the direct employment effect" of mining "is expected to be relatively modest." Thus, the economic benefits of growth in the mining industry, while positive, should be viewed with caution.[10]

To correct this problem, gross national income (GNI) can be used in place of GDP. GNI adjusts GDP to account for flows of income across country borders such as those described in the previous two paragraphs. To the extent that GNI data is available, it is a better indicator of the well-being of a country's citizens than GDP is.

Household consumption is an even better indicator of how well off a country's citizens are since it omits all the production that occurs in an economy that does not directly affect welfare. For example, consider a country engaged in armed conflict against insurgents compared to another country at peace. Suppose both countries have the same average household consumption, but the first country spends significantly more on security. One can argue that citizens in both countries are equally well off due to equal consumption or possibly that citizens of the second country are better off given there is less violence. GDP will be higher in the first country, however, as a result of the greater expenditures on security.

Implicit in the previous example is another limitation of GDP as a welfare measure—specifically, that government-provided services such as national defense, roads, and education are typically valued at the cost of producing them rather than for the economic benefit they provide. Suppose a government invests in a national system of roads to reduce the cost of transporting people and goods around the country. GDP values this investment based on the expenditures of the government. The project has the same impact on GDP whether the roads are built in an unpopulated region of the country and never used or they are built between two population centers and facilitate new trade between the two regions.

GDP also fails to capture the distribution of income and consumption. It is possible that GDP is increasing but that the majority of the population is experiencing declining living standards. This outcome will occur if the gains from rising GDP accrue to a small fraction of elite members of society. This problem is of particular importance in nation-building operations because new governments in war-torn countries are often plagued by corruption. Corrupt government officials can attempt to secure the benefits of economic growth for themselves and their supporters at the expense of the majority of the population.

There is one additional concern with GDP and related metrics that is specifically relevant in the context of nation building. Transfers into a country through foreign aid will tend to boost GDP, assuming these transfers lead to increased production. These transfers do in fact increase the welfare of citizens of a country. The concern from the perspective of nation-building operations, however, is that GDP is a backward-looking indicator of welfare in the past year; to the extent that numbers are inflated by aid transfers, GDP may give a false impression of future welfare after the operation ends and the foreign aid transfers cease. It may be a particularly large problem in Afghanistan, where foreign aid is unusually high at 40 percent of GDP.[11] We will return to the issue of assessing sustainability of welfare improvements in the final section of this chapter.

In many cases, per capita GDP is a good approximation of how well off people are despite the issues mentioned in this section.[12] Nonetheless, it is important to recognize that GDP is a flawed and imprecise measure of economic well-being, and it may be an especially poor measure in the context of nation building.

ALTERNATIVES TO GDP

Welfare economists have developed several alternatives for assessing the well-being of citizens of a country that take into account some of the previously discussed limitations to GDP.[13] The Human Development Index, an index developed by Mahbub ul Haq and the United Nations Development Programme for making cross-country comparisons regarding the welfare of each country's citizens, combines GNI with indexes of health and education that are important aspects of quality of life but are missing from a pure production-based measure like GNI.[14] The basic idea is that countries with very high per capita GNI but low levels of life expectancy and education do not offer the same opportunities to citizens as countries with lower incomes but better health and education systems.

Consider the case of Qatar, one of the wealthiest countries in the world, with extremely high per capita GNI due to oil exports. Qatar's population is made up of a wealthy and native minority and a large majority of immigrants who work without basic human rights.[15] Qatar is the wealthiest country in the world by per capita GNI, but it drops to thirty-sixth on the HDI ranking because of its low levels of education and life expectancy relative to other wealthy countries.

Although the HDI is a step in the right direction toward a better measure of economic well-being, the HDI relies on aggregate data that may be unavailable or inaccurate in many post-conflict settings or may not be published frequently enough for assessment purposes. Like GDP, it is a backward-looking indicator, which informs about the past state of the world but may not predict well how welfare will change following the completion of a nation-building operation. In the remaining sections of this chapter, we explore how to achieve sustainable welfare improvements following the withdrawal of US support, and we identify possible metrics to assess the sustainability of economic outcomes in a nation over time.

GAME THEORY AND THE ASSESSMENT OF ECONOMIC OUTCOMES

Up to this point, we have considered metrics that represent a snapshot of the current state of a country but offer only a limited glimpse into where the country is going in the future. When assessing an ongoing nation-building operation, there is a danger that these metrics will show positive progress as a result of the high level of foreign aid and support but that cessation of the nation-building operation will lead to a rapid decline in welfare. The US government can engage in policies that promote immediate increases in welfare that are not sustainable once the policies end, or it can choose policies that promote sustained increases in welfare that persist long after the US operation is complete. It is important to choose economic assessment metrics that can distinguish between the former and the latter. To analyze the sustainability of welfare improvements after an operation ends, we will use the tools of game theory.

Economists use game theory to describe situations where one agent's actions influence the outcomes of other agents and vice versa. The key insight is that one cannot ignore how a change in one's actions may in turn influence others to change their actions. Although this premise may seem simple, we will describe how this insight can improve assessment of economic outcomes.[16] Roger Myerson has used game theory to analyze the creation of stable governments in a nation-building setting. Decentralized governments can achieve greater legitimacy and stability because they allow local leaders to reward supporters with a share of government projects.[17] Patronage helps to overcome agency problems in which people at the local level would otherwise have no incentive to support the government. This insight is important: Legitimate governments often start at the local level, and US attempts to develop a strong central government instead may ultimately lead to failure. This point is especially relevant in Afghanistan, which has a long tradition of decentralized governance.

In this chapter, we look at a slightly different problem. Holding the structure of government fixed, we believe citizens on the ground often face a coordination problem in which they would collectively prefer to support a stable government that protects property rights and facilitates a market economy; however, their support also depends on their perceived level of support among the general population. To make an important point about assessing the sustainability of economic outcomes in a nation-building setting, we use a simple model about the choices the citizens of a country make. The model is based on an idea from the US Army's field manual *Counterinsurgency* and further developed by Gordon McCormick and Frank Giordano.[18] Suppose that we can divide the population of a country into three segments: a small group that is actively involved in the government, a small group of insurgents attempting to overthrow the government, and a large majority with no allegiance at the start of the conflict. We assume that the two small groups—the government and the insurgency—are intrinsically motivated to promote their respective groups and take actions without regard to the behavior of others; thus, their actions are not part of our model. We model the actions of the large majority as follows. To keep things simple, suppose each individual in the passive majority can choose to actively support the government, to actively support the insurgency, or to remain neutral. We further assume that the best outcome for each individual is for the government to achieve peace, stability, and legitimacy. In fact, all of the individuals recognize that it is in their collective mutual interest for the government to succeed; however, each individual's best choice in any given situation depends on the actions of the other individuals. Supporting the government amid a large insurgency carries a risk of personal harm. If everyone in the passive majority is supporting the government, this risk is small; however, if the insurgency has widespread support, then supporting the government makes an individual stand out and possibly leads to retribution against that individual. From the individual's perspective, the benefits of supporting the government increase as more of the other individuals support the government.

The setup described is similar to the discussion of critical mass games by Thomas Schelling.[19] Critical mass games have the feature that when enough other people make a certain choice, then everyone else wants to follow and make the same choice. The threshold number of people that makes everyone else want to jump on board is known as a tipping point, a term popularized by Malcolm Gladwell.[20] A small change from one side of the tipping point to the other can cause dramatic shifts in the final outcome. The reason for this is that critical mass games have two stable Nash equilibria, and a small change across the tipping point will change which equilibrium outcome prevails.

To illustrate this point, consider Schelling's example of ice hockey helmets. Prior to the league's rule mandating their use in 1979, some players in the National Hockey League expressed a preference for wearing helmets but worried that helmets gave them a disadvantage compared to players who did not wear them. On the one hand, if most of the other players wore helmets, then the disadvantage would be small, and the number wearing helmets would grow until most or all players chose to wear helmets. This result is the desirable equilibrium outcome for all players. On the other hand, if few players were initially wearing helmets, then other players would be less inclined to wear a helmet as the competitive disadvantage would trump the safety benefit. Their stance might even discourage the few who were wearing helmets and convince them to give up the helmets until ultimately none (or very few) of the players would wear helmets. This result is the second and less desirable equilibrium outcome. Although all the players prefer the safety provided by helmets, history or random chance can put the league on a path to the undesirable outcome that cannot be easily reversed. This unfortunate outcome is known as a coordination failure.[21] The key to overcoming a coordination failure and achieving the preferred equilibrium is to build a critical mass of players that surpasses the tipping point—that is, the threshold number of players after which other players will voluntarily choose helmets and the helmet equilibrium becomes self-sustaining. In the National Hockey League, the coordination failure was overcome following a tragic death, which tipped the league to the point that 70 percent of players were already wearing helmets by the time the league mandated their use.[22]

In our counterinsurgency example, the first, and more desirable, outcome is for everyone in the passive majority to support the government, a position that would lead to a weak insurgency and ultimately to a stable government. This outcome is best for everyone in the passive majority. The second possible equilibrium is for the tide to turn toward the insurgency and against the government. As more people support the insurgency, the incentive for others to also follow the insurgency increases until the insurgency gains power and the government becomes weak and unstable. This outcome is undesirable for the passive majority; however, once the country starts down this path, it is difficult to stop the process. Once the insurgency starts to grow and gain support, it will be in each individual's best interest not to support the government even if collectively everyone is worse off.

Figure 19.3 illustrates the coordination problem using a hypothetical example. The figure shows the fraction of people who will actively support the government as a function of their expectations about how many other people will actively support the government. If people expect that 30 percent of the population will support the government, then only 15 percent will actually support the government. This is not sustainable, as the 15 percent who support the government will find their expectations are not met. As they revise their expectations downward, fewer and fewer will support the government until we reach the stable equilibrium of no support. However, if people expect that 80 percent of the population will support the government, then 85 percent will actually support the government. In this case, the actual support exceeds expectations. As people revise their expectations upward, more and more people support the government until we reach the stable equilibrium of full support. Note that 40 percent support is a tipping point in this example. With initial expectations of slightly more than 40 percent support, the dynamics of the game will lead to the full support equilibrium. With expectations slightly less than 40 percent, the no support equilibrium will prevail.

Two questions arise—one about assessment and one about policy. The assessment question concerns how to determine if we are on the path to the full support equilibrium or not. Nation-building operations face potential pitfalls where traditional metrics of assessment will point toward success even

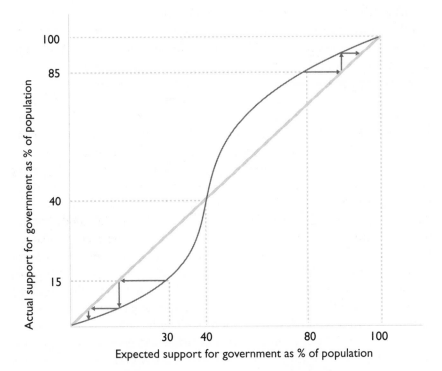

Figure 19.3. An example of government support as a critical mass game

as a country moves toward the undesirable equilibrium. The policy question is, if we are not on the right path, how can we adjust expectations and tip the game to the desirable equilibrium? We answer the policy question first by giving examples of the kinds of policies that can overcome the coordination problem and tip the game. In the following section, we address the assessment question with examples of how traditional metrics can go wrong and with a list of supplemental metrics that can provide the evidence that we are on a sustainable path to the desired equilibrium outcome.

How can nation-building operations spend money in ways that overcome the coordination failure, increase support for the government, and tip toward the preferred equilibrium outcome? In general, the key to overcoming a coordination failure is to build a large enough coalition of people who support the government that it will be in everyone else's interest to follow and to support the government as well.[23] In the context of nation building, how can such coalitions be formed? In our view, the key is to pursue initiatives in two areas—supporting markets and building human capital.

First, projects that support functioning markets should be pursued. Another kind of coordination failure can occur in war-torn countries concerning production decisions—for example, the choice of what kinds of crops to plant. In the absence of a functioning market to trade goods, individuals may focus on subsistence farming rather than reap the benefits of trade. One person cannot unilaterally reap the benefits of trade, but collectively everyone can improve their circumstances through specialization of production and trade. A nation-building operation can help coordinate individuals on the preferred "trading" equilibrium by creating an efficient transportation network for moving goods, promoting secure marketplaces, and creating a fair and effective criminal justice system to protect property rights. Individuals have a greater personal incentive to invest their time and resources in production (e.g., growing crops) when they feel assured that their goods will not be confiscated or destroyed and that they can safely bring them to market. If individuals see the government providing security and transport options, then such actions will help grow the economy and increase people's support for the government. It is very difficult for individuals to provide these projects on their own; collective action fostered by an effective government is necessary. This is true even in developed countries like the United States.

Second, equally important are projects that build *human capital*, a term economists use that broadly refers to the productivity of individuals. Projects that promote the health and education of workers are examples of human capital improvements. A healthy workforce loses fewer days due to sickness. Education increases the knowledge and skills of the workforce, lowering production costs and increasing the diversity of industries present in the domestic economy. While good health and education directly improve the quality of life for individuals, they also help the government achieve the preferred equilibrium outcome. Robust, literate workers have more to lose from the failure to sustain a stable government because the collapse of the government could jeopardize their health and eliminate the value of their education in labor markets. Both education and health are thus important investments to build coalitions of the population who support the government and to ensure sustained economic growth following the completion of the nation-building operation.

DEVELOPING METRICS TO ASSESS SUSTAINABILITY OF ECONOMIC OUTCOMES

The US government currently has a policy of making condolence payments of up to $2,500 to families of civilians who are killed by US forces in Afghanistan or Iraq.[24] This injection of cash into the hands of civilians increases consumption, and from a purely economic standpoint, these payments increase their welfare. However, there are reasons to believe that these increases in living standards can hide a reduction in support for the government. First, although civilian deaths cannot be completely prevented, they surely create resentment against US forces in the absence of condolence payments and possibly increase support for the insurgency or at least decrease active support for the US-allied government. Do the condolence payments successfully alleviate this resentment? It is not clear. At best, there may be a neutral impact on the families, but some families may feel negatively about being compensated for a lost family member with money, which in effect puts dollar values on lives. Either way, what our economic metrics show as an improvement in living standards is actually correlated with reduced support for the government and movement away from our desired equilibrium.

The difference between these condolence payments and the development projects described in the previous section is that the former gives the illusion of improved welfare that may evaporate when US forces leave the country while the latter promotes a stable equilibrium that can persist even after US forces leave. The following metrics can be used to assess whether nation-building operations are successful at creating a sufficiently stable government that can continue to function after the conclusion of the nation-building operation.

1. Infrastructure projects that are successfully completed and operational are a positive sign of progress in a nation-building operation. The special inspector general for Afghanistan reconstruction notes many projects are listed as "completed" but are not functional due to construction or maintenance problems.[25] It is important to assess the success of a project not only by the completion of the project but also by the continued use of the services that the completed project is supposed to provide. As noted earlier, projects should not be valued based on their costs and expenditures but by the benefits provided. For example, building a road that links two population centers and increases transport efficiency is a potentially welfare-improving project. To assess the success of this project, it is critical to monitor the use of the road after its completion. A useful metric would be the number of vehicles using the road per month, and the metric should be assessed continuously while the operation is in progress. Where an existing road is improved, increases in volume, savings in road user costs, and travel savings can also be measured. As another example, consider an irrigation project to deliver water to farmers in a rural area. Simply finishing the project is not a useful metric. Instead, tracking the crop yield or the number of farmers who plant crops while using the irrigation system are better metrics

to evaluate the project's success. It can be re-evaluated each season to monitor the continued progress of or the deterioration in the project's benefits.

2. Projects that build human capital include building hospitals, training medical workers, establishing schools, and training teachers. Again, assessment should not involve the number of projects completed; instead they should focus on the benefits received from the project such as the rate at which services are used. In this example, it could be the number of patients seen per month at a hospital or the number of children enrolled in schools each year. Even better, this data can be converted into dollar values with the help of empirical estimates on the value of education or the economic cost of illness, including missed time working and the discomfort of being ill. It should also be noted that a "completed" but unused hospital or school (see examples in the special inspector general for Afghanistan reconstruction's report[26]) would show up as a positive benefit using traditional metrics such as GDP but would have a neutral impact using the proposed metrics. In fact, empty buildings may actually have a negative impact on the nation-building operation by fostering feelings of frustration and resentment among members of the population who see them on a regular basis.

3. Some micro-level economic indicators provide useful information about how individuals feel about the state of the economy—for instance, whether they feel confident in the future and that their property is secure. These indicators can help assess whether we are moving toward a stable equilibrium that is sustainable or whether we are seeing temporary improvements in welfare due to the presence of US forces in the country. The most useful indicators are those that involve a costly action today that will reap benefits in the future. An individual will not sacrifice today to make a long-term investment if the individual anticipates that the economic situation will deteriorate in the near future. Taking a costly action indicates that the individual has confidence that the progress is sustainable. Examples of costly actions that signal sustainable progress are planting permanent crops, buying agricultural equipment, or making other kinds of large capital investments. Another example is the number of small business loans issued by private lenders, as lenders are hesitant to issue loans if the perceived likelihood of default is high. Related to this point, interest rates on small loans can also serve as indicators of lenders' confidence about the future. If lenders are pessimistic about the future, the perceived default risk will be high, and they will therefore demand higher interest rates. To reiterate, a common theme

in these examples is that we infer individual beliefs about the future by watching the actions they take today. We look for actions that would only be taken if individuals were optimistic regarding the future.

4. Finally surveys of the population can directly gauge how people feel about the current and future state of the economy. Surveys have the advantage of directly asking questions of interest that cannot be measured any other way. However, we urge caution in relying too heavily on surveys as an assessment tool because the hypothetical nature of surveys can lead to biased answers. Survey respondents might not carefully consider the question, they might give answers that they think the questioner wants to hear, or they might answer strategically, thinking about how the survey results will be used and giving answers that they perceive will increase the likelihood of some desired outcome. When survey respondents do not perceive there will be any consequences to their responses, the survey can be viewed as "cheap talk," and evidence shows that individuals will act differently in hypothetical surveys than they actually do when there are consequences to their choices or actions.[27] At times surveys may be useful as the only way to acquire some kinds of information, but, at best, they should be used as a complement to the metrics described in items 1–3 and not as a substitute in assessing whether nation-building operations are successful.

This chapter highlights some of the issues in measuring economic welfare in a post-conflict nation-building setting. We not only illustrate several limitations of metrics such as GDP and project expenditures but also provide suggestions for dealing with these limitations and implementing metrics that give an accurate picture of the state of the economy and the potential for sustained economic growth once an operation ends. Figure 19.4 summarizes our key prescriptions.

Assessment of economic outcomes in nation-building operations is an important aspect of the overall assessment of an operation. In fact, achieving a stable, growing economy may be one of the best predictors of attaining political stability and security. However, relying on traditional metrics like GDP may obfuscate the true state of the economy from the perspective of an average citizen; therefore, it might paint too rosy a picture of how well off people are now or how the economy is transitioning long term. More important, using a poor metric may lead policymakers to take actions that promote the metric but do not improve welfare or possibly even decrease welfare. Thus, choosing the right metric serves not only an informational purpose but also improves outcomes by helping decision makers choose the best course of action.

• Household consumption is better than GDP for measuring the current well-being of citizens in a country.
• Social indicators related to education and health should complement economic measures such as consumption and GDP when possible.
• Successful development projects in such areas as transportation, agriculture, health, and education are indicators of sustainable progress that will last beyond the nation-building operation.
• Measures of the success of a project should be based on the benefits of the project and not on its cost.
• Costly actions, or those actions that individuals would only find worthwhile if conditions were improving, are good indicators of sustainable progress.
• Hypothetical survey data (cheap talk) should be used with caution and only when no other data sources are available.

Figure 19.4. Key prescriptions on assessing economic welfare

NOTES

1. U.S. Army, *Counterinsurgency,* FM 3–24 (Washington DC: Government Printing Office, 2006), 1-21.
2. Christiaan Davids, Sebastiaan Rietjens, and Joseph Soeters, "Measuring Progress in Reconstructing Afghanistan," *Baltic Security and Defence Review* 21, no. 1 (2010); and the World Bank, *2014 World Development Indicators* (Washington DC: International Bank for Reconstruction and Development and World Bank, 2014), http://data.worldbank.org/sites/default/files/wdi-2014-book.pdf.
3. Special Inspector General for Afghanistan Reconstruction, *Commander's Emergency Response Program in Laghman Province Provided Some Benefits, but Oversight Weaknesses and Sustainment Concerns Led to Questionable Outcomes and Potential Waste*, Audit-11–7 (Crystal City VA: Office of the Special Inspector General for Afghanistan Reconstruction, January 2011).
4. Ellyn Creasey, Ahmed S. Rahman, and Katherine A. Smith, "Nation Building and Economic Growth," *American Economic Review* 102, no. 3 (2012): 278–82; and Paul Collier and Anke Hoeffler, "Aid, Policy, and Growth in Post-Conflict Societies," *European Economic Review* 48, no. 5 (2004): 1125–45.
5. James Dobbins et al., *The Beginner's Guide to Nation-Building* (Santa Monica: RAND, 2007), 179–82.

6. Department of Defense, *Report on Progress toward Security and Stability in Afghanistan*, Report to Congress (Washington DC: Department of Defense, December 2012).

7. For a detailed review of the limitations of GDP as a measure of well-being that are worth considering, see Joseph E. Stiglitz, Amartya Sen, and Jean-Paul Fitoussi, *Report by the Commission on the Measurement of Economic Performance and Social Progress*, 2009, http://www.stiglitz-sen-fitoussi.fr/en/index.htm.

8. Richard Hogg et al., *Afghanistan in Transition: Looking beyond 2014* (Washington DC: World Bank, 2013).

9. Department of Defense, *Report on Progress*, 134.

10. Hogg et al., *Afghanistan in Transition*, 2013.

11. Ibid., 2013.

12. William Nordhaus and James Tobin, "Is Growth Obsolete?," in *The Measurement of Economic and Social Performance*, ed. Milton Moss (New York: Columbia University/National Bureau of Economic Research, 1973).

13. The seminal work in this area is by Nordhaus and Tobin, who created an alternate index called the Measure of Economic Welfare (MEW). Examples of more recent work at developing indexes of economic well-being to replace GDP include: Herman E. Daly and John B. Cobb Jr., *For the Common Good: Redirecting the Economy toward Community, the Environment, and a Sustainable Future* (Boston: Beacon Press, 1989); and Lars Osberg and Andrew Sharpe, "An Index of Economic Well-being for Selected OECD Countries," *Review of Income and Wealth* 48, no. 3 (September 2001): 291–316.

14. UNDP, *Human Development Report, 1990: Concept and Measurement of Human Development* (New York: UNDP, 1990).

15. Amnesty International, *The Dark Side of Migration: Spotlight on Qatar's Construction Sector ahead of the World Cup* (New York: Amnesty International, 2013).

16. Roger B. Myerson, "A Field Manual for the Cradle of Civilization: Theory of Leadership and Lessons of Iraq," *Journal of Conflict Resolution* 53 (2009): 470–82; and Roger B. Myerson, "Toward a Theory of Leadership and State Building," *Proceedings of the National Academy of Sciences* 108, no. 4 (2011): 21297–301.

17. Ibid.

18. Gordon H. McCormick and Frank Giordano, "Things Come Together: Symbolic Violence and Guerrilla Mobilization," *Third World Quarterly* 28, no. 2 (2007): 295–329.

19. Thomas C. Schelling, *Micromotives and Macrobehavior* (New York: Norton, 1978).

20. Malcolm Gladwell, *The Tipping Point: How Little Things Can Make a Big Difference* (New York: Little, Brown, 2000).

21. Russell Cooper and Andrew John, "Coordinating Coordination Failures in Keynesian Models," *Quarterly Journal of Economics* 103, no. 3 (August 1988): 441–63.
22. "N.H.L. Rules New Players Now Must Wear Helmets," *New York Times*, August 7, 1979, C14.
23. See Geoffrey Heal and Howard Kunreuther, "Social Reinforcement: Cascades, Entrapment, and Tipping," *American Economic Journal: Microeconomics* 2, no. 1 (2010): 86–99; and Aric P. Shafran and Jason J. Lepore, "Subsidization to Induce Tipping," *Economics Letters* 110, no. 1 (2011): 32–35.
24. U.S. Forces Afghanistan, *Money as a Weapon System—Afghanistan*, USFOR-A Pub 1–06, 2009.
25. Special Inspector General for Afghanistan Reconstruction, *Commander's Emergency Response Program in Laghman Province Provided Some Benefits, but Oversight Weaknesses and Sustainment Concerns Led to Questionable Outcomes and Potential Waste*, Audit-11–7, January 2011.
26. Ibid.
27. See Christian A. Vossler and Sharon B. Watson, "Understanding the Consequences of Consequentiality: Testing the Validity of Stated Preferences in the Field," *Journal of Economic Behavior and Organization*, 2013, 86, 137–47; Erwin Bulte et al., "The Effect of Varying the Causes of Environmental Problems on Stated WTP Values: Evidence from a Field Study," *Journal of Environmental Economics and Management* 49 (2005): 330–42; and Richard T. Carson and Theodore Groves, "Incentive and Informational Properties of Preference Questions," *Environmental and Resource Economics* 37 (2007): 181–210.

CONCLUSION

CAN WE LEARN FROM THE ASSESSMENT OF WAR?

Anthony H. Cordesman and Hy Rothstein

THEORY OF VICTORY

Clausewitz continuously emphasized the unity between politics and war. And military strategy is simply the use, or threat of use, of force for policy ends. A similar unity exists between the goals of strategy and wartime assessments. It is impossible to do assessment without clear goals. While this point seems obvious, too often this requirement is not met. Furthermore, goals must be realistic or assessment becomes pointless as unrealistic goals cannot be achieved.

Since war aims and strategies are often fluid, a change in policy and strategy may necessitate a change in strategic assessment. Goal refinement should be an important part of the planning and assessment processes. Accordingly, good assessment starts in planning and continues throughout the campaign. It is the best way for the assessor and the commander to clearly define measurable and achievable goals that support the war's purpose. Both assessment and mission accomplishment are placed in jeopardy if poorly specified or ambiguous goals survive the planning process.

Successful prosecution of a military campaign does not necessarily indicate competence in the conduct of war. The significance of how war serves politics and how assessment serves war must always be front and center in the mind and actions of the commander.[1] Implicit to any strategy is the theory of victory or the underlying logic for how planners think elements of the military and associated activities will lead to desired political outcomes. This theory is simply a declaration of how you believe the things you are planning to do will lead to the goals you seek.

This declaration is central to the assessment plan because it allows assumptions to be turned into *hypotheses*, or conjectured relationships among key variables. These hypotheses can then be tested as part of the assessment process. Disproved hypotheses can be replaced until confirmed or the theory of victory can be modified until a validated logical chain connecting activities and goals is met.

The theory identifies what factors should be measured and how they work together to achieve goals. It helps determine what is worth measuring. In other words, the theory of victory shows a clear and logical connection between the activities and the desired outcomes. More important, it provides assessors with a window into breakdowns in the logic chain or which hypotheses are not substantiated.[2]

ARE WE WINNING?

The various chapters in this book cover many themes and provide both old and new insights about the challenges of wartime assessment. They also provide a useful warning as to just how different the tactical, strategic, and policy aspects of war can be, and they point to the importance of the civil-military element in given conflicts. These differences make it difficult, and perhaps dangerous, to present one simple set of lessons.

This in itself, however, is a key lesson. War is case specific and extremely complex. The search for simple assessments, narratives, and metrics—and the failure to deal with case-specific complexities—results in adding to the fog of war rather than reducing it. Command efforts to simplify the realities of war, analysts who fall in love with their own limited assessment models, and efforts to find clear historical parallels to past conflicts are inherently self-defeating. One can only simplify or prioritize what one actually understands.

This is particularly dangerous in the case of limited wars, where the nature and size of the US commitment is not clearly tied to American national security interests and when a frank and honest assessment of critical US strategic needs and requirements is deficient. As several chapters show, this trend is especially dangerous where early assessments understate the risks and growth of the threat, when best-case scenarios dominate the analysis, and when the risks and challenges of what is actually armed nation building are ignored.

As Hans Morgenthau warned decades ago, the United States has a strong tendency to turn conflicts into morality plays and crusades. Furthermore, we seem continuously to fail to articulate the purpose of our efforts to foreigners and to explain our actions using the internal logic of our intended targets, both friend and foe. As the wars in Korea, Vietnam, Iraq, and Afghanistan all warn in different ways, the United States also is prone to try to transform nations in both military and civil terms without regard to the difficulties and costs involved, the need to respect different cultures and values, and the calamitous cost of pursuing unobtainable civil and military goals.

LESSONS OF ASSESSMENT IN WAR

In the beginning of this chapter we noted the difficulty and potential danger associated with trying to reduce wartime assessment to a simple set of lessons. But this book would not be complete if we didn't cull some of the valuable insights identified by this book's scholarly contributors. Bernard Brodie said, "Strategic thinking, or 'theory' if one prefers, is nothing if not pragmatic."[3] Likewise, pragmatic lessons exist for designing and conducting wartime assessments.

THE ENEMY, PARTNERS AND ALLIES, AND OURSELVES

Looking through the book, one is struck by the fact that assessment reveals that the United States generally must deal with at least three threats in war: the enemy, our partners and allies, and ourselves.

THE ENEMY

The most familiar threat is the enemy, although the United States seems far more able to focus on the tactical threat from enemies than on the political threat they pose. In smaller wars and insurgencies, the United States seems to have found it extremely difficult to understand that enemies do not have to win tactically if they can steadily gain political influence and expand their presence. For example, in 2012–13 the only metric the International Security Assistance Force (ISAF) reported was on enemy-initiated attacks. The ISAF's failure to provide metrics on Taliban and insurgent areas of influence was a disaster long before it became apparent that its assessment of enemy-initiated attacks was misguided in every respect. Consequently it led the ISAF to cease such reporting altogether.

Assessments may be clouded by national stereotypes—for example, viewing one's enemy as weak willed or mercurial. At the strategic level, such self-deception can be disastrous. It is essential to know and understand the ideas that we are at war against—that is, why our enemy is fighting and what he is willing to die for.

Often initial success can happen very fast and even by surprise without US political or military leaders having accurate tools of assessment. Such was the case in the Philippines in the early 1900s and, arguably, early in the wars in Afghanistan and Iraq. Not understanding the reasons for initial success may lead American leadership to misunderstand the situation and rely more on intuition over informed decision-making processes.

A century ago poor communications between military headquarters and their subordinate units in the field complicated the acquisition of an accurate appreciation of local military conditions. The result was that small-unit commanders had more flexibility to craft wartime actions and policies that were applicable to their specific areas. This ability was certainly advantageous in attaining positive results in the Philippine case. Modern communications systems eliminate most information gaps today but not the fog of war. Accordingly, there is a constant demand, often emanating from Washington, for information to lift the fog. This never-ending demand for information can paralyze the war effort at the front and only adds to the fog of war.

In small wars, the need for comprehensive, localized intelligence includes information on the demographics of enemy, friendly, and neutral audiences; enemy infrastructure; enemy resources, as well as militia or police; and civilian morale. Collecting such information and making sense of it at a theater level are difficult tasks. Unfortunately an unintended negative consequence of modern communications is that theater commanders rarely defer to local commanders who possess critical knowledge unique to their areas of operations. Local commanders are simply boxed in by modern communications. Theater commanders need to delegate more authority to their subordinate commanders on today's differentiated battlefield, especially in the case where decisive battlefield victory is elusive.

PARTNERS AND ALLIES

The second threat is dealing with our partners and allies. The effective assessment of war requires a ruthlessly objective assessment of their strengths and weaknesses and of the differences between their strategic and tactical goals, values, and culture from that of the United States. Important differences will arise with even the best ally. In cases such as China and the Soviet Union in World War II, then Vietnam, and more recently Iraq, Pakistan, and Afghanistan, an objective net assessment should have been a critical element of every aspect of the assessment of war.

Furthermore, proxy troops fight for different reasons than one's own forces do; thus, assessments must account for very different incentives among proxy troops. Separate motivations create the need for consistent post-battle assessments as well as interpretations of those assessments. Proxy commanders have a strong incentive to manipulate reports and assessments in their favor to prove their worth and to justify continued material support. Far too often commanders blame their failures on poorly trained or undisciplined proxies without first knowing their motivations. Proxies can profoundly shape, either positively or negatively, the outcome of a campaign or war. Finally, making US support far more conditional should be a key part of US strategy and operations from the outset.

OURSELVES

As serious as the threat posed by the enemy and our allies, the third threat is the one Americans see in the mirror every day of a war and usually for years or decades after the war has ended—namely, ourselves. Entering a war properly prepared for all of the problems one may face is highly unlikely. The United States will never have all of the analytical tools available to assess a given conflict and might never have the key elements of the data it needs. Even the most objective effort makes it difficult to properly weigh all factors and data.

The chapters in this book warn that US prejudices, bureaucratic rigidities, and preconceptions are a constant threat. So is our tendency to politicize assessment, fight internal battles as well as real ones, use assessment for personal or bureaucratic ends, sell a given campaign or strategy, or request more forces.

Ideally a baseline assessment should take place before a conflict starts, if possible, and the assessment and analysis team should be involved in strategic planning from the beginning of the process. When initial assessments are not borne out, we should undertake reassessments grounded in that experience and adjust means and ends of policy accordingly. For example, in World War II the British government's decision to shift its bombing campaign from daytime missions against military, industrial, and transportation targets to nighttime missions against German cities was based largely on an assessment report showing the hopelessly inadequate results of targeted daylight bombing accompanied by high bomber losses.

It is equally important to review and adjust the assessment plan when the strategy changes; such changes should only be necessary if the political goals of the campaign shift and therefore the measures for determining if, or when, the new goals are achieved. Furthermore, distinguishing between enduring data that supports strategic assessment versus data that tactical units require for independent analysis is a nontrivial requirement of assessment.

If one is reduced to attrition as a means to win a war, then one must find reliable methods of measuring the amount of damage inflicted on an enemy versus the losses endured by one's own forces. Self-deception is a special danger here. Assessments must be built on more than impressionistic evidence, which all too often reinforces preexisting prejudices and preferences for policy. Erich von Falkenhayn certainly made this error at Verdun. Also when a war of attrition approaches its end, and one makes demands on an enemy seeking peace, it is important to balance the enemy's exhaustion with what is likely to be one's own vulnerable position, especially if an asymmetry of interests between the main protagonists exists.

Another key insight, and a grim one, is the inevitable and often unavoidable effort to sell the war using any narrative and metrics necessary to frame the conflict in a way that wins political and financial support. The chapters on Korea, Vietnam, Iraq, and Afghanistan all illustrate this lesson in different ways.

It is possible that senior military commanders will withhold the *full* truth when offering wartime assessments, believing it will prevent some future harm to the war's overriding objective. Given the nation's civil-military traditions, military commanders act as the chief advocates for their presidents' wars and face the dilemma of speaking to multiple audiences about the progress of the wars, especially those without visible decision points and identifiable milestones. However, policymakers, more so than their senior military commanders, seem likely to use less than candid language, based on a selective interpretation of the facts for political purposes, to publicize progress in limited wars that do not pose an existential threat to the nation.

Historians, journalists, and other external observers of war rarely have knowledge of private, candid disagreements between civilian and military leaders. While a senior military leader has a duty to be straightforward with his civilian boss, he also has a responsibility not to publically expose serious differences of opinion. To do so would violate appropriate civil-military relations and potentially undermine the health of American democracy. Thus, Americans might expect a "conversation gap" between private wartime assessments and public pronouncements of progress. Given that the credibility of a government is a precious commodity, there are dangers in overselling progress in wartime assessment, as best illustrated by the "credibility gap" created in the aftermath of the 1968 Tet Offensive.

Accordingly it is worth stating what is obvious: Military leaders need to improve their effectiveness in working with their civilian superiors and understanding their priorities. As they offer direct and frank advice, they should recommend appropriate courses of action even if they might not please their superiors. It is a senior officer's duty, not a violation of traditional civil-military relations. Not doing so risks assessments becoming nothing more than propaganda, and in the words of Neil Sheehan, a "bright shining lie."[4]

ADDITIONAL CHALLENGES

In addition to three main threats that the United States faces, the various chapters in this volume point to additional challenges that emerge in different ways.

WAR COSTS

One of these challenges is cost, a factor that is far less important in existential conflicts but became increasingly critical in Iraq and Afghanistan. It is more than casually ironic that the US Department of Defense argued before the Iraq War that its total cost would be less than $50 billion. Amy Belasco of the Congressional Research Service estimated that the United States spent some $1.4 trillion on the Iraq and Afghan wars between fiscal year 2001 and fiscal year 2011.[5] The cost through fiscal year 2015 currently is $1.66 trillion.[6]

Just as striking as these costs was the total failure, at every level, to consistently fund any given stream of activity, to establish proper accounting measures, to set up and track meaningful effectiveness measures, and to recognize the overall massive negative impact in terms of corruption, inflation, and the distortion of governance and the economy. Money can undermine the achievement of political goals if its use is not carefully scrutinized.

Furthermore, there are serious problems with using GDP as a welfare measure in nation-building operations. GDP includes profits earned by foreigners and production, such as defensive expenditures, that do not directly improve the lives of the domestic population. It also values government services based on expenditures instead of benefits provided to ordinary citizens. GDP also does not take into account inequality of income or consumption. It includes benefits of foreign aid that may not be sustainable after nation-building operations end. A better prescription than GDP for assessing economic welfare would include measuring household consumption, which more accurately assesses the well-being of citizens in a country.

Social indicators related to education and health should complement economic measures like consumption and GDP when possible. Successful development projects in areas such as transportation, agriculture, health, and education are indicators of sustainable progress that will last beyond the nation-building operation. In measuring the success of a project, metrics should be based on the benefits of the project, not its cost. Finally survey data ("cheap talk") should be used with caution and only when no other data sources are available.

Unfortunately one can effectively argue that the assessments of governance, economic progress, and legitimacy in Iraq and Afghanistan imply negative progress in conducting and assessing the civil side of war. In those wars, the US government was unprepared for the civil side of war. It set impossible goals, provided far too few resources, and developed assessments to show progress that either did not occur or was based on goals that might suit project aid in peacetime but had little value on a national basis in time of war.

ETHICAL CONSIDERATIONS AND JUST WAR THEORY

Proportionality assessments are at the heart of just war theory. But these assessments assume that we can estimate the number of deaths and grievous injuries innocents and soldiers will suffer as a result of going to war. Many of the chapters in this book, however, show that we do not assess potential damages very well. Just war theory needs to take stock of this uncertainty. One could introduce an error factor in assessments that would subject the moral assessment of war to higher cost estimates than we, in fact, hold. This factor may help to avoid a "war trap," where once wars have started, all further anticipated human costs are justified to honor those sacrifices already incurred. To avoid the war trap, the moral assessment of wars needs to exercise great discipline. Sunk costs are not a justification of further costs.

CYBER WARFARE AND IDEOLOGICAL FACTORS

The final chapters of the book warn that all of these problems may be compounded by new developments in war—for example, cyber warfare, new ideological factors, and innovative forms of information warfare. Cyber battle damages are assessed by examining the effects of cyber attacks on cyber systems, including damages to data, software, and hardware; and on organizations, including operational effects, monetary losses, and reputational effects. Cyber strength is assessed by applying risk assessment to determine the risk of adversary systems to our cyber attacks relative to the risk of our systems to an adversary's cyber attacks.

Ideological factors are at the forefront in both the Syrian civil war and the fighting in Iraq that led to an Islamist extremist conquest of Mosul and much of northern and western Iraq in June 2014. It is abundantly clear that any expected restraint in war may continue to fade in modern conflict and that wars will continue to be fought by actors who do not fit within standard

Western models of rationality. Understanding the enemy's ideology is important; indeed, it is almost as important as understanding our own and why we are willing to kill and be killed for a cause.

MILITARY DEPLOYMENT CYCLES

It is easy to talk about integrated civil-military relations and tying US tactics to a consistent strategy, but no assessment of recent US wars would indicate the United States had good ways of assessing the overall progress and coordination of such time streams. Iraq and Afghanistan also came very close to repeating the US experience in Vietnam, where "every year was the first year" of war, and constant changes in programs, leadership, and goals without giving the previous plan adequate time to play out meant starting over year after year.

ASSESSMENTS THAT SUPPORT DECISION MAKING

Wartime assessment is first and foremost designed to support the commander in making informed decisions about the conduct of war. It assumes that the assessment methodology adequately measures the change that must take place to achieve the war's purpose. If this is not the case, the measurement does not matter and will be irrelevant to decision making. Furthermore, should competent assessments fail to reach the decision maker in a usable form before the decision is made, they are useless.

In addition, the motivation behind assessments can be fatally flawed. For example, the assessment tool can be subverted to justify decisions already made, either for political posturing or for simply satisfying a higher authority's requirement to establish an assessment program. The result is an assessment tool that is disconnected from the decision-making process.

Finally, it is also necessary to be aware that any assessment mechanism will create incentives for units in the field. This mechanism could be either a powerful tool for guiding the soldiers' efforts or a source of serious pathology that subverts the decision-making process and undermines the conduct of war.

WHAT WILL BE THE AFTERMATH?

All of these issues, however, relate to a broader one. Wartime assessment almost inevitably focuses on the short-term priorities set by the need to achieve tactical victory, immediate political and economic stability, and a successful outcome as defined by the narrow goals of a campaign plan. What ultimately counts, however, is what happens after victory is achieved in the narrow short-term sense or what happens after US and allied forces withdraw.

The reality is that different and conflicting sets of time pressures affect assessment. The classic difference is that tactical time is generally very short term while strategic time may be much longer, and the blood spilled and mistakes made in tactical time are far more immediate than those occurring in strategic time. A focus on tactical time can produce an incentive structure for subordinate commanders that may undermine long-term goals.

The ultimate test in assessment is to tie assessment to some meaningful set of grand strategic goals that shape the outcome after the fighting ends—if it ends at all. In his book *Every War Must End*, Fred Iklé argued, quite correctly, that the key strategic goal in every war—and therefore in assessing a war—is to shape conflict termination in ways that achieve some lasting form of victory after the conflict ends.[7] The history of war, however, is the history of changing strategic goals throughout most conflicts. Since the end of World War II, the grim history of most irregular conflicts has been that they do not really end. Instead, they simply pause or mutate with continuing levels of violence and the substitution of political struggles and instability during the periods where some new form of fighting does not emerge.

As this book shows, the United States and its allies never set meaningful goals for conflict termination at any point of the Afghan and Iraq conflicts. The broad goals set in both wars—such as the Afghanistan Compact—were so ambitious and transformational that they were not only unachievable but also helped destabilize the countries, gave the enemy new windows of opportunity, and created a climate that made a stable and successful transition of power and US withdrawal far more difficult.

As time went on, the United States became more and more focused on withdrawal, limiting the duration of its role in the conflicts and its planned advisory and aid role after withdrawal. Wartime assessments progressively became less realistic and less transparent and pushed the assessment process to justify the accelerating speed and scale of withdrawal. Rather than undertaking a realistic assessment of what was actually happening or was likely to happen after withdrawal, assessments were shaded to support the desired political goal of ending US involvement in the wars.

The end result in Iraq was that the United States withdrew its military and police advisory missions precipitously during a significant level of ongoing civil conflict. The United States accepted and the president praised the authoritarian and sectarian government of Nouri al-Maliki, who then shaped the Iraqi Security Forces and the entire process of Iraqi governance to support his own power, Shi'ite sectarian interests, and, to some extent, those of Iran. This development triggered a new round of civil war that now overlaps the fighting in Syria, has drawn in Iran, and has pushed the United States into either finding new ways to support Iraq in a civil war or accepting major gains by the Islamic State of Iraq and Syria—a radical Sunni jihadist movement that threatens the entire region.

The end result in Afghanistan is still unclear. Unrealistic goals in reshaping the Afghan political process and structure of governance, however, do jeopardize any success the United States might have achieved after its forces have completely withdrawn. The failure to create a truly integrated civil-military plan and honest assessments of civil-military progress has left a level of corruption, failed governance, and rule of law that outside sources such as the World Bank and International Monetary Fund see as major threats to Afghan stability after the US and allied withdrawal.[8]

The United States can only be truly successful in assessing war by shaping that assessment around realistic goals, metrics, and narratives of the prospects for US withdrawal and conflict termination. So far the United States has not made any progress in this aspect of grand strategy since 1945. The Korean War has still not officially ended. Vietnam ended in defeat. US intervention in cases such as Cuba, Angola, the Democratic Republic of the Congo, and a variety of conflicts in Central America resulted in prolonged struggles that had mixed outcomes to say the least. The axiom "There is no strategy without grand strategy" applies to assessment as well.

ORGANIZING FOR ASSESSMENT

Organizations must value assessment for it to have any chance of contributing to success. New concepts and change in an organization are usually met with resistance. Organizations and individuals can be reticent to anything other than "business as usual." Creating an understanding of the value of assessment starts with an appreciation for what it can accomplish.

This process takes time, especially where an assessment culture never existed before. Key to successful assessment is a commitment from leadership. Leaders who make decisions supported by assessment output are willing to allocate resources for assessment. These resources include developing well-educated people capable of conducting sophisticated research. In addition, assessment requires getting over the fear of the results. Even the most transparent organization will cause its people to cringe just a little bit when its work is laid open to objective evaluation.

Yet a learning organization must develop a culture that is accepting of bad news and views such news as a means to correct its course. It is not a stretch to say that a good organization should take bad news in a positive way because it presents an opportunity to raise the organization's awareness of what it was not doing well and fix it.

Finally assessment requires resources. Military organizations operate in a constrained resource environment perhaps more today than since World War II. Assessment does not always make the resource cut. The reality, however, is that assessment is more important under conditions of resource scarcity. The military simply cannot afford to shortchange assessment. Trial and error is too costly a method to achieve success. Assessment as an essential requirement needs to permeate military thinking at all levels. The good news is that resources necessary for assessment, to include intelligence collection and analysis assets, are relatively small.[9]

LET THE SUN SHINE IN

One final issue is not directly addressed in this book, but every chapter makes some indirect contribution to the warning: The assessment of war cannot simply be an internal command activity or the business of the executive and legislative branches of government. The history of assessment shows that war can far too easily become a liar's contest and an exercise in the worst kind of public relations. Unless assessment is public in every area where it does not directly threaten to increase casualties or compromise operations, it may be corrupted to serve command or political ends and usually in ways that seriously increase the risk of defeat or some form of partial victory. In this sense, the restriction of reporting and overclassification may well be a final threat to the successful US conduct of war.

NOTES

1. Colin S. Gray, *War, Peace and International Relations: An Introduction to Strategic History* (New York: Routledge, 2008), 14–17.
2. Christopher Paul et al., *Assessing and Evaluating Department of Defense Efforts to Inform, Influence, and Persuade: An Annotated Reading List* (Santa Monica: RAND, 2014), 25–26.
3. Bernard Brodie, *War and Politics* (New York: Macmillan, 1973), 452.
4. Neil Sheehan, *A Bright Shining Lie: John Paul Vann and America in Vietnam* (New York: Vintage, 1988).

5. Amy Belasco, "The Cost of Iraq, Afghanistan, and Other Global War on Terror Operations since 9/11" (Washington DC: Congressional Research Service, March 29, 2011).

6. Anthony H. Cordesman, "Irregular Warfare: Learning the Lessons of 'Worst Case' Wars" (Washington DC: Center for Strategic and International Studies, June 11, 2014), 22, http://csis.org/files/publication/Lessons%20of%20 Worst%20Case%20Wars%20and%20Irregular%20Warfare%2010%20 JUNE%202014.pdf.

7. Fred Charles Iklé, *Every War Must End*, rev. ed. (New York: Columbia University Press, 2005).

8. For a detailed overview of the problems in the military, governance, and economic situation in Afghanistan in mid-2014, see Anthony H. Cordesman, "The Challenges to Afghan Transition: 2014–2016" (Washington DC: Center for Strategic and International Studies, 2014), http://csis.org/files/publica tion/140708_Transition_Afghanistan.pdf.

9. Ibid., 269–72, 303.

CONTRIBUTORS

Leo J. Blanken is an associate professor in the Defense Analysis Department at the Naval Postgraduate School. Dr. Blanken's current research focuses on the theoretical foundations of force structure planning. His book, *Rational Empires: Institutional Incentives and Imperial Expansion*, was published by the University of Chicago Press in 2012.

Anthony H. Cordesman holds the Arleigh A. Burke Chair in Strategy at the Center for Strategic and International Studies (CSIS), Washington, DC. During his time at CSIS, Cordesman has been the director of the Gulf Net Assessment Project and the Gulf in Transition Study, as well as the principal investigator of the CSIS Homeland Defense Project. He served as part of Gen. Stanley McChrystal's civilian advisory group during the formation of a new strategy in Afghanistan and has since acted as a consultant to various elements of the US military and the North Atlantic Treaty Organization. Cordesman is the author of more than fifty books, including a four-volume series on the lessons of modern war.

Conrad C. Crane is currently the chief of Historical Services at the US Army Heritage and Education Center of the US Army War College at Carlisle Barracks, Pennsylvania. Previously the director of the US Army Military History Institute there, he joined the War College in September 2006 after twenty-six years of military service, which concluded with a post as a professor of history at the US Military Academy. He has written or edited books on the Civil War, World War I, World War II, and Korea, and was the lead author for the groundbreaking US Army/Marine Corps *Counterinsurgency* field manual in 2006. Dr. Crane holds a BS from the US Military Academy and an MA and PhD from Stanford University.

Gregory A. Daddis is currently an academy professor of history at the US Military Academy at West Point and also serves as a colonel in the US Army. He is the author of *No Sure Victory: Measuring U.S. Army Effectiveness and Progress in the Vietnam War* (Oxford University Press, 2011) and *Westmoreland's War: Reassessing American Strategy in Vietnam* (Oxford University Press, 2014).

Dorothy E. Denning is a distinguished professor in the Defense Analysis Department at the Naval Postgraduate School and author of *Information Warfare and Security* (Addison-Wesley, 1999). Dr. Denning has been widely recognized for her contributions to cyber security and cyber conflict and is a member of the inaugural class of the National Cyber Security Hall of Fame.

Scott Sigmund Gartner is Director of the Penn State School of International Affairs. Professor Gartner studies war, assessment, and conflict resolution. He published *Strategic Assessment in War* (Yale University Press, 1997), *The Historical Statistics of the United States* (Cambridge University Press, 2006), and many other books and articles. Dr. Gartner's honors include the Jefferson Award for the best government resource, the Reference and User Services Association Outstanding Reference Award, Booklist Editor's Choice Award, Library Journal Best Reference Award, and the History News Network Book of the Month.

John Grenier is the author of *The First Way of War: American War Making on the Frontier, 1607–1814* (Cambridge University Press, 2005), which won the Society for Military History's Outstanding Book Award in American History in 2007. He is also the author of *The Far Reaches of Empire: War in Nova Scotia, 1710–1760* (2008), which is volume 16 of the prestigious Campaigns & Commanders series in military history from University of Oklahoma Press. Dr. Grenier is currently writing a biography of Maj. Robert Rogers, the "father of American special operations," and expects to see the book in print in 2016.

Alejandro S. Hernandez is an associate professor in the Systems Engineering Department at the Naval Postgraduate School. Dr. Hernandez retired as a colonel from the US Army and holds a BS in civil engineering from the US Military Academy, an MS and PhD in operations research from the Naval Postgraduate School, and a master's degree in strategic studies from the US Army War College. His research focus is on developing and applying a systems engineering approach to the design and analysis of simulation-based events.

William C. Hix is currently the director for strategy, plans, and policy in the Office of the Deputy Chief of Staff, US Army, Washington, DC. Major General Hix led troops in combat in Operations Desert Storm in Kuwait and Enduring Freedom in Afghanistan. He was a member of the Operation Iraqi Freedom joint lessons learned team and was chief of strategy at Multinational Force–Iraq Headquarters (2004–5). A former National Security Affairs Fellow at the Hoover Institution at Stanford University and a member of the International Institute for Strategic Studies, he holds a master's degree in military art and science from the US Army Command and General Staff College at Fort Leavenworth, Kansas.

Edward G. Lengel received his PhD in history from the University of Virginia in 1998 and is now a professor and director of the Papers of George Washington documentary editing project at the University of Virginia. In addition to editing several volumes of the *Papers of George Washington*, Dr. Lengel has written six books, including *General George Washington: A Military Life* (Random House, 2005), and numerous articles for *Military History* and other publications.

Jason J. Lepore is an associate professor of economics in the Orfalea College of Business at California Polytechnic State University–San Luis Obispo. Dr. Lepore earned his PhD in economics from the University of California–Davis in 2007. He has published research on various topics in game theory and defense economics in leading journals including the *Journal of Economic Theory*, *Journal of Mathematical Economics*, and *Defence and Peace Economics*.

Brian McAllister Linn is a professor of history at Texas A&M University. He received his BA from the University of Hawaii–Manoa and his MA and PhD from Ohio State University. Dr. Linn has been a John S. Guggenheim Fellow and the president of the Society for Military History, and he has also authored four books, including *The Philippine War, 1899–1902* (University Press of Kansas, 2000).

Russell Muirhead is the Robert Clements Associate Professor of Democracy and Politics at Dartmouth College. The author of *Just Work* (Harvard University Press, 2004), Dr. Muirhead is currently at work on a book on partisanship titled *A Defense of Party Spirit*. Previously Muirhead taught political theory at the University of Texas–Austin, Harvard University, and Williams College. He was a Radcliffe Institute Fellow (2005–6) and a winner of the Roslyn Abramson Teacher Award at Harvard College.

Christopher J. Nannini is the division chief for program evaluation at the Research Facilitation Laboratory. Lieutenant Colonel (Ret.) Nannini served as a military assistant professor at the Naval Postgraduate School. Mr. Nannini conducted an assessment of operational plans for the International Security Assistance Force (ISAF) in Afghanistan. He received an MS in operations research from the Naval Postgraduate School and an MS in medicinal chemistry and marine natural products from Oregon State University.

Julian Ouellet currently serves as a game director at the Joint Staff–Studies, Analysis, and Gaming Division. In his prior position Dr. Ouellet was Irregular Warfare Branch chief in the Joint Staff–Warfighting Analysis Division, where he provided strategic analysis to the International Security Assistance Force. He earned his PhD in political science from the University of Colorado in 2006.

Robert Reilly previously served as the director for Voice of America and is currently a senior fellow at the American Foreign Policy Council, Washington, DC. Mr. Reilly has also taught at the National Defense University and served in the Office of the Secretary of Defense, where he was a senior adviser for Information Strategy (2002–6).

Michael Richardson commanded a squadron in the US Army's Asymmetric Warfare Group and previously served as a military assistant professor in the Defense Analysis Department at the Naval Postgraduate School. Colonel Richardson is a PhD candidate in US history at the University of California–Los Angeles.

Hy Rothstein served in the US Army as a Special Forces officer for more than twenty-six years. Currently he teaches in the Defense Analysis Department at the Naval Postgraduate School. Dr. Rothstein earned his PhD in international relations from the Fletcher School at Tufts University. He has published several books, including *Afghanistan and the Troubled Future of Unconventional Warfare* (Naval Institute Press, 2006), *Afghan Endgames: Strategy and Policy Choices for America's Longest War* (Georgetown University Press, 2012), *Three Circles of War: Understanding the Dynamics of Conflict in Iraq* (Potomac Books, 2010), and *The Art and Science of Military Deception* (Artech House, 2013).

Kalev I. Sepp is a senior lecturer in defense analysis at the Naval Postgraduate School. He served as a deputy assistant secretary of defense for special operations and counterterrorism and was an expert member of the Baker-Hamilton Bipartisan Commission on Iraq (the Iraq Study Group). Dr. Sepp earned his PhD in history at Harvard University and his combat infantryman badge in the Salvadoran civil war.

Aric P. Shafran is an associate professor of economics at California Polytechnic State University–San Luis Obispo. He has published many articles on economic decision making under risk and uncertainty in *Games and Economic Behavior*, *Journal of Risk and Uncertainty*, and other journals. Dr.

Shafran holds a PhD and MA in economics from the University of Colorado and an MEng and BS in computer science from Cornell University.

Brooks D. Simpson is a Foundation Professor of History in the School of Historical, Philosophical, and Religious Studies at Arizona State University. He received his PhD (1989) in history from the University of Wisconsin. The author of six books, coauthor of two more, and editor or coeditor of five other book publications, Dr. Simpson was also a Fulbright Scholar (Leiden University, 1995).

D. Scott Stephenson is a professor in the Department of Military History at the US Army Command and General Staff College, Fort Leavenworth, Kansas. He received a BS from the US Military Academy, an MA from Syracuse University, and a PhD from the University of Kansas. Lieutenant Colonel (Ret.) Stephenson has served in command and staff positions in the United States and Europe. He is the author of *The Final Battle: Soldiers of the Western Front and the German Revolution of 1918* (Cambridge, 2009).

Mark Stout is a program director of the master of arts in global security studies at the Krieger School of Arts and Sciences, Johns Hopkins University. He has previously worked for the US Army, the Department of State, and the CIA. Dr. Stout is the lead author of *The Terrorist Perspectives Project: Strategic and Operational Views of Al Qaida and Associated Movements* (Naval Institute Press, 2008).

Bradley J. Strawser is an assistant professor of philosophy in the Defense Analysis Department at the Naval Postgraduate School and a research associate at the Oxford University Institute for Ethics, Law, and Armed Conflict. Dr. Strawser's most recent publication is *Killing by Remote Control: The Ethics of an Unmanned Military* (Oxford University Press, 2013).

Gerhard L. Weinberg served in the US Army in 1946–47, took a history PhD at the University of Chicago in 1951, worked on Columbia University's War Documentation Project, and established the program for microfilming the captured German documents. Dr. Weinberg has taught at the Universities of Chicago, Kentucky, Michigan, and North Carolina; has chaired several professional organizations; and has served on and chaired several US government advisory committees. Now retired, he is the author or editor of eleven books including *A World at Arms: A Global History of World War II* (Cambridge, 2005).

INDEX